T0261207

Computation in Bioinformatics

Scrivener Publishing
100 Cummings Center, Suite 541J
Beverly, MA 01915-6106

Artificial Intelligence and Soft Computing for Industrial Transformation

Series Editor: Dr S. Balamurugan (sbnbala@gmail.com)

Scope: Artificial Intelligence and Soft Computing Techniques play an impeccable role in industrial transformation. The topics to be covered in this book series include Artificial Intelligence, Machine Learning, Deep Learning, Neural Networks, Fuzzy Logic, Genetic Algorithms, Particle Swarm Optimization, Evolutionary Algorithms, Nature Inspired Algorithms, Simulated Annealing, Metaheuristics, Cuckoo Search, Firefly Optimization, Bio-inspired Algorithms, Ant Colony Optimization, Heuristic Search Techniques, Reinforcement Learning, Inductive Learning, Statistical Learning, Supervised and Unsupervised Learning, Association Learning and Clustering, Reasoning, Support Vector Machine, Differential Evolution Algorithms, Expert Systems, Neuro Fuzzy Hybrid Systems, Genetic Neuro Hybrid Systems, Genetic Fuzzy Hybrid Systems and other Hybridized Soft Computing Techniques and their applications for Industrial Transformation. The book series is aimed to provide comprehensive handbooks and reference books for the benefit of scientists, research scholars, students and industry professional working towards next generation industrial transformation.

Publishers at Scrivener
Martin Scrivener (martin@scrivenerpublishing.com)
Phillip Carmical (pcarmical@scrivenerpublishing.com)

Computation in Bioinformatics

Multidisciplinary Applications

Edited by

S. Balamurugan

*Founder & Chairman, Albert Einstein Engineering and Research Labs
(AEER Labs), Vice Chairman, Renewable Energy Society of India (RESI),
India*

Anand Krishnan

*NRF-DSI Innovation Fellow, Department of Chemical Pathology
University of the Free State (Bloemfontein Campus), Bloemfontein,
South Africa*

Dinesh Goyal

Poornima Institute of Engineering & Technology, Jaipur, India

Balakumar Chandrasekaran

Faculty of Pharmacy, Philadelphia University, Amman, Jordan
and

Boomi Pandi

Department of Bioinformatics, Alagappa University, Karaikudi, India

Scrivener
Publishing

Wiley Global Headquarters
111 River Street, Hoboken, NJ 07030, USA

For details of our global editorial offices, customer services, and more information about Wiley products visit us at www.wiley.com.

Limit of Liability/Disclaimer of Warranty
While the publisher and authors have used their best efforts in preparing this work, they make no representations or warranties with respect to the accuracy or completeness of the contents of this work and specifically disclaim all warranties, including without limitation any implied warranties of merchantability or fitness for a particular purpose. No warranty may be created or extended by sales representatives, written sales materials, or promotional statements for this work. The fact that an organization, website, or product is referred to in this work as a citation and/or potential source of further information does not mean that the publisher and authors endorse the information or services the organization, website, or product may provide or recommendations it may make. This work is sold with the understanding that the publisher is not engaged in rendering professional services. The advice and strategies contained herein may not be suitable for your situation. You should consult with a specialist where appropriate. Neither the publisher nor authors shall be liable for any loss of profit or any other commercial damages, including but not limited to special, incidental, consequential, or other damages. Further, readers should be aware that websites listed in this work may have changed or disappeared between when this work was written and when it is read.

Library of Congress Cataloging-in-Publication Data

ISBN 978-1-119-65471-1

Cover image: Pixabay.Com
Cover design by Russell Richardson

Set in size of 11pt and Minion Pro by Manila Typesetting Company, Makati, Philippines

10 9 8 7 6 5 4 3 2 1

Contents

Preface

The past couple of years will be remembered for the COVID-19 pandemic and ensuing lockdowns, wherein almost every country saw a series of lockdowns and consequent suffering. To overcome the pandemic, the discovery of vaccines and other alternative therapies were attempted worldwide. Currently, the discovery of new solutions to the pandemic can be facilitated through the use of promising bioinformatics techniques and integrated approaches. Hence, this book provides readers with an understanding of the use of bioinformatics tools in new drug design and the discoveries which are inevitable in the present situation. The book covers a broad spectrum of the bioinformatics field, starting with the basic principles, concepts, and application areas under multidisciplinary sections. Also covered is the role of bioinformatics in drug design and discovery, including aspects of molecular modeling. Some of the chapters provide detailed information on bioinformatics-related topics, such as silico design, protein modeling, DNA microarray analysis, DNA-RNA barcoding, and gene sequencing, all of which are currently needed in the industry. Also included are specialized topics, such as bioinformatics in cancer detection, genomics and proteomics, which are highly relevant to the present scenario. Moreover, a few chapters explain highly advanced topics, like machine learning and covalent approaches to drug design and discovery, all of which are significant in pharma and biotech research and development. Therefore, the contents of this book will be useful for students, scientists, researchers, and professionals working in the field of bioinformatics, drug design, pharmacoinformatics and medicinal chemistry under the umbrella of academia and industry.

Our sincere gratitude especially goes to all the contributors for their useful insights concerning bioinformatics and its multidisciplinary applications. We sincerely thank Scrivener Publishing for their assistance, constant support, and patience in finalizing this book.

S. Balamurugan
Coimbatore, India

Krishnan Anand
Bloemfontein, South Africa

Dinesh Goyal
Jaipur, India

Balakumar Chandrasekaran
Amman, Jordan

Boomi Pandi
Karaikudi, India

Bioinfomatics as a Tool in Drug Designing

Rene Barbie Browne, Shiny C. Thomas and Jayanti Datta Roy*

*Department of BioSciences, Assam Don Bosco University,
Sonapur, Assam, India*

Abstract

Drug discovery is the method of identifying and validating a disease target and discovering and developing a chemical compound which can interact with its specific target. This process is very complex and time consuming, requiring multidisciplinary expertise and innovative approaches. To overcome the difficulties and complexity, *in silico* approach is used that reduces the time and expenditure. This chapter addresses the importance of bioinformatics in drug designing. It focuses on bioinformatics tools like AutoDock, LigPlot, FlexX, and many other softwares which play an important role in rational designing of drug. Thus, the main goal of this chapter is to provide an overview of the importance of bioinformatics tools in designing a drug.

Keywords: AutoDock, LigPlot, FleX, GenBank, SWISS-PROT, PDB

1.1 Introduction

Bioinformatics is a multidisciplinary field of life sciences merging biology, computer science, and information technology into a single discipline [1]. A wide range of subject areas is included in this field. These subject areas are structural biology, gene expression studies, and genomics. Computational techniques play an important role analyzing information that are associated with biomolecules on a large scale [2].

The main goal of bioinformatics aims toward better understanding of living cells and how it functions at the molecular level. Besides being

---

Corresponding author: jayanti.roy@dbuniversity.ac.in

S. Balamurugan, Anand Krishnan, Dinesh Goyal, Balakumar Chandrasekaran and Booni Pandi (eds.)
Computation in Bioinformatics: Multidisciplinary Applications, (1–24) © 2021 Scrivener Publishing LLC

essential for basic genomic and molecular biology research, bioinformatics plays a pivotal role on many areas of biotechnology and biomedical sciences [3]. In this aspect, bioinformatics play a vital role in designing of novel drugs. The interactions between protein and ligand investigated computationally provide rational basis for rapidly identifying novel synthetic drugs [4]. Information available regarding the 3D structure of proteins makes it easier to design molecule in such a way that they are capable of binding to the receptor site of a target protein with great affinity and specificity. Consequently, it significantly reduces time and cost necessary to develop drugs with higher potency, fewer side effects, and less toxicity than using the traditional trial-and-error approach.

This field of computational study has also reduced the sacrifice of animals in research. Nowadays, the number of potential drug candidate molecules is increasing with the use of computational simulation and informatics methods. These methods help in reducing the number of animals sacrificed in drug discovery process [5]. By efficient use of existing knowledge, computational studies have also helped in reducing the number of animal experiments which is required in basic biological sciences [6].

Bioinformatics tools are now appreciably used for developing novel drugs, leading to a new variety of research. Discovery and development of a new drug is generally very complex process consuming a whole lot of time and resources. So, bioinformatics techniques in designing tools are now broadly used so as to growth the efficiency of designing and developing a novel synthetic drug [4]. Drug discovery is the method of identifying, validating a disease target, followed by designing a chemical compound which can interact with that target resulting in inhibition of biological response which increases the rate of the disease. All these processes can be supported by various computational tools and methodology. Some of the factors which need to be observed during identification of the drug target are sequences of protein and nucleotide, mapping information, functional prediction, and data of protein and gene expression. Bioinformatics tools have helped in collecting the information of all these factors leading to the development of primary and secondary databases of nucleic acid sequences, protein sequences, and structures. Some of the commonly used databases include GenBank, SWISS-PROT, PDB, PIR, SCOP, and CATH. These databases have become indispensable tools to accumulate information regarding disease target. Databases like PubChem and ChemFaces provide structural and biological information of known drug like compounds which helps to identify the drug target for designing drug in research field [7]. These databases help in saving time, money, and efforts of the researchers.

Designing of drugs using bioinformatics tools can be broadly classified into two main categories, *viz.*,

a) Structure-based drug design (SBDD)
b) Ligand-based drug design (LBDD)

a) **Structure-Based Drug Design (SBDD):** Designing of drugs using SBDD method utilizes the 3D structure of the biological target which can be acquired via X-ray crystallography or NMR spectroscopy techniques [8]. Candidate drugs can be predicted on the basis of its binding affinity to the target using the structural information of the biological target. If the structure of the biological target/receptor is unavailable, then in that case, the structure can be predicted using homology modeling. It usually requires the amino acid sequence of the target protein, which when submitted constructs models that can be compared with the 3D structure of similar homologous protein (template). In order to know the interactions or bio affinity for all tested compounds, molecular docking of each compound is performed into the binding site of the target, predicting the electrostatic fit between them.

b) **Ligand-Based Drug Design (LBDD):** In this method of designing drug, the structural information of the small molecule/compound is known which binds to the target. The compounds/ligands which help in developing a Pharmacophore model possess all the important structural features necessary for binding to a target active site. Most common techniques used in this approach are Pharmacophore modeling and quantitative structure activity relationships (3D QSAR). These techniques are used in developing models with predictive ability that are suitable for lead identification and optimization [9]. Compound which are similar in structure also possess the same biological interaction with their target protein.

1.2   Steps Involved in Drug Designing

The flowchart in Figure 1.1 has been constructed to outline the phases that are involved in drug designing using *in-silico* approaches.

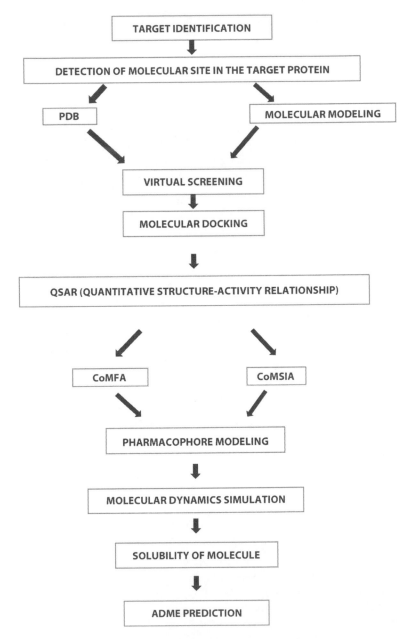

Figure 1.1 Flowchart of *in silico* approaches in drug designing.

1.2.1   Identification of the Target Protein/Enzyme

Before designing a novel synthetic drug, one needs to know all about the signaling pathways which lead to the disease. A novel drug needs to be designed in such a way that can interact with the target protein without interfering with normal metabolism. The most conventional method is to block the activity of the protein with a small molecule which can be the prospective drug. Virtual screenings of the target for compounds that can bind and inhibit the protein/enzyme are now performed using various bioinformatics softwares. Another strategy is to find other proteins which can regulate the activity of the target by binding and forming a complex, thereby controlling the disease.

- **PDB:** The Protein Data Bank (PDB) is the repository of information about the 3D structure structures of biological molecules which include nucleic acids and proteins (https://www.rcsb.org). The main function of this database is to provide 3D structural data of all the organisms which includes yeast, bacteria, plants, and other animals including humans. Techniques such as X-ray crystallography, electron microscopy, and nuclear magnetic resonance (NMR) spectroscopy help in extracting the information of the 3Dstructure of the macromolecules [10].
- **Swiss Target Prediction:** It is a web server which can accurately predict the targets of bioactive molecules based on similarity measures with known ligands [11]. In this web server, the predictions can be carried out in five different organisms, and mapping predictions by homology. The SwissTargetPrediction server is easily is accessible and is free of charge without any registration (www.swisstargetprediction.ch)
- **SPPIDER:** The SPPIDER protein interface recognition is a server that can be used to predict residues that needs to be in the putative protein interfaces by considering single protein chain with resolved 3D structure [12]. It can analyze protein-protein complex with given 3D structural information and can identify residues that are being in contact (http://sppider.cchmc.org/).

1.2.2   Detection of Molecular Site (Active Site) in the Target Protein

If a drug that needs to bind to a particular on a particular protein or nucleotide is known, then it can be tailor made to bind at that site. This is often performed computationally using several different techniques. Traditionally, the primary way is to identify compounds which can interact with the specific molecular site responsible for the disease. A second method is to test the specific compound against various molecular sites known for the occurrence of the disease. However, if the 3D structure of the protein target is not available, then the method of molecular modeling needs to be performed in order to construct the structure for further analysis.

- **CASTp:** Computed Atlas of Surface Topography of proteins (CASTp) is an online resource which is used for locating, delineating and measuring of concave surface regions on the 3D structures of protein [13]. It includes pockets which are located on protein surfaces. This server can be used to study surface features and functional regions of proteins. The server is updated daily and can be accessed at http://cast.engr.uic.edu
- **Active Site Prediction Server:** Active Site Prediction of Protein server help in computing the cavities in a given target protein. This sever can be easily accessed at http://www.scfbio-iitd.res.in/dock/ActiveSite_new.jsp.
- **3DLigandSite:** It is an automated method which can predict the ligand binding sites. One can submit a sequence or a protein structure and once submitted Phyre is run to predict the structure. The structure can then be used to search a structural library in order to identify homologous structures with bound ligands. These ligands are then superimposed onto the protein structure in order to predict a ligand binding site [14]. It can be accessed at http://www.sbg.bio.ic.ac.uk/3dligandsite.

1.2.3   Molecular Modeling

When desired structure of a target is not available, determining of the structure experimentally becomes difficult. In such conditions, designing of protein structure from pre-existing data and sequence becomes necessary. In designing of drugs, protein-ligand binding plays an important role. So, it is important to have a 3D structure of a protein. The 3D structures of protein are searched in a widely used database called PDB which provides a repository for all the known protein 3D structures [15]. X-ray crystallography and NMR spectroscopy are the two important techniques which determine the proteins 3D structure experimentally. This can be performed using *in silico* approach which provides a "homology-based modeling" method for protein modeling also referred as molecular modeling. It is an important computational technique which helps in designing the structure of a novel compound. It plays an important role in the study of various biological pathways which includes protein folding and stability, enzyme catalysis, identification of novel proteins, and other macromolecules [16]. This methodology works on the basis of sequence similarity, i.e., "proteins with similar sequences have similar structures". The models which are generated usually bear template significant sequence of more than 30% [17]. It is an accurate method allowing the researches to obtain an authenticated structure which might be useful as a drug after further validations. Because of this, virtual screening is necessary and has become an important part of drug discovery process [18]. The most common modeling softwares along with their description has been depicted in Table 1.1. Some of the important steps involved in molecular modeling are as follows:

a) Recognition of template and sequence alignment: Recognition of the template is the beginning step in homology modeling. To identify the homologous sequences of unknown protein, one can search the unknown against the pre-existing ones whose structure is known and identified. The homologous sequences can be identified by similarity searches which can be performed using sequence alignment programs such as BLAST (Basic Local Alignment Search Tool).

b) Model building: Some of the methods involved in building a model are spatial restraint, rigid-body assembly, segment matching, and artificial evolution.

c) Refinement modeling: Refinement of model involves addition, deletion, and substitution of amino acid residues, which includes loop modeling and side-chain modeling. This kind of modeling is based on molecular dynamics simulations, genetic algorithms, and Monte Carlo methods. AMBER, CHARMM22, and MM3 are commonly used force fields for energy minimization of modeled structures.

Table 1.1 The list of modeling softwares that are generally used in protein modeling is represented in tabular form.

S. no.	Name of software	Description	Reference
1	MODELLER	It involves homology modeling of the three-dimensional structures of the target protein.	[20]
2	UCSF Chimera	It helps in the visualization and analysis of molecular structures.	[21]
3	SWISS PDB VIEWER	It allows to analyze and model proteins.	[22]
4	Geno3D	It is an automatic web server for protein molecular modeling.	[23]
5	SWISS MODEL	Automated comparative modeling of protein structures can be performed.	[24]
6	CCP4	It helps in macromolecular structure determination.	[25]
7	Abalone	It is a modeling program which involves molecular dynamics of biopolymers	[26]
8	Tinker	It performs molecular mechanics and dynamics along with some unique features for biopolymers.	[27]

1. Loop modeling: In homologous protein sequences, insertion and substitution of amino acid residues in variable portion of the protein are referred as loops.
2. Side-chain modeling: It involves substitution of the side chains on the backbone structure of the protein. The substitution is analyzed by Root Mean Square Deviation (RMSD) values.

d) Validation of modeled protein structure: The protein structure obtained after homology modeling needs to be validated in order to check the accuracy of the modeling. This can be performed using web servers like WHATCHECK, WHAT IF, VADAR, and PROCHECK.

e) Small molecule databases: Screening of compounds in drug discovery to identify novel and drug-like properties can be performed using small molecule databases like NCBI, PubChem, and ChEMBL [19].

- **MODELLER:** It is a computer program which models 3D structures of proteins and their assemblies. This program is the most frequently used program for homology modeling. In order to construct, one needs to provide aligned sequence which will be modeled with known structures [27]. The program will then easily construct/build a model with no hydrogen atoms (https://salilab.org/modeller/).
- **SWISS PDB VIEWER:** The Swiss PDB Viewer is a free molecular graphics program that helps us to evaluate various proteins at the same time. The proteins can be placed one on top of another to reason the structural alignments and compare their active sites [28]. This program can be easily accessed at https://spdbv.vital-it.ch/.
- **SWISS MODEL:** It is a protein structure homology-modeling server which is fully automated. One can easily obtain it through ExPASy web server or from Swiss PDB Viewer. Their main aim is to model protein and make it easier to all researchers of life sciences [29]. It can be accessed at https://swissmodel.expasy.org.

1.2.4   Virtual Screening

Virtual screening is an *in silico* method used in drug designing. They are involved in identifying active compounds using chemical databases. It helps in identifying the structure of those compounds that may act as lead compounds with maximum affinity for a drug target [30]. The drug target may be a protein or enzyme. Virtual screening approaches are mainly of two types: structure-based and ligand-based. In structure-based virtual screening, molecular docking studies help in screening of target protein against ligands/compounds that are present in chemical libraries. The process of docking is usually based on the functional scores and binding strength of the compound with its target. Virtual screening uses computational programs to evaluate huge libraries of compounds automatically [31]. It is an accurate method allowing the researches to obtain an authenticated structure which might be useful as a drug after further validations. Because of this, virtual screening is necessary and has become an important part of drug discovery process [18].

- **MTiOpenScreen:** This approach involves docking of small molecules and virtual screening. The screening can be done in one run which can be up to 5,000 small molecules in different databases. The run can also be up to 10,000 molecules selected among 15,000 compounds that are prepared to be docked which is provided at MTiOpenScreen. The web server can be obtained from http://bioserv.rpbs.univ-paris-diderot.fr/services/MTiOpenScreen/.
- **ICM-VLS:** ICM Virtual Ligand Screening (VLS) is a combination of internal coordinate docking methodology with a sophisticated global optimization scheme. Its accuracy and fast potentials have led to an efficient virtual screening methodology in which ligands are fully and continuously flexible. It can be accessed at http://www.molsoft.com/vls.html.

1.2.5   Molecular Docking

Molecular docking is a computer simulation methodology which predicts the binding affinity of the target protein with the ligand at the atomistic level. The most important goal of molecular docking studies is to predict the binding conformation of protein-ligand and to estimate its interaction. It is also one of the main tools for virtual screening procedures, where a library of several compounds is "docked" against one drug target returning the best hit. Identifying the active site of the target protein where the ligand will bind is the first important step which needs to be performed before docking. This can be performed using programs like Q-SiteFinder, LigA Site, Meta Pocket, and CASTp [32]. A molecular docking study where the process of docking is performed without predicting the active site is referred as "Blind Docking" [33]. Here, Tables 1.2 and 1.3 show some of the most common Molecular docking software programs along with their specifications.

- **AutoDock:** It is an automated program to predict ligand and protein (bio-macromolecular targets) interactions. With recent advancement in bimolecular, X-ray crystallography is helping to provide structural information of complex biomolecules such as protein and nucleic acids. The structures can be taken/downloaded and can be used as targets for

Table 1.2 The list of molecular docking softwares is represented in tabular form.

S. no.	Name of software	Description	Reference
1	AutoDock	It performs automated docking of flexible ligands to macromolecules.	[34]
2	DockVision	It performs Monte Carlo, Genetic Algorithm, and database screening docking algorithms.	[35, 36]
3	GOLD	It helps in identifying correct binding modes of the active target molecules.	[37]
4	Docking Server	It provides a web-based interface for the molecular docking of protein and ligand.	[38]
5	SwissDock	It is a protein ligand server that is accessed through ExPASy.	[39]
6	CombiBUILD	It is a structure-based drug design program which helps in designing of combinatorial libraries.	[37]
7	QM Polarized Ligand Docking	It performs the function of both Glide and Q-Site applications of Schrodinger Suit.	[40]
8	Docking Server	It provides a web-based, easy to use interface for the molecular docking of protein and ligand.	[34]
10	Click2Drug	It is a protein ligand server that is accessed through ExPASy.	http://www.click2drug.org/

new drug molecules in controlling diseases and disorders of human, animal, and plant and understanding of fundamental aspects of biology [41]. It can be downloaded from http://www.scripps.edu/olson/forli/autodock_flex_rings.html (accessed 12.12.16).

Table 1.3 The list of molecular docking tools is represented in tabular form.

Tool	Brief description with uses
BLAST	Basic local alignment search tool; used for sequencing of DNA and protein.
RasMol	Raster molecule tool; used for molecular visualization of RNA/DNA and protein.
Discovery studio	Software; used for modeling and simulation.
Pub Med	Free search engine; used for searching matter related to medical and life sciences.
PDB	Protein Data Bank; used to collect information related to macromolecule.
Chem Draw	They are a part of the Chem office program which are used for drawing chemical molecule.
Marvin Sketch	These are advanced chemical editors that are used for drawing chemical structures and reactions.
PubChem	Database; used to collect information about structure and physiochemical properties of chemical compound.
AutoDock	Software; used for molecular docking.

- **GOLD:** Genetic Optimization for Ligand Docking is a genetic algorithm which provides docking of flexible ligand and a protein with flexible hydroxyl groups. The software uses a scoring function that is based on favorable conformations found in Cambridge Structural Database. The speed of GOLD and the reliability of its predictions depend on the control of different values of the genetic algorithm parameters. It provides reliable results both protein and ligand (http://www.ccdc.cam.ac.uk/Solutions/GoldSuite/Pages/GOLD.aspx) (accessed 20.12.16).

1.2.6 QSAR (Quantitative Structure-Activity Relationship)

It is a statistical approach which attempts to correlate relationships between physical and chemical properties of molecules to their biological activities. QSAR predicts the molecular properties from their structure without any need to perform the experiment using *in vitro* or *in vivo*. This method saves time and resources [39]. Descriptors which are commonly used are number of rotatable bonds LogP and molecular weight (MW). This approach is used in optimizing lead which is the most important step of discovering drugs. The two techniques in 3D QSAR developed for LBDD are comparative molecular field analysis (CoMFA) and Comparative molecular similarity indices analysis (CoMSIA). Based on the data dimensions many QSAR approaches range from 1D QSAR to 6D QSAR.

a) CoMFA (Comparative Molecular Field Analysis)

It is categorized as 3D QSAR computational technique in which incorporation of experimental activities (log units of KI or IC 50) and the 3D structures of the molecules are done in the study. For this study, a set of derivatives of bioactive compounds having different substitutions is first selected. All of these compounds are then distributed into 30% test set and 70% training set. For QSAR performance, several softwares are available. An important aspect in CoMFA analysis is that it requires a common substructure with good alignment having the same conformation in all molecules.

b) CoMSIA (Comparative Molecular Similarity Indices Analysis)

It is a more advanced method of CoMFA, having fewer limitations. In this approach, SEAL similarity method is used as descriptors. Some of the descriptors used in this method are steric, electrostatic, hydrophobic, and hydrogen bonding. In the ligand binding areas, the unfavored region or the favored regions are indicated by generated contours. Sybyl-X 2.0 and E-Dragon are the software used for QSAR studies.

- **OCHEM:** It is a web-based platform which aims to automate and simplify the typical steps that are required for QSAR modeling. It performs all the steps of a typical modeling workflow and provides facilities to use these data in the modeling process. It can be accessed at https://ochem.eu/home/show.do.
- **Discovery Studio:** This software helps in analyzing the molecular structures/sequences and modeling it. It provides tools for performing analysis of basic data including functionality for editing and viewing data. It is a free viewer which can be used to open data generated by other softwares in the Discovery Studio. It can be downloaded from https://www.3dsbiovia.com/products/collaborative-science/biovia-discovery-studio/visualization-download.php.

1.2.7   Pharmacophore Modeling

This is a powerful method which can easily categorize a group of molecules/ligands on the basis of active and inactive compounds. They provide set of molecular characteristics that is essential for the macromolecular recognition of ligands triggering a biological reaction. Some of the essential features modeled in pharmacophore are aromatic, hydrophobic, hydrogen bond acceptor (HBA), hydrogen bond donor (HBD), and anion and cation residues. Two main types of Pharmacophore modeling are structure-based modeling and ligand-based modeling.

Structure-based Pharmacophore modeling depends on the 3D structure of the protein obtained from PDB. These structures in PDB are provided by X-ray crystallography technique and/or NMR spectroscopy techniques. In the absence of 3D structure of protein, ligand-based Pharmacophore modeling is performed. Some of the softwares which are used for pharmacophore modeling are HypoGen, HipHop, DISCO, and PHASE.

- **PHASE:** It is a user friendly pharmacophore modeling solution for LBDD and SBDD. It creates hypotheses from protein-ligand complexes and apo proteins with Schrödinger's unique e-Pharmacophores technology. It can be accessed at https://www.schrodinger.com › phase.

1.2.8   Solubility of Molecule

Once the above steps have been done, the prospective compound is checked for whether the compound is water soluble or readily soluble in lipid which will affect the entry of the cells. The ability of a drug to make entrance into the cell and to bind to the target is an important factor which will determine its potency.

- **SwissADME:** This web tool can analyze drug-likeness and pharmacokinetics of molecules. It evaluates the affability of small molecules in order to compute the physicochemistry of one or several small molecules. It can be easily accessed at http://www.swissadme.ch/index.php.

1.2.9   Molecular Dynamic Simulation

It is a computational method which involves the solution of Newton's equation for motion to examine the dynamicity of the biological macromolecules. It provides comprehensive information on the fluctuations and conformational changes of proteins and nucleic acids. It helps in understanding the constancy of complexes of protein-ligand or of individual protein. Docking of protein-ligand complex with the ideal binding affinity is usually subjected to MD simulation. The protein topology is initially obtained by standard parameters using GROMACS or LEAP program. Online server PRODRG program is used for generating ligand topology [42]. It allows the study of interactions which occurs between different macromolecules during various cellular life processes and also analyzing of biological processes occurring in a living system. GROMACS is one of the most commonly used MD simulation softwares [43]. It produces trajectory files which carries the information of every conformational change that would have occurred on each atom during simulation. It provides a platform for the researchers to study the stability and minimization of energy of proteins as well as protein bound complexes. Some of software packages like NAMD, GROMACS, CHARMM, and AMBER are used for molecular dynamic simulation [44].

- **GROMACS:** It is one of the most commonly used molecular dynamic simulation softwares. Input files are taken in PDB format which then produces trajectory files that carry the information of each and every conformational changes taking place that would have occurred on each atom during simulation. It requires several commands to process this software. Using this software, researchers are able to study the stability and minimization of energy of proteins as well as protein bound complexes. It can be downloaded from http://www.gromacs.org.

1.2.10   ADME Prediction

It plays an important role in the process of drug discovery. Most drugs with poor pharmacokinetic and toxicity predictions fail in the clinical trials. The toxicity and the molecular property are important properties in a drug whose prediction will help in determining the positivity or negativity of the drug during clinical trials. This method of prediction follows Lipinski's rule of five [45]. The Lipinski's rule of five states that HBAs must be less than 10, HBDs must be less than 5, MW of the ligand must not be more than 500 Daltons; the number of rotatable bonds should be less than 10 and the milogP value must be less than five. The Lipinski's rule accepts compounds with one violation and those satisfying these rules can be orally available for humans. Softwares like PreADMET, VolSurf, admet-SAR, QikProp, PASS, and Molinspiration are used for ADME prediction [46, 47].

- **MOLINSPIRATION:** It provides a wide range of cheminformatic softwares and tools which supports manipulation and processing of molecules. It also includes SD file conversion, SMILES, fragmentation of molecules, creation of tautomers, and calculating molecular properties that are required in QSAR, modeling and designing of drugs, depiction of high quality molecule, and molecular database tools which supports substructure and similarity searches. Molinspiration is user friendly and can be easily accessed at https://www.molinspiration.com/.

1.3   Various Softwares Used in the Steps of Drug Designing

Bioinformatics tools provides information about potential targets that include nucleotide and protein sequencing information, protein and gene expression data, prediction of the function, information of the pathway, mapping information, disease associations, information of the structure, and taxonomic distribution, among others. This helps in reducing time, effort, and money in characterization of different targets. The field of bioinformatics has thus become a major component of the drug discovery pipeline, playing a vital role for validating drug targets. Table 1.4 illustrates some of the most commonly used software for drug design, along with their descriptions.

Table 1.4 The list of softwares used in the steps of drug designing is represented in tabular form.

Sr. no.	Software name	Description
1	DDDPlus	It helps in dissolution and disintegration study.
2	GastroPlus	Correlation for various formulations in *in vivo* and *in vitro*.
3	MapCheck	It helps in comparing dose or fluency measurement.

(Continued)

Table 1.4 The list of softwares used in the steps of drug designing is represented in tabular form. (*Continued*)

Sr. no.	Software name	Description
4	AutoDock	They help in evaluating the ligand-protein interaction.
5	Schrodinger	They perform ligand-receptor docking.
6	GOLD	They perform protein-ligand docking.
7	BioSuite	It performs genome analyzing and sequence analyzing.
8	Maestro	It involves molecular modeling analysis.
9	ArgusLab	They perform Molecular docking calculations and provides molecular modeling package.
10	GRAMM	Protein-protein docking and protein-ligand docking.
11	SYBYL-X Suite	It involves molecular modeling and ligand-based designing.
12	Sanjeevini	It can predict protein-ligand binding affinity.
13	PASS	It can create and analysis of SAR models.
14	AMIDE (A Medical Image Data Examiner)	They provide medical image analysis in molecular imaging.
15	Discovery Studio® Visualizer	It helps in viewing and analyzing protein data.
16	Imaging Software SCGE-Pro	They perform cytogenetic and DNA damage analysis.
17	Xenogen Living Image Software	It involves *in vivo* imaging display and analysis.
18	GeneSpring	It can identify variation across set of sample and for correction method in samples.
19	QSARPro	It involves protein-protein interaction study.

(Continued)

Table 1.4 The list of softwares used in the steps of drug designing is represented in tabular form. (*Continued*)

Sr. no.	Software name	Description
20	REST 2009 Software	They perform analysis of gene expression data.
21	EthoWatcher	It performs behavior analysis.
22	MARS (Multimodal Animal Rotation System)	It can perform animal activity tracking, enzyme activity, and nanoparticle tracking and delivery study.

1.4   Applications

Bioinformatics plays an important role in defining and classifying the nucleotide compositions of human genome sequence. This field helps in identifying and analyzing a large number of biological drug targets, thereby greatly increasing the possibility of potential drugs. This approach provides strategies and algorithm to predict new drug targets and also stores and control available drug target information. The annual expenditure of developing a new drug has been reduced due to the application of bioinformatics in drug discovery. They play a major role in determining the variation of species on the basis of similarity or dissimilarity of gene structure or amino acid sequence in protein. The level of sequence similarity can also be determined using bioinformatics analysis tools. Bioinformatics techniques are mainly applied in two different phases of drug discovery. First is extracting interesting information. Second is finding important genes and proteins, thereby speeding the process of drug discovery.

Genome sequencing of various organisms has become possible due to bioinformatics. There are almost hundred organisms whose genome has been mapped so far using bioinformatics tools [48]. The databases of these organisms are increasing day by day as every day a new information about any organism. Bioinformatics and genomics have been adopted by pharmaceutical industries for drug targets and drug discovery. The possibility of designing and developing drugs is due to the understanding of molecular biology with the help of bioinformatics tools. In the recent years, bioinformatics has made it easier for the researchers to easily target the molecules in the *in vitro* environment. Screening of newly developed compounds can now be done against the molecules of the proteins or genetically modified cells thereby giving efficient results. This way of drug development has made the process of identification of the disease easier in an organism.

Several studies have been carried which highlights the role and application of bioinformatics tools in drug designing. Some of these are as follows.

In 2013, an investigation was done to evaluate the activity of anti-dengue in compounds that are isolated from eight *Carica papaya* [49]. It was investigated against NS2B-NS3 protease of dengue 2 virus (DENV-2). In this study, admetSAR was used to screen the ADMET properties of the compounds extracted from *Carica papaya* [49].

In 2014, molecular dynamics study was carried out to evaluate the constancy of the complexes of protein-ligand and individual protein. The study was also carried out for double mutant (toho-1-R274N/R276N in Escherichia coli) and triple mutant (toho-1-E166A/R274N/R276N in Escherichia coli) systems of class A β-lactamases and also for point mutant (SHV-E166A in Klebsiella pneumoniae) [50].

In 2014, to reveal the potential anti-mycobacterium activity of pyrrole hydrazine derivatives which acts on enoyl-acyl carrier protein reductase was carried out using CoMFA and CoMSIA analysis [51].

In 2016, Malathi and Ramaiah performed structure-based virtual screening to analyze the inhibtors that are potential for OXA-10 ESBL expressing *P. aeruginosa*. This was done in opposition to millions of compounds that are present in ZINC database. For this study, Molinspiration tool was used. The tool was used to filter the imipenem analogs that is based on the Lipinski's rule of five [52].

In 2016, identification of novel inhibitors for Penicillin binding protein 2a (PBP2a) of ceftaroline-resistant methicillin-resistant *Staphylococcus aureus* (MRSA) was used for virtual screening using Dock blaster server [53].

Acinetobacter baumannii (*A. baumannii*), a Gram negative, coccobacilli which is associated with nosocomial infections has developed resistance to all known classes of antibiotics. The infections have been treated with the carbapenem group of antibiotics like imipenem and meropenem. According to the reports, *A. baumannii* has obtained resistance to imipenem due to the secretion of carbapenem hydrolysing class D beta-lactamases (CHDLs). A study was carried out in 2016, to search for the possible mechanism of imipenem resistance in OXA-143 and OXA-231 (D224A) CHDLs expressing *A. baumannii*. This was performed using molecular docking and dynamics simulation studies.

Malathi *et al.*, in 2016, carried out a study to find the possible mechanism of imipenem resistance in OXA-143 and OXA-231 (D224A) CHDLs expressing *A. baumannii* by implementing molecular docking and dynamics study. Their study revealed that OXA-143 CHDL-imipenem complex has better binding affinity than OXA-231 (D224A) CHDL-imipenem complex. Their results also indicated that binding affinity of OXA-143 with imipenem was strong when compared with OXA-243. Hence, they could conclude that this mechanism might be the probable reason for imipenem resistance in OXA-143 expressing *A. baumannii* strains [54].

In 2017, Suganya *et al.* investigated the anti-dyslipidemic property. This property was studied on plant compounds against HMG-CoA reductase. Molecular dynamic study was performed to analyze the stability of the rutin-HMG CoA complex. It was observed that the resulted plots reveal the constancy of the Epicatechin-HMG CoA complex instead of the free HMG CoA [55].

In 2018, Kist *et al.* have performed a search which was ligand-based Pharmacophore in order to investigate non-ATP competitive inhibitors for mammalian or mechanistic target of rapamycin (mTOR).

The spatial arrangement of protein model and ligand model was generated in order to design a model by ZINCPharmer platform.

This was done with the help of hydrophobic interactions of residues like C19, C5, C21, C45, C43, and C49 of rapamycin. Thus, it results in the generation of eight new inhibitors with better activity [56].

1.5   Conclusion

The field of bioinformatics plays a pivotal role in designing novel synthetic drugs. Bioinformatics is providing a huge support in order to overcome the cost and time in drug discovery and development. A broad range of softwares and databases related to drug can be obtained using bioinformatics, thereby helping in drug designing purposes. For drug designing, the tools which were discussed in this chapter are playing a major role in the enhancement of modified drugs development. With the use of bioinformatics tools in designing drugs, promising drug candidates can be constructed thereby providing a hope for betterment in drug discovery area.

References

1. Younus W., M., Ganie, N.A., Rani, S., Mehraj, S., M.R., Baqual, M.F., Sahaf, K.A., Malik, F.A., Dar, K.A., Advances and applications of Bioinformatics in various fields of life. *Int. J. Fauna Biol. Stud.*, 5, 2, 03–10, 2018.

2. Luscombe, N.M., Greenbaum, D., Gerstein, M., What is Bioinformatics? A Proposed Definition and Overview of the Field. *Methods Inf. Med.*, 40, 4, 346–58, 2001.

3. Kumar, A. and Chordia, N., Role of Bioinformatics in Biotechnology. *Res. Rev. Biosci.*, 12, 1, 116, 2017.

4. Sliwoski, G., Kothiwale, S., Meiler, J., Lowe Jr., E.W., Computational methods in drug discovery. *Pharmacol. Rev. Jan*, 66, 1, 334–395, 2014.

5. Raia, J. and Kaushikb, K., Reduction of Animal Sacrifice in Biomedical Science & Research through Alternative Design of Animal Experiments. *Saudi Pharm. J.*, 26, 6, 896–902, 2018.

6. Kwong, P.D., Chuang, G.Y., DeKosky, B.J., Gindin, T., Georgiev, I.S., Lemmin, T., Schramm, C.A., Sheng, Z., Soto, C., Yang, A.S., Mascola, J.R., Shapiro, L., Antibodyomics: bioinformatics technologies for understanding B-cell immunity to HIV- 1. *Immunol. Rev.*, 275, 108–128, 2017.

7. Kim, S., Thiessen, P.A., Bolton, E.E., Chen, J., Fu, G., Gindulyte, A., Bryant, S.H., PubChem substance and compound databases. *Nucleic Acids Res.*, 44, D1202–1213, 2016.

8. Leach, A.R. and Harren, J., *Structure-Based Drug Discovery*, Springer, Berlin, 2007.

9. Hughes, J.P., Rees, S., Kalindjian, S.B., Philpott, K.L., Principles of early drug discovery. *Br. J. Pharmacol.*, 162, 6, 1239–1249, 2011.

10. Dutta, S., Burkhardt, K, Young, J., Swaminathan, G.J., Matsuura, T., Henrick, K., Nakamura, H., Berman, H.M., Data deposition and annotation at the worldwide protein data bank. *Mol. Biotechnol.*, 42, 1, 1–13, 2009.

11. Gfeller, D., Grosdidier, A., Wirth, M., Daina, A., Michielin, O., Zoete, V., SwissTargetPrediction: a web server for target prediction of bioactive small molecules. *Nucleic Acids Res.*, 42, Web Server issue, W32–8, 2014.

12. Porollo, J.M., Prediction-based Fingerprints of Protein-Protein Interactions. *Proteins: Struct. Funct. Bioinf.*, 66, 630–45, 2007.

13. Andrew Binkowski, T., Naghibzadeh, S., Liang, J., CASTp: Computed Atlas of Surface Topography of proteins. *Nucleic Acids Res.*, 1, 31, 13, 3352–3355, 2007.

14. Wass, M.N., Kelley, L.A., Sternberg, M.J.E., 3DLigandSite: predicting ligand-binding sites using similar structures. *Nucleic Acids Res.*, Jul 1, 38, Web Server issue, W469–W473, 2010.

15. Berman, H.M., Westbrook, J., Feng, Z., Gilliland, G., Bhat, T.N., Weissig, H., Bourne, P.E., The Protein Data Bank. *Nucleic Acids Res.*, 28, 235–242, 2000.

16. Ramachandran, K.I., Deepa, G., Namboori, K., *Computational Chemistry and Molecular Modeling Principles and Applications*, Springer-Verlag GmbH, Berlin, 2008.

17. Cavasotto, C.N. and Phatak, S.S., Homology modeling in drug discovery: current trends and applications. *Drug Discovery Today*, 676–683, 2009.

18. Malcolm, J.M., Zhaowen, L., Xuliang, J., Virtual screening in drug discovery, in: *Drug Discovery Research. New Frontiers in the Post-Genomic Era*, pp. 63–88, 2007.

19. Kim, S., Thiessen, P.A., Bolton, E.E., Chen, J., Fu, G., Gindulyte, A., Bryant, S.H., PubChem substance and compound databases. *Nucleic Acids Res.*, 44, D1202–1213, 2016.

20. Eswar, N., Marti-Renom, M.A., Webb, B., Madhusudhan, M.S., Eramian, D. *et al.*, Comparative Protein Structure Modeling with MODELLER. *Curr. Protoc. Bioinf.*, 15, 5.6.1–5.6.30, 2006.

21. Lin, J., Okada, K., Raytchev, M., Smith, M.C., Nicastro, D., Structural mechanism of the dynein power stroke. *Nat. Cell Biol.*, 16, 479–485, 2014.

22. Johansson, M.U., Zoete, V., Michielin, O., Guex, N., Defining and searching for structural motifs using DeepView/Swiss-PdbViewer. *BMC Bioinf.*, 13, 173, 2012.

23. Combet, C., Jambon, M., Deléage, G., Geourjon, C., Geno3D: automatic comparative molecular modelling of protein. *Bioinformatics*, 18, 213–214, 2002.

24. Schwede, T., Kopp, J., Guex, N., Peitsch, M.C., SWISS-MODEL: an automated protein homology-modeling server. *Nucleic Acids Res.*, 31, 13, 3381–3385, 2003.

25. Winn, M.D., Ballard, C.C., Cowtan, K.D., Dodson, E.J., Emsley, P. *et al.*, Overview of the CCP4 suite and current developments. *Acta Crystallogr. D Biol. Crystallogr.*, 67, 235–242, 2011.

26. Qureshi, R.H. and Noman, B., SZABIST., Is Abalone, Bio designer and Fold it, the best software for Protein Structure Prediction of AIDS Virus? *J. Indep. Stud. Res. – Comput.*, 9, 2, 36–43, 2011.

27. Rackers, J.A., Wang, Z., Lu, C., Laury, M.L., Lagardère, L., Schnieders, M.J., Schnieders, M.J., Tinker 8: Software Tools for Molecular Design. *J. Chem. Theory Comput.*, 14, 10, 5273–5289, 2018.

28. Eswar, N., Webb, B., Marti-Renom, M.A., Madhusudhan, M.S., Eramian, D., Shen, M.-y., Pieper, U., Sali, A., Comparative Protein Structure Modeling Using Modeller. *Curr. Protoc. Bioinf.*, 15, 1, 5.6.1–5.6.30, 2006.

29. Kaplan, W. and Littlejohn, T.G., Swiss-PDB Viewer (Deep View). *Brief Bioinform.*, 2, 2, 195–7, 2001.

30. Rester, U., From virtuality to reality - Virtual screening in lead discovery and lead optimization: a medicinal chemistry perspective. *Curr. Opin. Drug Discovery Devel.*, 11, 559–568, 2008.

31. Walters, W.P., Stahl, M.T., Murcko, M.A., Virtual screening – an overview. *Drug Discovery Today*, 3, 160–178, 1998.

32. Laurie, A.T. and Jackson, R.M., Q-SiteFinder: An energy-based method for the prediction of protein-ligand binding sites. *Bioinformatics*, 21, 1908–1916, 2005.

33. Malathi, K., Anbarasu, A., Ramaiah, S., Ethyl Iso-allocholate from a medicinal rice karungkavuni inhibits dihydropteroate synthase in escherichia coli:

A molecular docking and dynamics study. *Indian J. Pharm. Sci.*, 78, 780–788, 2016.

34. Forli, S., Huey, R., Pique, M.E., Sanner, M., Goodsell, D.S., Olson, A.J., Computational protein-ligand docking and virtual drug screening with the AutoDock suite. *Nat. Protoc.*, 11, 5, 905–919, 2016.

35. Hart, T.N. and Read, R.J., A multiple-start Monte Carlo docking method. *Proteins*, 13, 206–22, 1992.

36. Hart, T.N., Ness, S.R., Read, R.J., Critical evaluation of the research docking program for the CASP2 challenge. *Proteins*, Suppl 1, 29, 205–9, 1997.

37. Pagadala, N.S., Syed, K., Tuszynski, J., Software for molecular docking: a review. *Biophys. Rev.*, 9, 2, 91–102, 2017.

38. Bikadi, Z. and Hazai, E., Application of the PM6 semi-empirical method to modeling proteins enhances docking accuracy of AutoDock. *J. Cheminform.*, 1, 15, 2009.

39. Grosdidier, A., Zoete, V., Michielin, O., SwissDock, a protein-small molecule docking web service based on EADock DSS. *Nucleic Acids Res.*, 39, Web Server issue, W270–W277, 2011.

40. Singh, K.D. and Muthusamy, K., Molecular modeling, quantum polarized ligand docking and structure-based 3D-QSAR analysis of the imidazole series as dual AT1 and ETA receptor antagonists. *Acta Pharmacol. Sin.*, 34, 12, 1592–1606, 2013.

41. Rizvi, S.M.D., Shakil, S., Haneef, M., A simple click by click protocol to perform docking: Autodock 4.2 made easy for non- Bioinformaticians. *Excli J.*, 12, 831–857, 2013.

42. Schuttelkopf, A.W. and van Aalten, D.M., PRODRG: A tool for high-throughput crystallography of protein-ligand complexes. *Acta Crystallogr. Sect. D: Biol. Crystallogr.*, 60, 1355–1363, 2004.

43. Alder, B.J. and Wainwright, T.E., Studies in Molecular Dynamics. I. General Method. *J. Chem. Phys.*, 27, 1208, 1957.

44. Van der Spoel, D., Lindahl, E., Hess, B., Groenhof, G., Mark, A.E., Berendsen, H.J., GROMACS: Fast, flexible, and free. *J. Comput. Chem.*, 26, 1701–1718, 2005.

45. Gimenez, B.G., Santos, M.S., Ferrarini, M., Fernandes, J.P., Evaluation of blockbuster drugs under the rule-of-five. *Pharmazie*, 65, 148–152, 2010.

46. Cheng, F., Li, W., Zhou, Y., Shen, J., Wu, Z., Liu, G., Tang, Y., AdmetSAR: A comprehensive source and free tool for assessment of chemical ADMET properties. *J. Chem. Inf. Model.*, 52, 3099–3105, 2012.

47. Lagunin, A., Stepanchikova, A., Filimonov, D., Poroikov, V., PASS: Prediction of activity spectra for biologically active substances. *Bioinformatics*, 16, 747–748, 2000.

48. Mychaleckyj, J.C., Genome Mapping Statistics and Bioinformatics. *Methods Mol. Biol.*, 404, 461–488, 2007.

49. Senthilvel, P., Lavanya, P., Kalavathi Murugan, K., Swetha, R., Anitha, P. et al., Flavonoid from *Carica papaya* inhibits NS2B-NS3 protease and prevents Dengue 2 viral assembly. *Bioinformation*, 9, 18, 889–895, 2013.

50. Kumar, K.M., Lavanya, P., Anbarasu, A., Ramaiah, S., Molecular dynamics and molecular docking studies on E166A point mutant, R274N/R276N double mutant, and E166A/R274N/R276N triple mutant forms of class A β-lactamases. *J. Biomol. Struct. Dyn.*, 32, 12, 1953–1968, 2014.

51. Joshi, S.D., More, U.A., Dixit, S.R., Korat, H.H., Aminabhavi, T.M., Badiger, A.M., Synthesis, characterization, biological activity, and 3D-QSAR studies on some novel class of pyrrole derivatives as antitubercular agents. *Med. Chem. Res.*, 23, 3, 1123–1147, 2013.

52. Malathi, K. and Ramaiah, S., Molecular Docking and Molecular Dynamics Studies to Identify Potential OXA-10 Extended Spectrum β-Lactamase Non-hydrolysing Inhibitors for Pseudomonas aeruginosa. *Cell Biochem. Biophys.*, 74, 2, 141–55, 2016.

53. Lavanya, P., Ramaiah, S., Anbarasu, A., A Molecular Docking and Dynamics Study to Screen Potent Anti-Staphylococcal Compounds Against Ceftaroline Resistant MRSA. *J. Cell Biochem.*, 117, 2, 542–8, 2016.

54. Malathi, K., Anbarasu, A., Ramaiah, S., Exploring the resistance mechanism of imipenem in carbapenem hydrolysing class D beta-lactamases OXA-143 and its variant OXA-231 (D224A) expressing Acinetobacter baumannii: An *in-silico* approach. *Comput. Biol. Chem.*, 67, 1–8, 2017.

55. Baskaran, G., Salvamani, S., Ahmad, S.A., Shaharuddin, N.A., Pattiram, P.D., Shukor, M.Y., HMG-CoA reductase inhibitory activity and phytocomponent investigation of Basella alba leaf extract as a treatment for hypercholesterolemia. *Drug Des. Devel. Ther.*, 14, 9, 509–17, 2014.

56. Kist, R., Timmers, L.F.S.M., Caceres, R.A., Searching for potential mTOR inhibitors: Ligand-based drug design, docking and molecular dynamics studies of rapamycin binding site. *J. Mol. Graph Model.*, 80, 251–263, 2018.

New Strategies in Drug Discovery

Vivek Chavda[1], Yogita Thalkari[2]* and Swati Marwadi[3]

[1]*Formulation and Protein Characterization Lab, Dr. Reddys Laboratory, Hyderabad, India*
[2]*Analytical Research and Development Lab, Lupin Research Park, Pune, India*
[3]*Formulation and Protein Characterization Lab, Lupin Research Park, Pune, India*

Abstract

The procedure involved in drug discovery is intricate, tedious, and cost incurring and requires multi-disciplinary expertize and inventive methodologies. Computational drug discovery process is a successful technique for quickening and streamlining drug disclosure and improvement process. Due to substantial increment in the accessibility of natural macromolecule and little atom data, the materialness of computational drug discovery has been stretched out and comprehensively applied to about each phase of the drug discovery and further advancement work process, including objective recognizable proof and approval, lead revelation and improvement, and preclinical tests. Over the previous decades, computational medication disclosure strategies, for example, atomic docking, pharmacophore displaying and mapping, again plan, sub-atomic likeness figuring, and succession-based virtual screening, have been extraordinarily improved. In this section, we present a review of these significant computational strategies, stages, and effective applications in this field.

Keywords: Drug discovery, computational methodologies, high throughput screening, virtual screening, OMICS technology, etc.

Corresponding author: yogitathalkari@gmail.com

S. Balamurugan, Anand Krishnan, Dinesh Goyal, Balakumar Chandrasekaran and Boomi Pandi (eds.) *Computation in Bioinformatics: Multidisciplinary Applications*, (25–48) © 2021 Scrivener Publishing LLC

2.1   Introduction

Drug discovery involves the range of processes start from cogent target choice to its approval and also the post approval changes. While complete medication revelation work processes (Drug Discovery) are actualized prevalently in the large pharma sectors, early disclosure center in the scholarly community (Academia) serves to recognize test molecules that can fill in as apparatuses to think about targets or pathways. Regardless of contrasts in a definitive objective of the private and scholarly divisions, a similar essential standard characterizes the accepted procedures in early drug revelation process. An effective early disclosure program is based on solid objective definition and approval utilizing an assorted arrangement of biochemical and cell-based measures with practical pertinence to the natural framework being examined [1].

The molecules identified as targets or hits undergo extensive scaffold optimization and are characterized for their target specific action and off-target effects in *in vitro* and in animal models [1, 2]. While the active molecule from screening campaigns pass through highly stringent chemical studies and pharmacokinetic and pharmacodynamic studies such as Absorption, Distribution, Metabolism, and Excretion (ADME) filters for lead identification, the probe discovery involves limited medicinal chemistry optimization [2].

The purpose of probe discovery is identification of a molecule with sub-μM activity and reasonable selectivity in the context of the target being studied. The molecules identified from probe discovery can serve as starting scaffolds for lead identification and optimization studies. Structuring of medication is not really depending on the PC demonstrating methods and bioinformatics approaches in the huge information as these are useful and steady devices yet we cannot completely depend on that.

Similarly, biopharmaceuticals and particularly therapeutic antibodies are an undeniably significant class of medications and computational techniques for improving the proclivity, selectivity, and solidness of these protein-based therapeutics have additionally increased biologics dominance in the therapeutic market.

Procedure of medication advancement and discovery comprises of preclinical research using cell-based assays and animal models and initial clinical trials on people along with administrative endorsement.

Present day drug discovery process includes the distinguishing proof and screening of focuses on, its science and advancement of those objectives to build the liking, selectivity (to diminish the capability of symptoms), viability/intensity, metabolic dependability (to expand the half-life), and oral bioavailability. All these improvement processes are generally carried out before commencement of the clinical trials so as to get the desired therapeutic outcome.

2.2   Road Toward Advancement

Bioinformatic examination can fasten up the drug target identification and drug candidate screening and refinement process, and it likewise also helps in the identification of antagonistic consequences [2, 3]. High-throughput screening information, for example, genomic, epigenetic, genome design, cistromic, transcriptomic, proteomic, and ribosome profiling information have all made critical commitments possible towards advanced instrument based medication revelation and medication repurposing [3, 4].

Amassing of protein and RNA structures, just as improvement of homology demonstrating and protein structure reproduction, combined with huge structure databases of little particles and metabolites, made ready for increasingly sensible protein-ligand docking tests and progressively instructive virtual screening. In this chapter, we present the reasonable structure that drives the assortment of these high-throughput information, abridge the utility and capability of mining these information in drug discovery, diagram a couple of intrinsic impediments in information and programming mining these information, call attention to new approaches to refine examination of these various kinds of information, and feature normally utilized programming and databases applicable to substantiate drug discovery process. Bioinformaticians in novel drug discovery utilize high-throughput atomic information (Figure 2.1) having correlations between side effect transporters (patients, creature malady models, disease cell lines, and so on) and ordinary controls.

The key objectives of such comparisons are as follows [1–5]:

1. To connect side effects to hereditary transformations, epigenetic alterations, and other natural elements regulating gene expression.
2. To select and identify drug targets that can either restore cellular function or eliminate malfunctioning cells, e.g., cancer cells.
3. To foresee, refine, or rebuild treatment that can follow up on the medication focus to accomplish the planned restorative outcome and limit adverse reactions.

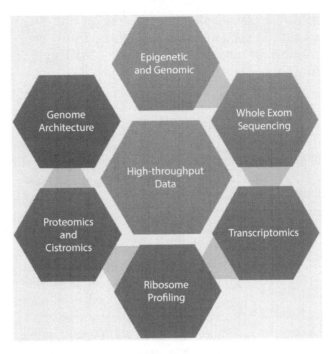

Figure 2.1 High-throughput data used in bioinformatics.

4. To assess the impact on environmental health and the potential of drug resistance.

Despite whether the objective of translational research is novel drug revelation, the two endpoints require the distinguishing proof of an objective or a pathway by means of fundamental or clinical research. Concentrates on the sub-atomic levels system of illness unwind focuses on that are applicable to infection advancement and movement [4, 5].

The objective ranges from proteins, molecular level changes in proteins and genes or polymorphisms in the coding or non-coding loci of the genome or transcriptional or post-translational alteration procedures. Toward one side of the objective range, characterizing the job of target is generally clearer in basic mono-factorial ailments, which are described by one causative allele, and regulating that solitary quality or factor hypothetically builds the likelihood of focusing on the problem viably. At the opposite finish of the objective range, characterizing an objective in complex multifactorial problems is very testing [4–6].

Complex infections, including disease, neurodegenerative issue, and Type 2 diabetes, are for the most part heterogeneous and have variable phenotypes from chance factors that are an element of hereditary qualities, age, sex, and diet or way of life decisions. The difficulties in distinguishing an exceptional objective fundamental complex illness emerge from cell cross-talks between flagging pathways and collaboration organizes that outcome in useful redundancies and other compensatory components [3, 5].

As the business endeavors to always improve its capacities and prescient powers in medicate/drug discovery to deliver more secure and increasingly cogent medications, it has become exceptionally evident that target data seems to be very precise to provide desire safety and efficacy later on. The significance of securing increasingly far reaching data on focuses of intrigue cannot be downplayed. An objective is considered druggable when it is agreeable to balance either through hereditary as well as experimentation. Tweak of the objective should inspire a quantifiable reaction, which sets up a solid, unequivocal connection between the objective and disease advancement or movement [1–6]. The field of target recognizable proof systems has been evaluated widely.

So, an objective in illness or pathogenesis can be estimated through the hereditary control of cells or creature model living beings utilizing bunched normally interspaced short palindromic rehashes (CRISPR-Cas9), translation activator-like effector nucleases (TALENs), and zinc-finger nucleases (ZFNs), RNA obstruction, or microRNAs. Concoction approval of the objective can be performed utilizing known mixes or accessible antibodies. The likelihood of recognizing an atom that has high capability of connecting with an objective viably requires solid objective approval information and aides in by and large hazard appraisal. The achievement of planning pertinent examine frameworks requires describing the objective in both ordinary and pathogenic states: arrangement and structure, practical or auxiliary repetition, portrayal of joined isoforms, posttranslational adjustments, subcellular dispersion, and mRNA and protein articulation levels crosswise over tissues, their half-lives, and guideline [1–4].

Target deconvolution can likewise be endeavored utilizing mass spectrometry following protein adjustment (CETSA) or partialiy enhancement strategies in the nearness or nonappearance of a medication, trailed by hereditary approval.

Target recognizable proof as of late can likewise be bolstered from extraction and incorporation of important data accessible from various datasets.

Broad research and clinical perceptions throughout the years have made accessible huge volume "omics" datasets, which may demonstrate basic in target and medication disclosure. Correlative reconciliations crosswise over omics databases are ventured to encourage the structure of increasingly extensive models of focuses in ailment. The high-throughput genomics, transcriptomics, epigenomics, proteomics, and metabolomics can help set up solid quality/protein variation affiliations and can help in biomarker revelation [7]. Eventually, models rising up out of solid correlative datasets may help distinguish right patient population and characterize important clinical endpoints for the diagnostics, avoidance, or treatment of sicknesses.

2.3   Methodology

Some potential procedures and stages concentrated on computational medication disclosure (Drug Discovery) and improvement have been created and developed. In this segment, a few approaches and stages that include target proof, docking-based virtual screening, compliance testing, scoring capacities, atomic comparability count, virtual library structure, and succession-based medication configuration are condensed, consolidated and summarized. These perspectives are personally connected, and upgrades in any angle could profit the others.

2.3.1   Target Identification

As the main stage in the drug discovery pipeline, the recognizable proof of medication that focuses from enormous amounts of applicant macromolecules is both significant and testing. The present significant devices for target recognizable proof are genomic and proteomic approaches, which are arduous and tedious. In this manner, to supplement the test techniques, computational instruments and stages, including reverse docking and pharmacophore mapping, have been created [2, 3].

TarFisDock is a web server that recognizes potential targets utilizing a switch docking system to look for all conceivable restricting proteins for a given little molecule. The advancement of TarFisDock depended on the generally utilized docking program, DOCK (form 4.0). This stage comprises of a front-end web interface written in PHP and HTML with MySQL as database framework. DOCK is utilized as a back-end instrument for turn around docking [1–3].

The benefit of TarFisDock is self-evident; it could be a significant apparatus for distinguishing potential focuses for a compound with known organic movement, a recently confined characteristic item or a current medication whose pharmacological system is unknown. Moreover, this stage is additionally ready to discover potential focuses on that could be liable for the poisonous quality and reactions of a medication, which could take into account the expectation of the off-target impacts of a medication competitor.

For sure, review have indicated that off-target impacts have been to a great extent answerable for the high whittling down rate in target improvement. Moreover, TarFisDock could give important data to building drug target arranges so as to ponder the medication target collaboration in a progressively efficient manner. The unwavering quality of this technique has been tried on nutrient E and 4H-tamoxifen by distinguishing their putative restricting proteins.

The outcomes showed that TarFisDock could anticipate half of the revealed comparing targets. In any case, this technique still has certain constraints [1–5]:

1. The protein passages are not adequate to cover all the protein data of disease related genomes.
2. The adaptability of the proteins is not considered during the docking strategy.
3. The scoring capacity, which was planned to assess little atoms, may not be exact enough for assessing reverse docking.

A web-open potential medication target database (PDTD) was developed for TarFisDock. This database at present contains in excess of 1,100 protein sections with 3D structures acquired from the Protein Data Bank. The general data for these proteins was extricated from the writing and a few online databases, for example, TTD, Drug Bank, and Thomson Pharma. This database contains assorted data on in excess of 830 potential medication targets, and each medication target has structures in both the PDB and MOL positions.

Data on related sicknesses, organic capacities, and related flagging pathways has additionally been gathered. The entirety of the objectives was arranged by their capacity and their related sicknesses. PDTD has a catchphrase look work for parameters, for example, the PDB ID, the objective name, and the ailment name. As an extensive and one of a kind archive of medication targets, it could be utilized for *in silico* target objective ID, virtual screening, and the disclosure of auxiliary impacts for existing medications [2–4].

Another significant issue in target ID is finding the best connection mode between the potential objective and the little atom tests. Notwithstanding the invert docking strategy, pharmacophore displaying and mapping can be utilized to distinguish the ideal cooperation mode. A pharmacophore model is the spatial course of action of highlights fundamental for an atom to associate with a particular objective receptor. Pharm Mapper is the primary online device to utilize an "invert" pharmacophore mapping way to deal with foresee potential medication focuses against some random little atom. In any case, the Pharm Mapper server requires an adequate number of accessible pharmacophore models that portray the coupling methods of known ligands at the coupling locales. In this way, a huge, in-house database of pharmacophore models commented on with their objective data was developed (Pharm Target DB). The objective protein structures in complex with little atoms were deliberately separated from the Drug Bank, Binding DB, PDB Bind, and PDTD databases, and more than 7,000 pharmacophore models (covering data for more than 1,500 medication targets) in light of the mind-boggling structures were created.

A consecutive mix of triangle hashing (TriHash) and hereditary calculation (GA) enhancement was received to distinguish the pharmacophore that best fit the errand. Profiting by the exceptionally effective and vigorous triangle hash mapping technique, Pharm Mapper is computationally productive and can-do high throughput screens. The calculation is profoundly computerized, and the interface is easy to understand. For experienced clients, discretionary parameters controlling pace and exactness and the competitor targets subset can be unreservedly tweaked. The significant constraint of the program is that the pharmacophore database just incorporates medicate focuses on that have PDB structures with a co-solidified ligand. Be that as it may, Pharm Target DB is refreshed intermittently as the quantity of structures saved in PDB develops.

2.3.2   Docking-Based Virtual Screening

Virtual screening dependent on atomic docking has gotten one of the most generally utilized techniques for SBDD. The essential criteria for any docking strategy are docking exactness, scoring precision, and computational effectiveness, which are for the most part firmly affected by the conformational looking through techniques. Molecular docking is a run of the mill streamlining issue; accordingly, it is hard to get the worldwide ideal arrangement. Most conformational advancement strategies in docking projects can just manage a solitary goal, for example, the coupling vitality, shape complementarity, or synthetic complementarity. This kind of strategy is not powerful for tackling true issues, which typically include numerous goals. Thusly, an improvement calculation that involves a few goals and results in increasingly sensible and strong restricting modes among ligands and macromolecules is desperately required.

A recently created docking procedure, GAsDock, utilizes an entropy-based multi-populace GA to enhance the coupling presents between little atoms and macromolecule receptors. Data entropy was utilized in the GA for advancement, and contracted space was utilized as the union foundation, guaranteeing that GAsDock can merge quickly and consistently. An approval test docking known inhibitors into the coupling pockets of thymidine kinase (TK) and HIV-1 turn around RT showed that GAsDock is more precise than other docking programs, for example, GOLD, FlexX, DOCK, Surflex, and Glide. To expand the precision and speed of the procedure, an improved versatile hereditary calculation has been built up that supports an adaptable docking technique.

Some propelled methods, for example, multi-populace hereditary system, entropy-based looking through strategy with self-adaption, and semi accurate evaluation, were brought into this calculation. Another cycle plot was likewise utilized related to these systems to accelerate the enhancement and assembly forms, making this strategy fundamentally quicker than the old technique. What is more, two arrangements of multi-target enhancement (MO) techniques, meant MOSFOM (Multi-Objective Scoring Function Optimization Methodology), that at the same time consider both the vitality score and the contact score were created. MOSFOM principally stresses another system to acquire the most sensible restricting adaptation and increment the hit rates as opposed to precisely foreseeing the coupling free vitality.

2.3.3   Conformation Sampling

One of the basic parts of medication structure elucidation and improvement is to see the bioactive adaptations of the little atoms that decide the physical and organic properties of the particles. A large number of the medication disclosure strategies, for example, atomic docking, pharmacophore development and coordinating, 3D database looking, 3D-QSAR, and sub-atomic similitude investigation, include a conformational testing system to produce adaptations of little particles in the coupling pocket and a scoring stage to rank these compliances. A down to earth compliance group should ensure that the conformers are vitality sensible and length the conformational space in a proper measure of time. Other advanced criteria, for example, pharmacophore and restricting pocket mapping, have likewise been executed to test the conformers, making the adaptation age process a multi-target enhancement process [1–3].

A profoundly effective conformational age strategy named Cyndi, which depends on the multi-target advancement calculation (MOEA), has been created. Utilizing various goals to control vitality openness just as geometric assorted variety, Cyndi is fit for looking the conformational space in almost steady time and of inspecting the Pareto outskirts at which both the vitality and decent variety highlights are favored. The conformers are encoded into GA people with data on the dihedral torsions of the rotatable securities; the VDW and the torsional vitality terms are two particular goals for isolating the created conformers in vitality space utilizing the Tripos power field [2–5]. Cyndi guarantees that the produced compliance group at the same time meets numerous criteria, for example, low vitality and geometric decent variety, rather than focusing on only one criteria. As of late, Cyndi was refreshed to consolidate the MMFF power field to all the more objectively evaluate the conformational vitality.

An examination among Cyndi and MacroModel coordinated in Maestro V7.5 (Schrodinger Inc), concentrating on the harmony between the inspecting profundity of the conformational space and the conformational costs as for the calculation technique utilized has been performed. MacroModel was appeared to have similar execution to Cyndi as far as recovering the bioactive compliances, while Cyndi performed better at finding bioactive adaptations in the briefest measure of time as to the productivity of the compliance testing.

2.3.4   Scoring Function

The scoring capacity is a basic segment in virtual screening. One significant scoring strategy is the information-based scoring technique, which normally removes basic data from tentatively decided protein-ligand edifices and utilizes the Boltzmann law to change the molecule pair inclinations into separation subordinate pairwise possibilities. The capability of mean power (PMF) scoring capacity can change over basic data into free vitality with no information on the coupling affinities and is in this way expected to be progressively material. This strategy verifiably balances many contradicting commitments to authoritative, for example, solvation impacts, conformational entropy, and communication enthalpy. A few wonderful approaches concentrated on these fields are presented beneath.

A kinase family-explicit PMF scoring capacity named kinase-PMF was created with a kinase informational index of 872 edifices from the PDB database to evaluate the authoritative of ATP-focused kinase inhibitors. This scoring capacity acquires the useful structure and iota sort of PMF0443. Contrasted with eight others regularly utilized scoring strategies, kinase-PMF had the most elevated achievement rate in distinguishing positive mixes from fakes as well as gem adaptations. Subsequently, this strategy could enable analysts to screen and upgrade hit mixes in kinase inhibitor improvement.

An improved PMF scoring capacity named KScore, which depends on a few various preparing sets and a recently characterized particle composing plan utilizing 23 re-imagined ligand iota types, 17 protein molecule types, and 28 recently presented iota types for nucleic acids, has been created. In examination with the current PMF possibilities, for example, PMF99 and PMF04, the pairwise possibilities for various particle types utilized in KScore have been fundamentally improved, especially in the field of reflecting exploratory marvels, including the cooperation separations and the qualities of hydrogen holding, electrostatic connections, VDW associations, cation-π communications, and fragrant stacking. KScore is an integral asset for recognizing solid covers from a progression of mixes and can be applied to enormous scale virtual screening. What is more, further upgrades should be conceivable by changing the molecule composing plan and various preparing sets. KScore has been incorporated into the recently referenced atomic docking program GAsDock. Based on the idea and formalism of PMF and a novel emphasis technique, an information-based scoring capacity named IPMF was created. This scoring capacity incorporates extra exploratory restricting partiality data into the information base as reciprocal information to the for the most part utilized auxiliary data.

The utilized emphasis strategy is to remove the 3D basic data and the coupling proclivity data so as to yield an "improved" information-based model. The presentation of IPMF was assessed by scoring a various arrangement of 219 protein-ligand edifices and contrasting the outcomes with seven normally utilized scoring capacities. Accordingly, the IPMF score performs best in the action forecast test. Likewise, when re-positioning restricting postures, IPMF additionally exhibited negligible upgrades over the other assessed information-based scoring capacities. These outcomes recommend that the extra restricting liking data can be utilized for creating scoring capacities as well as for improving their capacity to foresee restricting affinities.

The IPMF approach gives a well-characterized plan to bring restricting data into common factual possibilities, which might be pertinent to other information-based scoring capacities.

2.3.5 Molecular Similarity Methods

As the foundation of structure-movement relationship (SAR) and basic grouping examination, sub-atomic likeness is a significant idea in LBDD.

Closeness-based virtual screening and molecular positioning are viewed as one of the most incredible assets in restorative science and have been effectively applied in various cases. Comparability looking through projects can by and large be classified into 2D and 3D similitude as indicated by whether 3D adaptation data is considered. 2D likeness techniques are productive for rapidly profiling neighboring mixes. Be that as it may, it might somewhat give various hits to indistinguishable questions from various 2D likeness definitions target various parts of the data. This strategy likewise will, in general, find close auxiliary analogs rather than novel platform hits. Notwithstanding, 3D comparability techniques ordinarily think about different parts of the 3D adaptation, including pharmacophores, atomic shapes, and sub-atomic fields. 3D strategies can be advantageously used to achieve platform jumping to distinguish novel mixes.

In light of the pharmacophore coordinating methodology, which was utilized as the motor of the recently referenced PharmMapper Server, a strategy named SHAFTS (SHApe-FeaTure Similarity) has been created for quick 3D sub-atomic closeness figuring. This technique embraces cross-breed similitude measurements of sub-atomic shape and hued (or marked) science bunches commented on by pharmacophore highlights for 3D computation and positioning so as to incorporate the quality of both pharmacophore coordinating and volumetric likeness draws near. The triplet hashing technique is utilized to count quick sub-atomic arrangement presents. The cross-breed likeness comprises of shape-density covers and pharmacophore highlight fit qualities and is utilized to score and rank arrangement modes. SHAFTS accomplished unrivaled execution as far as both by and large and beginning time improvements of known actives and chemotypes contrasted with other ligand-based strategies. SHAFTS has been incorporated into ChemMapper Server (unpublished outcome). Spherical harmonic (SH) is a lot of symmetrical round capacities that can without much of a stretch speak to the state of a shut bend surface, for example, a sub-atomic surface. SH extension hypothesis has been effectively applied in virtual screening, protein-ligand acknowledgment, restricting pocket displaying, atomic section closeness, etc. SHeMS is a novel atomic shape comparability correlation technique got from SH extension. In this technique, the SH extension coefficients are weighted to compute closeness, prompting an unmistakable commitment of generally and point by point highlights to the last score. What is more, the reference set for improvement can be designed by the client, which takes into consideration framework explicit and redid correlations. A retrospective VS experiment on the directory of useful decoys (DUD) database and principal component analysis (PCA) reveals that SHeMS provides dramatically improved performance over the original SH (OSH) and ultra-fast shape recognition (USR) methods.

2.3.6   Virtual Library Construction

All over again, de novo drug design tranquilize configuration plans to synthetically fill the coupling destinations of target macromolecules. One of the basic difficulties of this procedure is to choose piece sets that have the best potential to be portions of new medication leads for a given objective. Virtual library development including centered library, directed library, and essential screening library has been proposed as one approach to beat this test. Another test is to set up legitimate criteria for item judgment. To take care of this issue, target similarity and basic assorted variety have been acquainted into library structure with decrease the size and increment the screening proficiency of the built libraries.

Concentrated libraries focus on one specific objective and are based on a lead compound or pharmacophore, while focused on libraries are intended to look for tranquilize leads against explicit targets. Another productive methodology that receives the benefits of both centered and focused on libraries and incorporates advancements from docking-based virtual screening and medication like examination was built up to construct, advance, and survey centered libraries. A product bundle named LD1.0 was effectively created utilizing the new approach. Building squares are chosen from given piece databases to make a progression of virtual libraries. The virtual libraries are then advanced by library-put together GA and assessed with respect to the premise of determined criteria, for example, docking vitality, sub-atomic assorted variety, and medication similarity. GA holds libraries with higher scores and makes new libraries to shape the up and coming age of centered libraries. When the end condition is fulfilled, GA improvement closes.

2.3.7   Sequence-Based Drug Design

The 3D structures of most proteins have not recently been resolved, and huge numbers of the proteins do not have a known ligand. In this circumstance, neither structure-based strategies nor ligand-based techniques can be utilized to lead identification and advancement. Along these lines, a technique to foresee ligand-protein interactions (LPIs) without 3D or ligand data is earnestly required. As of late, a succession-based medication configuration model for LPI was developed exclusively based on the essential grouping of proteins and the basic highlights of little particles utilizing the help support vector machine (SVM) approach. This model was prepared utilizing 15,000 LPIs between 626 proteins and more than 10,000 dynamic mixes gathered from the Binding Database. In the approval trial of this model, nine novel dynamic mixes against four pharmacologically significant targets were discovered utilizing just the arrangement of the objective. This is the principal case of a fruitful arrangement-based medication configuration crusade.

2.4   Role of OMICS Technology

Presently, current pharmaceutical businesses are confronting unsustainable program disappointment in spite of critical increments in venture due to waning revelation pipelines, quickly growing R&D focuses, increasing spending plans, expanding administrative recording systems and expenses, and foresee noteworthy holes later on tranquilize markets. The procedure of drug discovery from idea to commercialization is dull and extensive and adds to the extending emergency. The animal models which are accessible now a days which are foreseeing clinical interpretations are basic, exceptionally reductionist and, subsequently, not fit for reason. Presently, there is obstruction produced for different illness like jungle fever, tuberculosis, and HIV which prompts calamitous results of expanding steady loss rates. The transitioning of omics-based applications makes accessible an imposing mechanical asset to additionally grow our insight into the complexities of human illness.

The institutionalization, investigation, and far reaching examination of the "information substantial" yields of these sciences are for sure testing. A reestablished spotlight on expanding reproducibility by understanding inalienable organic, methodological, specialized, and diagnostic factors is urgent if dependable and helpful inductions with potential for interpretation are to be accomplished. The individual omics sciences—genomics, transcriptomics, proteomics, and metabolomics—have the solitary preferred position of being complimentary for cross approval, and together might empower a genuinely necessary frameworks science point of view of the bother's fundamental malady forms. In the event that current antagonistic patterns are to be turned around, it is basic that a move in the R&D center from speed to quality is accomplished. Omics advances are an essential piece of educated pharmaceutical R&D, and their job in R&D will keep on growing. There are still difficulties to be routed to completely use omics advancements, particularly for treating complex maladies, for example, neurological and immune system illnesses (Figures 2.2 and 2.3).

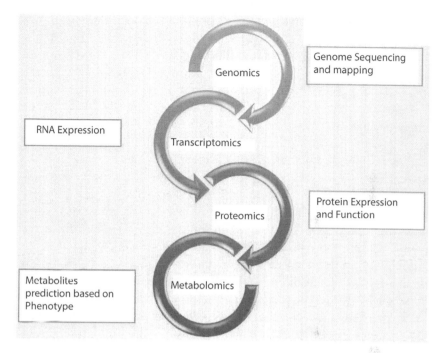

Figure 2.2 Integrated OMICS in drug discovery.

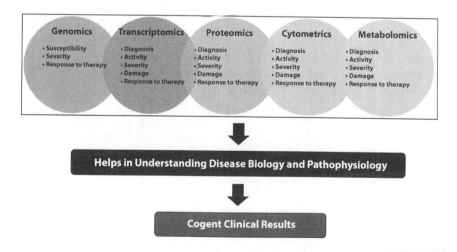

Figure 2.3 Role of integrated omics in clinical biology.

Just to give some examples. How to build up omics information norms to diminish between lab changeability and to expand trust in particularly characterizing illness subtypes to help the plan of clinical preliminaries? How to translationally connect omics information in obsessive conditions and clinical phenotypes of individual illnesses? How to coordinate different layers of omics data and phenotypic portrayals, including neurotic biomarkers of a malady, pharmacodynamics reactions to a medication treatment? How to interface omics information to cerebrum pictures or subjective scores for neurological or mental sicknesses? Computational and factual strategies will without a doubt keep on assuming a job. Looking forward, quantitative frameworks pharmacology may help cross over any barrier. It is foreseen that the atomic systems portrayed by omics information and the physiological/obsessive systems displayed by clinical tests/analysis will be quantitatively coordinated to educate R&D.

As biomedical advances develop, omics advances should be coordinated with new advancements. The advances of a malady on-chip are not too far off. A malady on-chip is a novel living infection model that can be developed to catch the neurotic highlights of an illness over the span of its common history and to connect omic profiles and clinical phenotypes. Related to tests for transcriptomics, proteomics, microRNAs, and post-translational alteration data, illness on-chip advances can uncover the sub-atomic etiology of a malady, distinguish tranquilize targets, and, above all, uncover the reactions to a medication over the frameworks (viability and security). Alzheimer's sickness is a model where an infection on-chip can be instrumental. A few hereditary changes in the β-amyloid forerunner protein quality have been recognized in familial Alzheimer's sickness. Possibly, utilization of hereditary control to actuate explicit changes of cells and make explicit malady on-chip probably would not be implausible. Sooner rather than later, a 3D Alzheimer's sickness "cerebrum on-chip" will build our capacity to decide the atomic systems related with its etiology and to find a novel therapeutic item to forestall its beginning and additionally capture its movement.

2.5 High-Throughput Screening and Its Tools

High-throughput screening (HTS) is a basic empowering innovation for translational research that can have endpoints of medication revelation or test disclosure. The end purpose of new drug discovery process is a exceptional process that prompts recognizable proof of a medication applicant that has potential for turning into an advertised medication (Figure

2.4). New drug discovery is both an expensive and time-concentrated procedure that requires joining of mastery from different particular groups and can take as long as 15 years to carry a competitor and efficacious molecule to the market [1, 2]. Regardless of multi-million-dollar interests in innovative work (R&D) and in executing guidelines, medicate revelation and improvement is an extremely hazardous procedure for huge pharma. Dangers emerge from clinical preliminary disappointments because of absence of medication target commitment, absence of connection amongst objective and illness, and deficient endpoint and patient determination. Different dangers incorporate patent terminations and rivalry from generics, tranquilize end because of long haul wellbeing issues, and poor efficacies crosswise over a lot of bigger hereditarily assorted populaces [1–4]. The significant expenses and hazards and long courses of events of genuine medication disclosure are not perfect with a lot of shorter task achievements and little research spending plans of the scholastic world. Striking special cases to this speculation incorporate scholarly labs that seek after exhaustive early and pre-clinical medication disclosure look into programs. The second endpoint of translational research, test revelation, is a progressively suitable option in scholarly settings. Test revelation can be seen as a middle of the road momentary

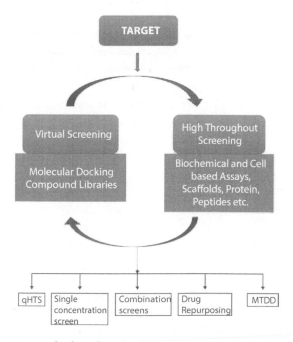

Figure 2.4 Screening methods in drug discovery.

procedure of compound recognizable proof, where the applicant atom is utilized as an apparatus to dismember a natural procedure or pathway of intrigue. The procedure of test disclosure is appropriate to working inside constrained spending plans, catching momentary achievements characterized by test revelation productions and new target entries. Test revelation likewise suits the huge swath of targets and organic frameworks that scholastics seek after paying little heed to business rate of return esteem.

When the examiner meets the set up measurable acknowledgment standard for screening (e.g., signal windows, coefficient of inconstancy, reproducibility, Z' factor, consistency, and so forth), the test is first utilized for screening a little preparing set of mixes (~2,000–10,000), to check that the test is performing acceptably. The test compound assortments can fluctuate with the screening office or can be directed by the objective class. The approval or test library can contain an assortment of little atoms illustrative of frameworks present in a lot bigger compound sets, may incorporate an assortment of known bioactives that incorporate mixes with in any event one known sub-atomic objective, and may incorporate kinase or phosphatase inhibitors or inhibitors of a cell cycle, proteasomes, and so forth. The information from the approval screening is assessed for different parameters like the Z' scores, signal consistency, hit rates, recurrence of bogus positives, and test obstruction mixes.

When the test passes all approval screening parameters, bigger compound assortments are screened at least one fixation. The essential screening can be performed at a solitary focus or can be performed at 6–8 fixations in quantitative HTS group (qHTS) (Figure 2.4). The qHTS, however more cost- and time-escalated, helps in producing portion reaction bends for every one of the mixes tried. The qHTS group additionally limits the determination of bogus positive hits. Blend screening is one more method of screening in which the synergistic mix of mixes is distinguished by joining either single or different centralizations of compound or medication of enthusiasm with different medications or bioactive or decent variety platforms from centered libraries. Mix screening can likewise be performed for sedate repurposing ventures where a clinical standard of care is utilized to screen different US Food and Drug Administration (FDA)–affirmed tranquilize assortments to recognize progressively strong synergistic mixes of medications for new signs or for improving adequacy of existing standard of care [1–5]. New blends may help distinguish at least two medications that target multifactorial issue and improve the nature of care. Notwithstanding the wet seat HTS crusades, virtual screening can likewise be performed to choose essential hits. The certainty of hit ID by means of virtual screens increments if the screening model is upheld by X-beam precious stone structures of restricting areas or co-gem models with ligands. The difficulties of characterizing a hypothetical low vitality model without precious stone structure data makes genuine positive recognizable proof from virtual screening all the more testing. Rather than HTS, which is reliant on real accessible compound libraries, virtual screens can get to a lot of bigger compound assortments from databases. Negligible synthetic platforms can show restricting indiscrimination and can adjust a few focuses on that offer utilitarian areas and restricting locales crosswise over target families. The numerous objective regulations by a medication or polypharmacology is abused in screens for tranquilize repositioning that help in the recognizable proof of new signs for showcased drugs. Recognizable proof of new movement for an advertised medication by means of trial and *in silico*–based methodologies fits well inside the extent of scholarly disclosure ventures, as the security, danger profiles, details, and pharmacology of promoted drugs are as of now settled. A mix of at least two FDA-endorsed drugs against an objective may improve results particularly if the mixes focus on the crosstalk between pathways that are initiated or quelled in infection settings [1–3].

Another form of multi-target drug discovery (MTDD) screening includes distinguishing proof of single mixes with action against at least two focuses on that dwell in a similar tissue or cell compartment. In such screens, the hit mixes recognized from the primary screen against an objective are utilized against the second focus important to distinguish frameworks with movement against the two targets. Both exploratory just as virtual *in silico* approaches can be utilized to configuration screens to recognize intensifies that are dynamic against different focuses of intrigue. A few judiciously based structures, computationally based docking, and virtual screening approaches are accessible for recognizing drugs with numerous capacities. The forecast of collaborations between a substance compound and other potential natural targets require a mining of "omics" datasets, sub-atomic docking utilizing X-beam precious stone structures or models, ligand-based quantitative structure–activity relationship (QSAR) comparability expectation of a few dimensional fingerprints of little particles, and restricting pocket sub-cavities that have been appeared to oblige known medications crosswise over proteins that need grouping likeness. Polypharmacology-based screens can help in the choice of atoms that have higher viability and lower harmfulness.

The appearance of innovations, for example, ongoing reverse transcriptase polymerase chain reaction (RT-PCR) and cDNA microarrays, is a messenger for another period in the investigation of organic frameworks. In immunobiology, these advances have started to affect investigations of irresistible ailments, provocative procedures, and insusceptible cell work. In any case, an absence of hereditary reagents for local and partner creatures has blocked across the board utilization of new innovations to contemplates in these frameworks. We have as of late depicted improvement of cDNA microarrays for contemplating ox-like immunobiology. Albeit incredible in uncovering qualities associated with immunological marvels in cows, these assets were constrained by an absence of qualities known to work in resistant reactions from different species, for example, mouse and human. To address this deficiency, we utilized a blend of bioinformatics and high throughput RT-PCR to make amplicons speaking to more than 270 cow-like qualities whose orthologs in different species were known to work in invulnerable reactions.

Amplified gene segments were prepared from cDNA representing RNA isolated from either unstimulated or concanavalin A (ConA) stimulated peripheral blood mononuclear cells (PBMCs). In total, 276 genes were amplified from cDNA representing unstimulated bovine PBMC RNA or from cDNA representing ConA stimulated bovine PBMC RNA.

A web-accessible resource (http://gowhite.ans.msu.edu/public_php/gd-bovine-immunology.php) has been created to assist in dissemination of this novel resource. The web-accessible resource contains information on gene name, the forward and reverse primers used to amplify each segment, expected product size, and if the gene was found in unstimulated PBMCs or only in ConA stimulated PBMCs. Gene names appear as hyperlinks to the Gene bank pages representing the bovine gene or expressed sequence tag (EST) used to generate each primer pair.

2.6   Chemoinformatic

There are seven stages in the medication disclosure process: sickness/disease determination, target speculation, lead compound recognizable proof (screening), lead optimization, pre-clinical development, and clinical developments and pharmacogenomic improvement [6]. Generally, these means are completed consecutively, and on the off chance that one of the means is moderate, it hinders the whole procedure (Figure 2.5). So as to make a compound library with incredible substance with decent variety, an assortment of basic handling innovations for decent variety investigations were made and applied. These computational methodologies are the parts of cheminformatics. After 1990, numerous concoction decent variety related methodologies were grown, for example, auxiliary descriptor calculations, basic likeness calculations, order calculations, enhanced compound choices, and library counts. Nonetheless, help from these decent variety examinations approaches has been constrained. More hits have

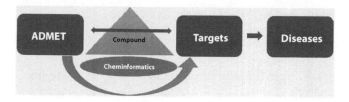

Figure 2.5 Chemoinformatic in drug discovery.

been found from these artificially various libraries, yet the greater part of these hits does not bring about new medications [2, 4, 6].

In this way, the way toward making and screening drug-like mixes went under question. As the human genome venture was finished, many new focuses for tranquilize disclosure have been created through genomics and current atomic science [1]. The present truth is that the pharmaceutical drug discovery business is confronting numerous objectives, however with minimal auxiliary data. One currently sees as an excessive number of hits while scanning for lead identification, in this way lead enhancement is obstructed. To get more target auxiliary data, high-throughput protein crystallization has been investigated. Be that as it may, numerous objectives are layer proteins and it is exceptionally hard to acquire auxiliary data for these proteins. Subsequently, lead improvement remains the most genuine bottleneck. Moreover, we realize that, around 40% of all improvement up-and-comers flop because of absorption, distribution, metabolism, excretion, and toxicity ("ADMET") issues. This new Drug discovery technique challenges cheminformatics in the accompanying viewpoints [6]: (1) cheminformatics ought to have the option to separate information from enormous scale crude HTS databases in a shorter timeframes and (2) cheminformatics ought to have the option to give productive *in silico* devices to anticipate ADMET properties. This is ordinarily exceptionally difficult to do. Cheminformatics has accomplished numerous accomplishments in assorted variety examination, SAR, and virtual screening during the previous decade. It is additionally seen as helpful in the accompanying field from information mining to medicate revelation.

2.6.1 Exploratory Data Analysis

The purposes of this stage are to derive features (descriptors), to select relevant features (bioactivities related descriptors), and to systematically identify the relations among the features.

2.6.2 Example Discovery

This stage utilizes different multivariable arrangement innovations, straight or non-direct relapse advancements, master framework approaches, and AI advances to find the examples, which can clarify the information in incredible detail.

2.6.3 Pattern Explanation

Any outcome ought to be logical to scientific experts or researcher. A few information mining results can be straight forward for physicists, for example, topological data. Nonetheless, the outcomes from measurable methodologies or AI strategies may seem hard for physicists to comprehend. In this manner, de-convolution or information perception advances are required to decipher the dynamic example, for example, neural system designs with the goal that scientific experts can take synthetic activities.

2.6.4 New Technologies

New technologies, such as SVMs, are appearing in recent scientific applications. SVM is one of the discriminant approaches. This method eliminates many problems (such as local minima, un-robust results and too many parameter settings) experienced with other inference methodologies like neural networks and decision trees. However, more investigations are required for applying SVM in cheminformatics.

2.7 Concluding Remarks and Future Prospects

Chemical probes generated through academic programs can provide valuable information on target biology and translatability. The NIH Molecular Libraries Program contributed significantly toward probe discovery and developed 375 probes against a large number of targets. The academic drug discovery consortium (ADCC) lists 149 drug discovery centers across the world. While some of the screening centers focus on specific diseases or capabilities, a vast majority of the screening facilities works on a wide range of targets and diseases. The screening centers differ in the size of screening resources (compound collections, advanced equipments, and platform detection technologies and capabilities) as well as extent of a university's drug discovery infrastructure support. The extent to which an academic discovery project is taken along the course of mid- to late-stage discovery depends largely on resources and an interest in establishing multidisciplinary collaborations. Obtaining funds for medicinal chemistry optimization, ADME, pharmacokinetics and pharmacodynamics, formulations, and toxicology are bottlenecks for majority of the academic programs. The most profitable molecule emerges in the academia if the identified molecule move forward for the late stage drug development at the industry. Around 24% of FDA-endorsed drug discovery programs somewhere in the range of 1998 and 2007 were accounted for to have risen up logically creative college licenses to biotechnology and pharmaceutical organizations. Academic drug discovery programs are not limited to scholarly research but have additionally acquired advanced analytical methodologies into conventional medication revelation forms. Substantial change in the experiment design and computational methodologies with the use of advanced instrumentation leads to major change in academic as well as industrial drug discovery program. Exploiting computational strategies, strong hits can be acquired in only weeks. Looking for new concoction elements has prompted the development of top-notch datasets and libraries that can be streamlined for either sub-atomic assorted variety or likeness with available candidates. What is more, disseminated processing has gotten progressively famous in enormous scale virtual screening, partially on account of progressively ground-breaking innovation.

Although it is apparent that computational drug discovery methods have great potential, one should not rely on computational techniques in a black box manner and should beware of the Garbage In–Garbage Out (GIGO) phenomenon. The *in silico* segments genererally inquire about virtual screening of the potential candidates followed by use of high-throughput instruments to check the few potential candidates for pharmacological effect however this process is not the substitute for the potential *in vivo* evaluation. Later on, notwithstanding expanding the precision and adequacy of existing advances, the most significant inclination in computational medication disclosure field will be the incorporation of computational science and science together with chemoinformatics and bioinformatics, which will bring about another field known as pharmacoinformatics. Motivated by the fulfillment of the human genome and various pathogen genomes, incredible endeavors will be made to comprehend the job of quality items so as to misuse their capacities, which could be of extraordinary assistance for finding new medication targets. Computational strategies including objective distinguishing proof will turn out to be more enticing, and planned little atoms will likewise be widely utilized as tests for useful research.

References

1. Augen, J., The evolving role of information technology in the drug discovery process. *Drug Discovery Today*, 7, 315–323, 2002.
2. Hecht, P., High-throughput screening: beating the odds with informatics-driven chemistry. *Curr. Drug Discovery*, 7(8), 21–24, 2002 Jan.
3. Xu, J. and Stevenson, J., Drug-like Index: A New Approach To Measure Drug-like Compounds and Their Diversity. *J. Chem. Inf. Comput. Sci.*, 40, 1177–1187, 2000.
4. Matter, H., Baringhaus, K.-H., Naumann, T., Klabunde, T., Pirard, B., Computational approaches towards the rational design of drug-like compound libraries. *Comb. Chem. High Throughput Screen.*, 4, 453–475, 2001.
5. Wikel, J.H. and Higgs, R.E., Applications of molecular diversity analysis in high throughput screening. *J. Biomol. Screen.*, 2, 65–67, 1997.
6. Engel, T., Basic Overview of Chemoinformatics. *J. Chem. Inf. Model.*, 2267–2277, 2006. Varnek, A. and Baskin, I., Chemoinformatics as a Theoretical Chemistry Discipline. *Mol. Inf.*, 30, 1, 20–32, 2011.
7. Nirmalan, N., Hanison, J., Matthews, H., "Omics"-Informed Drug and Biomarker Discovery: Opportunities, Challenges and Future Perspectives. *Proteomes*, 4, 3, 28, 2016 Sep.

3

Role of Bioinformatics in Early Drug Discovery: An Overview and Perspective

Shasank S. Swain* and Tahziba Hussain

Division of Microbiology and NCDs, ICMR-Regional Medical Research Centre, Chandrasekharpur, Bhubaneswar, Odisha, India

Abstract

Today, medicine is essential for humans to live far away from diseases caused by several pathogenic bacteria, viruses, fungus, and some lifestyle-associated health disorders or non-communicable diseases such as diabetes and cancer, including several autoimmune diseases. Thus, several drugs have been introduced continuously by innovative medicinal chemists, pharmacologists, and pharmaceutical companies to counter-attack the newly emerged strains/serotypes/diseases. After a widespread use and genetic variance within pathogens, every drug appeared active for a short period against a particular disease. Thus, the development of a newer drug is a continuous process. But the event of new drug development from original innovation to market is a complicated, time-consuming, and resource-consuming process. At that time, the bioinformatics or computer-aided drug design (CADD) tool is one of the renovated platforms in current drug discovery. The virtual-cum-theoretical assessment of biological activity by cost-effective throughput screening, target identification, and lead optimization process guided and shortened the existing drug development modules. The consecutive growth in bioinformatics technologies was widely assumed pioneer the newer drug development platform. Overall, this is systematic information of different bioinformatics tools useful in early drug discovery. Undoubtedly, individual bioinformatics tools and databases provided biological, chemical, and toxicological information to streamline the early drug discovery.

Keywords: Computer-aided drug design, high-throughput screening, bioinformatics, chemoinformatic tools

Corresponding author: swain.shasanksekhar86@gmail.com

S. Balamurugan, Anand Krishnan, Dinesh Goyal, Balakumar Chandrasekaran and Boomi Pandi (eds.)
Computation in Bioinformatics: Multidisciplinary Applications, (49–68) © 2021 Scrivener Publishing LLC

3.1   Introduction

A drug is a chemical or natural or semi-synthetic substance, has been used to control disease via inhibition of disease-associated enzyme/pathway. At present, the development or identification of a potential lead drug molecule against any disorders is a challenge [1–4]. The current drug discovery has started with a target-specific and should be active, less-toxic, with balanced pharmacokinetics, and Absorption, Distribution, Metabolism, Excretion/Toxicity (ADME/T) properties [5–7]. Before targeting a disease, we need to identify the cause, symptoms, and biological mechanism and medical datasheets, if available earlier. Indeed, drug discovery is a complicated, long-term step-by-step validation procedure with a significant commercial deal. From the history of drug discovery, the traditional hit-and-trial validation method for any drug molecule was a time-consuming process associated with high risks and a nominal output [5, 8].

In the 19th century, drug discovery was an accidental output and a god-gifted asset. The anti-infective agent penicillin was the revolutionary discovery by Sir Alexander Flemings in 1928 during an experiment on the influenza virus at St. Mary's Hospital in London [9, 10]. Nevertheless, conventional drug discovery is the mother of the current drug discovery. The discovery of the microscope by Antony Leeuwenhoek in the 1600s, cells by Robert Hooke in 1665, the report of the first anesthetic agent, nitrous oxide (NO_2) by Joseph Priestly in 1772, first anti-malarial agent, quinine, by Pierre Joseph Pelletier and Joseph Bienaimé Caventou in 1820, first smallpox Vaccine by Dr. John Clinch and the first report on malaria parasite from blood samples in 1800, first successful human blood transfusion by James Blundell in 1818, the discovery of the potent anti-inflammatory drug, Aspirin by Charles Henri Leroux in 1829, Cholera Vaccines by Jaume Ferran Clua in 1884, X-rays by Wilhelm Rontgen in 1895 along with the first synthetic antibacterial, Prontosil by Gerhard Domagk in 1932, etc., are some suitable and scientific examples of appreciated discoveries. Thus, the current drug discovery influenced and made a strong base from the above findings [3, 9, 11, 12].

Currently, the expertise of modern combinatorial medicinal chemistry has been associated with many successful pharmaceutical discoveries in the form of novel drugs/remedies against several deadly diseases [13, 14]. For example, it was not noticed until the mid to late 1800s that the active plant chemical salicylic acid converts to a marketed drug, Aspirin, for pain and inflammation cure. Like that, the computational tool is not a new model for the pharmaceutical industry and drug discovery. Even the word

"Rational Drug Design (RDD)" has been introduced in the early 1980s, and later, computational chemistry, protein crystallography, and molecular biology were slowly incorporated into drug discovery. As a result, today, advanced computational biology and chemistry make an ideal shape by tools of bioinformatics, chemoinformatic, and multi-omics data sets and play a significant role in reducing both time and resources in ongoing drug development modules [15–17].

3.2   Bioinformatics and Drug Discovery

From last decades, several pharmaceutical companies partially minimize their research and development efforts and investment in antibiotic/drug development due to technical difficulties in drug identification, screening; particularly significantly failure in clinical trials due to toxicity and drug-delivery issues with newly introduced drug candidates [18, 19]. Nevertheless, the advanced bandwagon of bioinformatics analysis and time-killing validation process opens a new direction in current drug discovery toward the pharmaceutical companies' benefits. Briefly, the traditional hit-and-trial method known as "forward pharmacology", associated with a lot of validation in both druggable and non-druggable candidates, while the advanced RDD method is known as "reverse pharmacology" selected some specific druggable candidates followed a systematic and target specific approach [17, 20, 21].

Generally, a pathogen can create its survival system in the host-body through activating pathogenic enzymes associated with specific pathways responsible for the disease dissemination. Thus, the analysis of existing medical records and genomics-proteomics information on such enzymes is vital for selecting any putative drug target. On the other hand, the potential drug candidates are always chosen based on solid binding affinity against targeted enzymes through bioinformatics tools [15, 17, 22]. The elimination of unwanted/unsuitable drug candidates at the early-stage through bioinformatics reduces both times/resources to accelerate the drug development module. Thus, the three-dimensional (3D) structure of enzyme/protein and ligand or drug candidates are more essential components for computer-aided drug discovery (CADD). Overall, the broad computational based drug discovery divided into two types, namely, structure-based drug design (SBDD) and ligand-based drug design (LBDD), with specific advantage (Figure 3.1).

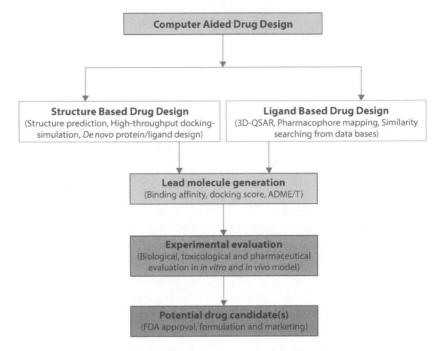

Figure 3.1 Schematic demonstration of a computer-aided drug discovery.

3.2.1 Structure-Based Drug Design (SBDD)

The well-developed programmers and techniques can be used in every drug design stage and guide to achieving the desired goals [17, 20, 23, 24]. Moreover, the advancements in current structural biology through bioinformatics tools reveal several diseases information for drug development. The Protein Data Bank (PDB) is a vast open assessable source of NMR, X-ray, and cryo-EM crystallographic 3D structure of a protein, enzyme, and DNA as a drug target for any research application. However, the above crystallographic methods for 3D structure prediction are more expensive and cannot predict specific protein structures. Simultaneously, the bioinformatics approach called "homology modeling" and "*de novo* protein modeling" generates complicated theoretical protein 3D models to accelerate the drug screening procedure. However, proper modeling and analysis of integral membrane protein drug targets still a challenge for computational biology or bioinformatics [25, 26].

Briefly, the SBDD is one of the methods used in computational-based drug discovery during selecting a potent inhibitor(s) from a bunch of chemical entities/drug candidates against a particular/desired target

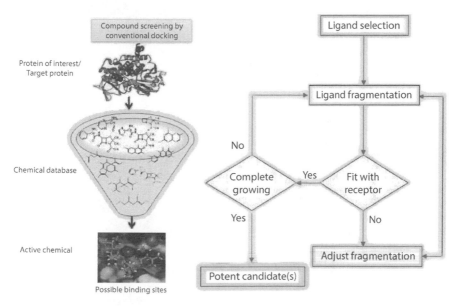

Figure 3.2 Schematic presentation of structure-based drug design.

protein/enzyme/DNA linked with the disease [27, 28] (Figure 3.2). The potential chemical entity or lead drug is selected based on the molecular interaction or binding affinity or docking score (kcal/mol) with the target protein through a computational platform known as "molecular docking" or "virtual screening". Mainly, ligand efficacy, type and site of binding, and biding distance between protein-ligand are essential parameters used during the selection of any potential lead drug candidates. Additionally, ligand modification is also an alternative technique employed to overcome unstable interactions or enhance biological potency or reduce drug candidates' toxic profiles, known as lead optimization [29, 30]. Overall, currently used virtual screening and molecular docking-simulation able to locate potent drug candidates in minimum time and resource to accelerate development modules [28, 31–33].

3.2.2   Ligand-Based Drug Design (LBDD)

Similarly, LBDD also an indirect drug design method based on a known ligand against unknown targets [34, 35] (Figure 3.3). LBDD drug development platform is primarily a preferable approach for repurposing drug discovery to minimize the drug requirements at any emerging/pandemic time. The exploration of a known drug candidate's unknown potency is the

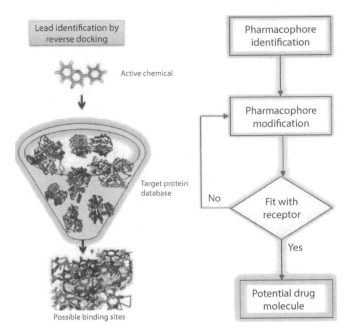

Figure 3.3 Schematic presentation of ligand-based drug design.

ideal platform in ongoing drug discovery. The same ligand interactions, ligand efficacy, and interaction type are an ideal parameters for selecting multi-potential chemical entities in the LBDD platform. The advantage of this method is to play with specific know ligands having some existing data to use against any other diseases/purpose. Still in SBDD cases, the selection of unknown ligand may increases a higher chance of failure during toxicity/side effect validation stages even after most significant interaction with our target of interest. The versatile quantitative structure-activity relationships (QSAR) and pharmacophore modeling are essential in LBDD to improve any selected candidate's potency and efficacy [36, 37]. Thus, the virtual platform–based SBDD and LBDD possess both advantages-cum-disadvantages but are cost-effective and need proper utilization for a specific purpose.

3.3   Bioinformatics Tools in Early Drug Discovery

Today, advanced machine learning and artificial intelligence techniques mimic the biological system significantly and give more reliable early drug discovery results. On the other hand, after physical evaluation, both toxicity and ADME/T profiles are the most common reason-cum-obstacles for the failure of most newly introduced drug candidates in the clinical trial. In this stage, the high-throughput computational screening and prediction of possible toxicity and ADME/T properties in the preclinical stage are more advantageous in drug discovery [29, 38]. As a result, CADD or computational tools are cost-effective, time-saving, and user-friendly [39].

3.3.1   Possible Biological Activity Prediction Tools

Biological activity is defined as the supremacy of any chemical entity/substance to change the natural process of a biological system [40]. Substances/drugs may be active against two or more biological targets or diseases, simultaneous in different characteristics. For example, the first line antimycobacterial drug, Rifampicin, was used against *Mycobacterium tuberculosis* in directly observed treatment, short-course (DOTS), as well as against *M. leprae* in multi-drug therapy (MDT) synergistically with different substances in different doses. The biological activity of material proved through an experimental method as per objective and activity calculated by the concentration/quantity of elements able to change/control disease state without any adverse effects.

Presently, computational tools and software can predict the possible biological activity of a chemical entity. For example, the widely used Prediction of Activity Spectra for Substances (PASS) tool able to estimates several probable biological-activity profiles of compounds based on their structural composition or formulae with an "average accuracy of prediction" is about 95 %. The PASS prediction is designed based on the knowledge of the structure-activity relationship (SAR) of about 260,000 compounds with known biological activities [41]. According to PASS prediction, when the Pa value was > 0.7, the chemical structure probably would exhibit well biological activity in an experimental model. In contrast, a chemical with 0.5 < Pa < 0.7 value would exhibit considerably lesser activity. Alternately, when the Pa value was < 0.5, the compound would not be active in any experimental model. The PASS program predicts with reasonable accuracy about 400 types of biological activities at the molecular level to identify potential targets for an unknown compound [41].

Similarly, molecular docking is a crucial method to verify the biological activity of a chemical through molecular interaction with the targeted enzyme [42]. The concept of docking has been developed on the principle of the lock-and-key theory. During the docking study, the interaction between a target enzyme with any small chemical entity generates an energy value (known as docking score) and an indicator of that chemical entity's biological activity against the target. According to docking software, AutoDock Vina, the docking score is represented in the negative sign and more in the negative score indicates a higher potency. Several free and purchase software/tools are available for docking and simulation study (Table 3.1). Docking-based virtual selection guided some essential aspects of drug designing through the inherent binding affinity between drug and target enzyme, which is useful for speeding up optimization of the lead molecule in the least time and resources [1, 31] (Figure 3.4). Molecular docking has been applied for the last two decades and located several potential drug molecules effortlessly than the traditional approach [43]. Thus, it plays an essential role in selecting active chemicals early for clinical validation.

Molecular dynamics (MD) simulations have been used in CADD to check the docking complex intermolecular stability in a pre-generated

Table 3.1 List of some widely and freely available tools and software's for molecular docking.

Name of tool	Brief description	Web information
AutoDock and AutoDock Vina	Molecular docking between protein-ligand interactions based on Lamarckian genetic algorithm and free energy scoring function.	http://autodock.scripps.edu/ http://vina.scripps.edu/download.html
ArgusLab	A molecular modeling, docking and quantum analysis user friendly software	http://www.arguslab.com/arguslab.com/ArgusLab.html
DOCK Blaster	Docking study especially with chemicals compound presented in ZINC data based against any biological target structure	https://blaster.docking.org/
BSP-SLIM	A blind molecular docking platform especially for low resolution protein structure with any drug candidates	https://zhanglab.ccmb.med.umich.edu/BSP-SLIM/

(Continued)

Table 3.1 List of some widely and freely available tools and software's for molecular docking. (*Continued*)

Name of tool	Brief description	Web information
HADDOCK	An information-driven flexible docking approach for bio-molecular complexes	https://haddock.science.uu.nl/
Hex and Hex Server	A quick active and powerful visualization docking server for protein-protein study	http://hexserver.loria.fr/
iGEMDOCK	A user-friendly docking server for identifying lead compounds and understanding ligand binding mechanisms	http://gemdock.life.nctu.edu.tw/dock/igemdock.php
PatchDock	An algorithm-based docking study for protein, DNA, peptide, and drug	https://bioinfo3d.cs.tau.ac.il/PatchDock/php.php
SwissDock	A web-based docking server for prediction of the molecular-ligand interactions	http://www.swissdock.ch/
ZDOCK	An interactive docking prediction tool for protein-protein study	http://zdock.umassmed.edu/

Figure 3.4 A schematic presentation of protein-ligand interaction visualization with two different software PyMOL and BIOVIO-DVS.

environment [31]. Moreover, thermodynamic integration and free energy perturbation methods are more accurate analyses for protein-ligand complexes stability but still quite limited for large complex bio-molecular recognition [29, 33]. Nowadays, MD simulation methods have become a routine practice in CADD to analyzing structural flexibility and entropic effects as thermodynamics and kinetics associated with receptor-drug recognition precisely [31]. Overall, some MD analyses varied from software to software, as each software was established, followed by specific algorithms and force fields. Currently, GROMACS is one the most liable and freely assessable software for a beginner. Indeed, programming hands/knowledge of computational coding is essential in the computational platform, most specifically during MD simulation.

3.3.2   Possible Physicochemical and Drug-Likeness Properties Verification Tools

Several potent drug candidates were removed in clinical trials for lack of drug-suitability profiles, such as low bioavailability, high toxicity, poor pharmacokinetics, or drug-drug interactions. Thus, all balanced form is known as the character of drug ability or drug-likeness property [44]. CADD has always focused on searing and screening potential lead chemical entities based on the ideal drug-likeness properties and strong binding affinity against the target protein. During 1990–2010, drug ability prediction in the early stage is impossible, and the FDA drug approval rates also significantly reduce [45, 46]. Predicting likely drug profiles through computational tools decreases the time-consuming and expensive *in vitro* and *in vivo* experiments with unwanted drug candidates.

Solubility, stability, pharmacokinetics, and ADME/T profiles are determinant factors for drug ability [47, 48]. The Lipinski's rule of five (RO5) or Pfizer rule considers molecular weight (MW), number of hydrogen bond acceptors (H-BA), number of hydrogen bond donors (H-BD), and octanol/water partition coefficient (ClogP) value during analysis. The RO5 parameters also directly influenced pharmacokinetics profiles and ADME/T properties statistically and experimentally [44]. According to RO5, the MW of the prospective chemical must have ≤ 500 g/mol, with H-BD ≤ 5, H-BA ≤ 10, and ClogP ≤ 5. If a compound violates two or more rules, then it may not be orally active for the human body. Thus, RO5 standardization is a regular analysis in an ongoing computational drug development platform.

As follows, most of the marketed drugs have been promoted through/obeys the principle of RO5 because it is a pre-defined process for validating drug-likeness of designed chemical(s), computationally before synthesis, and subjective for pharmacological validations. Thus, predicting the drug-likeness value for a new chemical entity is a statistical output of existing drugs placed in World Drug Index documents. Today, Molspiration (https://www.molinspiration.com/), MolSoft (https://www.molsoft.com/), and SwissADME (http://www.swissadme.ch/) are widely used user-friendly tools for the drug-likeness prediction by uploading the newly designed chemical structure or using Simplified Molecular Input Line Entry System (SMILE) notation, according to tools (Table 3.2).

Table 3.2 List of some widely and freely used tools for physicochemical, toxicity, and ADMET-pharmacokinetics profile prediction.

Name of tool	Brief description	Web information
admetSAR	For the prediction of ADME/T profiling by structure similarity search QSAR models	http://lmmd. ecust.edu.cn/ admetsar2
Lazar	A QSRA-based framework for prediction of toxicity, lethal dose, and recommended dose for a desired chemical	http://lazar.in-silico. de
Molinspiration	A fragment-based virtual screening platform for physicochemical properties, bioactivity prediction of a chemical entity	https://www. molinspiration. com/
MolSoft	A high-speed molecular properties and drug likeness score calculator tool for a chemical	https://www. molsoft.com/
OECD Toolbox	For prediction of several end points as well as experimental data for reference study	http://toolbox. oasis-lmc.org
OSIRIS-property explore	Prediction of solubility, toxicity physicochemical properties for a chemical	https://www. organic-chemistry.org/ prog/peo/
PreADMET	It is a drug-likeness, ADME/T and toxicity prediction tool based on training set data	https://preadmet. bmdrc.kr/

(Continued)

Table 3.2 List of some widely and freely used tools for physicochemical, toxicity, and ADMET-pharmacokinetics profile prediction. (*Continued*)

Name of tool	Brief description	Web information
ProTox-II	Welcome to ProTox-II, a virtual lab for the prediction of toxicities of small molecules	http://tox.charite. de/protox_II/
ToxiM	A machine learning approach for perdition of solubility, toxicity profile of a molecule	http:// metagenomics. iiserb.ac.in/ ToxiM/index. html
Swiss-ADME	Prediction of ADMET-pharmacokinetics, bioavailability and drug-likeness properties for any chemical entity	http://www. swissadme.ch/

3.3.3   Possible Toxicity and ADME/T Profile Prediction Tools

Toxicity-related adverse effects continue to challenge any newly intro-duced drug candidates to pass the clinical trial evaluation stages to become a marketed drug [45, 46]. Moreover, a pharmaceutical company based on the business profile is directly proportional to the achievement of introduced drugs in clinical trials. Thus, identifying safety issues ear-lier or in a preclinical stage is a great advantage, wherein *in silico* toxicity prediction plays a crucial role [33, 34]. Using advanced high-throughput algorithms, artificial intelligence techniques, multi-omic clinical data set increases the quality and efficacy of computational toxicity predic-tion, which is more beneficial for the pharmaceutical industry to remove unwanted toxic chemicals in the preclinical stage.

Several training set databases, namely, ACuteTox (http://www.acu-tetox.eu/), Open PHACTS (https://www.openphactsfoundation.org/), OpenTox (https://www.opentox.net/), ToxBank (http://www.toxbank.net/), RepDose (https://repdose.item.fraunhofer.de/), RISCTOX: (http://risc-tox.istas.net/en/), and TOXNET (https://toxnet.nlm.nih.gov/), gather a huge volume of clinical facts and free to assess for any research guidance. The primary objectives of the above reference databases are to increase the reliability of toxicity prediction, reduce experimental toxicological testing, and select safer chemicals for drug development for experimental study [23, 30, 49]. Several tools are already available in the public domain to predict the possible toxicity based on the presented training data (Table 3.2).

However, toxicity prediction of the desired drug candidates through the computational tool is a heavy task because of all toxicological properties associated with multiple physiological processes through ADME/T profiles. The biological system also varies from mice to rats, pigs, rats, bats, monkeys, and humans; thus, predicting the accurate toxicity profiles is always an expensive and time-consuming procedure. Concomitantly, the entire drug delivery validation system, such as pharmacokinetics (PK), pharmacodynamics (PD), half-life period (T½), drug-drug interaction, and drug excretion profiles recognized under ADME/T as a crucial parameter during drug validation. Example tools are ADMETlab (http://admet. scbdd.com/calcpre/index/), admetSAR (http://lmmd.ecust.edu.cn/admet-sar2), PreADMET (https://preadmet.bmdrc.kr/), SwissADME (http://www.swissadme.ch/), and vNN (https://vnnadmet.bhsai.org/). Indeed, several commercial spoon-feeding/more user-friendly/reliable computational tool/software is also available for molecular docking, toxicity prediction, drug-likeness score, toxicity, and pharmacokinetic profiles predication. Nevertheless, AutoDock like free software for molecular docking, GROMACS for MD-simulation, PyMOL for molecular interaction visualization, PASS for biological activity prediction, Molsoft for drug-likeness score prediction, ProTox for toxicity prediction, and SwissADME for ADME/T profile assessment and, on the other hand, PDB for relevant 3D-protein structure information, DrugBank and PubChem for drug/chemical structure information, and KEGG database for reference pathway mapping are most widely useable/assessable several freely bioinformatics tools/software and databases, worldwide.

3.4 Future Directions With Bioinformatics Tool

A researcher or scientist always aims to target and identify the safe, efficient compounds with perfect pharmacokinetic profiles to convert a rational market drug in their associated drug discovery field. For the last two decades, the traditional method, the "one-target-one approach", is an expensive, time-taking, practice in drug discovery [50, 51]. The currently used integral approach taking the information of literature, disease, target, compound, mechanisms, and parameters with advanced computational expertise is a more comprehensive and holistic methodology for developing suitable drug candidates [32, 34, 50, 52]. Computational tools promise for gaining, policing, and promising to simplify the conventional drug discovery method continuously. Additionally, the freely assessable massive amount of data sets from PDB, NCBI, UniProtKB, PubChem, ZINC, KEGG, and PubChem Drug Bank along with previous research/medical information from literature databases, namely, PubMed, Scopus, Sci-Hub, play a crucial role in early drug discovery [29, 32, 53, 54].

However, a chemical that is screened *in vitro* for efficacy against disease may fail in clinical trial stages due to the lack of drug-likeness profile/ score. A maximum number of pipeline drugs were removed in different stages of clinical trials before FDA approval for a marketed drug, even after an investment of >2.6 billion dollars for a drug candidate [45, 46, 55]. The high-throughput screening (HTS) screening is an alternative way to determine the active drug molecules from a bank of chemicals with a high possibility for a marketed drug [33]. However, HTS is still expensive and requires abundant resources, which are not accessible in academic settings regularly. It is now converted into a virtual screening or virtual shortcuts as a more robust and energetic tool in the pharmaceutical sector after advanced computational tools or CADD with HTS. Thus, to save resources and time during the selection of potent-lead-drug molecule(s) or avoiding unwanted-drug-molecule(s) in the pre-clinical stage. Today, CADD tools are not used in the pharmaceutical company and in most popular in every academic to reduce expensive experimental assays during productive outputs [17, 34]. The CADD program guided to predict the possible side effects, bioavailability, and associated crucial clinical parameters in drug development modules. Successively, in the modern genomic era, the combination of a sufficient number of multilevel biological and chemical data sets from tissue, DNA, protein, and the whole organism will help to predict the most nearby results by advanced computational machine learning hypothesis, tools, and algorithms [21, 23, 28, 30].

The addition of medicinal chemistry with bioinformatics tools has revolutionized current drug discovery toward the designing or screening a lead drug within minimum time and resources [1, 13, 14]. In combination, both the "MedChem-BioChem" model provides a professional environment of drug discovery with a high degree of scientific heterogeneity and a compelling manner toward improving modern drug discovery platforms. This is a new era of drug discovery to uncover links between diseases through transcriptome analysis, protein expression, and multi-omic networking profiles of target enzymes. Several studies have confirmed that the computational approach followed by experimental assessment had been efficaciously executed to identify novel therapeutic agents [1, 31, 35]. The method needs to be analyzed before implementing different computational tools for fruitful results because every technique has its field of applicability and limitations. Thus, we cannot depend only on computational outputs to avoid the original hypothesis and investigation. The computational approach is used to find out some possible clues or links between drugs and diseases. Incorporating the vast and amount of chemical, biological, and clinical data with computational hypothesis-prediction is challenging. For example, sometimes, computationally predicted novel compound(s) cannot be synthesized in the laboratory and cannot exhibit significant *in vitro* and *in vivo* studies [56, 57]. Thus, experimental assessment is only and one of the main methods to validate the computational prediction. To find out more links between drug, target and disease is the primary focus for a computational chemist or biologist to simplify the current drug discovery method [6, 17, 28, 49, 58].

3.5   Conclusion

Today, several advanced molecular techniques, along with time-killing assays were introduced in place of the traditional hit-and-trial method for isolation, selection, and validation of potent therapeutic agents for early diagnosis and control. Indeed, the CADD is specifically used to discover biological active lead chemical/drugable agent(s) based on computational chemistry, predicted docking pose, and strong molecular binding affinity-stability against a target disease through SBDD or LBDD method. Associated pre-characterized activity, function, and mechanism accelerated the drug discovery procedure. Additionally, "systems pharmacology" is an innovative drug research model where both ligand and protein information are combined to generate a novel drug molecule. Progressively, MD simulation and quantum mechanical study are most often use to study minute conformational changes between protein-ligand complexes in a pre-defined environment at different intervals. Overall, the CADD method can reduce the time and resources through systematic-cum-optimized processes in current drug discovery; however, a potential drug is always approved based on experimental (*in vitro* and *in vivo*) results. Thus, bioinformatics is the value-added virtual feature to speed up the current drug discovery procedure to design safer and more effective drugs from the preliminary stage.

Acknowledgements

ICMR-Young Scientist Research Scheme supports this work (FTS No. 3128113/No.R.12014/14/2017-HR), awarded to Dr. S. S. Swain by Department of Health Research (Indian Council of Medical Research), Govt. of India, New Delhi.

References

1. Swain, S.S., Paidesetty, S.K., Padhy, R.N., Development of antibacterial conjugates using sulfamethoxazole with monocyclic terpenes: A systematic medicinal chemistry based computational approach. *Comput. Methods Programs Biomed.*, 140, 185, 2017.
2. Atanasov, A.G., Waltenberger, B., Pferschy-Wenzig, E.M., Linder, T., Wawrosch, C., Uhrin, P., Temml, V., Wang, L., Schwaiger, S., Heiss, E.H., Rollinger, J.M., Schuster, D., Breuss, J.M., Bochkov, V., Mihovilovic, M.D., Kopp, B., Bauer, R., Dirsch, V.M., Stuppner, H., Discovery and resupply of pharmacologically active plant-derived natural products: A review. *Biotechnol. Adv.*, 33, 1582, 2015.
3. Arrowsmith, J., A decade of change. *Nat. Rev. Drug Discovery*, 11, 17, 2012.
4. Brodniewicz, T. and Grynkiewicz, G., Preclinical drug development. *Acta Pol. Pharm.*, 67, 578, 2010.
5. Gajdács, M., The Concept of an ideal antibiotic: Implications for drug design. *Molecules*, 24, E892, 2019.
6. Elebring, T., Gill, A., Plowright, A.T., What is the most important approach in current drug discovery: doing the right things or doing things right? *Drug Discovery Today*, 17, 1166, 2012.
7. Swinney, D.C. and Anthony, J., How were new medicines discovered? *Nat. Rev. Drug Discovery*, 10, 507, 2011.
8. Mohs, R.C. and Greig, N.H., Drug discovery and development: Role of basic biological research. *Alzheimers Dement (N Y)*, 3, 651, 2017.
9. Hutchings, M., Truman, A., Wilkinson, B., Antibiotics: past, present and future. *Curr. Opin. Microbiol.*, 51, 72, 2019.
10. Tan, S.Y. and Tatsumura, Y., Alexander Fleming (1881–1955): Discoverer of penicillin. *Singapore Med. J.*, 56, 366, 2015.
11. Schuhmacher, A., Gassmann, O., Hinder, M., Changing R&D models in research-based pharmaceutical companies. *J. Transl. Med.*, 14, 105, 2016.
12. Patwardhan, B. and Mashelkar, R.A., Traditional medicine-inspired approaches to drug discovery: can *Ayurveda* show the way forward? *Drug Discovery Today*, 14, 804, 2009.

13. Campbell, I.B., Macdonald, S.J.F., Procopiou, P.A., Medicinal chemistry in drug discovery in big pharma: past, present and future. *Drug Discovery Today*, 23, 219, 2018.
14. Itoh, Y. and Suzuki, T., "Drug" discovery with the help of organic chemistry. *Yakugaku Zasshi*, 137, 283, 2017.
15. Romano, J.D. and Tatonetti, N.P., Informatics and computational methods in natural product drug discovery: A review and perspectives. *Front. Genet.*, 10, 368, 2019.
16. Hasin, Y., Seldin, M., Lusis, A., Multi-omics approaches to disease. *Genome Biol.*, 18, 83, 2017.
17. Macalino, S.J., Gosu, V., Hong, S., Choi, S., Role of computer aided drug design in modern drug discovery. *Arch. Pharm. Res.*, 38, 1686, 2015.
18. Simpkin, V.L., Renwick, M.J., Kelly, R., Mossialos, E., Incentivising innovation in antibiotic drug discovery and development: progress, challenges and next steps. *J. Antibiot. (Tokyo)*, 70, 1087, 2017.
19. Taylor, D., The pharmaceutical industry and the future of drug development, in: *pharmaceuticals in the environment*, pp. 1–33, Environmental Science and Technology, 2015.
20. Lage, O.M., Ramos, M.C., Calisto, R., Almeida, E., Vasconcelos, V., Vicente, F., Current screening methodologies in drug discovery for selected human diseases. *Mar. Drugs*, 16, E279, 2018.
21. Zhou, J., Li, Q., Wu, M., Chen, C., Cen, S., Progress in the rational design for polly-pharmacology drug. *Curr. Pharm. Des.*, 22, 3182, 2016.
22. Aparoy, P., Reddy, K.K., Reddanna, P., Structural and ligand based drug design strategies in the development of novel 5- LOX inhibitors. *Curr. Med. Chem.*, 19, 3763, 2012.
23. Patel, C.N., Kumar, S.P., Rawal, R.M., Patel, D.P., Gonzalez, F.J., Pandya, H.A., A multiparametric organ toxicity predictor for drug discovery. *Toxicol. Mech. Methods.*, 30, 159, 2020.
24. Xia, X., Bioinformatics and drug discovery. *Curr. Top. Med. Chem.*, 17, 1709, 2017.
25. Yin, H. and Flynn, A.D., Drugging membrane protein interactions. *Annu. Rev. Biomed. Eng.*, 18, 51, 2016.
26. Arinaminpathy, Y., Khurana, E., Engelman, D.M., Gerstein, M.B., Computational analysis of membrane proteins: the largest class of drug targets. *Drug Discovery Today*, 14, 1130, 2009.
27. Rawson, S., Bisson, C., Hurdiss, D.L., Fazal, A., McPhillie, M.J., Sedelnikova, S.E., Baker, P.J., Rice, D.W., Muench, S.P., Elucidating the structure basis for different enzyme inhibitor enzyme inhibitor potency by cryo-EM. *Proc. Natl. Acad. Sci. U.S.A.*, 115, 1795, 2018.

28. Lionta, E., Spyrou, G., Vassilatis, D.K., Cournia, Z., Structure-based virtual screening for drug discovery: principles, applications and recent advances. *Curr. Top. Med. Chem.*, 14, 1923, 2014.

29. Sliwoski, G., Kothiwale, S., Meiler, J., Lowe, E.W., Jr, Computational methods in drug discovery. *Pharmacol. Rev.*, 66, 334, 2013.

30. Hughes, J.P., Rees, S., Kalindjian, S.B., Philpott, K.L., Principles of early drug discovery. *Br. J. Pharmacol.*, 162, 1239, 2011.

31. Swain, S.S., Paidesetty, S.K., Dehury, B., Sahoo, J., Chaitanya, S.V., Mahapatra, N., Hussain, T., Padhy, R.N., Molecular docking and simulation study for synthesis of alternative dapsone derivative as a newer anti-leprosy drug in multidrug therapy. *J. Cell. Biochem.*, 119, 9838, 2018.

32. Leelananda, S.P. and Lindert, S., Computational methods in drug discovery. *Beilstein J. Org. Chem.*, 12, 2694, 2016.

33. Ge, H., Wang, Y., Li, C., Chen, N., Xie, Y., Xu, M., He, Y., Gu, X., Wu, R., Gu, Q., Zeng, L., Xu, J., Molecular dynamics-based virtual screening: accelerating the drug discovery process by high-performance computing. *J. Chem. Inf. Model.*, 53, 2757, 2013.

34. Yu, W. and MacKerell, A.D., Jr., Computer-aided drug design methods. *Methods Mol. Biol.*, 1520, 85, 2017.

35. Aparoy, P., Reddy, K.K., Reddanna, P., Structure and ligand based drug design strategies in the development of novel 5-LOX inhibitors. *Curr. Med. Chem.*, 19, 3763, 2012.

36. Baig, M.H., Ahmad, K., Rabbani, G., Danishuddin, M., Choi, I., Computer-aided drug design and its application to the development of potential drugs for neurodegenerative disorder. *Curr. Neuropharmacol.*, 16, 740, 2018.

37. Shim, J. and Mackerell, A.D., Jr., Computational ligand based rational design: Role of conformational sampling and force fields in model development. *MedChemComm*, 2, 356, 2011.

38. Nantasenamat, C. and Prachayasittikul, V., Maximizing computational tools for successful discovery. *Expert. Opin. Drug Discovery*, 10, 321, 2015.

39. Roy, A., Early probe and drug discovery in academia: A minireview. *High Throughput*, 7, pii:E4, 2018, doi: 10.3390/ht7010004.

40. Schenone, M., Dančík, V., Wagner, B.K., Clemons, P.A., Target identification and mechanism of action in chemical biology and drug discovery. *Nat. Chem. Biol.*, 9, 232, 2013.

41. Khurana, E., Devane, R.H., Dal Peraro, M., Klein, M.L., Computational study of drug binding to the membrane-bound tetrameric M2 peptide bundle from influenza-A virus. *Biochim. Biophys. Acta*, 1808, 530, 2011.

42. Meng, X.Y., Zhang, H.X., Mezei, M., Cui, M., Molecular docking: a powerful approach for structure-based drug discovery. *Curr. Comput. Aided Drug Des.*, 7, 146, 2011.

43. Jorgensen, W.L., The many roles of computation in drug discovery. *Science*, 303, 1813, 2004.

44. Benet, L.Z., Hosey, C.M., Ursu, O., Oprea, T.I., BDDCS, the rule of 5 and drugability. *Adv. Drug Delivery Rev.*, 101, 89, 2016.

45. Drago, T., Cahill, K., Grealy, A., Lucey, K., Mahmoud, M., Pharmaceutical company in-house research and licensing transaction review. *Adv. J. Soc. Sci.*, 8, 77, 2021.

46. Takebe, T., Imai, R., Ono, S., The current status of drug discovery and development as originated in united states academia: The influence of industrial and academic collaboration on drug discovery and development. *Clin. Transl. Sci.*, 11, 597, 2018.

47. Tian, S., Wang, J., Li, Y., Li, D., Xu, L., Hou, T., The application of *in silico* drug-likeness predictions in pharmaceutical research. *Adv. Drug Delivery Rev.*, 86, 2, 2015.

48. Lipinski, C.A., Lead- and drug-like compounds: the rule-of-five revolution. *Drug Discovery Today Technol.*, 1, 337, 2004.

49. Russell, R.B. and Eggleston, D.S., New roles for structure in biology and drug discovery. *Nat. Struct. Biol.*, 7, 928, 2000.

50. Earm, K. and Earm, Y.E., Integrative approach in the era of failing drug discovery and development. *Integr. Med. Res.*, 3, 211, 2014.

51. Cressey, D., Traditional drug-discovery model ripe for reform. *Nature*, 471, 17, 2011.

52. Yang, S.Y., Pharmacophore modeling and applications in drug discovery: challenges and recent advances. *Drug Discovery Today*, 15, 444, 2010.

53. Zheng, S., Dharssi, S., Wu, M., Li, J., Lu, Z., Text mining for drug discovery. *Methods Mol. Biol.*, 1939, 231, 2019.

54. Agarwal, P. and Searls, D.B., Literature mining in support of drug discovery. *Brief. Bioinform.*, 9, 479, 2008.

55. Schuhmacher, A., Gassmann, O., Hinder, M., Changing R&D models in research-based pharmaceutical companies. *J. Transl. Med.*, 14, 105, 2016.

56. Kügler, P., Rast, G., Guth, B.D., Comparison of *in vitro and* computational experiments on the relation of inter-beat interval and duration of repolarization in a specific type of human induced pluripotent stem cell-derived cardiomyocytes. *PLoS One*, 14, e0221763, 2019, doi: 10.1371/journal.pone.0221763.

57. Banerjee, P., Siramshetty, V.B., Drwal, M.N., Preissner, R., Computational methods for prediction *in vitro* effects of new chemical structures. *J. Cheminform.*, 29, 8, 2016.

58. Grootendorst, P., How should we support pharmaceutical innovation? *Expert Rev. Pharmacoecon. Outcomes Res.*, 9, 313, 2009.

4

Role of Data Mining in Bioinformatics

Vivek P. Chavda[1]*, Amit Sorathiya[2], Disha Valu[3] and Swati Marwadi[4]

[1]Department of Pharmaceutics, L.M. College of Pharmacy, Ahmedabad, India
[2]Formulation & Development, Sun Pharma Advanced Research Centre,
Vadodara, India
[3]Analytical Development, Orbicular Pharmaceutical Ltd, Hyderabad, India
[4]Department of Biotechnology, Sinhgad College of Engineering, Pune, India

Abstract

In the recent days, the term which was very challenging in the discipline of informational science is data mining, which includes extraction of tremendous amount of data. Data mining is very useful and interesting in accessing the different patterns of data from the pre-existing data in the database to get knowledge based information using different software techniques. Data mining looks most suitable for bioinformatics, as bioinformatics is enrichment of data, though the evolutionary phases of human existence at molecular level are lacking.

Nevertheless, gathering information from different databases is very helpful and informative in informational science which is affected by the several different aspects of the data stored in the libraries. These libraries involves the persistent data with the relevant domain of science. Also, it consists of various factors such as diversity, count, dimension, etc. Later on, it is not that much easier to manage and access the data which is most useful in data discovery as it requires the cogent scientific skills and deep insight for the body of knowledge around that data. The biological databases compilation is also difficult. The most effective way for accessing the databases in informational science and developing new technologies for studying the biotic system at molecular level includes extracting the raw data from the other relevant databases and also its further evaluation has become more important and crucial concept in informational science.

Keywords: Data mining, proteomics, DNA, RNA, gene expression, analysis, etc.

---

*Corresponding author: Vivek7chavda@gmail.com

S. Balamurugan, Anand Krishnan, Dinesh Goyal, Balakumar Chandrasekaran and Boomi Pandi (eds.)
Computation in Bioinformatics: Multidisciplinary Applications, (69–84) © 2021 Scrivener Publishing LLC

4.1   Introduction

The Data Science is extraction of useful information from the huge amount of data which leads to identify the fresh and understandable data models and patterns out of it [1]. Bioinformatics is the computer-assisted science aiming at managing a huge volume of genomic data, which combines the power of computerized science of storing, analyzing, and utilizing information from biological data such as molecules, sequences, gene expressions, and pathways to solve multiple genetic puzzles [2]. The approaches of improvement to provide some important details about the rapidly expanding sources of biological data in data mining (DM) will play a vital role [3]. DM is the fundamental science of discovery of new interesting configurations and correlation in huge amount of data. It is defined as "the process of finding meaningful new relationships, patterns, and trends by digging into large amounts of data stored in storerooms" [4]. Knowledge Discovery in Databases (KDD) is the word sometime used for DM. These processes are blood for the future research as well as driving force for the technological paradigm. It is the need of the hour which is consistently evolving for identifying the probability of hidden knowledge that exist in the data which is already generated by the science and technology [5].

DM methodologies have paved the futuristic advancement for bioinformatics and an appropriate tool for the same which provides deep insight for the data at the molecular level for recognizing patterns and making algorithms around it. The wide-ranging databases of biological information create both challenges and opportunities for development of novel KDD methods [6, 7]. Biological data handling will be beneficial for identifying the appropriate targets and generating therapeutics around the identified target in a sort span. The entire human genome, the complete set of genetic information within each human cell, has now been determined [8]. Understanding these genetic instructions promises to permit scientists to better understand the nature of diseases and their cures, to identify the mechanisms underlying biological processes such as growth and ageing and to clearly track our evolution and its relationship with other species [9]. The main hindrance lying between investigators and the knowledge they seek is the sheer volume of data available. This is evident from the rapid increase in the number of base pairs and DNA sequences in the repository of GenBank [10].

4.2   Data Mining Methods/Techniques

Selection of DM technique is very crucial in the context of studies being undertaken and in the complexity of the identified problem and business type. Various DM techniques are summarized in Figure 4.1, and a common platform approach is adopted generally for the accuracy and cost-effectiveness of the entire process.

4.2.1   Classification

4.2.1.1   Statistical Techniques

Statistical techniques of DM is a branch of mathematics mainly deals with collection and description of data [11]. Despite of the above fact, many data scientists are against it for being considered as DM technique. But still, it assists to determine the patterns of data evaluated and can build a predictive models around it [12]. For this reason, data analyst should possess some knowledge about the different statistical techniques. In today's world, people have to deal with a large amount of data and have to derive important patterns from it. The application of statistical analysis is given in Figure 4.2, while the different data collection methods are summarized in Figure 4.3.

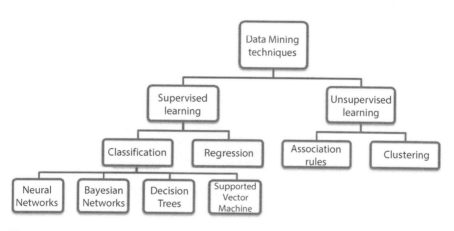

Figure 4.1 Data mining techniques.

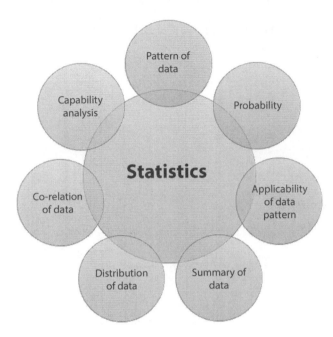

Figure 4.2 Application of statistics in data mining.

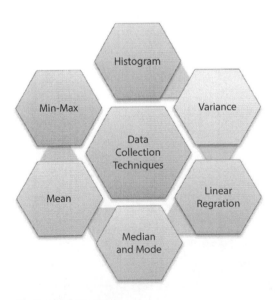

Figure 4.3 Data collection techniques.

For data analysis, statistics is the essential component to understand and evaluate the data. Statistics will help the scientist to identify the data pattern while DM process through data visualization. This will further help in detecting the noise and then in optimizing and identifying the significant finding out of the data jargon.

4.2.1.2   Clustering Technique

Clustering technique (segmentation) is one of the oldest DM techniques where the data which are similar in nature being are treated as a cluster. This will assist to comprehend the differences and similarities between the data and it is very accurate method of DM [13]. It seems to be pretty useful when pattern recognition is needed between the same kinds of data to draw a meaningful conclusion. For instance, an insurance firm can group its consumers based on their income, age, nature of policy, and type of claims. There are different types of clustering methods used for the DM process (Figure 4.4).

Figure 4.4 Types of clustering methods.

4.2.1.3   Visualization

Data visualization is the primary and most common method of the DM which is applied at the beginning of the DM process [14]. Many types of research are going on these days to produce an interesting projection of databases, which is called Projection Pursuit. Data visualization is very useful tool which will give the holistic overview of the analyzed data and helps the scientist to remove the data which are not suitable for the further process. It is equally useful for the recognition of the hidden patterns [12].

4.2.1.4   Induction Decision Tree Technique

As the name suggest, the decision tree technique has the tree-like structure which can generate predictive model [15]. In this technique, the data to be evaluated shall be classified as the branch of the tree and the leaves of the trees are considered as partitions of the data set related to that particular classification. This technique can be used for exploration analysis, data pre-processing, and prediction work [16]. The data are classified as the segment or the branch which possesses some similarities in their information being predicted. On a closer look, one can see that it has pretty good potential for correlate the problem statement with that of the desired outcome; hence, it is popularly used by the statistician for predictive data analysis as well as for the data pre-processing.

The first and foremost step in this technique is growing the tree. The basic of growing the tree depends on finding the best possible question to be asked at each branch of the tree. The decision tree stops growing under any one of the below circumstances.

a) If the segment contains only one record
b) All the records contain identical features
c) The growth is not enough to make any further spilt

CART which stands for Classification and Regression Trees is a data exploration and prediction algorithm which picks the questions in a more complex way. It tries them all and then selects one best question which is used to split the data into two or more segments. After deciding on the segments, it again asks questions on each of the new segment individually. Another popular decision tree technology is CHAID (Chi-Square Automatic Interaction Detector). It is similar to CART but it differs in one way. CART helps in choosing the best questions, whereas CHAID helps in choosing the splits [17].

4.2.1.5   Neural Network

Another significant approach used by individuals these days is the neural network. In the early stages of DM technology, this method is most commonly used. Neural networks are very user friendly as it is sequential process where it does not demand the scientist to be technically sound in the domain of data generated [18, 19].

A set of interconnected neurons is a neural network. A single layer or multiple layers can form. The architecture of the network is called the creation of neurons and their interconnections. There are a wide range of models of neural networks and each model has its own benefits and drawbacks. There are distinct architectures in of neural network model, and these architectures use distinct learning processes. Neural networks are a very solid method of predictive modelling. But even for specialists, it is not quite easy to comprehend. It produces very complicated models that are difficult to completely comprehend. Companies are therefore seeking new solutions to grasp the Neural Network Methodology (NNM).

Two possibilities have already been proposed [20]. The first approach is to bundle the neural network into a complete solution that will allow it to be used for a single application. The second approach is that it is related to specialist advisory services. In numerous types of applications, the neural network has been used [15].

4.2.1.6   Association Rule Technique

It is the different techniques of all techniques in DM which identify the hidden pattern in the data set through which one can find out the variable of interest. Even one can also find out the appearance frequency of any particular variable [21]. Different types of association rules are depicted in Figure 4.5. It will give the frequency as well as correctness of the same rule for particular problem.

This rule technique extends up to a two-step process. First, Step-Find all the data sets which are occurring regularly or repeatedly. Second, Step-Over the time it creates strong association rules from the data sets which appear constantly.

4.2.1.7   Classification

Among all DM techniques, it is the most common and widely used specially to generate model from a large data set (Figure 4.6). Also, the other advantage of this technique is to obtain important information about data

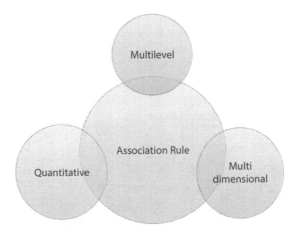

Figure 4.5 Type of association rules.

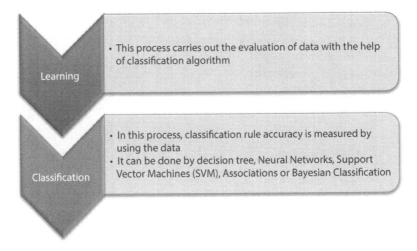

Figure 4.6 Classification technique.

and metadata (data about data). If you evaluate it closely, then it is very much similar to cluster analysis technique, but here, it utilizes decision tree or neural network system. This technique includes two main processes, i.e., Learning and Classification [16, 22].

4.3   DNA Data Analysis

DNA, RNA, and protein are three important elements of life science; they set the groundwork of all living organisms [23]. Tons of researchers are working together to explain the nature of life, and lots of study has been performed to define interactions between structures and their properties [24]. For microbiologists, information encoded in nucleic acid molecular sequences is important because not only it transmits genetic information from generation to generation and furthermore affects transcription and translation activity [25]. Without gathering and processing such DNA sequences, research on the origins of life sciences cannot be performed, which involves identifying the exact order and proportion of the four nitrogen bases in a DNA strand: adenine, thymine, guanine, and cytosine [26].

The most interesting advances in the area of life science research is the isolation of DNA fragments which are exist in large numbers and identification of biologically active using recombinant DNA technology which is the most advantageous aspect in the area of molecular biology. Large DNA molecules could be split into multiple small fragments in an organized manner using restriction endonucleases [16]. Recombinant DNA techniques also help in the purification and classification of independent mixture of restriction fragments and most significantly, at least three steps are required to do DNA sequencing: cloning, sequencing, and analyzing. In DNA sequencing, there are two main techniques: Maxam-Gilbert sequencing (also known as chemical sequencing) and the process of chain termination (also known as Sanger sequencing). The previous approach applies radioactive labels to the 50th end of DNA and produces subsequent breaks at specific bases by using chemical process [27, 28]. In the form of dark bands, which reflect radiolabeled DNA fragments, autoradiography helps to generate a sequence or chain of fragments. Sanger's mechanism, on the other hand, requires modified di-deoxynucleoside triphosphates (ddNTPs).

Although using computers for data analysis has obvious advantages, there still exist weaknesses (Figure 4.7). Despite of so called technological advancement in the field, it has certain disadvantages also which are summarized in Figure 4.8.

Figure 4.7 Importance of DNA sequence data analysis.

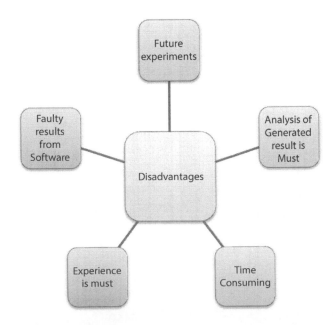

Figure 4.8 Disadvantages of next-generation sequencing data analysis.

4.4   RNA Data Analysis

When we are stating RNA sequencing (RNA-Seq), it is mainly related to transcriptome of a cell. This is mainly done with virtual screening and high-throughput screening method [29]. In comparison with previous Sanger sequencing– and microarray-based techniques, it provides good resolution and greater data coverage for RNA data. These data are very useful for identifying novel transcripts, identifying alternative spliced genes, and detecting allele-specific expression [30, 31]. All the recent advancement in this field like RNA workflow, libraries for sample preparation, and data analysis suits have enabled the scientist to get the functional transcript and transcription process [32]. RNA-Seq may be performed to estimate different RNA populations, including complete RNA, pre-mRNA, and non-coding RNA, including certain microRNA and long ncRNA, in addition to polyadenylated messenger RNA (mRNA) transcripts. A high-throughput approach is mostly used for now a days, which has some additional benefits, such as having more understanding of the complex and dynamic existence of the transcriptome [33, 34]. Elucidation of the different physiological and pathological conditions is now possible with such advanced techniques. With the aid of new mapping techniques, longer reads becomes a reality. Since prolonged readings can extend several exon-exon junctions, with the additional information encoded in longer reads, the recognition and quantification of alternative isoforms can dramatically improve. Soon, one will see the same applications as an extension in the clinical diagnosis like screening of cancer, pregnancy even for personalized medicine [35, 36].

4.5   Protein Data Analysis

Entire units of cellular components, such as the genome, transcriptome, and, more recently, the proteome, can be analyzed now due to advancement in technology, instrumentation, molecular biology, and bioinformatics [37]. With advancement, it is now possible to monitor changes in the human tissue proteomes that are associated with differentiation, apoptosis, disease, and other important biological modifications [38]. The proteomics arm of the OMICS technology is mainly used to elucidate protein structure, its functionality, interactions, and post-translational modifications. When we compare these data with genomics, it is 100-fold complex and dynamic which contribute to the enormity of the challenge of proteomics and the very modest progress to date [39]. Development of proteomic technologies having different sides can be depicted from relatively broad proteomics experience of the authors and the proteomics reports of others. To increase the overall number of identified and quantified proteins, multiple complimentary approaches need to be taken with any protein-profiling technology. More than one approach can be used to increase the validity of the quantitation of expressed proteins in different samples [40]. To increase the understanding of the quantitation differences arising from biological effects, a multiple-approach strategy would be preferred rather than having experimental approaches [41].

Although the reported number of identified proteins per study may range from a few hundred to a few thousand, the amount of time and material it takes to profile that many proteins is not of less importance [42]. One can see the evolution in both side means analyzing by different mode of mass spectrometry as well as proteomics approaches to be ahead of time still there is a need of better platform based approach for the same [43]. At initial stage, a platform where any raw data file format from any instrument can be deposited and converted into a common file format for preliminary spectral analysis would be extremely valuable. Adding to the same, a good reporting arm for the statistical evaluation of the data is needed [44]. Combination of both these element will surely give us the desired outcome.

4.6   Biomedical Data Analysis

Unprecedented amount of data has been generated with advancement in structural bioinformatics, molecular biology, and pharmacogenomics research in the biomedical field. In short, biomedical data can be available in varieties of sub domains. The major arm of the same is data related to gene expression, DNA sequence, and protein primary structure [27]. Apart from that, addition of the high throughput sequencing methods and cDNA microarray technology has provided efficiency in both data generation as well as its analysis. Virtual screening is also an added star to the same bucket of research tool. There are many algorithms available which can deal with bifurcation of sequences, checking similarities, and get read of weak candidates among them, separating protein coding regions from non-coding regions in DNA sequences, prediction of protein structure as well as function, and reconstructing the underlying evolutionary history [45]. There are four components of a DNA sequence, namely, adenine (A), cytosine (C), guanine (G), and thymine (T), which specifies the code of life.

Similarly, when we talk about proteins primary structure, it mainly grafted from the 20 amino acids. These amino acids will be incorporated for the gene coding of the DNA sequence. On the other side, gene expression data will be useful to understand the expression profile in terms of its regulation under specific conditions in a cell [46]. The research in this field can be accelerated if a good database is created along with a capable software.

4.7 Conclusion and Future Prospects

Bioinformatics and DM are the two side of the same coin. If we consider one side, i.e., Bioinformatics which is having huge amount of data but devoid of molecular level organizational theory to organize such data, these gaps are filled by the other side of the coin, i.e., DM. However, DM in bioinformatics is mainly affected by the heterogeneous nature of data, which make it difficult at reaching quality output some times. Not only this but data integration and level of expertise require to do the same is also the concern. It is useful for the identification of the gene, transcription process, protein function elucidation, function motif detection etc. Apart form that, it is useful for the diagnosis, prognosis and treatment optimization of a particular ailment. It also has potential to detect the interaction, sorting of the database generated and protein sub-cellular location prediction. If we talk about future of the same, the it is surely bright. There is need of an efficient scoring algorithm which can be able to execute all the data dump efficiently and in comprehensive manner is highly desirable.

References

1. Hayashi, C., What is Data Science? Fundamental Concepts and a Heuristic Example. In: *Data Science, Classification, and Related Methods*. Hayashi, C., Yajima, K., Bock, H.-H., Ohsumi, N., Tanaka, Y., Baba, Y. (eds.). Studies in Classification, Data Analysis, and Knowledge Organization, pp. 40–51, Springer, Japan, 1998.
2. Grothaus, G.A., Mufti, A., Murali, T., Automatic layout and visualization of biclusters. *Algorithms Mol. Biol.*, 1, 15, 2006.
3. Murzin, A.G., Brenner, S.E., Hubbard, T., Chothia, C., SCOP: a structural classification of proteins database for the investigation of sequences and structures. *J. Mol. Biol.*, 247, 536–540, 1995.
4. Greiner, L., *What is Data Analysis and Data Mining?*, http://www.dbta. com/Editorial/Trends-and-Applications/What-is-Data-Analysis-and-Data-Mining-73503.aspx, 2019. Jan 7, 2011.

5. Hwang, W., Cho, Y.R., Zhang, A., Ramanathan, M., A novel functional module detection algorithm for protein-protein interaction networks. *Algorithms Mol. Biol.*, 1, 24, 2006.

6. Fayyad, U., Haussler, D., Stolorz, P., Mining scientific data. *Commun. ACM*, 39, 51–57, 1996.

7. Han, J. and Kamber, M., *Data Mining: Concepts and Techniques*, 2nd Ed., Morgan Kaufmann, 2006.

8. Mount, D.W., *Bioinformatics – Sequence and Genome Analysis*, Cold Spring Harbor Laboratory Press, New York, 2001.

9. Li, J., Wong, L., Yang, Q., *Data Mining in Bioinformatics*, IEEE Intelligent System, IEEE Computer Society, 2005.

10. Edwards, D., Hansen, D., Stajich, J.E., DNA Sequence Databases. In: *Bioinformatics*, Edwards, D., Stajich, J., Hansen, D. (eds). Springer, New York, NY, 2009. https://doi.org/10.1007/978-0-387-92738-1_1.

11. Tang, H. and Kim, S., *Bioinformatics: mining the massive data from high throughput genomics experiments, analysis of biological data: a soft computing approach*, S. Bandyopadhyay (Ed.), Indian Statistical Institute, India, 2007.

12. Guillet, F., *Quality measures in data mining*, 1st ed., Springer, Berlin, 2007.

13. Tramontano, A., *Introduction to bioinformatics*, 1st ed., Chapman & Hall/ CRC, London, 2007.

14. Larose, D. and Larose, C., *Discovering Knowledge in Data: An Introduction to Data Mining*, 1st ed., Wiley Publication, 2014.

15. Zhang, Y. and Rajapakse, C.J., *Machine Learning in Bioinformatics*, Wiley, 456, 2008.

16. Han, and Kamber, *Data Mining concepts and techniques*, Morgan Kaufmann Publishers, 2006.

17. Lever, J., Krzywinski, M., Altman, Model selection and overfitting. *N. Nat. Methods*, 13, 703–704, 2016.

18. Lancashire, L.J., Lemetre, C., Ball, G.R., An introduction to artificial neural networks in bioinformatics–application to complex microarray and mass spectrometry datasets in cancer studies. *Brief. Bioinform.*, 10, 3, 315–29, 2009.

19. Yang, Q., Data Mining and Bioinformatics: Some Challenges, 2012, http://www.cse.ust.hk/~qyang (Date of access: 25 Nov 2019).

20. https://www.educba.com/data-mining-techniques/.

21. Baxevanis, A.D., Petsko, G.A., Stein, L.D., Stormo, G.D. (Eds.), *Current Protocols in Bioinformatics*, Wiley, 2007.

22. Hand, D.J., Mannila, H., Smyth, P., *Principles of Data Mining*, MIT Press, p. 578, 2001.

23. Adams, M.D., Kerlavage, A.R., Fleischmann, R.D., Fuldner, R.A., Bult, C.J., Lee, N.H., Kirkness, E.F., Weinstock, K.G., Gocayne, J.D., White, O. *et al.*, Initial assessment of human gene diversity and expression patterns based upon 83 million nucleotides of cDNA sequence. *Nature*, 377, 3–174, 1995.

24. Cristianini, N. and Hahn, M., *Introduction to Computational Genomics*, Cambridge University Press, 2006.
25. Abbott, A., Genome sequence of the nematode C. elegans: a platform for investigating biology. The C. elegans Sequencing Consortium. *Science*, 282, 2012–2018, 1998.
26. Velculescu, V.E., Zhang, L., Vogelstein, B., Kinzler, K.W., Serial analysis of gene expression. *Science*, 270, 484–487, 1995.
27. Abecasis, G.R., Cherny, S.S., Cookson, W.O., Cardon, L.R., Merlin—Rapid analysis of dense genetic maps using sparse gene flow trees. *Nat. Genet.*, 30, 97–101, 2002.
28. Adams, M.D., Kelley, J.M., Gocayne, J.D., Dubnick, M., Polymeropoulos, M.H., Xiao, H., Merril, C.R., Wu, A., Olde, B., Moreno, R.F. *et al.*, Complementary DNA sequencing: Expressed sequence tags and human genome project. *Science*, 252, 1651–1656, 1991.
29. Auer, P.L. and Doerge, R.W., Statistical design and analysis of RNA sequencing data. *Genetics*, 185, 405–416, 2010.
30. Battle, A., Mostafavi, S., Zhu, X., Potash, J.B., Weissman, M.M., McCormick, C., Haudenschild, C.D., Beckman, K.B., Shi, J., Mei, R. *et al.*, Characterizing the genetic basis of transcriptome diversity through RNA-sequencing of 922 individuals. *Genome Res.*, 24, 14–24, 2013.
31. Blencowe, B.J., Ahmad, S., Lee, L.J., Current-generation high-throughput sequencing: Deepening insights into mammalian transcriptomes. *Genes Dev.*, 23, 1379–1386, 2009.
32. Brennecke, P., Anders, S., Kim, J.K., Kolodziejczyk, A.A., Zhang, X., Proserpio, V., Baying, B., Benes, V., Teichmann, S.A., Marioni, J.C. *et al.*, Accounting for technical noise in single-cell RNA-seq experiments. *Nat. Methods*, 10, 1093–1095, 2013.
33. Crick, F., Central dogma of molecular biology. *Nature*, 227, 561–563, 1970.
34. Zeng, W. and Mortazavi, A., Technical considerations for functional sequencing assays. *Nat. Immunol.*, 13, 802–807, 2012.
35. Wang, Z., Gerstein, M., Snyder, M., RNA-Seq: A revolutionary tool for transcriptomics. *Nat. Rev. Genet.*, 10, 57–63, 2009.
36. Rudloff, U., Bhanot, U., Gerald, W., Klimstra, D.S., Jarnagin, W.R., Brennan, M.F., Allen, P.J., Biobanking of human pancreas cancer tissue: Impact of *ex-vivo* procurement times on RNA quality. *Ann. Surg. Oncol.*, 17, 2229–2236, 2010.
37. Wodak, S.J. and Janin, J., Computer Analysis of Protein-Protein Interactions. *J. Mol. Biol.*, 124, 2, 323–42, 1978.
38. Lee, K., Computational Study for Protein-Protein Docking Using Global Optimization and Empirical Potentials. *Int. J. Mol. Sci.*, 9, 65–77, 2008.
39. Abbott, A., A post-genomic challenge: learning to read patterns of protein synthesis. *Nature*, 402, 715–720, 1999.
40. Aebersold, R., Rist, B., Gygi, S.P., Quantitative proteome analysis: methods and applications. *Ann. N. Y. Acad. Sci.*, 919, 33–47, 2000.

41. Yates, J.R., III, Protein structure analysis by mass spectrometry. *Methods Enzymol.*, 271, 351–377, 1996.

42. Aebersold, R., A mass spectrometric journey into protein and proteome research. *J. Am. Soc. Mass. Spectrom.*, 14, 685–695, 2003b.

43. Bischoff, R. and Luider, T.M., Methodological advances in the discovery of protein and peptide disease markers. *J. Chromatogr. B Analyt. Technol. Biomed. Life Sci.*, 803, 27–40, 2004.

44. MacBeath, G. and Schreiber, S.L., Printing proteins as microarrays for high-throughput function determination. *Science*, 289, 1760–1763, 2000.

45. Watson, J.D., Hopkins, N.H., Roberts, J.W. *et al.*, *Molecular Biology of the Gene*, 4th edn., Benjamin-Cummings, Menlo Park, CA, 1987.

46. Aluru, S. (Ed.), *Handbook of Computational Molecular Biology*, Chapman & Hall/CRC Press, 2006.

5

In Silico Protein Design and Virtual Screening

Vivek P. Chavda³, Zeel Patel¹*, Yashti Parmar² and Disha Chavda⁴

*¹Department of Electromechanical, Sheridan Collage of Engineering,
Toronto, Canada*
*²Department of Pharmacology and Medicines, Weifang Medical University,
Shandong, China*
*³Formulation & Development, Dr. Reddy's Laboratory (Biotech division),
Hyderabad, India*
⁴Analytical Development, Orbicular Pharmaceutical Ltd, Hyderabad, India

Abstract

If we look back in the last decade, there are so many achievements been made in the field of molecular biology and computational design to make functional modification of proteins a reality. The journey so far is really long and being cherished from structure based virtual screening (SBVS) which is used at early-stage drug discovery for finding the actual reason of Mutagenesis or even improvement of protein purity and quality. Docking-based virtual screening is most widely used nowadays followed by high-throughput screening. Virtual screening is basically a screening tool at the early phase of drug discovery for sequence selection considering desired protein function. These technological advancements have brought the cost of drug discovery down along with tremendous speed and control over the protein design part which brings the artificial proteins engineering at an evolutionary phase. Software packages for *in silico* protein design have been engineered for the academic usage.

Keywords: Protein design, docking, *in silico*, virtual screening, high-throughput screening

*Corresponding author: Patelzeel1394@gmail.com

S. Balamurugan, Anand Krishnan, Dinesh Goyal, Balakumar Chandrasekaran and Boomi Pandi (eds.)
Computation in Bioinformatics: Multidisciplinary Applications, (85–100) © 2021 Scrivener Publishing LLC

5.1   Introduction

Protein-based drug design, which starts from virtual screening (VS) and ends at commercialization, is a very complex and time-consuming process (10–15 years); here, it also affects the pocket about $1–3 billion. Due to availability of huge protein data and the academic research, lot of information is available which has shortened the path for the target identification of protein design [1]. Computational (*in silico*) methods have been evolved so much that database search, activity relationship, pharmacophores, homology models, and molecular modeling become handy and easy. The initial VS is either ligand based or structure based (Figure 5.1).

Lead compound identification which is shoving sufficient biological activity and effector function is keen in the early stage optimization where various optimization tolls are being explored (Figure 5.2). *In silico* drug discovery presents a rich range of opportunities that will assist in prioritizing targets and compounds for validation *in vitro* and *in vivo*. There is simultaneous development in the robotic technology, and machine learning has paved the way for protein crystallography-based evaluation which is, sometimes, referred as structural bioinformatics [2]. Nowadays, during early stage of discovery protein-protein interaction, inhibitors are also taken in to the consideration.

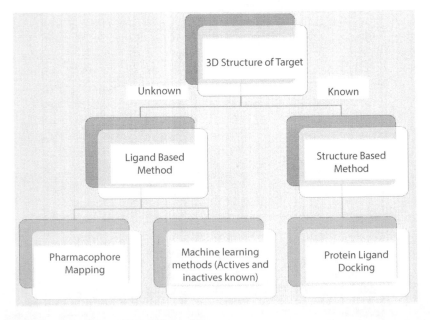

Figure 5.1 Approaches for virtual screening.

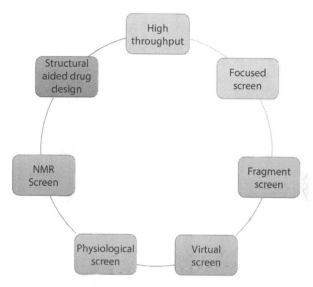

Figure 5.2 Screening strategies.

When we consider small-molecule industry, they have adopted high-throughput screening (HTS) which is based on chemical library as a means to identify new lead compounds. HTS is the second line method after VS for the evaluation for lead optimization process even though it is costly and time consuming [3]. Structure-based drug design (SBDD) with the use of computational methods is the another option to solve the same purpose [4]. Structure-based drug discovery (SBDD) has provided attractive niche for fast and cost-efficient lead discovery and optimization (Figure 5.3) [5]. There are different approaches for the VS like structure-based VS (SBVS), ligand-based VS, and fragment-based VS. Amalgamation of computational methods with 3D structural information of the protein target, one can easily device the underlying molecular interactions involved in ligand-protein binding and thus interpret experimental results in atomic-level detail. Structure-based drug design includes VS but not HTS. In VS, the screening of target is done against already available libraries of drug-like compounds [6]. The compounds which are found promising are further being evaluated experimentally. When it comes to de novo drug design approach, the novel molecule is being grafted using the 3D structure of the receptor [5].

Computer-aided drug discovery has achieved higher hit rates than with HTS [7–9]. When we specifically talk about protein-based drug design, obviously one cannot deny the role of *in silico* methodologies [10–12].

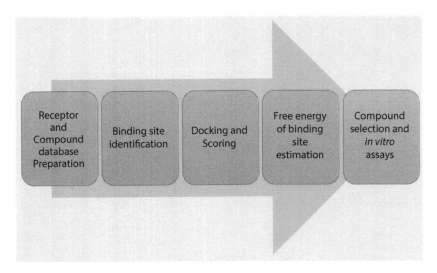

Figure 5.3 Structure-based virtual screening workflow.

Application of X-ray crystallography and nuclear magnetic resonance spectroscopy for the computational drug design has elucidated interactions of target and ligands [13, 14]. SBVS has achieved a solid success as a part of new drug discovery programs, among which docking-based VS (DBVS) is arguably the most widely applied one in practice [15, 16].

5.2   Virtual Screening Process

These are the time-saving tools for the screening of novel biologics as well as the small molecules. The most obvious tools for drug repurposing are HTS and its computational twin: VS. For the bioactivity screening, these are the must in place tools [17]. The major aim of these tool is screening of the compound of interest from the millions of candidates [18]. When we look in to this, it looks pretty simple but it is a very exhaustive process where some computational screening is also done in order to remove some unwanted reactive candidate (Figure 5.4) [19].

The "rule of five" (Ro5) is mostly applied specially in case of small-molecule synthesis where design space is defined by ClogP (octanol/water

Figure 5.4 Road map for high-throughput screening.

partition coefficient), molecular weight, HDO (number of hydrogen bond donors), and HAC (number of hydrogen bond acceptors). The property distribution of chemical and drug databases in the Ro5 space is well characterized [17, 20]. In short, through VS one can identify real, high-affinity ligands with unmatched cost-effectiveness and efficiency [21]. Automated protein docking using three-dimensional or SBVS has paved the ways for bring new protein therapeutics early in the real world [22]. It is really easy through these tools to optimize the molecules on a specific binding site. SBVS is unusually logistically efficient, saving significant labour and resources. One of the biggest advantages of this robotic screen is that one needs to analyze only selected protein molecules for efficacy and binding [23]. Nowadays, combination of machine learning and VS is gaining lot of momentum in biotech industry in predicting protein structure [24]. Song and Co-workers have defined an ensemble learning algorithm "imDC" for prediction of binding proteins [25]. Lin *et al.* defined the state-of-the-art strategy for the classifying protein folding sequentially by merging *K*-means, static selective strategy, and ensemble forward sequential selection which is 74.21% accurate [26].

Table 5.1 Types of screening modes [27].

Screening mode	Number of samples tested per day	Examples
Low-throughput screening	1–500	Animal models, assays for CYP-mediated metabolism combined with LC/MS/MS
Medium-throughput screening	500–10,000	Fluorescent cellular microscopic imaging assay, assays for determination of catalytic activities of oxygen-consuming enzymes
High-throughput screening	10,000–100,000	Fluorescent enzymatic inhibition assay, luciferase reporter gene assays
Ultrahigh-throughput screening	≥100,000	β-lactamase cell reporter assay, assay for quantification of 5-HT2C receptor editing

Drug repositioning propelled by pharmacovigilance and VS may, in some way, provided the right path for the candidate selection with narrow downing the clinical trial study arm [23]. Under the umbrella of computer aided drug design, VS due to its low-cost and time-saving modules being explored nowadays. The different type of screening modes is explained in the Table 5.1. Here, mostly, HTS is used in conjunction with VS vertical.

5.2.1   Before Virtual Screening

It is very much important that before one start working on the VS platform, some knowledge gathering and understanding is requires with respect to Reals, Tangibles, and Virtual [28]. The largest collection of Virtuals and Tangibles is represented by the ChemNavigator database [29]. Genedata Biologics® is a first-in-class workflow system that boosts the efficiency of the biologics discovery process [30]. Cleaning up the collection (Figure 5.5) is very tedious and skillful task to be performed before staring actual screening process.

5.2.2   General Process of Virtual Screening

VS is nothing but the computer-based screening process in order to reduce the number of screening molecules considering protein binding and efficacy so as to bring a good lead compound in to the real world. The workflow of VS process is shown in Figure 5.6.

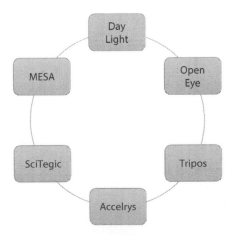

Figure 5.5 Softwares for removing garbage from the collection.

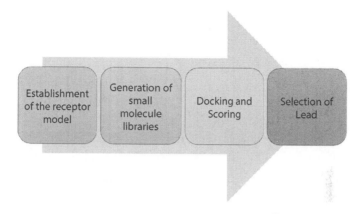

Figure 5.6 Workflow of virtual screening process.

5.2.2.1 Step 1 (The Establishment of the Receptor Model)

Obtaining macromolecular structure and binding site description are the two most important factors for the establishment of receptor model; the key point for the success of a structure-based VS. A typical PDB structure file, if one looks at it closely, is made up of heavy atoms, ligands, water molecules, cofactors, activators, and subunits of protein. The information missing here is like charge density, bond order, as well as topological hierarchy. Terminal amide groups and asparagine residues may be mis-arranged as X-ray structures cannot unambiguously distinguish between O and NH2 groups. Ionization is also one of the factors which need to be considered and evaluated along with stearic factors. Such structure related issues can be solved by determinig protonation states of the amino acids using softwares [31, 32] (PROPKA, H++, SPORES) followed by software (PDB2PQR)–based hydrogen bond optimization [33].

Apart from the above-mentioned factors, one should also consider capping of the residues, metal ion effects, missing side chains, etc., during molecular docking. In addition, a decision needs to be made regarding whether water molecules will be left in or removed from the binding site [34]. There are cases where binding site is not known or allosteric modulators are present and then solution can be derived by static approach (SiteMap, FTMap, Fpocket, MDpocket, QsiteFinder, MED-SUMO, and SiteHound-web), dynamic approach (MDMix, SILCS, and MixMD), mixed approach (FTFlex), and based on inhomogeneous solvation theory [JAWS, WaterMap, WATMD (Novartis), 3D-RISM, and SZMAP] [34].

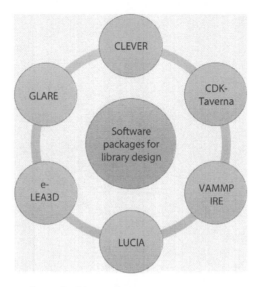

Figure 5.7 Software packages for library design.

5.2.2.2   Step 2 (The Generation of Small-Molecule Libraries)

The next goal is to convert the two-dimensional protein structure to three-dimensional structure which is generally done by conversion program [35]. After getting protein 3D structures, it has been modified by adding the hydrogen atoms and charges, in order to get it ready for the docking process (Figure 5.7) [8]. "Protein Preparation Wizard" is used to generate libraries of variety of protein structures for SBVS, e.g., WebPDB [34, 36].

5.2.2.3   Step 3 (Molecular Docking)

The molecular docking as the name suggests mainly used to check the atomic level interactions of target with its counterpart inshore molecular mechanism of binding processes [37]. Docking is a two-step process which includes the optimization of protein conformation (its position and orientation) and binding site/affinity. Sampling methods are mainly related with the conformation part while scoring is related to binding (Figure 5.8 and 5.9). The conformational attributes of the molecule and its receptor interaction can be evaluated by docking algorithm. Docking efficiency can be further increased if the binding site well characterized and its information is handy [38]. As an evolutionary path docking starts in early days with Rigid Lock

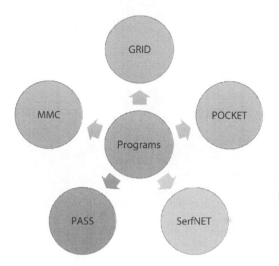

Figure 5.8 Binding sites detection programs [38, 41–43].

Key theory by Fisher to "induced-fit" theory stating that the active site of the protein is continually reshaped by interactions with the ligands as the ligands interact with the protein [39, 40].

Nowadays, Local Move Monte Carlo (LMMC) approach is used as a potential solution to flexible receptor docking problems [44]. The purpose

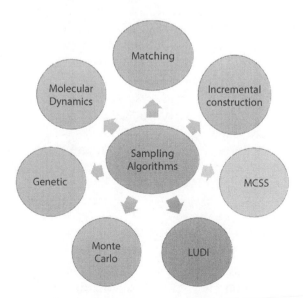

Figure 5.9 Sampling algorithms for molecular docking.

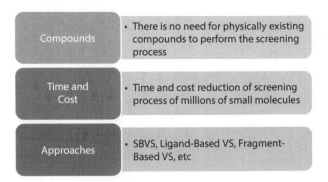

Figure 5.10 Advantages of virtual screening process over HTS.

of the scoring function is to fetch high affinity candidate in a quick and efficient manner. Scoring function is purely assumption based as there is no calculation of the binding affinity between the protein and ligand being done (Figures 5.8 and 5.9). Scoring functions can be divided in force-field-based, empirical, and knowledge-based scoring functions [45].

5.2.2.4   Step 4 (Selection of Lead Protein Compounds)

Once molecular docking is completed then next step is *Selection of Lead Protein Compounds.* It is a vigorous analysis of the data generated to be done by subject matter expert to judge more suitable candidates and concise the findings. The purpose of this analysis and post-processing is as accurate as possible to assess protein-ligand binding free energies. The generated complex candidate set is classified, and the error results are distinguished [46]. The scoring function is really critical for the lead identification as sometimes wrong selection of scoring function will not be able to provide cogent information with respect to effector function and adequate conformational data. It may also lead to wrong structural selection, improper ligand idea with respect to stearic hindrance, twisted amides, E/Z esters, imperfect hydrogen-bonding network, and poses based on shape complementarity [47]. Advantages of virtual screening is summarized in Figure 5.10.

5.3   Machine Learning and Scoring Functions

Machine learning techniques are the best tools for the optimization and grafting of predictive models through scoring function. For the derivatization of the scoring pattern, it generally considers ligand-target binding interactions in conjunction with solvation and entropic effects. Moreover, machine learning techniques such as neural networks (NNs), support vector machines (SVMs), and random forest (RF) are able to account for the nonlinear dependence among the various interactions involved in ligand-target binding. It is one of the classic techniques for the binding affinity estimation.

In silico simulation of the microscopic organization of human brain based on NN is the scoring function idea by Durrant and McCammon [48]. In order to get close to information related to ligand-target interactions, 194 neurodes for input layer are defined. Kinnings *et al.* have find out the inhibitors associated with *Mycobacterium tuberculosis* using SVM for scoring where they obtained individual energy terms directly from the built-in scoring function of eHiTS [49]. Amini *et al.* have grafted system-specific scoring functions using inductive logical algorithm along with the support vector [50]. Tang *et al.* have engineered PHOENIX scoring function using thermodynamic principals to map binding free energy (ΔG), enthalpy (ΔH), and the change of entropy ($T\Delta S$) as descriptors [51].

Li and Coworkers have developed target-specific scoring rather than using occurrence count of ligand-target atom pair as geometric descriptor to generate a scoring function [52]. SVM is basically made up of 135 amino acids, and its (SVM-SP) effectiveness is already being proven for epidermal growth factor receptor where three novel hits being produced. Ballester and Mitchell have engineered RF scoring which works around ligand-protein atom pairing using a set of descriptors [53]. Among all the 16 scoring functions available, RF scoring is proved to be the best although it only considers atomic number with no concern about distance dependence [54].

5.4   Conclusion and Future Prospects

Discovery of protein molecule is a very time consuming and costly process. One of the most widely used *in silico* methods for drug discovery includes docking and ligand-based methods for VS. In an ideal world, computational prediction would give the right answer for potential candidates and drug discovery would be better for it. Unfortunately, this is not the case and the probability of success is much lower; however, the methods themselves are generally more efficient than HTS alone and can be a useful as a tool to focus experimental efforts and lead to screening enrichment with actives. It is imperative that those embarking on drug discovery projects understand this; otherwise, they are neglecting a potentially powerful method for idea generation. Machine learning scoring function is really helpful for the interactions and effector function optimization. Still more works need to be done for the topological part as well as getting well verse with post translation modification, side chain optimization, etc.

References

1. Hughes, J.P. *et al.*, Principles of early drug discovery. *Br. J. Pharmacol.*, 162, 1239–1249, 2011.
2. Chandra, N., Anand, P., Yeturu, K., Structural bioinformatics: deriving biological insights from protein structures. *Interdiscip. Sci.*, 2, 4, 347–66, 2010.
3. Reddy, A.S., Pati, S.P., Kumar, P.P., Pradeep, H.N., Sastry, G.N., Virtual screening in drug discovery — a computational perspective. *Curr. Protein Pept. Sci.*, 8, 4, 329–351, 2007.
4. Lavecchia, A. and Di Giovanni, C., Virtual screening strategies in drug discovery: a critical review. *Curr. Med. Chem.*, 20, 23, 2839–2860, 2013.
5. Jorgensen, W.L., The many roles of computation in drug discovery. *Science*, 303, 5665, 1813–1818, 2004.
6. Ripphausen, P., Nisius, B., Peltason, L., Bajorath Jr., Quo vadis, virtual screening? A comprehensive survey of prospective applications. *J. Med. Chem.*, 53, 24, 8461–8467, 2010.
7. Benod, C., Carlsson, J., Uthayaruban, R., Hwang, P., Irwin, J.J., Doak, A.K., Shoichet, B.K., Sablin, E.P., Fletterick, R.J., Structure-based discovery of antagonists of nuclear receptor LRH-1. *J. Biol. Chem.*, 288, 27, 19830–19844, 2013.
8. Cheng, T., Li, Q., Zhou, Z., Wang, Y., Bryant, S.H., Structure-based virtual screening for drug discovery: a problem-centric review. *AAPS J.*, 14, 1, 133–141, 2012.
9. Clark, D.E., What has virtual screening ever done for drug discovery? *Expert Opin. Drug Discovery*, 3, 841–851, 2008.
10. Heifetz, A., Barker, O., Verquin, G., Wimmer, N., Meutermans, W., Pal, S., Law, R.J., Whittaker, M., Fighting obesity with a sugar-based library: discovery of novel MCH-1R antagonists by a new computational-VAST approach for exploration of GPCR binding sites. *J. Chem. Inf. Model.*, 53, 5, 1084–1099, 2013.
11. chröder, J., Klinger, A., Oellien, F., Marhöfer, R.J., Duszenko, M., Selzer, P.M., Docking-based virtual screening of covalently binding ligands: an orthogonal lead discovery approach. *J. Med. Chem.*, 56, 4, 1478–1490, 2013.
12. Kolb, P., Rosenbaum, D.M., Irwin, J.J., Fung, J.J., Kobilka, B.K., Shoichet, B.K., Structure-based discovery of beta2-adrenergic receptor ligands. *Proc. Natl. Acad. Sci. U.S.A.*, 106, 16, 6843–6848, 2009.

13. Villoutreix, B.O., Eudes, R., Miteva, M.A., Structure-based virtual ligand screening: recent success stories. *Comb. Chem. High Throughput Screen.*, 12, 10, 1000–1016, 2009.

14. Ghosh, S., Nie, A., An, J., Huang, Z., Structure-based virtual screening of chemical libraries for drug discovery. *Curr. Opin. Chem. Biol.*, 10, 3, 194–202, 2006.

15. Seifert, M.H.J. and Lang, M., Essential factors for successful virtual screening. *Mini Rev. Med. Chem.*, 8, 63–72, 2007.

16. Tuccinardi, T., Docking-based virtual screening: recent developments. *Comb. Chem. High Throughput Screen.*, 12, 3, 303–314, 2009.

17. Mestres, J., Virtual screening: a real screening complement to high-throughput screening. *Biochem. Soc. Trans.*, 30, 797–799, 2002.

18. Bologa, C.G., Olah, M.M., Oprea, T.I., Chemical Database Preparation for Compound Acquisition or Virtual Screening, in: *Methods in Molecular Biology*, R.S. Larson (Ed.), pp. 375–384, Humana Press Inc., Totowa, NJ, 2018.

19. Oprea, T., Lead structure searching: Are we looking for the appropriate properties? *J. Comput.-Aided Mol. Des.*, 16, 325–334, 2002.

20. Lipinski, C.A. *et al.*, Experimental and computational approaches to estimate solubility and permeability in drug discovery and development settings. *Adv. Drug Deliv. Rev.*, 23, 3–25, 1997.

21. Hattotuwagama, C.K., Davies, M.N., Flower, D.R., Receptor-ligand binding sites and virtual screening. *Curr. Med. Chem.*, 13, 1283–1304, 2006.

22. McInnes, C., Virtual screening strategies in drug discovery. *Curr. Opin. Chem. Biol.*, 11, 494–502, 2007.

23. Flower, D.R., Pharmacovigilance, Drug Repositioning, and Virtual Screening. *J. Pharmacovigil.*, 1, 1, 1–3, 2013.

24. Bilsland, A.E., Pugliese, A., Liu, Y., Identification of a selective G1-phase benzimidazolone inhibitor by a senescencetargeted virtual screen using artificial neural networks. *Neoplasia*, 17, 9, 704–715, 2015.

25. Song L, L.D., Zeng, X., Guo, L., nDNA-prot: identification of DNA-binding proteins based on unbalanced classification. *BMC Bioinform.*, 15, 1, 10, 2014.

26. Lin, C., Zou, Y., Qin, J., Hierarchical classification of protein folds using a novel ensemble classifier. *PLoS One*, 8, 2, e56499, 2013.

27. Szymański, P., Markowicz, M., Mikiciuk-Olasik, E., Adaptation of High-Throughput Screening in Drug Discovery—Toxicological Screening Tests. *Int. J. Mol. Sci.*, 13, 427–452, 2012.

28. Hann, M.M. and Oprea, T.I., Pursuing the leadlikeness concept in pharmaceutical research. *Curr. Opin. Chem. Biol.*, 8, 255–263, 2004.

29. iResearch™ Library, ChemNavigator, Inc., (Date of Access; 20 February, 2021) www.chemnavigator.com/cnc/products/IRL.asp.

30. Genedata Biologics, Transform Biopharma Discovery, (Date of Access; 20 February, 2021), https://www.genedata.com/products/biologics/.

31. Li, H., Robertson, A.D., Jensen, J.H., Very fast empirical prediction and rationalization of protein pKa values. *Proteins*, 61, 4, 704–721, 2005.

32. Anandakrishnan, R., Aguilar, B., Onufriev, A.V., Onufriev, A.V., H++ 3.0: automating pK prediction and the preparation of biomolecular structures for atomistic molecular modeling and simulation. *Nucleic Acids Res.*, 40, W537-41–W541, 2012.

33. Dolinsky, T.J., Czodrowski, P., Li, H., Nielsen, J.E., Jensen, J.H., Klebe, G., Baker, N.A., PDB2PQR: expanding and upgrading automated preparation of biomolecular structures for molecular simulations. *Nucleic Acids Res.*, 35, Web Server issue, W522–5, 2007.

34. Lionta, E. *et al.*, Structure-Based Virtual Screening for Drug Discovery: Principles, Applications and Recent Advances. *Curr. Top. Med. Chem.*, 14, 16, 1923–1938, 2014.

35. Lavecchia, A. and Di Giovanni, C., Virtual screening strategies in drug discovery: a critical review. *Curr. Med. Chem.*, 20, 23, 2839–2860, 2013.

36. Kovalenko, A., Three-dimensional RISM theory for molecular liquids and solid-liquid interfaces, in: F. Hirata and P.G. Mezey (Eds.), 360, Vol. 24, pp. 169–275, Kluwer Academic Publishers, Dordrecht, 2003.

37. McConkey, B.J., Sobolev, V., Edelman, M., The performance of current methods in ligand-protein docking. *Curr. Sci.*, 83, 845–855, 2002.

38. Goodford, P.J., A computational procedure for determining energetically favorable binding sites on biologically important macromolecules. *J. Med. Chem.*, 28, 7, 849–857, 1985.

39. Fischer, E., Einfluss der configuration auf die wirkung derenzyme. *Ber. Dtsch. Chem. Ges.*, 27, 2985–2993, 1894.

40. Koshland, D.E., Jr., Correlation of Structure and Function in Enzyme Action. *Science*, 142, 1533–1541, 1963.

41. Levitt, D.G. and Banaszak, L.J., POCKET: a computer graphics method for identifying and displaying protein cavities and their surrounding amino acids. *J. Mol. Graphics*, 10, 4, 229–234, 1992.

42. Glaser, F., Morris, R.J., Najmanovich, R.J., Laskowski, R.A., Thornton, J.M., A method for localizing ligand binding pockets in protein structures. *Proteins*, 62, 2, 479–488, 2006.

43. Mezei, M., A new method for mapping macromolecular topography. *J. Mol. Graph. Model.*, 21, 5, 463–472, 2003.

44. Xuan-Yu, M. *et al.*, Molecular Docking: A powerful approach for structure-based drug discovery. *Curr. Comput. Aided Drug Des.*, 7, 2, 146–157, 2011.

45. Kitchen, D.B., Decornez, H., Furr, J.R., Bajorath, J., Docking and scoring in virtual screening for drug discovery: methods and applications. *Nat. Rev. Drug Discovery*, 3, 11, 935–949, 2004.

46. Moitessier, N., Englebienne, P., Lee, D., Lawandi, J., Corbeil, C.R., Towards the development of universal, fast and highly accurate docking/scoring methods: a long way to go. *Br. J. Pharmacol.*, 153, Suppl 1, S7–26, 2008.

47. Athanasiadis, E., Cournia, Z., Spyrou, G., ChemBioServer: a web-based pipeline for filtering, clustering and visualization of chemical compounds used in drug discovery. *Bioinformatics*, 28, 22, 3002–3003, 2012.

48. Durrant, J.D. and McCammon, J.A., NNScore: a neural-network-based scoring function for the characterization of protein–ligand complexes. *J. Chem. Inf. Model.*, 50, 10, 1865–1871, 2010.

49. Kinnings, S.L., Liu, N., Tonge, P.J., Jackson, R.M., Xie, L., Bourne, P.E., A machine learning-based method to improve docking scoring functions and its application to drug repurposing. *J. Chem. Inf. Model.*, 51, 2, 408–419, 2011.

50. Tang, Y.T. and Marshall, G.R., PHOENIX: a scoring function for affinity prediction derived using high-resolution crystal structures and calorimetry measurements. *J. Chem. Inf. Model.*, 51, 2, 214–228, 2011.

51. Deng, W., Breneman, C., Embrechts, M.J., Predicting protein–ligand binding affinities using novel geometrical descriptors and machine-learning methods. *J. Chem. Inf. Comput. Sci.*, 44, 2, 699–703, 2004.

52. Li, L., Khanna, M., Jo, I., Wang, F., Ashpole, N.M., Hudmon, A. *et al.*, Target-specific support vector machine scoring in structure-based virtual screening: computational validation, *in vitro* testing in kinases, and effects on lung cancer cell proliferation. *J. Chem. Inf. Model.*, 51, 4, 755–759, 2011.

53. Ballester, P.J. and Mitchell, J.B.O., A machine learning approach to predicting protein–ligand binding affinity with applications to molecular docking. *Bioinformatics*, 26, 9, 1169–1175, 2010.

54. Cheng, T., Li, X., Li, Y., Liu, Z., Wang, R., Comparative assessment of scoring functions on a diverse test set. *J. Chem. Inf. Model.*, 49, 4, 1079–1093, 2009.

6

New Bioinformatics Platform-Based Approach for Drug Design

Vivek Chavda[2†], Soham Sheta[1*], Divyesh Changani[3] and Disha Chavda[4]

[1]*Formulation and Development, Zydus Cadila,
Ahmedabad, India*
[2]*Department of Pharmaceutics, L.M. College of Pharmacy,
Ahmedabad, India*
[3]*Regulatory Affairs (Biologics), Mylan Laboratories Ltd.,
Hyderabad, India*
[4]*Analytical Development, Orbicular Pharmaceutical Ltd.,
Hyderabad, India*

Abstract

There is ample growth potential in the current biologics era. There are more than 1,600 biologics under evaluation where over 250 approved drugs and many more drugs are in the pipeline. Many genomes have been mapped with the aid of bioinformatics tools. Such advancements have triggered the research at the level of transcriptome and protein engineering. The journey of finding new viable protein drug starts from the virtual screening of the targets/lead, optimizing them, and making them commercially viable. An approach called rational drug design is now integrated with computer-aided drug design under the umbrella of molecular docking. Computer-aided drug design which is also known as *in silico* method is further being bifurcated in to ligand-based and structure-based screening. Nowadays, ligand-based (pharmacophore) and structure-based (molecular docking) screening have merged into a platform that involves the processes of finding new target discovery for achieving promising leads. This chapter encompasses current approaches for drug design and their interrelationship for drug discovery process.

Keywords: Platform-based approach, gene, lead, computer-aided drug discovery

Corresponding author: sohamsheta@gmail.com
†*Corresponding author*: Vivek7chavda@gmail.com

S. Balamurugan, Anand Krishnan, Dinesh Goyal, Balakumar Chandrasekaran and Boomi Pandi (eds.)
Computation in Bioinformatics: Multidisciplinary Applications, (101–120) © 2021 Scrivener Publishing LLC

6.1　Introduction

The approval of Eilly Lilly's Humulin® (Insulin) in 1982 by USFDA (US Food and Drug Administration) as the first recombinant therapeutic protein was a landmark for biotechnology [1]. After that, biologic drug development has reached many milestones. Many complex biologicals were discovered afterward due to unmet medical needs. To include in the list, the products are early traditional replacement proteins (Insulin) to more recent, complexly structured antibodies (adalimumab and infliximab for inflammatory condition), oligonucleotides, fusion proteins (etanercept and infliximab), and gene constructs [2]. Many biologics agents have been delivered despite having developmental, scientific and technological challenges [3, 4]. The development of therapeutic proteins is difficult task as antidrug antibodies (ADAs) may develop [5]. Sometimes, the neutralizing antibody for a targeted protein may alter its pharmacokinetics [6]. Also, the development of ADAs tends to neutralize the endogenous proteins, thereby it may create endogenous substance deficiency which is harmful to the patient [7]. It was observed with recombinant hormones (Erythropoietin and thrombopoietin) therapies where ADAs neutralized the protein produced within patients. Modernistic treatments and advanced protein engineering technology are required to prevent generation of antibodies to therapeutic proteins, which improves the efficacy in many patients and which results in more therapeutic adherence [8]. In the past 30 to 40 years, the thirst for developing targeted protein therapeutics is increasing, thereby it promoted the development of monoclonal antibodies (mAbs), particularly for cancer and immunological disorders, e.g., breast cancer medication trastuzumab (Herceptin) [9]. The mAbs have been primarily used as diagnostic medicine, in as a laboratory tool in biochemistry and in molecular biology. The strategic thinking has shifted due to the increasing knowledge of biologics, benefit based on their distinctive features (e.g., high specificity, no inherent variability, low lot to lot inconsistencies, long half-life, and safety), and advanced technology for production and purification [10]. Research in the clinical field is making incessant efforts for making the rich health level of the people. There is an agile increase in chronic diseases like cancer, immunological disorders, hepatitis, and HIV, causing high morbidity and mortality [11, 12]. Bioinformatics tool and protein engineering technology are the essential elements for drug development program. To confirm therapeutic efficacy and to check pharmacokinetic profile clinical trials are performed. It is a complex and capital-intensive process and requires huge investment by the pharmaceutical industry [13]. It starts with the identification of potential drug candidate, optimization of that drug candidate with safety, efficacy, selectivity, and stability (Figure 6.1) [14]. This is followed by three phases, i.e., the preclinical study, clinical study, and, last but not the least, post-marketing surveillance. Bioinformatics tools has important place in the drug discovery, drug development and clinical development. Bioinformatics is an interconnecting field that develops and uses methods and computer softwares to understand biological data [15]. It combines the field biology, information technology, computer science, statistics, and mathematics to interpret the biological data. It uses informatics to understand health and disease and also helps to gain new knowledge pertaining to health and disease [16].

It makes data management easier during clinical trials. In addition, cutting edge technologies like molecular docking, proteomics, and quantitative structure–activity relationship (QSAR) in clinical research results in an expeditious and easier process. Softwares like EasyTrial, CloudLIMS, MakroCare, EdeTek, and CTMS are used for smooth conductance of clinical trials. Electronic data capture (EDC) is one of the ways to save the clinical data digitally. EDC replaces conventional document-based data collection methodology, to streamline the patient's data and make possible the time for drug/device to come to market much faster. Electronic

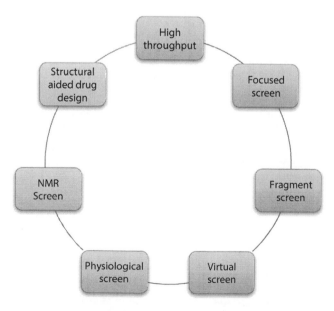

Figure 6.1 Screening strategies for the targets for the drug discovery process.

case report form (eCRF, e.g., Ennov eCRF) has also played a primary role in clinical trial data management. It assembles and organizes diverse data from electronic and paper-based platforms and allows to study patient data in very effortless manner. Softwares like Siebel CTMS is used for clinical data management and statistical analysis of the data [17, 18]. After the marketing of the drug, a vital component of the drug development process, the safety of a drug could be monitored by drug safety software like EasySafteyTM, Lifesafety®. Later in this chapter, reader will have insight at multifactorial points related to use of computronics and bioinformatics in drug discovery and development, finished formulation design, and clinical research.

6.2   Platform-Based Approach and Regulatory Perspective

The unstoppable progress has occurred in biotechnology and medical field and its journey continues on the novel developmental pathway (Figure 6.2). But simultaneously, it requires that such novel products developed should be safe, effective, and economical for patients. Regulatory agencies should ensure and evaluate such benefits previously mentioned [19]. USFDA came up with many expedited drug review programs like fast track designation, accelerated approval and priority review designation, and breakthrough therapy designation (BTD). For fast track designation, drug should show its efficacy to fulfill unmet medical needs and its indication should be for serious condition [20]. For accelerated approval, the drug should be for serious condition; it should have more advantage over conventional therapy and should have the beneficial effects.

The drug is considered for priority review unless and until it has increased evidence in safety, treatments, prevention, or diagnosis of condition. Food and Drug Administration Safety and Innovation Act (FDASIA) comes in 2012. FDASIA gave FDA new and dynamic tool known as BTD. The candidature selection process is based on the outcome which must have a considerable improvement over conventional therapies for patients with serious or chronic diseases like cancer and immunological disorders [21].

The BTD program has resulted in faster innovation and review of advanced medicine. The manufacturing and production of therapeutic proteins requires state-of-the-art facility as it is highly complicated process. For example, a typical protein drug manufacturing includes culture

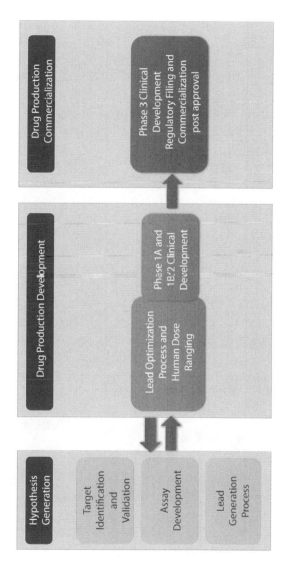

Figure 6.2 Overview on drug discovery process.

development, fermentation, extraction or recovery of proteins, concentration and purification, final formulation, drying, and packaging [22–25]. A number of critical process steps are higher than small molecules due to their very complex and delicate structures. Examples of protein therapeutics include antibody-drug conjugates, blood clotting factors, fc fusion proteins, interferons, enzymes, and interleukins [26]. A number of biologics technologies are currently in use to increase the half-life, selectivity, and functionality of advanced therapeutic protein drugs as well as to increase its large-scale feasibility to make it commercially viable [26, 27]. For example, the conjugation of protein modification approaches, including Fc-fusion, albumin-fusion, and PEGylation, is currently being used to extend a drug's half-life which is particularly taken care for patients undergoing factor or hormone replacement therapy to increase patient compliance [28–31]. For drug targeting, novel approach is antibody-drug conjugates, thereby limiting the adverse effects of cytotoxic drugs. Considering current market scenario, platform-based approach is highly effective practice for drug discovery of biologics (Figure 6.3).

Functional modification of protein through protein engineering can exploit particular functionality of proteins. For example, changing glycosylation pattern of protein through engineering strategies may result in modification of the protein's ligand binding properties, function, and corresponding therapeutic effect produced (Figure 6.4) [32, 33].

In the future, protein engineering will be uprooted profoundly which will give birth to many protein therapeutics with changing generation.

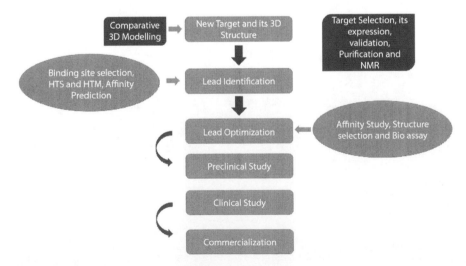

Figure 6.3 Platform-based drug development process.

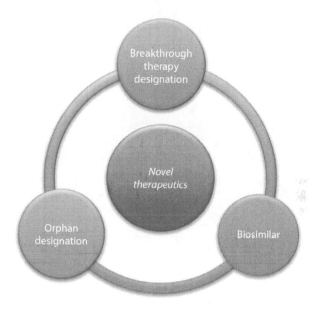

Figure 6.4 Pathways for the development of novel biotherapeutics.

At the same time, it increases the load toward new technologies for immunogenicity risk assessment and mitigation [34, 35]. Protein engineering considers codon optimization, conformational optimization, and side chain modification apart from primary sequencing in order to improve the protein synthesis and increase protein production [36–38].

Finally, an assemblage of advanced computational and experimental methods for protein-engineering and readily available platform technologies has provided new opportunities to develop safer, effective, and more patient compliant protein therapeutics [26].

6.3   Bioinformatics Tools and Computer-Aided Drug Design

Computer-aided drug design (CADD) is computer modeling assisted through computer simulation discovery. It is one of the methods for drug design by rational, lucid way by using computronics. There are two types of design, namely, 1) structure-based and 2) ligand-based drug design (Figure 6.5). Structure-based drug design is generally used for the development of

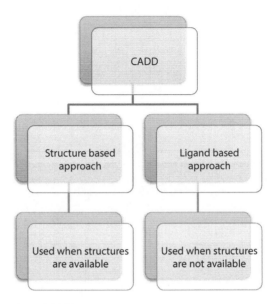

Figure 6.5 Bifurcation of CADD.

novel biologics using molecular docking while small molecules are gener-ally designed using ligand-based approach.

The main center point of CADD is to get the suitable molecule by reduc-ing capital expenditure. It includes the following [39]:

1) Application of well-organized approaches for the drug target identification and validation.
2) Effector function evaluation.
3) Codon optimization for getting better yield.
4) Generation of new biochemical information databases about ligands and targets (e.g., receptors) to identify and optimize adventitious medicinal agents.
5) Making new software and tools to establish ADME (Absorption, Distribution, Metabolism, and Excretion) properties of drugs.
6) Methods to detect the entry of less efficacious drug candi-dates which are more likely to fail in clinical research phase.

There are many reasons in addition to reduced capital expenditure and time to use the CADD [40]. There are many molecules that fail in initial phase of the development or even during clinical trial. In order to screen the initial molecules, computational methods (*in silico*) are developed [41].

Several softwares have been developed for characterization of protein structure and functionality to identify interacting compounds and active site residues and to study protein-compound interactions, which may, eventually, ushered in the identification of new drugs [42]. The 3D protein structure can be predicted using homology modeling, while molecular docking is explored to predict protein interaction. The preferred orientation of the docked protein is one which has overall minimum energy. CADD has provide attractive niche for the identification of potential drugs for various diseases [43].

6.4   Target Identification

Identifying precise drug receptor or target is an essential part of drug discovery process [44, 45]. It includes getting a knowledge of biochemistry

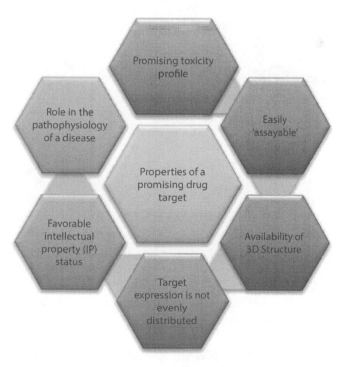

Figure 6.6 Properties of a promising drug target [48].

and of a specific disease or disorder, like amino acid sequence identification of target, expression, and metabolite [46]. The target identification process is basically targeted to identify binding targets for receptors to be cogent biologics (Figure 6.6). Drug development process only progresses when the particular drug target(s) or receptors for a disease has been discovered and understood. With the help of duo, i.e., biotechnology and information technology tools, now, it is possible to find out the potential biologics for wide targets in a sort time span and with less expenditure [47].

In current biotherapeutic setup for target identification, many data analytics tools are available which will fasten up the process. For the identification of the metabolic profile of the identified molecule, HMDB (Human Metabolome Database) is used which precisely provide the human metabolome data, while for protein structure prediction, PDB (Protein Data Bank) is explored and found to be efficient. Apart from that the pathway analysis, KEGG (Kyoto Encyclopedia of Genes and Genomes), Gene Ontology, PantherDB, Reactome, and Biocarta are popular choice. There are database and software's like PharmGKB for Pharmacogenomic data, Protein Atlas for protein expression information, CTD (Comparative Toxicogenomics Database) and T3DB (Target-Toxin Database) for toxic databases, and ChEMBL and Pubchem for Chemgenomic data are used widely [39].

6.5   Target Validation

Biotechnology and information technology is being increasingly used to support target validation by providing functional intelligence through information sourced from databases and experimental datasets using a variety of computer engineering tools [39]. The predictive power of these approaches are at peak when information from vast range of database and experimental data sets are combined [49]. The aim of this chapter is to highlight and discuss the key approaches available in this very fast-growing field to help in the selection of the right bioinformatics tools and databases [50]. Target validation is a capital-demanding and costly process. Usage of data filtering and statistics will ease the process of target validation at cellular level [51]. On the other side, network plugins like Cytoscape2.6.3 will help in network validation when 80–100 random networks of interest are there. Network validation is also one of the key elements of the drug discovery process. RNAi and CRISPR-Cas9 are the examples of genomic validation approach, which is useful for identifying gene function and/or gene regulatory networks [52]. Data is the blood for the process; it may be freely available or sometimes paid one. Certain medical records and

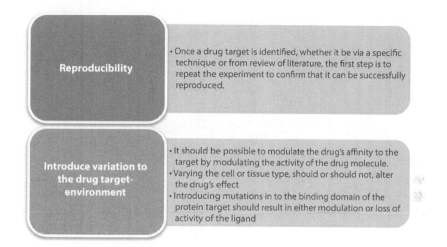

Figure 6.7 Target validation steps.

clinical trials data will be useful for ascertaining inter-individual variability upon drug administration (Figure 6.7). There are certain targets whose role in the disease pathology is unknown and can be targeted to design the effective therapeutic alternative [51, 53, 54].

The role and action of the candidate molecule as well as how it cures potential disease can be easily decoded by the usage of bioinformatics tools. This will make the target validation process cogent and fast. Integration of intensive biochemical, genetic, and animal studies in bioinformatics will serve as booster tool for drug design and drug discovery process [55]. There are approaches like target interaction, sense reversal, and proteomic approach that utilize small interfering RNAs (siRNAs) and *in vivo* validation which are mainly used for the target validation.

6.6   Lead Identification and Optimization

Once the particular protein target is identified and validated, then it has to crack the lead identification process where it is being evaluated for its biological and pharmacological activity along with effector function. High-throughput screening (HTS) which use the cutting edge technology for the identification of the lead molecule is the current practice for drug discovery [56]. Ultra High-Throughput Screening (UHTS) can screen up to 100,000 assays per day [57–59]. Tag-lite® technology can be used to study cell-based binding assay using which homogeneous and non-radioactive ligand binding can be evaluated [60, 61]. In addition to this, the system named IntelliCyt® HTFC screening has the same features. High yielding flow cytometry, using non-adherent cells or beads in either 96 or 384 well format, can be conducted. The technology is highly responsive with a wide range and allows the use of small volumes of cells or beads [62]. The samples can be purified by Bravo liquid handler (Agilent) or Multitrap™ (GE Healthcare), but these are currently costly [63]. As the complexity of drug and targets increases, it may be possible that label free technologies will play a supporting role to conventional label technologies. The list of various label-free technologies includes the xCELLigence from Roche (It uses sophisticatedly designed microliter plates containing gold microelectrodes which monitors viability of cultured cells noninvasively with electrical impedance as readouts.) and the Enspire® from Perkin Elmer which is based on optical waveguide technology of the Corning Epic® system [63–65]. Suitability of such technique should be checked for screening of biologics and it needs time and evaluation. For the evaluation of the newer generation monoclonal antibodies, affinity to the binding site is the desired criteria for the candidature selection of the particular class of the monoclonal antibodies. Traditionally, relatively small panel of antibody candidates (<10) can be measured using technique such as BiaCore (based on the surface plasma resonance). However, the entry of the most advanced high-throughput technology Octet RED System (ForteBio) has resulted in large number of affinity-based screening of antibodies [66, 67]. After optimization of drug candidate for efficacy, selectivity, and potency, the next step is to check its pharmacokinetic properties [68]. If a molecule is safe regards to toxicity and mutagenicity, then it becomes a prior choice for lead molecule [69]. Combination of analytical techniques are used in structural elucidation of compounds, namely, FIA/DI-MS, MALDI-FT-MS, DI-NMR, HPLC-UV/MS, HPLC-NMR, SFC-MS, and ESI-FT-ICR-MS. MolMind combines *in silico* and laboratory methods. In this platform, a genetic algorithm helps a lot to guide a robotic synthesis system. Furthermore, chemical and biological screening is used to obtain molecules with the desired pharmacokinetic and pharmacodynamic properties [70].

6.7   High-Throughput Methods (HTM)

New high-throughput technologies serve as boon for the generation, selection, and optimization of novel targets [71]. With advent of the artificial intelligence and robotic systems (Figure 6.8), it is now possible to handle "n" number of the compounds per day (roughly 100,000 compounds per day).

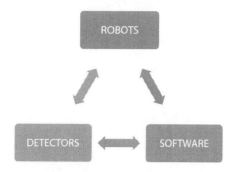

Figure 6.8 Arms of high-throughput methods (HTM).

The Omics branches like genomic, transcriptomics, proteomic, and metabolomics have been applied along with high-throughput target validation approaches in order to get potential protein candidates [72]. There are libraries of the potential biological targets against which libraries of the potential biologics molecule are evaluated by automation process of screening with big data analytics and limited volume bioassays [73].

Drug target (gene) validation is generally elucidated by proteomics analysis, transgenic KOs, siRNA-based methods, antisense technology, and aptamers, which is then linked with HTS where HTM like NMR, DNA Microarray, and DNA Chips LC/MS are being applied for the further evaluation [74, 75]. The use of technologies such as real-time reverse transcriptase polymerase chain reaction (RT-PCR) and cDNA microarrays has created a new era in the study of biological systems. The techniques are available for identification of targets are fluorescence resonance energy transfer (FRET) and homogeneous time resolved fluorescence (HTRF) [76]. Various *in silico* models are available for the toxicological evaluation of the drug candidate (Figure 6.9) [77].

In addition, a more responsive primary HTS method that can screen crude preparations is quite desirable. During the initial screening process, protein libraries used are not of purified moieties but it encompasses bacterial lysates or extracts, or hybridoma supernatants. Components in bacterial preparations hybridoma supernatants can interfere with HTS performance, resulting in decreased sensitivity and accuracy [78]. There are instances which required purified antibodies for their bioanalytical evaluation especially cell-based assays, leading to delay or hampering of the drug discovery process. IgG reformatting which is basically reformatting phage-displayed antibody fragments to full-length IgG is used to solve the same purpose [79].

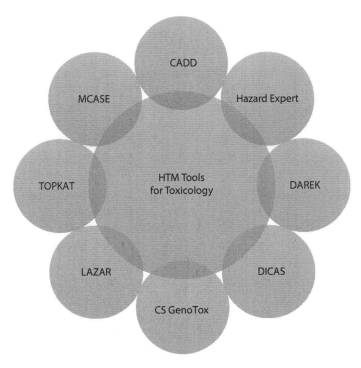

Figure 6.9 HTM tools for toxicological evaluation.

6.8　Conclusion and Future Prospects

In the last three and half decades, the focus of drug discovery and development has gradually shifted away from small, well-defined chemical molecules to large, complex molecular entities—therapeutic biologics [79]. The area of biologics is non-ending in nature. Out of top 10 selling molecule of 2019, 8 are biologics; it means that, clinically, it has proven its potential. More number of pharmaceutical industries has started working on the development of biologics as well as its counterpart biosimilar. The field of molecular engineering has noticed a revolutionary trend in the last decade starting from HTS to virtual screening with molecular docking. As these agents are more complex and dynamic in nature, nonclinical safety evaluation is must and challenging, often unexpected safety issues, which will require significant efforts to understand and monitor. Biotherapeutics are now playing an increasingly prominent role in combating cancer, diabetes, and autoimmune diseases. The recent entry of cellular and gene therapy products has opened the door for biologics to tap into complex areas like genetic disorder, regenerative therapy, and tailored medicine [80, 81].

In the future, novel biological therapeutics will continue to improve our quality of life by enriching our medicinal needs for serious diseases. The screening of the target is now become easy due to availability of molecular docking. There is still to be done in these field especially prediction of post-translation modification, conformational stability, and side chain design [80]. It is commonly believed that better disease targets are essential to develop more effective therapies, improve R&D efficiency, boost success rate, and reduce costs [82]. Another approach for boosting up the drug discovery relies on the development of more responsive and accurate assay methodology that simplifies and expedites the process. In addition, a more sensitive primary high-throughput screen (HTS) that can footprint preparations is quite desirable. Targeting intracellular molecules has been a long-standing challenge for biologics [78]. When we consider the therapeutic difficulties of such biologics agent, then two factors come in to the picture: high molecular weight and high structure complexity. These will hamper their interaction with cellular targets due to their inability to cross the cell membrane and sometimes intracellular protein-protein interactions (PPIs). We hope that next-generation biologics will overcomes such lacunas [83]. Another future challenge is Target Central Nervous System (CNS) and the Blood-Brain Barrier (BBB). Finally, the future the area of antibody-drug conjugates and its related objects is a niche therapeutics domain due to multiple technological trends.

References

1. Andrews, L. et al., A snapshot of biologic drug development: Challenges and opportunities. Hum. Exp. Toxicol., 34, 12, 1279–1285, 2015.
2. Morrow, T., Defining the difference: What Makes Biologics Unique. Biotechnol. Healthc., 1, 4, 28–29, 2004.
3. Alshekhlee, A., Basiri, K., Miles, J.D., Ahmad, S.A., Katirji, B., Chronic inflammatory demyelinating polyneuropathy associated with tumor necrosis factor-alpha antagonists. Muscle Nerve, 41, 723–727, 2010.
4. Antony, G.K. and Dudek, A.Z., Interleukin 2 in cancer therapy. Curr. Med. Chem., 17, 3297–3302, 2010.
5. Hwang, W.Y.K. and Foote, J., Immunogenicity of engineered antibodies. Methods, 36, 3–10, 2005.
6. Vultaggio, A., Nencini, F., Pratesi, S., Petroni, G., Maggi, E., Matucci, A., Manifestations of antidrug antibodies response: Hypersensitivity and infusion reactions. J. Interf. Cytok. Res., 34, 12, 946–952, 2014.
7. Radstake, T., Svenson, M., Eijsbouts, A.M., van den Hoogen, F.H.J., Enevold, C., van Riel, P.L.C.M., Bendtzen, K., Formation of antibodies against

infliximab and adalimumab strongly correlates with functional drug levels and clinical responses in rheumatoid arthritis. *Ann. Rheumatol. Dis.*, 68, 11, 1739–1745, 2009.

8. Tovey, M.G., Immunogenicity and other problems associated with the use of biopharmaceuticals. *Ther. Adv. Drug Saf.*, 2, 3, 113–128, 2011.

9. Wolbink, G.J., Aarden, L.A., Dijkmans, B., Dealing with immunogenicity of biologicals: Assessment and clinical relevance. *Curr. Opin. Rheumatol.*, 21, 3, 211–215, 2009.

10. Alkhalfioui, F., Magnin, T., Wagner, R., From purified GPCRs to drug discovery: the promise of protein-based methodologies. *Curr. Opin. Pharmacol.*, 9, 629–635, 2009.

11. Alqahtani, S., Mohamed, L.A., Kaddoumi, A., Experimental models for predicting drug absorption and metabolism. *Expert Opin. Drug Metab. Toxicol.*, 9, 1241–1254, 2013.

12. Lee, K., Silva, E.A., Mooney, D.J., Growth factor delivery-based tissue engineering: general approaches and a review of recent developments. *J. R. Soc. Interface*, 8, 153–170, 2011.

13. Dawson, J.I. and Oreffo, R.O., Bridging the regeneration gap: stem cells, biomaterials and clinical translation in bone tissue engineering. *Arch. Biochem. Biophys.*, 473, 124–131, 2008.

14. teenholdt, C., Bendtzen, K., Brynskov, J., Thomsen, O.E., Ainsworth, M.A., Clinical implications of measuring drug and anti-drug antibodies by different assays when optimizing infliximab treatment failure in Crohn's disease: Post hoc analysis of a randomized controlled trial. *Am. J. Gastroenterol.*, 109, 7, 1055–1064, 2014.

15. Gill, S.K. *et al.*, Emerging role of bioinformatics tools and software in evolution of clinical research. *Perspect. Clin. Res.*, 7, 3, 115–122, 2016.

16. Mohs, R.C. and Greigb, N.G., Drug discovery and development: Role of basic biological research. *Alzheimers Dement.: Trans. Res. & Clin. Interventions*, 3, 4, 651–657, 2017.

17. US FDA, *Guidance for Industry Computerized Systems Used in Clinical Investigations,* U.S. Department of Health and Human Services Food and Drug Administration Office of the Commissioner (OC), May 2007. Available from: https://www.fda.gov/media/70970/download. Accessed on May 5th 2021.

18. Shah, J. *et al.*, Electronic Data Capture for Registries and Clinical Trials in Orthopaedic Surgery: Open Source versus Commercial Systems. *Clin. Orthop. Relat. Res.*®, 468, 10, 2664–2671, 2010.

19. U.S. Department of Health & Human Services, Food and Drug Administration, *Frequently Asked Questions: Breakthrough Therapies,* U.S. Food and Drug Administration, April 2nd 2021.

20. Kepplinger, E.E., FDA's Expedited Approval Mechanisms for New Drug Products. *Biotechnol. Law Rep.*, 34, 1, 15–37, 2015.

21. Food and Drug Administration, *Breakthrough therapy,* U.S. Food and Drug Administration, April 1st 2018. Available from: https://www.fda.gov/patients/fast-track-breakthrough-therapy-accelerated-approval-priority-review/breakthrough-therapy. Accessed on May 5th 2021.
22. Bandaranayake, A.D. and Almo, S.C., Recent advances in mammalian protein production. *FEBS Lett.,* 588, 2, 253–260, 2014.
23. Butler, M. and Meneses-Acosta, A., Recent advances in technology supporting biopharmaceutical production from mammalian cells. *Appl. Microbiol. Biotechnol.,* 96, 4, 885–894, 2012.
24. Zhu, J., Mammalian cell protein expression for biopharmaceutical production. *Biotechnol. Adv.,* 30, 5, 1158–1170, 2012.
25. Cipriano, D., Burnham, M., Hughes, J.V., Effectiveness of various processing steps for viral clearance of therapeutic proteins: database analyses of commonly used steps. *Methods Mol. Biol.,* 899, 277–292, 2012.
26. Sauna, Z.E., Alexaki, A., Katagiri, N.H., Recent advances in (therapeutic protein) drug development. Version 1. *F1000Res.,* 6, 113, 2017.
27. Turecek, P.L., Bossard, M.J., Schoetens, F. *et al.,* PEGylation of Biopharmaceuticals: A Review of Chemistry and Nonclinical Safety Information of Approved Drugs. *J. Pharm. Sci.,* 105, 2, 460–475, 2016.
28. Casi, G. and Neri, D., Antibody-drug conjugates: basic concepts, examples and future perspectives. *J. Control. Release,* 161, 2, 422–428. 10, 2012.
29. Levin, D., Golding, B., Strome, S.E. *et al.,* Fc fusion as a platform technology: potential for modulating immunogenicity. *Trends Biotechnol.,* 33, 1, 27–34, 2015.
30. Rath, T., Baker, K., Dumont, J.A. *et al.,* Fc-fusion proteins and FcRn: structural insights for longer-lasting and more effective therapeutics. *Crit. Rev. Biotechnol.,* 35, 2, 235–254, 2015.
31. Andersen, J.T., Pehrson, R., Tolmachev, V. *et al.,* Extending half-life by indirect targeting of the neonatal Fc receptor (FcRn) using a minimal albumin binding domain. *J. Biol. Chem.,* 286, 7, 5234–5241, 2011.
32. Jefferis, R., Glycosylation as a strategy to improve antibody-based therapeutics. *Nat. Rev. Drug Discovery,* 8, 8, 226–234, 2009.
33. Costa, A.R., Rodrigues, M.E., Henriques, M. *et al.,* Glycosylation: impact, control and improvement during therapeutic protein production. *Crit. Rev. Biotechnol.,* 34, 4, 281–299, 2014.
34. Shankar, G., Pendley, C., Stein, K.E., A risk-based bioanalytical strategy for the assessment of antibody immune responses against biological drugs. *Nat. Biotechnol.,* 25, 5, 555–561, 2007.
35. Yin, L., Chen, X., Vicini, P. *et al.,* Therapeutic outcomes, assessments, risk factors and mitigation efforts of immunogenicity of therapeutic protein products. *Cell. Immunol.,* 295, 2, 118–126, 2015.
36. Maertens, B., Spriestersbach, A., von Groll, U. *et al.,* Gene optimization mechanisms: a multi-gene study reveals a high success rate of full-length

human proteins expressed in Escherichia coli. *Protein Sci.*, 19, 7, 1312–1326, 2010.

37. Mauro, V.P. and Chappell, S.A., A critical analysis of codon optimization in human therapeutics. *Trends Mol. Med.*, 20, 11, 604–613, 2014.

38. Sauna, Z.E. and Kimchi-Sarfaty, C., Understanding the contribution of synonymous mutations to human disease. *Nat. Rev. Genet.*, 12, 10, 683–691, 2011.

39. Kumar, A. and Chordia, N., Bioinformatics in Drug Discovery. *SciFed J. Protein Sci.*, 12, 1, 116, 2017.

40. Terstappen, G.C. and Reggiani, A., In silico research in drug discovery. *Trends Pharmacol. Sci.*, 22, 23–26, 2001.

41. Vu, L.A., Quyen, P.T.A., Huong, N.T., In silico Drug Design: Prospective for Drug Lead Discovery. *IJESI*, 4, 60–70, 2015.

42. Schneider, G. and Fechner, U., Computer-based de novo design of drug-like molecules. *Nat. Rev. Drug Discovery*, 4, 649–663, 2005.

43. Gore, M. and Desai, N.S., Computer-aided drug designing. *Methods Mol. Biol.*, 1168, 313–321, 2014.

44. Arfken, G., *Mathematical Methods for Physicists*, 3rd, pp. 428–436, Academic Press, Orlando, 1985.

45. Yu, W., Lakkaraju, S., Raman, E.P., MacKerell, A., Jr, Site-Identification by Ligand Competitive Saturation (SILCS) assisted pharmacophore modeling. *J. Comput. Aided Mol. Des.*, 28, 491–507, 2014.

46. Schneider, G. and Fechner, U., Computer-based de novo design of drug-like molecules. *Nat. Rev. Drug Discovery*, 4, 649–663, 2005.

47. Yu, W., Guvench, O., MacKerell, A.D., Computational approaches for the design of protein–protein interaction inhibitors, in: *Understanding and exploiting protein–protein interactions as drug targets*, G. Zinzalla (Ed.), pp. 99–102, Future Science Ltd, London, UK, 2013.

48. Gashaw, I., Ellinghaus, P., Sommer, A., Asadullah, K., What makes a good drug target? *Drug Discovery Today*, 17, S24–S30, 2012.

49. Wermuth, C., Aldous, D., Raboisson, P., Rognan, D., *The Practice of Medicinal Chemistry*, 4th ed., Elsevier ltd, pp. 45–70, 2015.

50. Lindsay, M.A., Target discovery. *Nat. Rev. Drug Discovery*, 2, 831–838, 2003.

51. Croston, G., The utility of target-based discovery. *Expert Opin. Drug Discovery*, 12, 5, 427–429, 2017.

52. Jain, K., RNAi and siRNA in target validation. *Drug Discovery Today*, 9, 7, 307–309, 2004.

53. Moffat, J., Vincent, F., Lee, J., Eder, J., Prunotto, M., Opportunities and challenges in phenotypic drug discovery: an industry perspective. *Nat. Rev. Drug Discovery*, 16, 8, 531–543, 2017.

54. Gashaw, I., Ellinghaus, P., Sommer, A., Asadullah, K., What makes a good drug target? *Drug Discovery Today*, 17, S24–S30, 2012.

55. Blake, R.A., Target validation in drug discovery. *Methods Mol. Biol.*, 356, 367–77, 2007.

56. Vedani, A., Dobler, M., Lill, M.A., The challenge of predicting drug toxicity in silico. *Basic Clin. Pharmacol. Toxicol.*, 99, 195–208, 2006.
57. Ekins, S., Algorithms for network analysis in systems—ADME/Tox using the MetaCore and MetaDrug platforms. *Xenobiotica*, 36, 877–901, 2006.
58. Koh, H.L., Yau, W.P., Ong, P.S., Hegde, A., Current trends in modern pharmaceutical analysis for drug discovery. *Drug Discovery Today*, 8, 889–897, 2003.
59. Hillisch, A., Protein structure-based drug design: applications, limitations and future developments. *Chem. Cent. J.*, 2, Suppl 1, S15, 2008.
60. Zwier, J.M., Roux, T., Cottet, M., Durroux, T., Douzon, S., Bdioui, S., Gregor, N., Bourrier, M., Oueslati, N., Nicolas, L. *et al.*, A fluorescent ligand-binding alternative using tag-lite® technology. *J. Biomol. Screening*, 15, 1248–1259, 2010.
61. Yan, H., Gu, W., Yang, J., Bi, V., Shen, Y., Lee, E., Winters, K.A., Komorowski, R., Zhang, C., Patel, J.J. *et al.*, Fully human monoclonal antibodies antagonizing the glucagon receptor improve glucose homeostasis in mice and monkeys. *Pharmacol. Ther.*, 329, 102–111, 2009.
62. Black, C.B., Duesing, T.B., Trinkle, L.S., Dunlay, T.R., Cell-Based screening using high-throughput flow cytometry. *Assay Drug Dev. Technol.*, 9, 13–20, 2011.
63. Cariuk, P., Gardener, M.J., Vaughan, T.J., Evolution of Biologics Screening Technologies. *Pharmaceuticals (Basel)*, 6, 5, 681–688, 2013.
64. Asphahani, F. and Zhang, M., Cellular impedance biosensors for drug screening and toxin detection. *Analyst*, 132, 835–841, 2007.
65. Lee, P.H., Gao, A., van Staden, C., Ly, J., Salon, J., Xu, A., Fang, Y., Verklecren, R., Evaluation of dynamic mass redistribution technology for pharmacological studies of recombinant and endogenously expressed g protein-coupled 0receptors. *Assay Drug Dev. Technol.*, 6, 83–94, 2008.
66. Karlsson, R., Michaelsson, A., Mattsson, L., Kinetic analysis of monoclonal antibody-antigen interactions with a new biosensor based analytical system. *J. Immunol. Methods*, 145, 229–240, 1991.
67. Abdiche, Y., Malashock, D., Pinkerton, A., Pons, J., Determining kinetics and affinities of protein interactions using a parallel real-time label-free biosensor, the Octet. *Anal. Biochem.*, 377, 209–217, 2008.
68. Martis, E.A., Radhakrishnan, R., Badve, R.R., High-throughput screening: The hits and leads of drug discovery—An overview. *J. Appl. Pharm. Sci.*, 1, 2–10, 2011.
69. Gribbon, P. and Sewing, A., High-throughput drug discovery: What can we expect from HTS? *Drug Discovery Today*, 10, 17–22, 2005.
70. Weber, L., Multi-component reactions and evolutionary chemistry. *Drug Discovery Today*, 7, 143–147, 2002.

71. Martis, E.A., Radhakrishnan, R., Badve, R.R., High-throughput screening: The hits and leads of drug discovery—An overview. *J. Appl. Pharm. Sci.*, 1, 2–10, 2011.

72. Fara, D.C., Oprea, T., Prossnitz, E.R., Bologa, C.G., Edwards, B.S., Sklar, L.A., Integration of virtual and physical screening. *Drug Discovery Today*, 3, 337–385, 2006.

73. Mayr, L.M. and Bojanic, D., Novel trends in high-throughput screening. *Curr. Opin. Pharmacol.*, 9, 5, 580–588, 2009.

74. Mayr, L.M. and Fuerst, P., The future of high-throughput screening. *J. Biomol. Screening*, 13, 443–448, 2008.

75. Hubbell, J.A., Biomaterials science and high-throughput screening. *Nat. Biotechnol.*, 22, 828–829, 2004.

76. Armstrong, J.W., A review of high-throughput screening approaches for drug discovery. *Am. Biotechnol. Lab.*, 17, 26–28, 1999.

77. Olasik, E.M. and Marcowikz, M., Adaptation of High-Throughput Screening in Drug Discovery—Toxicological Screening Tests. *Int. J. Mol. Sci.*, 13, 1, 427–452, 2012.

78. Smith, A.J., New horizons in therapeutic antibody discovery: opportunities and challenges versus small-molecule therapeutics. *J. Biomol. Screening*, 20, 4, 437–453, 2015. Web.

79. Challner, C.A. and Branch, E., Challenges for Next-Generation Biological Therapeutics in Discovery and Development, *Pharma's Almanac*, May 29th 2018. Available from: https://www.pharmasalmanac.com/articles/challenges-for-next-generation-biological-therapeutics-discovery-and-development#:~:text=There%20are%20several%20limitations%20embedded,be%20introduced%20between%20each%20step. Accessed on May 9th 2021.

80. Altevogt, B.M., Davis, M., Pankevich, D.E., Norris, S.M. (Eds.), *Improving and Accelerating Therapeutic Development for Nervous System Disorders: Workshop Summary*, pp. 30–42, National Academies Press, February 6th 2014.

81. Schuhmacher, A., Gassmann, O., Hinder, M., Changing R&D models in research-based pharmaceutical companies. *J. Transl. Med.*, 14, 1, 105, 2016. Web.

82. Fan, F., *Biologics Drug Discovery: Steps to producing an antibody drug candidate*, GeneScript Webinar, 2014, Available from: https://www.genscript.com/gsfiles/techfiles/GenScript_Biologics_Webinar.pdf.

83. *Better Antibody Screening Using IntelliCyt's iQue Screener*, IntelliCyt, Doc Number 11600.C, 2014. Available from: https://slidelegend.com/download/better-antibody-screening-using-intellicyts-ique-screener_5a1bcbd51723dde0275d1509.html.

7

Bioinformatics and Its Application Areas

Ragini Bhardwaj[1], Mohit Sharma[2,3] and Nikhil Agrawal[4]*

[1]Department of Bioscience, Banasthali Vidyapith University,
Tonk, Rajasthan, India
[2]Postgraduate School for Molecular Medicine, Medical University of Warsaw,
Warsaw, Poland
[3]Małopolskie Centre of Biotechnology Jagiellonian University, Kraków, Poland
[4]College of Health Sciences, University of KwaZulu, Natal, Durban, South Africa

Abstract

Bioinformatics is a computer-based science, which handles data related to the biological field. Its diverse applications in the field of biology make it one of the most crucial disciplines of biological sciences. Bioinformatics techniques have wide applications in different domains of biotechnology, microbial genomics, medical-related filed, agriculture gene therapy, etc. Bioinformatics advances our understanding in the basic biological process and treatment and prevention of many genetic diseases. Modern biology and related sciences are increasingly dependent on bioinformatics. Bioinformatics techniques such as molecular dynamics simulations (MD) help to understand proteins structures at molecular level. That is not possible to understand by any other means. Thus, bioinformatics exhibits excellent potential in the future development of science and technology.

Keywords: Microbial genome application, medicine, gene therapy, agriculture

7.1 Introduction

Bioinformatics deals with the analysis of biological data using the computer and statistical techniques. In bioinformatics computer algorithms are employed to speed up analysis of biological related data. Bioinformatics

---

*Corresponding author: nikhil.08oct@gmail.com

S. Balamurugan, Anand Krishnan, Dinesh Goyal, Balakumar Chandrasekaran and Boomi Pandi (eds.)
Computation in Bioinformatics: Multidisciplinary Applications, (121–138) © 2021 Scrivener Publishing LLC

deals with several subjects, e.g., biochemistry, biophysics, genetics biotechnology, structural biology, pharmacogenomics, microbiology, mathematics, statistics, and computer sciences. Bioinformatics involves compilation and storage of biological data generated from across the globe by different research labs and companies in a very orderly manner. It includes analysis of various biological data including protein domains, protein structure, and nucleotide sequence [1–2]. It also involves the development of a new algorithm to establish the relationship among the members of different biological data sets. Bioinformatics enhance our knowledge and understating of different plants, animals and human beings, and this new knowledge can be employed in the field of medicine. Bioinformatics helps in data integration and cross-linking of different domains of sciences, e.g. cross-linking mass spectrometry with protein modeling. Since the emergence of genomics, there has been a large amount of data pertaining to DNA sequencing including the human genome project. Side by side, there has been an emergence in the field called transcriptomics, which focuses on studying the expression level of different messenger RNA from a particular organism or tissue at a particular point of time. Different techniques of bioinformatics assist in the analysis of a large amount of data generated in the above-mentioned fields. The field of RNA-seq allows us analysis such as SNP identification, RNA editing and differential gene expression analysis. Proteomics which pertains to the studying of proteins in detail analysis of their expression, structure, function, and interactions. The data generated from above mentioned different fields called as biological data. Units of information on biological data pertain to three important molecules DNA, RNA, and the proteins. We can get much information from this molecule. In the case of DNA, sequence analysis, mutations, polymorphism studies, identification of regulatory regions, genome annotations, gene finding, and comparative genomics are studied. In the case of RNA, splice variant, tissue expression level, microarray, single-gene analysis, and sequence contigs are studied. Finally, in the case of protein structure and function prediction, ligand docking, protein-protein interactions, protein expression, and phylogenetic analysis are studied. Study of these molecules have been the interface between informatics and modern biology. Bioinformatics involves discovery, expansion, and implementation of computational algorithms and software tools that help us to enhance our knowledge about the behavior of these biomolecules. Bioinformatics has its importance in agriculture also; in developing country like India, it plays a significant role in agriculture when it can be used to increase the nutritional content and to increase the production and to get resistance against diseases. In the pharmaceutical area, bioinformatics helps to lessen time and cost concerns for different analysis and drug discovery [3–7]. The use of bioinformatics is threefold: (1) to collect and organize the data in a way that allow researchers to access the information and to enter new results as it is produced; (2) to develop tools to analyze this data in the required way; (3) to analyze these data using these tools and understand the results in a biologically meaningful manner. Using bioinformatics, we can conduct a global analysis of all the available data. The experiment results from the biological laboratory will be stored into the bioinformatics databases, and then, analysis of these data can be done by using different computational technique and tools. The data can be analyzed in terms of sequence, structure, function, evolution, pathway, etc. The result of the analysis will be then compared with the biological data and the experiment result. Biological databases contains following data. (1) Collection of DNA sequences, protein sequences, macromolecule structures, genome sequences, etc. DNA sequence strings with four based letters A, T, C, and G, which comprises genes. (2) Protein sequences are nothing but a collection of 20 amino acids letter. The most sophisticated form of information is the macromolecular structural data. (3) Genome sequence information is the collection of raw DNA sequences ranging from 1.6 million bases to 3 billion bases [8–11].

Some issues are related to the organization of this massive amount of biological data. Firstly, most of the data can be group together based on the biological similarity, e.g., genes can be grouped together according to their function, pathway, etc. So, the major aspect of managing this data is developing a method to access the similarity between these biomolecules and identifying those that are related. There are different databases available to deposit these data according to the information it carries. Each database contains a different type of data. Some examples for the databases are (1) protein sequence databases, (2) nucleotide sequence databases, and (3) structural databases. So, according to the types of data, these can be stored in different databases. The information stored in databases is meaningless unless it is analyzed. There are different types of analysis that can be done using these data sets. The raw DNA sequences data can be analyzed to find the coding and non-coding region (introns and exons) of DNA sequences. Proteins sequences can be compared using bioinformatics algorithm. Multiple sequence alignment can also be performed on proteins sequences to identify similar regions [12–16].

Annotation and encoding of the sequence is the way to explain a whole genome. The relationship between proteins, the biological pathways of different genes, and details about the gene products are core research areas in bioinformatics. The gene expression level is a way to understand the protein and mRNA that are produced by the cell. The main application of this research is in the area of human diseases diagnosis. Bioinformatics algorithms can find the shared sequences between different gene and proteins. The research on gene expression is trying to solve problem related to gene expression [17–19].

7.2   Review of Bioinformatics

Bioinformatics is a multidisciplinary field that develops method and software tools for considerate biological data. Bioinformatics combines computer science, mathematics, statistics, and engineering to study and process biological data. 1951 - Sequencing peptide (Frederick Sanger). 1965 - Sequencing RNA (Robert Holley). 1970 - Term bioinformatics coined by Paulin Hogewey and Ben Hesper. 1977 - Sequencing DNA (Frederick Sanger). 1990 - Human genome project started (expected duration 15 years) and in 2003 - Human genome project completed (Table 7.1) [20–22].

The field of bioinformatics has many practical uses in the modern-day world (Figure 7.1). These include agriculture, molecular medicine, microbial genome application, animals, and comparative studies. Bioinformatics

Table 7.1 Milestones in bioinformatics [22].

1856 & 1863	Rules of heredity by Gregor Mendel
1953	DNA double helix model by Watson & Crick
1955	DNA sequencing
1955	First protein sequencing by F. Sanger
1972	Paul berg first recombinant DNA molecule using ligase
1973	Protein data bank is announced
1977	rDNA technology by Herbert Boyer and Stanley Cohen
1981	579 human genes had been mapped and mapping by Marvin Carruthers and Leory Hood
1988	NCBI was founded
1990	The BLAST program by S. Karatin and Altahul
1991	Human genome project

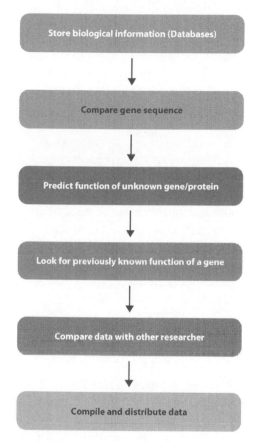

Figure 7.1 Bioinformatics use in six steps [23, 24].

is being used in interpretation and analysis of various kinds of data including nucleotides and an amino acid sequence, protein structure, and protein domain. And an expansion of new algorithms and statistics tools which helps in establishing relationship amongst different biomolecules databases. Bioinformatics also involves tools that help to locate a gene within a gene sequence, predict protein structure, clustering protein structures and sequences. In gene therapy, mutations are easily detected and quantified through next-generation sequencing technology in a heterogeneous sample. Thus, a cost-effective precision medicine, a right drug at the right dose to the right patient at the right time, can be administered. Bioinformatics technique such as data mining is used to analyze and interpret data faster thus reduces the cost and time of drug discovery. Gene identification by sequence inspection and prediction of splice site allows mutations to correct easily. This is much used in the analysis of mutations that causes cancer.

The increasing level of carbon dioxide release is considered to contribute to global climate change. One way to lower the level of atmospheric carbon dioxide (CO_2) to identify organisms that utilize CO_2 as the sole energy source and study their gene expressions that will aid in identifying other organisms that use CO_2 as the main energy source. Bioinformatics helps in creating genome databases of these microbes and also provide insight into their gene expression. Bioinformatics also employed in DNA microarrays analysis that provides us details of transcription for every gene in a genome of a species and further allows us to compare the gene expression between species [25, 26]. One of significant use of bioinformatics is in computational evolutionary biology, data-driven biology in which functional genomics, comparative genomics, and system biology are studied [25–29].

We use bioinformatics in six steps: (1) store biological information (databases), (2) compare gene sequences, (3) forecast function of unknown genes/proteins, (4) look for previously known functions of a gene, (5) compare data with other researchers, and (6) compile and distribute data for other researchers [23, 24].

7.3   Bioinformatics Applications in Different Areas

There are many applications of bioinformatics in different field including biology, biotechnology, microbial genome application, resequencing, comparative analysis, genome assembly personalized medicine, preventive medicine, waste cleanup, and many others. The goal of bioinformatics is to connect the core and tools with the surrounding discipline. The tools and data manipulation are needed for each applied discipline. Using bioinformatics, we can process and store information in a way that is beneficial to the objectives of our work. The manipulation of this information in the creation of modals makes bioinformatics essential to modern science (Figure 7.2) [29, 30].

7.3.1   Microbial Genome Application

Microorganisms are found everywhere, i.e., they are ubiquitous. They can survive and exhibit adverse conditions like extremes in temperature, cold, radiation, salty, acidic, pressure, and pH. So, studying the genetic material of microorganisms can help to understand their nature at a very primary level. And further identification of genes that give them exclusive ability to survive under extreme conditions will help to design more efficient inhibitors against them [31–33]. Bioinformatics uses the below mentions methods to understand microorganisms.

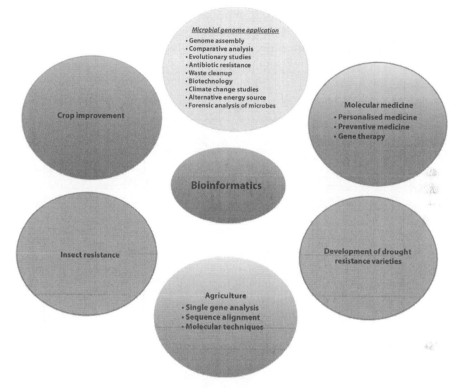

Figure 7.2 Bioinformatics applications in different areas [34].

Genome assembly: Due to the enormous amount of data, genome assembly is one of the complex computational analyses, among all. In genome assembly, a assemble program produce contigs for every chromosome of the genome being further sequenced. But due to the complex character of genome, it leads to a gap in the genome in ideal condition. Some assembly challenges include the presence of repeats in the genome at a different location and are often seen in varying length in the multiple copies. E.g. interspersed repeats and tandem repeats are very common in human DNA. The most common errors caused by these repeats are slipped-strand mispairing, errors in sequence alignment etc [35, 36].

Comparative analysis: In a comparative analysis, scientists use a variety of bioinformatics tool to compare genome sequences of different species. By carefully comparing the characteristics that describe the various organisms, including the genome of the organism, researchers can pinpoint the region of similarity and differences. This information can assist the scientist in understanding the structure and function of a gene which is extremely important—identifying the DNA sequences that have been conserved many years ago. So, it is an important step toward understanding genome. It helps to identify the genes that are essential for life. In highlight, genomic signals manage gene function across many species. Moreover, it also helps us to further of genes that are associated with specific diseases which may lead to the production of more effective medicine [37–40].

Evolutionary studies: In evolutionary genetic studies, MEGA software is most commonly used. First, it computes pairwise distances for the alignment of gene sequences. Then it constructs the phylogenetic tree from all three domain of life (eukaryote, bacteria, and archaea). After that, it analyzes gene duplication and estimates the evolutionary probability [41].

Antibiotics resistance: Antibiotic resistance is one of the biggest problems for food security and global health. So, scientists have been examining the genome of certain bacteria like *Enterococcus faecalis*, a primary source of bacterial infection among hospital patients. Scientists have discovered a virulence region that is made up of several antibiotic-resistant genes that may contribute to the bacterium's transformation from harmless gut bacteria to threatening attacker known as Pathogenicity Island that could provide useful markers for detecting pathogenic strains and help to establish controls to prevent the increase of infection in the world [42, 43].

Waste cleanup: Some bacteria and microbes have the potential to repair damaged DNA and a small fragment of the chromosome by separating damaged segments concentrated areas. Some organisms are responsible for sewage treatment (e.g., *C. cresentus*). And some bacteria are responsible for environmental cleanup. In bioinformatics, we study about genes and proteins of these bacterias [44].

Biotechnology: Bioinformatics has many applications that make it so unique discipline among all. Bioinformatics has so many applications in biotechnology field including genome sequencing, identification of the function of the gene, predicting the 3D structure modeling, prediction of promoter coding region of the genome, and identification of genes. Without using bioinformatics, handling and interpretation of these genes would be unthinkable [45].

Climate change studies: Bioinformatics has played an important role in the control of climate change at some level from the past few years.

Carbon dioxide level is increasing day by day, and this is because of the use of fossil fuel for energy, and this results in the global climate change. To decrease atmospheric carbon dioxide level, the Department of Energy, USA has launched a program, which utilizes bioinformatics to study genomes of microorganisms that uses carbon dioxide as their sole carbon source [46–48].

Alternative energy sources: Bioinformatics can also be used in the study of the genome of microbe, which can generate energy from different natural sources. Recently, scientists are studying the genome of *Chlorobium tepidum* which can generate energy from light. It will give the immense contribution for producing the alternative energy sources [49, 50].

Forensic analysis of microbes: Bioinformatics field in forensic is based on statistical and technological advances such as DNA microarray sequencing and machine learning algorithm. It addresses hypothesis based formulation on DNA samples, decides the least population of similar units of evidence, and determines the statistical meaning of the outcomes of tests. Scientist used their genomic tools to distinguish between strains of one microorganism with the closely related strains [51–53].

7.3.2 Molecular Medicine

Every disease has a genetic component, and any type of gene alteration causes a specific type of diseases. Fortunately, scientists have sequenced complete human genome so we can easily identify the disease directly associated with the genes and can understand the molecular basis of diseases very easily [54–56].

Personalized medicine: Personalized medicine is a healthcare approach in which treatment is customized for an individual patient. The individual gene is compared with the reference DNA. This uncovers any specific genetic mutations that the patient may possess. This can determine the individual's susceptibility to specific diseases. Some drugs are unsuccessful to reach the market because they have shown adverse effects on the patients due to the sequence variant in the patient DNA [57, 58].

Preventive medicine: Preventive medicine is an important part of the healthcare provider over a patient lifetime. It is a branch of medicine dealing with the prevention of diseases and the maintenance of good health and medical practices. Preventive actions such as change of way of life or having treatment at the initial possible stages when they are more likely to be successful could result in massive advances in our struggle to conquer diseases [59–63].

Gene therapy: A, T, G, and C nucleotides are used in gene therapy technology to develop long-lasting therapy for people of severe diseases. Genes are segments of DNA that direct the cell to produce a protein that performs a vast function in the body. Many diseases have genetic bases meaning that mutated genes provide incorrect instruction that causes the cell to produce an abnormal protein that will further cause a variety of diseases. So, gene therapy is an approach used to treat or even prevent disease by varying the expression of a person's gene [64–66].

7.3.3   Agriculture

In agriculture, bioinformatics can allow to enhance the nutritional quality of food and develop a crop that can handle poor soil growing condition. Bioinformatics tool can be used to make comparison between the numbers, locations, and biochemical functions of genes in different organisms. The bioinformatics tools used in agriculture involves the following [67–71].

Single gene analysis: This involves analyzing and comparing the genetic material of different species and studying the functions of the genes, mechanism of inherited diseases, and species evolution. Various bioinformatics tools are used to make a comparison between a number of genes, their location, and their biochemical function in different life form [71–74].

Sequence alignment: Sequence alignment is of two types the first is pairwise alignment, e.g., BLAST and FASTA, and the second is multiple alignments, e.g. PSI-BLAST [75–78].

Molecular techniques: There are several tools dedicated to serving molecular biologist, design efficient PCR and primer design which are freely available [79, 80].

Crop improvement: Bioinformatics techniques are widely used for crop improvement, they not only help in improving overall crop productions but also help in improvement of nutritional quality of crops. The bioinformatics tools help in providing rational annotation of genes, proteins, and phenotypes. Various tools are available to identify the genes, to learn physiology, and to study comparative genomics and expression profiling. So, the final objective of bioinformatics is to incorporate large-scale data for understanding the molecular mechanism concerned in the various developmental processes [81–83].

Insect resistance: Genes of one organism that can manage several dangerous pests are transferred into the desired plant. This new plant can resist the attack of insect. By using different bioinformatics tools, it is possible to analyze the genes that have insect resistance quality. This may help to reduce the use of insecticide and hence may improve the nutritional quality of crops. For example, genes of *Bacillus thuringiensis* are transferred to cotton, maize, and potato. Some toxin gene has also been genetically engineered in several crops [84, 85].

Development of drought-resistant varieties: Genes of particular variety can be identified which are responsible to survive in adverse condition like extreme heat condition, which is further transfer into another crop. Later on, this new crop can be able to survive in extreme heat, or it can be further grown as a drought tolerance variety [85–88].

7.4   Conclusion

There are different applications of bioinformatics in the field of agriculture, medicine, and microbial genome etc. Employing bioinformatics tools allows scientists and researchers to work fast and more efficient than before.

References

1. Fenstermacher, D., Introduction to bioinformatics. *J. Am. Soc. Inform. Sci. Tech.*, 56, 5, 440–446, 2005.
2. Chen C., Huang H., Wu C.H., Protein Bioinformatics Databases and Resources. In: Wu C., Arighi C., Ross K. (eds) Protein Bioinformatics. Methods in Molecular Biology, vol. 1558, Humana Press, New York, NY, 2017. https://doi.org/10.1007/978-1-4939-6783-4_1.
3. Sinchaikul, S., Sookkheo, B., Topanuruk, S., Juan, H.-F., Phutrakul, S., Chen, S.-T., Bioinformatics, functional genomics, and proteomics study of Bacillus sp. *J. Chromatogr. B*, 771, 1-2, 261–287, 2002.
4. Ji, F. and Sadreyev, R.I., RNA-seq: Basic bioinformatics analysis. *Curr. Protoc. Mol. Biol.*, 124, 1, e68, 2018.

5. Blueggel, M., Chamrad, D., Meyer, H.E., Bioinformatics in proteomics. *Curr. Pharm. Biotechnol.*, 5, 1, 79–88, 2004.

6. Xue, J., Zhao, S., Liang, Y., Hou, C., Wang, J., Bioinformatics and its Applications in Agriculture, in: *International Conference on Computer and Computing Technologies in Agriculture*, pp. 977–982, Springer, 2007.

7. Shah, V.A., Rathod, D.N., Basuri, T., Modi, V.S., Parmar, I.J., Applications of bioinformatics in pharmaceutical product designing: a review. *World J. Pharm. Phar. Sci.*, 4, 477–493, 2015.

8. Mehmood, M.A., Sehar, U., Ahmad, N., Use of bioinformatics tools in different spheres of life sciences. *J. Data Min. Genomics Proteomics*, 5, 2, 1, 2014.

9. Bilotta, M., Tradigo, G., Veltri, P., Bioinformatics Data Models, Representation and Storage, in: *Encyclopedia of Bioinformatics and Computational Biology: ABC of Bioinformatics*, p. 110, 2018.

10. Berman, H.M., Bhat, T.N., Bourne, P.E., Feng, Z., Gilliland, G., Weissig, H., Westbrook, J., The Protein Data Bank and the challenge of structural genomics. *Nat. Struct. Biol.*, 7, 11, 957–959, 2000.

11. Lander, E.S., Linton, L.M., Birren, B., Nusbaum, C., Zody, M.C., Baldwin, J., Devon, K., Dewar, K., Doyle, M., FitzHugh, W., Initial sequencing and analysis of the human genome. International Human Genome Sequencing Consortium. *Nature,* 409, 860–921, 2001. https://doi.org/10.1038/35057062.

12. Gill, P., Fereday, L., Morling, N., Schneider, P.M., The evolution of DNA databases—recommendations for new European STR loci. *Forensic Sci. Int.*, 156, 2-3, 242–244, 2006.

13. Pearson W.R. Using the FASTA Program to Search Protein and DNA Sequence Databases. In: Computer Analysis of Sequence Data. Methods in Molecular Biology, vol. 25, Springer, Totowa, NJ, 1994. https://doi.org/10.1385/0-89603-276-0:365.

14. Apweiler, R., Bairoch, A., Wu, C.H., Protein sequence databases. *Curr. Opin. Chem. Biol.*, 8, 1, 76–80, 2004.

15. Nakamura, Y., Gojobori, T., Ikemura, T., Codon usage tabulated from international DNA sequence databases: status for the year 2000. *Nucleic Acids Res.*, 28, 1, 292–292, 2000.

16. Pearson, W.R., Comparison of methods for searching protein sequence databases. *Protein Sci.*, 4, 6, 1145–1160, 1995.

17. Ye, Y. and Doak, T.G., A parsimony approach to biological pathway reconstruction/inference for genomes and metagenomes. *PloS Comput. Biol.*, 5, 8, e1000465, 2009.

18. Creighton, C.J., Nagaraja, A.K., Hanash, S.M., Matzuk, M.M., Gunaratne, P.H., A bioinformatics tool for linking gene expression profiling results with public databases of microRNA target predictions. *Rna*, 14, 11, 2290–2296, 2008.

19. Wasserman, W.W. and Sandelin, A., Applied bioinformatics for the identification of regulatory elements. *Nat. Rev. Genet.*, 5, 4, 276–287, 2004.

20. Gobalan, K. and John, A., Applications of Bioinformatics in Genomics and Proteomics. *J. Adv. Appl. Sci. Res.*, 1, 3, 29–42, 2016.

21. Collins, F.S. and McKusick, V.A., Implications of the Human Genome Project for medical science. *Jama*, *285*, 5, 540–544, 2001.
22. Attwood, T.K., Gisel, A., Eriksson, N.-E., Bongcam-Rudloff, E., Concepts, historical milestones and the central place of bioinformatics in modern biology: a European perspective, in: *Bioinformatics-trends and methodologies*, vol. 1, 2011.
23. Hernández-Domínguez, E.M., Castillo-Ortega, L.S., García-Esquivel, Y., Virginia Mandujano-González, V., Díaz-Godínez, G. and Álvarez-Cervantes, J. (October 22nd 2019). Bioinformatics as a Tool for the Structural and Evolutionary Analysis of Proteins, Computational Biology and Chemistry, Payam Behzadi and Nicola Bernabò, IntechOpen, DOI: 10.5772/intechopen.89594. Available from: https://www.intechopen.com/chapters/69666.
24. Rehm, B., Bioinformatic tools for DNA/protein sequence analysis, functional assignment of genes and protein classification. *Appl. Microbiol. Biotechnol.*, *57*, 5, 579–592, 2001.
25. Madhukar N.S., Elemento O. Bioinformatics Approaches to Predict Drug Responses from Genomic Sequencing. In: von Stechow L. (eds.) Cancer Systems Biology. Methods in Molecular Biology, vol. 1711, Humana Press, New York, NY, 2018. https://doi.org/10.1007/978-1-4939-7493-1_14.
26. Sobhy, H., A bioinformatics pipeline to search functional motifs within whole-proteome data: a case study of poxviruses. *Virus Genes*, *53*, 2, 173–178, 2017.
27. Carriço, J., Rossi, M., Moran-Gilad, J., Van Domselaar, G., Ramirez, M., A primer on microbial bioinformatics for nonbioinformaticians. *Clin. Microbiol. Infect.*, *24*, 4, 342–349, 2018.
28. Wu, D., Rice, C.M. & Wang, X. Cancer bioinformatics: A new approach to systems clinical medicine. *BMC Bioinformatics*, 13, 71, 2012. https://doi.org/10.1186/1471-2105-13-71.
29. Sinha, S., Role of bioinformatics in climate change studies. *J. Sci.*, *1*, 1–8, 2015.
30. de Carvalho, L., Borelli, G., Camargo, A., de Assis, M., de Ferraz, S., Fiamenghi, M., José, J., Mofatto, L., Nagamatsu, S., Persinoti, G., Bioinformatics applied to biotechnology: A review towards bioenergy research. *Biomass Bioenergy*, *123*, 195–224, 2019.
31. Rampelotto, P.H., Resistance of microorganisms to extreme environmental conditions and its contribution to astrobiology. *Sustainability*, *2*, 6, 1602–1623, 2010.
32. Bansal, A.K., Bioinformatics in microbial biotechnology–a mini review. *Microb. Cell Fact.*, *4*, 1, 1–11, 2005.
33. Zhaurova, K. Genomes of other organisms: DNA barcoding and metagenomics. *Nat. Edu.*, *1*, 1, 2008, 2008, https://www.nature.com/scitable/topicpage/genomes-of-other-organisms-dna-barcoding-and-662/.
34. Korobeynikov, A. and Lapidus, A., Third international conference Bioinformatics from Algorithms to Applications (BiATA 2019). *BMC Bioinf.*, *20*, Suppl 17, 516, 2019.

35. Pop, M., Genome assembly reborn: recent computational challenges. *Briefings Bioinf.*, *10*, 4, 354–366, 2009.
36. Levinson, G. and Gutman, G.A., Slipped-strand mispairing: a major mechanism for DNA sequence evolution. *Mol. Biol. Evol.*, *4*, 3, 203–221, 1987.
37. Bellgard, M., Ye, J., Gojobori, T., Appels, R., The bioinformatics challenges in comparative analysis of cereal genomes—an overview. *Funct. Integr. Genomics*, *4*, 1, 1–11, 2004.
38. Bernt, M., Braband, A., Middendorf, M., Misof, B., Rota-Stabelli, O., Stadler, P.F., Bioinformatics methods for the comparative analysis of metazoan mitochondrial genome sequences. *Mol. Phylogenet. Evol.*, *69*, 2, 320–327, 2013.
39. Cheng, J., Zeng, X., Ren, G., Liu, Z., CGAP: a new comprehensive platform for the comparative analysis of chloroplast genomes. *BMC Bioinf.*, *14*, 1, 1–8, 2013.
40. Davis, J.J., Wattam, A.R., Aziz, R.K., Brettin, T., Butler, R., Butler, R.M., Chlenski, P., Conrad, N., Dickerman, A., Dietrich, E.M., The PATRIC Bioinformatics Resource Center: expanding data and analysis capabilities. *Nucleic Acids Res.*, *48*, D1, D606–D612, 2020.
41. Kumar, S., Nei, M., Dudley, J., Tamura, K., MEGA: a biologist-centric software for evolutionary analysis of DNA and protein sequences. *Briefings Bioinf.*, *9*, 4, 299–306, 2008.
42. Ndagi, U., Falaki, A.A., Abdullahi, M., Lawal, M.M., Soliman, M.E., Antibiotic resistance: bioinformatics-based understanding as a functional strategy for drug design. *RSC Adv.*, *10*, 31, 18451–18468, 2020.
43. Dozmorov, M. G., Kyker, K. D., Saban, R., Shankar, N., Baghdayan, A. S., Centola, M. B., & Hurst, R. E. Systems biology approach for mapping the response of human urothelial cells to infection by Enterococcus faecalis. In BMC bioinformatics, Vol. 8, No. 7, pp. 1-15, BioMed Central 2007, December.
44. Umadevi, S., Emmanuel, A., Ayyasamy, P., Rajakumar, S., Computational approaches in waste management: Special emphasis in microbial degradation. *Res. Rev. J. Ecol. Environ. Sci.*, 22–27, 2015 https://www.rroij.com/open-access/computational-approaches-in-waste-management-special-emphasis-inmicrobial-degradation.pdf.
45. Kumar, A. and Chordia, N., Role of bioinformatics in biotechnology. *Res. Rev. Biosci.*, *12*, 1, 1–6, 2017.
46. Drell, D., The Department of Energy Microbial Cell Project: a 180 paradigm shift for biology. *Omics: J. Integr. Biol.*, *6*, 1, 3–9, 2002.
47. Batley, J. and Edwards, D., The application of genomics and bioinformatics to accelerate crop improvement in a changing climate. *Curr. Opin. Plant Biol.*, *30*, 78–81, 2016.
48. Kumar, G.R. and Chowdhary, N., Biotechnological and bioinformatics approaches for augmentation of biohydrogen production: A review. *Renew. Sustain. Energy Rev.*, *56*, 1194–1206, 2016.

49. Dahiya, B.P. and Lata, M., Bioinformatics impacts on medicine, microbial genome and agriculture. *J. Pharmacogn. Phytochem.*, 6, 1938–1942, 1938.

50. Gupta, O. and Rani, S., Bioinformatics applications and Tools: An Overview. *CiiT-Int. J. Biom. Bioinf.*, 3, 3, 107–110, 2010.

51. Bianchi, L. and Liò, P., Forensic, DNA and bioinformatics. *Briefings Bioinf.*, 8, 2, 117–128, 2007.

52. Liu, Y.-Y. and Harbison, S., A review of bioinformatic methods for forensic DNA analyses. *Forensic Sci. Int.: Genet.*, 33, 117–128, 2018.

53. Muntaha, S.T., Hasnain, M.J.U., Khan, W.A., Rafiq, F., Pervez, M.T., Role of bioinformatics in forensic science. *FUUAST J. Biol.*, 8, 1, 133–138, 2018.

54. Altman, R.B., Bioinformatics in support of molecular medicine. *Proc. AMIA Symp., American Medical Informatics Association*, 53, 1998. https://www.ncbi.nlm.nih.gov/pmc/articles/PMC2232090/.

55. Ostrowski, J. and Wyrwicz, L.S., Integrating genomics, proteomics and bioinformatics in translational studies of molecular medicine. *Expert Rev. Mol. Diagn.*, 9, 6, 623–630, 2009.

56. Teufel, A., Krupp, M., Weinmann, A., Galle, P.R., Current bioinformatics tools in genomic biomedical research. *Int. J. Mol. Med.*, 17, 6, 967–973, 2006.

57. Molidor, R., Sturn, A., Maurer, M., Trajanoski, Z., New trends in bioinformatics: from genome sequence to personalized medicine. *Exp. Gerontol.*, 38, 10, 1031–1036, 2003.

58. Fernald, G.H., Capriotti, E., Daneshjou, R., Karczewski, K.J., Altman, R.B., Bioinformatics challenges for personalized medicine. *Bioinformatics*, 27, 13, 1741–1748, 2011.

59. Cantor, C.R., The use of genetic SNPs as new diagnostic markers in preventive medicine. *Ann. N. Y. Acad. Sci.*, 1055, 1, 48–57, 2005.

60. Yu, C., Liu, Z., McKenna, T., Reisner, A.T., Reifman, J., A method for automatic identification of reliable heart rates calculated from ECG and PPG waveforms. *J. Am. Med. Inf. Assoc.*, 13, 3, 309–320, 2006.

61. Xie, Q., Bai, Q., Zou, L.Y., Zhang, Q.Y., Zhou, Y., Chang, H., Yi, L., Zhu, J.D., Mi, M.T., Genistein inhibits DNA methylation and increases expression of tumor suppressor genes in human breast cancer cells. *Genes Chromosomes Cancer*, 53, 5, 422–431, 2014.

62. Bouchard, C., Antunes-Correa, L.M., Ashley, E.A., Franklin, N., Hwang, P.M., Mattsson, C.M., Negrao, C.E., Phillips, S.A., Sarzynski, M.A., Wang, P.-y., Personalized preventive medicine: genetics and the response to regular exercise in preventive interventions. *Prog. Cardiovasc. Dis.*, 57, 4, 337–346, 2015.

63. Shah, N.H. and Tenenbaum, J.D., Focus on translational bioinformatics: The coming age of data-driven medicine: translational bioinformatics' next frontier. *J. Am. Med. Inf. Assoc.: JAMIA*, 19, e1, e2, 2012.

64. Giordano, F., Hotz-Wagenblatt, A., Lauterborn, D., Appelt, J.-U., Fellenberg, K., Nagy, K., Zeller, W., Suhai, S., Fruehauf, S., Laufs, S., New bioinformatic strategies to rapidly characterize retroviral integration sites of gene therapy vectors. *Methods Inf. Med.*, 46, 05, 542–547, 2007.

65. Xue, K., Cao, J., Wang, Y., Zhao, X., Yu, D., Jin, C., Xu, C., Identification of potential therapeutic gene markers in nasopharyngeal carcinoma based on bioinformatics analysis. *Clin. Transl. Sci.*, *13*, 2, 265–274, 2020.

66. Seto, J., Walsh, M.P., Mahadevan, P., Zhang, Q., Seto, D., Applying genomic and bioinformatic resources to human adenovirus genomes for use in vaccine development and for applications in vector development for gene delivery. *Viruses*, *2*, 1, 1–26, 2010.

67. Esposito, A., Colantuono, C., Ruggieri, V., Chiusano, M.L., Bioinformatics for agriculture in the Next-Generation sequencing era. *Chem. Biol. Technol. Agric.*, *3*, 1, 1–12, 2016.

68. Singh, V., Singh, A., Chand, R., Kushwaha, C., Role of bioinformatics in agriculture and sustainable development. *Int. J. Bioinform. Res.*, *3*, 2, 221–226, 2011.

69. Iquebal M.A., Jaiswal S., Mukhopadhyay C.S., Sarkar C., Rai A., Kumar D. Applications of Bioinformatics in Plant and Agriculture. In: Barh D., Khan M., Davies E. (eds.) PlantOmics: The Omics of Plant Science. Springer, New Delhi, 2015. https://doi.org/10.1007/978-81-322-2172-2_27.

70. Prabha R., Verma M.K., Singh D.P., Bioinformatics in Agriculture: Translating Alphabets for Transformation in the Field. In: Hakeem K., Malik A., Vardar-Sukan F., Ozturk M. (eds.) Plant Bioinformatics. Springer, Cham, 2017. https://doi.org/10.1007/978-3-319-67156-7_7.

71. Aslam Z., Khattak J.Z.K., Ahmed M., Asif M., A Role of Bioinformatics in Agriculture. In: Ahmed M., Stockle C. (eds.) Quantification of Climate Variability, Adaptation and Mitigation for Agricultural Sustainability. Springer, Cham, 2017. https://doi.org/10.1007/978-3-319-32059-5_17.

72. Luscombe, N.M., Greenbaum, D., Gerstein, M., What is bioinformatics? A proposed definition and overview of the field. *Methods Inf. Med.*, *40*, 04, 346–358, 2001.

73. Ozbudak, E.M., Thattai, M., Kurtser, I., Grossman, A.D., Van Oudenaarden, A., Regulation of noise in the expression of a single gene. *Nat. Genet.*, *31*, 1, 69–73, 2002.

74. Hoballah, M.E., Gübitz, T., Stuurman, J., Broger, L., Barone, M., Mandel, T., Dell'Olivo, A., Arnold, M., Kuhlemeier, C., Single gene–mediated shift in pollinator attraction in Petunia. *Plant Cell*, *19*, 3, 779–790, 2007.

75. Mount D.W., Using the Basic Local Alignment Search Tool (BLAST). *CSH Protoc.*, 2007 Jul 1;2007:pdb.top17. doi: 10.1101/pdb.top17. PMID: 21357135.

76. Pearson, W.R., Finding protein and nucleotide similarities with FASTA. *Curr. Protoc. Bioinf.*, *53*, 1, 3.9. 1–3.9. 25, 2016.

77. Edgar, R.C. and Batzoglou, S., Multiple sequence alignment. *Curr. Opin. Struct. Biol.*, *16*, 3, 368–373, 2006.

78. Jeanmougin, F., Thompson, J.D., Gouy, M., Higgins, D.G., Gibson, T.J., Multiple sequence alignment with Clustal X. *Trends Biochem. Sci.*, *23*, 10, 403–405, 1998.

79. Abd-Elsalam, K.A., Bioinformatic tools and guideline for PCR primer design. *Afr. J. Biotechnol.*, 2, 5, 91–95, 2003.
80. You, F.M., Huo, N., Gu, Y.Q., Luo, M.-c., Ma, Y., Hane, D., Lazo, G.R., Dvorak, J., Anderson, O.D., BatchPrimer3: a high throughput web application for PCR and sequencing primer design. *BMC Bioinf.*, 9, 1, 1–13, 2008.
81. Mochida, K. and Shinozaki, K., Genomics and bioinformatics resources for crop improvement. *Plant Cell Physiol.*, 51, 4, 497–523, 2010.
82. Lai, K., Lorenc, M.T., Edwards, D., Genomic databases for crop improvement. *Agronomy*, 2, 1, 62–73, 2012.
83. Okii, D., Chilagane, L., Tukamuhabwa, P., Maphosa, M., Application of bioinformatics in crop improvement: annotating the putative soybean rust resistance gene Rpp3 for enhancing marker assisted selection. *J. Proteomics Bioinform.*, 7, 001–009, 2014.
84. Randhawa, G.J., Singh, M., Grover, M., Bioinformatic analysis for allergenicity assessment of Bacillus thuringiensis Cry proteins expressed in insect-resistant food crops. *Food Chem. Toxicol.*, 49, 2, 356–362, 2011.
85. Afolabi-Balogun, N., Inuwa, H., Ishiyaku, M., Bakare-Odunoola, M., Nok, A., Isolation and characterization of a mannose-binding insecticidal lectin gene from Allium sativum (garlic) and its putative role in insect resistance using bioinformatics tools. *Infect. Genet. Evol.*, 12, 7, 1508–1512, 2012.
86. Vassilev, D.; Leunissen, J.; Atanassov, A.; Nenov, A.; Dimov, G., Application of Bioinformatics in Plant Breeding. Biotechnology & Biotechnological Equipment, 19 (sup 3), 139–152, 2005. https://www.tandfonline.com/doi/abs/10.1080/13102818.2005.10817293.
87. Zeli, W., Hengyue, Z., Xianxi, Y., Xiuling, J., Xinzheng, L., Anatomical studies on the drought resistant varieties in maize. *Acta Bot. Boreal.-Occid. Sin.*, 18, 4, 581–583, 1998.
88. Gao Y. *et al.*, Identification of Rice Drought-Resistant Gene Based on Gene Expression Profiles and Network Analysis Algorithm. In: Huang DS., Jo KH. (eds.) Intelligent Computing Theories and Application. ICIC 2020. Lecture Notes in Computer Science, vol. 12464. Springer, Cham, 2020. https://doi.org/10.1007/978-3-030-60802-6_26.

8

DNA Microarray Analysis: From Affymetrix CEL Files to Comparative Gene Expression

Sandeep Kumar[1]*, Shruti Shandilya[2], Suman Kapila[3], Mohit Sharma[4,5] and Nikhil Agrawal[6†]

[1]*International Institute of Veterinary Education & Research, Haryana, Rohtak, India*
[2]*Department of Applied Physics, Aalto University, Espoo, Finland*
[3]*ICAR-National Dairy Research Institute, Haryana, India*
[4]*Post Graduate School of Molecular Medicine, Medical University of Warsaw, Warsaw, Poland*
[5]*Malopolskie Centre of Biotechnology, Jagiellonian University, Krakow, Poland*
[6]*College of Health Sciences, University of KwaZulu-Natal, Westville, Durban, South Africa*

Abstract

Microarray technique is widely used for the rapid detection and comparison of expression of thousands of genes at the same time. For the microarray data analysis, robust and reproducible protocols are being generated day by day. Bioconductor provides several free microarray data analysis packages. The analysis includes the following processes: quality control, normalization, and calculation of differential gene expression. This chapter demonstrates a protocol to find out the differentially expressed genes from the raw data (.CEL files) using the Bioconductor tools.

Keywords: Microarray, bioconductor, genes

*Corresponding author: sandeepvermma@gmail.com
†Corresponding author: nikhil.08oct@gmail.com

S. Balamurugan, Anand Krishnan, Dinesh Goyal, Balakumar Chandrasekaran and Boomi Pandi (eds.)
Computation in Bioinformatics: Multidisciplinary Applications, (139–154) © 2021 Scrivener Publishing LLC

8.1   Introduction

DNA microarray, also known as DNA chip, is a molecular technique used to quantify mRNA expression in the cells/tissues [1]. In this technique, an array of hundreds of known DNA fragments called as probes is immobilized on a chip in defined positions. This chip can be made up of either silicon or nylon. Using the microarray technique, thousands of genes can be studied simultaneously to compare different conditions [2]. Spotted microarray and oligonucleotide chips are the most popular types of microarray among the users for expression study, and the difference between these is the way to immobilize the probe on the slide. In spotted or DNA microarray, the probes are synthesized separately and immobilized mechanically to the chip. However, in oligonucleotide chips, the probes are directly synthesized on the slide. A probe set is used in the oligonucleotide chip instead of a single probe [3]. Microarray data analysis includes image analysis, quality control, normalization, and differential gene expression. In this chapter, the pipeline for the analysis of microarray data is developed and run in RStudio, an integrated development environment (IDE) for R. The packages are downloaded from Bioconductor. It provides advance tools for microarray data analysis. Bioconductor is built on an open-source platform, R programming language. Bioconductor software constituents are available as R packages. Here, we will use affy, affyQCReport, limma, gdata, and gplots packages for the analysis. This chapter will provide a detailed methodology for the analysis of Affymetrix microarray data [5].

8.2   Data Processing

8.2.1   Installation of Workflow

The packages are installed via the BiocManager using the following commands in R studio.

```
>if (!requireNamespace("BiocManager", quietly = TRUE))
 install.packages("BiocManager")
>BiocManager::install("affy")
>BiocManager::install("affyQCReport")
>BiocManager::install("limma")
>BiocManager::install("gdata")
>BiocManager::install("gplot")
```

After the successful installation of packages, all packages are loaded in order. To call the packages, **library** () function is used. This will also load all the other packages necessary to run the workflow.

```
>library(affy)
>library(affyQCReport)
>library(limma)
>library(gdata)
>library(gplots)
```

If several packages with the same functionality are loaded, e.g., oligo and affy, then R will not be able to identify the package. Affy and oligo packages have functions with the similar name, e.g., **intensity()**, **MAplot()**, and **rma()**. If a function intensity(data) is called, then the package name should be specified before calling the function, e.g.,

```
>oligo::intensity(data)
```

Otherwise, it chooses affy over oligo by default.

8.2.2   Importing the Raw Data for Processing

The working directory is specified using the **setwd** function, where all .CEL files are downloaded.

```
>setwd("Path to the working directory")
```

To see the path of the working directory, the **getwd** function is used.

```
>getwd()
```

The next step is to import .CEL files that contain raw probe-level data into AffyBatch object. **ReadAffy** function can be employed to import the data

```
>data <- ReadAffy()
```

To see the loaded data, type **data** in the console

```
>data
```

This function will give the information about the array size, affy IDs, annotation, and number of samples and genes.

AffyBatch object
size of arrays=1164x1164 features (20 kb)
cdf=HG-U133_Plus_2 (54675 affyids)
number of samples=6
number of genes=54675
annotation=hgu133plus2

8.2.3   Retrieving Sample Annotation of the Data

Microarray data sets not only include expression data but also comprise information of samples hybridized to the arrays, e.g., sample labels. AffyBatch objects contain many slots, and phenoData is one of these. It contains samples labels.

>ph = data@phenoData
>ph

This function will give information about phenotypic data and metadata of the experiment.

An object of class 'AnnotatedDataFrame'
sampleNames: Control 1.CEL Control 2.CEL ... Treated 3.CEL (6 total)
varLabels: sample
varMetadata: labelDescription
ph is a data frame and a column of a data frame can be selected using the $ sign. To see the number of samples in the experiment, use

>ph$sample

[1] 1 2 3 4 5 6

And to observe the data in the data frame, use

>ph@data

It will show the name and number of samples used in the experiment
          sample
Control 1.CEL   1

Control 2.CEL   2
Control 3.CEL   3
Treated 1.CEL   4
Treated 2.CEL   5
Treated 3.CEL   6

To retrieve the probe IDs (Affymetrix IDs), **featureName** function is used

>featureNames(data)

```
[1] "1007_s_at" "1053_at"  "117_at"
[4] "121_at"   "1255_g_at" "1294_at"
[7] "1316_at"  "1320_at"  "1405_i_at"
[10] "1431_at"  "1438_at"  "1487_at"
[13] "1494_f_at" "1552256_a_at" "1552257_a_at"
[16] "1552258_at" "1552261_at" "1552263_at"
[19] "1552264_a_at" "1552266_at" "1552269_at"
[22] "1552271_at" "1552272_a_at" "1552274_at"
[25] "1552275_s_at" "1552276_a_at" "1552277_a_at"
[28] "1552278_a_at" "1552279_a_at" "1552280_at"
[31] "1552281_at" "1552283_s_at" "1552286_at"
[34] "1552287_s_at" "1552288_at" "1552289_a_at"
```

To fetch the number of probe sets represented on the arrays

>length(featureNames(data))

[1] 54675

8.2.4   Quality Control

The first step before the calculation of the differential gene expression is quality assessment. To check the integrity of the chip, the following code is used.

```
>for (i in 1:6)
    {
name = paste("image",i,".jpg",sep="")
jpeg(name)
image(data[,i],main=ph@data$sample[i])
dev.off()
    }
```

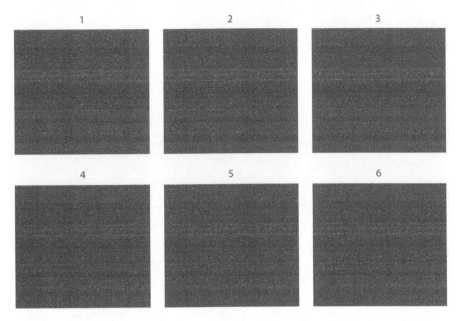

Figure 8.1 Image analysis of chips. To check the integrity of microarray chips, image analysis is done. Six samples are used to demonstrate the analysis of microarray data.

In results, the images of the chips are produced as shown in Figure 8.1. These figures show the quality of the chips. The foreground and background signals should be clear. The quality of raw data must be accessed to check the biasness, intensity, RNA degradation, etc. Quality control of Affymetrix uses simple graphical exploration methods for quality assessment before and after the normalization. The function **affyQAReport** is used to check the quality of microarray data

>affyQAReport(data)

It creates a folder named as affyQC containing all the quality checks in pdf files: Boxplots, Histogram, MAPlots, MADimage, RNA degradation plot, and QCstat.

8.2.4.1   Boxplot

Boxplots are the graphical representation of log-intensity distribution to compare the different arrays (Figure 8.2a). These boxplots evaluate the normalization process; therefore, boxplots are drawn before and after the normalization.

8.2.4.2   Density Histogram

In addition to boxplot, affyQAReport also generates the histogram of log-intensity (Figure 8.2b). The density curves of raw data are unsmoothed, while after the normalization, the curves become smooth.

8.2.4.3   MA Plot

The MA plots are used to identify log-intensity dependent biasness. The MA plots compare the log-intensity of each array to their reference array (Figure 8.2c). The plot Y-axis has the log-ratio intensity of one array to the reference median array ("M"), and X-axis has the average log-intensity of both arrays ("A"). The probe levels are not expected to differ much within a group of replicates, so we expect an MA plot centred on the $Y = 0$ axis from low to high intensities. The MA plots for each replicate separately show that the references array is the median array of each group. These plots are used to check the efficiency of normalization method because normalization is expected to correct the log-intensity dependent biasness.

8.2.4.4   NUSE Plot

This plot shows the probe set homogeneity. Normalized Unscaled Standard Error (NUSE) plot is used for the visualization of standard error from probe-level model fit (Figure 8.2d). For each gene, the value of the median standard error is 1. The bad quality arrays have a higher median, standard error.

8.2.4.5   RLE Plot

RLE (Relative Log Expression) plot represents the ratio of estimated and median expression of gene or probe set. It is supposed that all probes are not differentially expressed; therefore, the RLE plots are centred at 0 (Figure 8.2e). If the plot is not centred at 0, then the array is of low quality.

8.2.4.6   RNA Degradation Plot

For the accuracy of results, the RNA should be of good quality to be used in microarray experiments. The RNA degradation plot used to access the

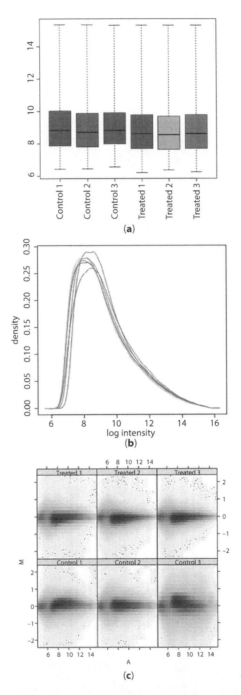

Figure 8.2 (a to c) Boxplot (a), Density histogram (b), and MA plot (c). These plots are used to check the data biasness in samples before normalization.

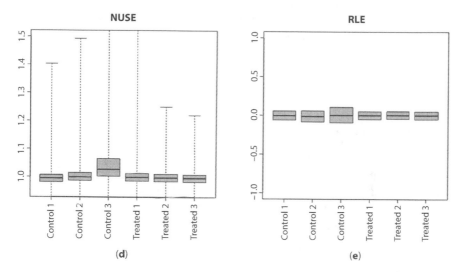

(d)

(e)

Figure 8.2 (d and e) NUSE plot (d) and RLE plot (e) are used to determine the probe set homogeneity. The standard error from the probe-level model is visualized as boxplots in the NUSE plot. The deviation from the median of gene expression is visualized as boxplots in RLE plot. The RLE plots should be centered near 0. In low-quality arrays, the patterns of the RLE plots are not being centered near 0.

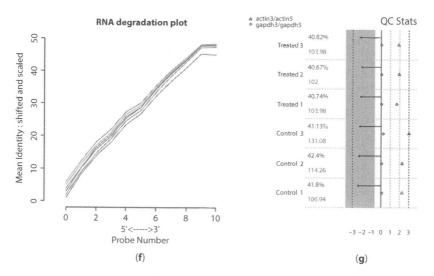

(f)

(g)

Figure 8.2 (f and g) RNA degradation plot (f) and QC stat plot (g). RNA degradation plot is used to visualize the average intensity of each probe from 5′ to 3′ end across all the probe sets. The quality control parameters used in the arrays are visualized in QC stats plot.

RNA quality used in the experiments. This plot can also be used to identify the artefact in the microarray. The arrays with similar RNA degradation pattern can be used for further analysis. The bad RNA quality array will have a very steeper slope from 5′ to 3′ (Figure 8.2f).

8.2.4.7   QCstat

QC plot provides information about average background, scale factor, number of genes called present, 3′:5′ ratios of control genes (β-actin and GAPDH), and values for spike-in control transcripts. The graph is plotted from the bottom, i.e., the first chip is plotted at the base and last chip is plotted at the top. Each plot separated by horizontal dotted lines represents each sample. Each plot contains the information for an individual chip. Blue region represents the area where scale factors are within three-fold of the mean scale factor for all chips. The scale factors are plotted as horizontal blue lines raised from the centre line. If the scale factors fall outside the blue region, then they are plotted as a red line (Figure 8.2g).

8.3   Normalization of Microarray Data Using the RMA Method

Raw data is always biased due to many unknown sources of variations. To get rid of biasness, data normalization is performed. This process removes the biasness to ensure the results with the highest accuracy. Robust multi-array average (RMA) method is used here for the data normalization [4]. This method involves the three steps to transform log-intensity values to gene expression values.

8.3.1   Background Correction

This step generally corrects the background noise and intensity. The background noise can be raised from many sources such as fluorescence due to non-specific binding of probes and poor washing. Different methods are being used to correct the background noise and robust multi-array average (RMA) algorithm is popular among them. This step is required for the accurate measurements of specific hybridization.

8.3.2   Normalization

The next step after background correction is data normalization to normalize the technical variations because, during the hybridization process, there is always a discrepancy in arrays which lead to the difference in the log-intensity between the arrays.

8.3.3   Summarization

It is needed because all transcripts are represented by multiple probes. For each gene, the normalized probe intensities and background adjusted need to be summarized into expression set with one value.

```
>data.rma = rma(data)
```

Background correcting
Normalizing
Calculating Expression

Boxplot is drawn from the normalized data to evaluate the normalization process as shown in Figure 8.3.

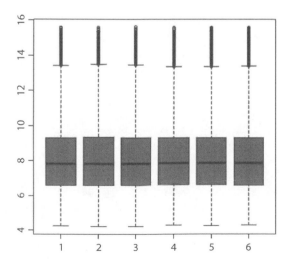

Figure 8.3 Boxplots of array data after normalization.

```
>name = "boxplotnorm.jpg"
>jpeg(name)
>boxplot(data.matrix,col='ed',names=ph@data$sample)
>dev.off()
```

MA plots are drawn to compare raw and normalized data in affy as shown in Figure 8.4. The red line shows the deviation from the central blue line. This below-given code is used to produce MA plots from raw data (Figure 8.4a).

```
>for (i in 1:6)
{
name = paste("MAplot",i,".jpg",sep="")
jpeg(name)
MAplot(data,which=i)
dev.off()
}
```

This code is used to produce MA plots from normalized data (Figure 8.4b).

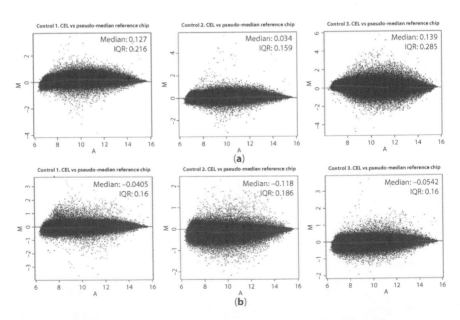

Figure 8.4 MA plots to compare the normalization method. Before normalization (a) and after normalization (b).

```
>for (i in 1:6)
{
name = paste("MAplotnorm",i,".jpg",sep="")
jpeg(name)
MAplot(data.rma,which=i)
dev.off()
}
```

8.4   Statistical Analysis for Differential Gene Expression

For the statistical analysis, the limma package is used. It estimates the fold changes and standard errors by fitting a linear model for each gene. A design matrix is created, and column names are assigned. The design matrix indicates which arrays are dye-swaps.

```
> design <- model.matrix(~ -1+factor(c(1,1,1,2,2,2))); colnames(design) <- c("S1", "S2")
```

To compare treated Vs control, a contrast matrix is created

```
> contrast.matrix <- makeContrasts(S2-S1, levels=design)
```

To fit a linear model for each gene based on the given series of arrays, the following code is used.

```
> fit <- lmFit(data.rma, design)
```

Estimated coefficients and standard errors are computed for a given set of contrasts.

```
> fit2 <- contrasts.fit(fit, contrast.matrix)
```

Compute moderated t-statistics and log-odds of differential expression by empirical Bayes shrinkage of the standard errors toward a common value.

```
> fit2 <- eBayes(fit2)
```

The following code is used to see the list of top 10 differentially expressed genes (Figure 8.5).

```
> topTable(fit2, coef=1, adjust="fdr", sort.by="B", number=10)
```

To summarize the result, the summary() function is used.

```
>results <- decideTests(fit2)
>summary(results)
```

S2 - S1
Down   1490
NotSig 52026
Up   1159

It shows the significantly upregulated, downregulated, and non-significant gene expression. There are 1,490 genes that are downregulated and 1,159 genes that are upregulated. To see the graphical representation of the differential expression of genes, volcano plot is used. It plots significance versus fold-change on the y- and x-axes, respectively (Figure 8.6).

```
>volcanoplot(fit2)
```

```
              logFC    AveExpr         t        P.Value
231577_s_at  3.131748  6.995678  41.47926  4.401322e-09
225803_at    3.451597 11.467331  41.14197  4.638800e-09
232573_at    2.171975  9.163857  32.24667  2.221742e-08
241762_at    3.571207  8.247122  31.32270  2.677756e-08
222457_s_at  1.540784  9.732538  28.24943  5.194529e-08
225328_at    2.573676 10.006275  27.89953  5.626654e-08
202269_x_at  2.895364  7.837827  25.94534  8.960302e-08
219553_at   -2.216859 10.729335 -25.68445  9.559320e-08
213413_at    1.819140  8.551729  24.90736  1.163673e-07
228152_s_at  1.218098  9.495411  24.18247  1.405692e-07
                   adj.P.Val         B
231577_s_at  0.0001268132  9.215275
225803_at    0.0001268132  9.198143
232573_at    0.0003660157  8.589701
241762_at    0.0003660157  8.503793
222457_s_at  0.0005127289  8.174490
225328_at    0.0005127289  8.132172
202269_x_at  0.0006533198  7.874512
219553_at    0.0006533198  7.837151
213413_at    0.0007069314  7.721332
228152_s_at  0.0007685619  7.606813
```

Figure 8.5 Result showing log fold change in gene expression along with p-value.

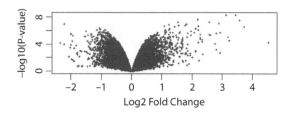

Figure 8.6 Volcano plot of the log fold change in gene expression. The scattered plot on the right-hand side (positive values) indicates the upregulated genes, and scattered plot on the left-hand side (negative values) indicates the downregulated genes.

8.5   Conclusion

Microarray is a promising molecular technique to identify the target genes and pathways involved in a variety of processes. It also explains the pattern of gene expression in different conditions. In this chapter, a pipeline is demonstrated to analyze the microarray data using the Bioconductor tools. This pipeline demonstrates the calculation of differential gene expression between two different conditions however it is not limited for two conditions only, a number of samples can be analyzed using this pipeline. This chapter shows the flexibility of Bioconductor in the analysis of microarray data.

References

1. Hardiman, G., Microarray technologies–an overview. *Pharmacogenomics*, 3, 3, 293–297, 2002.
2. Li, Z., Analysis of Gene Regulatory Circuits, in: *Microarray Technology and Its Applications. Biological and Medical Physics, Biomedical Engineering*, U.R. Müller and D.V. Nicolau (Eds.), Springer, Berlin, Heidelberg, 2005.
3. Woo, Y., Affourtit, J., Daigle, S., Viale, A., Johnson, K., Naggert, J., Churchill, G., A comparison of cDNA, oligonucleotide, and Affymetrix GeneChip gene expression microarray platforms. *J. Biomol. Tech.: JBT*, 15, 4, 276, 2004.
4. Bolstad, B.M., Irizarry, R.A., Åstrand, M., Speed, T.P., A comparison of normalization methods for high density oligonucleotide array data based on variance and bias. *Bioinformatics*, 19, 2, 185–193, 2003.
5. Gentleman, R.C., Carey, V.J., Bates, D.M., Bolstad, B., Dettling, M., Dudoit, S., Ellis, B., Gautier, L., Ge, Y., Gentry, J., Hornik, K., Bioconductor: open software development for computational biology and bioinformatics. *Genome Biol.*, 5, 10, R80, 2004.

9

Machine Learning in Bioinformatics

Rahul Yadav[1], Mohit Sharma[2,3] and Nikhil Agrawal[4]*

[1]SRM University, SRM Nagar, Kattankulathur, Tamil Nadu, India
[2]Postgraduate School for Molecular Medicine, Medical University
of Warsaw, Warszawa, Poland
[3]Poland Malopolskie Centre of Biotechnology Jagiellonian University,
Krakow, Poland
[4]College of Health Sciences, University of KwaZulu-Natal, Westville,
Durban, South Africa

Abstract

Human evolution has seen different stages, and at present, we are in the information Age. The revolution to this age started with the advent of the internet. In the present age, data is generated in huge amount in different domains of science. Specially, in biological sciences e.g., genomics, proteomics, molecular modeling etc. The data generated for genomics different from that of molecular modeling. However, the information's can be linked to obtain a better insight into the functionality even at the cellular level. It has become tough to analyze such massive data and conclude in a short period. The present-day scenario is changing with the implementation of Machine Learning methods. Machine Learning provides more in-depth insight into the problems backed up by mathematically models to take a short amount of time in terms of analysis. Machine Learning has been implemented in detection and medication suggestions for cancer patients. In drug discovery, Machine Learning models have been developed to design potential drug molecules. In the present chapter, we have tried to provide an understanding and importance of Machine Learning in the field of bioinformatics and its different domains.

Keywords: Machine learning, bioinformatics, drug discovery, genomics

*Corresponding author: nikhil.08oct@gmail.com

S. Balamurugan, Anand Krishnan, Dinesh Goyal, Balakumar Chandrasekaran and Boomi Pandi (eds.)
Computation in Bioinformatics: Multidisciplinary Applications, (155–164) © 2021 Scrivener Publishing LLC

9.1   Introduction and Background

Humans have developed their standards of living in due course of evolution with their invention. Throughout our evolution, humans have lived through four primary ages. The first, the "Stone Age" or commonly known as the "Hunter and the Gatherer Age", basically comprised of the humans hunting and gathering food for a living. During the later stages of the Stone Age, humans started to have a more stable life focusing on farming skills as well as other developments like making weapons and utensils during the Mesolithic and the Neolithic phases. The second age is the "Bronze Age" and this age marked to be very important in human evolution. Humans evolved to develop metal tools and weapons as compared to the Stone Age, where the tools and weapons were mostly comprised of stones and wood. The Bronze Age is also known as the Industrial Age. It was during the later stages of this age when humans first started to make industrial machines. This age has not been far behind, and now, we are in the third age of human evolution, the "Computer Age".

The Stone Age remained for a couple of millions of years of age, the Bronze Age for a few thousand years, but the Computer Age has only been a started a few decades ago. Information is being gathered and collected for a long period. However, the past few decades proved to be the most decisive of them all. The first steam-driven computing machine was built by the famous English Mathematician Charles Babbage in the year 1822. Nevertheless, age is not considered as the Computer Age. In the year 1936, Dr. Alan Turing, another mathematician, during World War II made a machine capable of anything computable. Since then, the Computer Age began. Several companies were founded in later years. Most notable are Hewlett-Packard by David Packard and Bill Hewlett and IBM (International Business Machines).

Today's age is the age of the computer, "The Computer Age" also known as the Information Age". The Information Age has seen a significant transformation with the inventions of the modern-day computer. With the advancements during this age, the computers grew in terms of computing capabilities and high information processing speed. However, computers grew smaller in size but became more compact and powerful. Nowadays, we have high-performance computing systems with RAM's of ranging up-to terabytes (TB).

This was enough until recently. With the vast amount of information being gathered each second, the need for computers to be robust and smart became inevitable. Since the past decade, the amount of data that is being generated in each domain of science has drastically engorged.

Artificial Intelligence (AI) is a program, so designed as to solve a complex problem in order to obtain interesting, valuable information. It comprises of two parts. The first part is to find what is the problem and why do we need to solve that problem. The second part is the implementation of particular algorithms for solving the problem and getting the desired output. Various algorithms can be used for solving these problems. The algorithms are backed by mathematical models [1].

The physical limitation of computers led to the innovation of algorithms commonly known as AI. With the amount of data being generated each day, finding necessary information has become like finding a needle out of a haystack. However, digging out information nowadays is becoming comfortable with the use of such programs.

So, what is Artificial Intelligence? Artificial Intelligence or more commonly known as AI is a program so designed which is trained in order to find particular information from an enormous amount of data using less time and space based on some mathematical models. The program is previously trained using a model data set before actually being used. These programs can adapt and act according to the data without any human intervention. An example is Apple's Siri. At the moment, a particular AI program can only be used to perform the task that it was built for. AI itself has two subsets to itself, namely, Machine Learning (ML) and Deep Learning (DL).

A ML program is a somewhat more intelligent artificially intelligent program that can rectify itself with the exposure of data. Although they also need to be trained over a training dataset, yet ML programs are so designed with mathematical models that it can rectify itself with the exposure to data. One of the best examples is IBM's Watson Health. Watson Health is an ML program for cancer diagnostics and treatment. It is used to recommend the treatment of cancer patients by considering the genome, history, and pathology of the patient. The program then recommends a probable treatment with the help of the information previously present.

DL programs are a subset of ML. DL programs are so-called due to the fact that the number of neural networks used in such programs is much more as compared to ML programs. An example of the DL program is the detection of faces from images [4]. Below is an image to provide a brief overview between AI, ML, and DL(Figure 9.1). AI is being used in almost all fields in the present day. Few examples of fields where AI is used are as below.

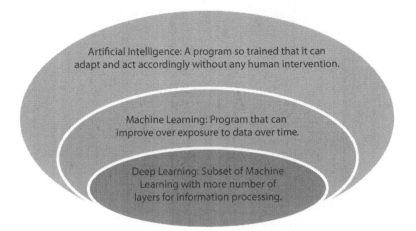

Figure 9.1 Typical example of the correlation between Artificial Intelligence, Machine Learning, and Deep Learning [1–4].

9.1.1   Bioinformatics

In the last few decades, bioinformatics has evolved and is playing a significant role in the fields of biotechnology, drug designing, and related fields. The most notable advancement was the invention of a technique known as DNA sequencing. It was made possible by Dr. Sanger to sequence the DNA of any organism. This technique led us to sequence the human genome comprising of approximately 3.2 billion bases of nucleotides. But with various companies founded during this time, the time has significantly reduced to merely a few days, and the amount of data being produced from the machines is greatly increased to TB. In order to process such data, there is a need for high computing systems as well as better algorithms. Various advancements have also been made in the field of clinical genomics. IBM's Watson is one such example. ML programs are used to identify, diagnose, and provide a probable treatment to the patients [4].

In the field of bioinformatics, ML is also used in the field of computational biology drug discovery is another field, which requires high computational speed as well as a considerable amount of memory in order to perform its task. Support vector machine, a ML algorithm, can be implemented in order to achieve such tasks. SVMs work on regression-based models and are generally supervised based programs. These types of ML programs have gained popularity in the computational biology community. Sometimes, a probabilistic approach based on hidden

Markov models is also used for predictions in the field of computational biology [5].

9.1.2 Text Mining

Another field that uses ML is the field of text mining. The term is first mentioned by Ronen Faldman. Although the actual term coined by Ronen was Knowledge Discovery in Databases, it is a data mining process whose main aim was to extract information that is potentially useful data [6]. ML methods for text mining, retrieval, or extraction of information are also known as natural language processing which uses algorithms, ML methods, and statistics in order to derive important information from a particular text. It uses a method called tokenization, where a document is split into words and all the punctuations are replaced by tabs or other white spaces. These tokenized words form a part of a dictionary. This dictionary is then reduced in size by the use of dimension reduction algorithms where less important words are removed. SVM are used on clean, dimension-reduced, and indexed data [7].

9.1.3 IoT Devices

The best examples in the modern days are the inventions of IoT devices that are small, single units of machines designed in order to perform specific tasks. One such task can be collecting the weather information of a particular geographic location. Hundreds of such devices can be placed at various places within the geographic location. Information such as the air pollution index, CO_2 levels, temperature, and moisture can be collected. Companies are combining data produced from hundreds of such devices. This information gathered through these devices collectively becomes vast. Thus, it increases the processing time and needs more memory of the computers [2].

9.2 Machine Learning Applications in Bioinformatics

Bioinformatics is a rapidly emerging field with an ocean of data being generated in each of its domains that needs to be analyzed. This vast amount of data that is being generated has led to the implementation of the ML approach. Pattern recognition is one of the most recognizable aspects of the field of bioinformatics. There are two major categories of data generated in terms of the problem and the approach made toward solving the problem. One is the type of data that is already present and has some information on the approach toward solving the problem is already known. The approach used for types of data is more or less established already. The second type of data is any novel data, any information of which is not known previously. Such type of data requires some novel approach which may also lead to developing entirely new techniques to approach such problems.

Genomics has become one of the most prominent and eminent fields in bioinformatics. In the early phase of bioinformatics, a large amount of data was generated using the microarray. This was because it gained popularity and as an emerging technology within the computational biologists. Microarrays technology allowed us to study the expression of several genes over a panel. The mRNA was first reverse transcribed to DNA which was then attached with a fluorescently labeled dye. On excitation, the fluorescently labeled dyes emitted a particular color that is captured by a sensor. The fluorescent labels were of two colors: green and red. The green color depicts upregulation, and red color depicts downregulation. This is known as the two system hybridization technique. Since it used the property of mRNA expressions, it was found to have applications in the field of medical diagnostics. This method was also used to find the difference between healthy and diseased individuals. The training data for such a problem was the already known information on the expression levels of a particular gene within a normal individual. The ML approach applied to such a problem where a training dataset can be used is known as the supervised learning method. Microarray technology triggered the use of SVM which is based on a supervised learning method. Other applications of ML include the detection of single nucleotide polymorphisms in case of cancer data, prediction of various properties of amino acid residues in a protein, classification, and prediction of cancer. All of this data can be analyzed using artificial neural networks (ANNs).

SVMs are used for the classification of various gene expression data as well as the classification of protein quaternary structures [8].

Computing the phylogenetic distances and plotting of a phylogenetic tree is a daunting task in the field of bioinformatics. The phylogenetic tree represents the closeness or distances between organisms. This is performed by a method called multiple sequence alignment wherein all the sequences comprising of at least more than three organisms are aligned together, and a score is calculated. The sequences are then rearranged and realigned. This process is performed iteratively in order to obtain the best alignment to represent precise distances between the organisms. ML approaches are used in order to perform such tasks implementing various algorithms [9].

9.3   Machine Learning Approaches

ML uses two different approaches, in general, for the processing of data and infers usable information from it. The two different approaches are supervised learning and unsupervised learning. Supervised learning is a ML approach that is trained on similar example data in order to learn how to infer useful information from a dataset. Whereas unsupervised learning is an approach where the ML program is not trained before, yet it tries to infer solutions to the problem [10]. One of the examples of supervised learning in bioinformatics is the use of gene-finding algorithms. A gene finding algorithm is usually trained on a known set of sequences. The transcription start sites and transcription end sites of the genes are already known for these sequences. The splice site information between the genes is also known for the sequences. The programs then predict the genes of any unknown sequences provided to it based on the information derived by the training dataset like the DNA sequence arrangement, the start codons, and stop codons along with the information of 5' and 3' UTR and the introns [10]. When such pieces of information are not available, it comes to the use of unsupervised ML programs. One of the best examples of unsupervised learning methods in bioinformatics would be explained when talking about epigenetics data. Encyclopedia of DNA elements (ENCODE) consortium and the Roadmap Egipegomics Project produce a heterogenous collection of epigenomics data. When working on such a heterogeneous mixture of data to find certain patterns of information, it is best to use unsupervised learning methods. In such cases, the program itself trains on a set of iteration in order to find a particular set of patterns, which it then uses for deriving similar patterns when fed with similar datasets [11]. One of the best examples of such a ML program is a gene-finding tool named GeneMark. GeneMark has both a web-based and a stand-alone version. GeneMark generally has two different variants: one of it uses a supervised learning approach, while the other uses an unsupervised learning approach for *in silico*–based gene finding. The supervised based model is GeneMark.hmm, which uses a type of supervised learning known as the hidden Markov model for gene prediction. Both methods produce quite accurate results. The supervised based model uses a predefined set of information where the start codons and stop codon 5' and 3'

UTR regions of similar data are already known to the program. It then uses the information to find similar patterns in the query dataset and to predict the genes. It is best for the use of already known organisms whose genomic region information is known [11].

Another variant of GeneMark is the GeneMark S which is an abbreviation for GeneMark self-learning and uses an unsupervised based approach for gene finding. The GeneMark S uses two different sets of algorithms for gene finding. First, it uses general GeneMark.hmm, a method with known information for gene finding. It then tries to find patterns from the unknown sequences which, in turn, are used to match with the results obtained from that of GeneMark.hmm with high accuracy of 99% or till the stability of gene finding is saturated at a particular level. If the percentage of accuracy starts to drop, then it stops its iterations [12].

9.4   Conclusion and Closing Remarks

Newer and better algorithms are being developed in order to predict precise results. The ML approach is being implemented in almost all aspects of bioinformatics. Several gene prediction programs make use of ML models in order to predict CDS regions of unknown genes. In next-generation sequencing machine, learning-based methods are used for analyzing data. One such example is the implementation of ML method for analyzing 16S rRNA sequences in QIIME2. The developers of the program have used ML model in order to analyze such data. ML is being used more and more in each field of science. In the field of bioinformatics, it has gained huge popularity due to the vast diversity in the type of data being generated. The vast amount of data being generated in each domain of bioinformatics requires continuously improving ways to analyze with precision. In the real world, the molecules may act in certain ways. In order to reflect the same results, more research is needed to understand the biological function.

References

1. Marr, D., Artificial intelligence—a personal view. *Artif. Intell.*, 9, 1, 37–48, 1977.
2. Desai, N.S. and Alex, J.S.R., IoT based air pollution monitoring and predictor system on Beagle bone black, in: *2017 International Conference on Nextgen Electronic Technologies: Silicon to Software (ICNETS2)*, IEEE, pp. 367–370, 2017, March.

3. Meidan, Y., Bohadana, M., Shabtai, A., Guarnizo, J.D., Ochoa, M., Tippenhauer, N.O., Elovici, Y., ProfilIoT: a machine learning approach for IoT device identification based on network traffic analysis. In: *Proceedings of the symposium on applied computing*, pp. 506–509, 2017 Apr 3.

4. Bini, S.A., Artificial intelligence, machine learning, deep learning, and cognitive computing: what do these terms mean and how will they impact health care? *J. Arthroplasty*, 33, 8, 2358–2361, 2018.

5. Vert, J.P. and Jacob, L., Machine learning for in silico virtual screening and chemical genomics: new strategies. *Comb. Chem. High Throughput Screen.*, 11, 8, 677–685, 2008.

6. Feldman, R., Fresko, M., Kinar, Y., Lindell, Y., Liphstat, O., Rajman, M., Zamir, O., Text mining at the term level, in: *European Symposium on Principles of Data Mining and Knowledge Discovery*, 1998, September, Springer, Berlin, Heidelberg, pp. 65–73.

7. Hotho, A., Nürnberger, A., Paaß, G., A brief survey of text mining, in: *Ldv Forum*, 2005, May, vol. 20, No. 1, pp. 19–62.

8. Bhaskar, H., Hoyle, D.C., Singh, S., Machine learning in bioinformatics: A brief survey and recommendations for practitioners. *Comput. Biol. Med.*, 36, 10, 1104–1125, 2006.

9. Larranaga, P., Calvo, B., Santana, R., Bielza, C., Galdiano, J., Inza, I., Robles, V., Machine learning in bioinformatics. *Brief. Bioinform.*, 7, 1, 86–112, 2006.

10. Lloyd, S., Mohseni, M., Rebentrost, P.. Quantum algorithms for supervised and unsupervised machine learning. arXiv preprint arXiv:1307.0411, 2013 Jul 1.

11. Libbrecht, M.W. and Noble, W.S., Machine learning applications in genetics and genomics. *Nat. Rev. Genet.*, 16, 6, 321–332, 2015.

12. Besemer, J., Lomsadze, A., Borodovsky, M., GeneMarkS: a self-training method for prediction of gene starts in microbial genomes. Implications for finding sequence motifs in regulatory regions. *Nucleic Acids Res.*, 29, 12, 2607–2618, 2001.

10

DNA-RNA Barcoding and Gene Sequencing

Gifty Sawhney[1,2], Mohit Sharma[3,4] and Nikhil Agarwal[5*]

[1]*Inflammation Pharmacology Division, CSIR-Indian Institute of Integrative Medicine, Jammu, J&K, India*
[2]*Academy of Scientific and Innovative Research (AcSIR), CSIR-Indian Institute of Integrative Medicine, Jammu, J&K, India*
[3]*Postgraduate School for Molecular Medicine, Medical University of Warsaw, Warszawa, Poland*
[4]*Małopolska Centre of Biotechnology, Jagiellonian University, Krakow, Poland*
[5]*College of Health Sciences, University of KwaZulu-Natal, Westville, Duran, South Africa*

Abstract

DNA barcoding, a new way of quickly identifying any species based on the collection of a DNA sequence from the minuscule tissue sample of any individual, is now extended to taxa throughout the tree of life. DNA barcoding helps to identify organisms as a taxonomist research tool by enhancing the ability to analyze organisms by including all phases of the life history of an organism. DNA barcoding promotes the exploration of biodiversity by identifying species that are theoretically new to science. DNA barcoding is used as a biological technique for solving fundamental ecological and evolutionary issues, such as the formation of organisms in plant communities. There are two basic steps in the DNA barcoding process: (1) creating the DNA barcode library of the identified organisms and (2) comparing the unidentified barcode sequence with the barcode library for authentication. While DNA barcoding has been used as a methodology for less than a decade, it has grown significantly in proportion to the number of sequences produced as barcodes and their applications. This volume presents protists, bacteria, and plants with the latest information about the production, use, and study of DNA barcodes across the tree of life.

Corresponding author: nikhil.08oct@gmail.com

S. Balamurugan, Anand Krishnan, Dinesh Goyal, Balakumar Chandrasekaran and Boomi Pandi (eds.)
Computation in Bioinformatics: Multidisciplinary Applications, (165–228) © 2021 Scrivener Publishing LLC

Keywords: DNA barcoding, RNA barcoding, gene sequence, human genome, chromosomes

10.1   Introduction

A living organism's heritable component is its genome, a large sequence of deoxyribonucleic acid (DNA), which contains the whole collection of inherited data carried by the individual and its individual cells. In early 2000s, at the Natural History Museum in London (UK), the first international conference on "Barcoding Life" was attended by more than 200 delegates from around 50 nations, and it was reported that a compact DNA sequencing system is accessible now to classify all life [1]. Identifying 1.7 million species took taxonomists for two centuries, but it was found that this figure could be a blatant misrepresentation of the real biological diversity of Earth [2, 3]. While taxonomists may classify most of the species they are acquainted with, an emergent society needs data for a wide range taxonomical classification of species. The creation of RNA/DNA repositories has great prospective to categorize and classify species and promote environmental and biodiversity support study projects. In the early 2000s, Taxonomy Workshop of DNA at the Munich Deutsche Staatssammlung was sponsored by the German Science Association (DFG) amid the involvement of approximately 100 scientists primarily from European nations [4]. The issues at this preliminary stage were the mainly useful indicators for the DNA taxonomy (i.e., a DNA-based universal categorization mechanism throughout the species), the challenges of connecting known names to entities within a genetic code–based system [5].

Genomes can possess approximately 500 genes (for mycoplasma, a form of bacterium), about 20,000 to 25,000 for a person, or about 50,000 to 60,000 for rice. W. Sutton in 1903 has proposed the theory that there are genes on chromosomes and in this context. Sutton got experimental support from T.H. Morgan in 1910. By 1922, Morgan and his co-workers developed gene mapping techniques and analyzed the relative positions of more than 2,000 genes on the four chromosomes of *Drosophila melanogaster*. Although these classic genetic studies have been successful, and until the 1940s, there was no real understanding of the gene's molecular existence. Nevertheless, nobody believed that DNA was a genetic material, but it had been widely assumed that protein-composed chromosome until the studies by Avery, MacLeod, and McCarty in 1944 and the experiments by Hershey and Chase in 1952. The breakthrough of the DNA function was a huge incentive for biomedical research. The discovery of DNA functionality was an important catalyst for genetic engineering, and many important scientists were introduced into the subsequent generation (Figure 10.1) (the most powerful of them are Delbrück, Chargaff, Crick, and Monod).

The genome is made up of chromosomal DNA and plasmid eukaryotic. DNA is found in mitochondria and chloroplast in eukaryotic organisms. The evolution of genome is influenced by the substances within the genome that express nucleotide sequences. The DNA genome generates all the proteins of the body at the proper time and within the required cells by means of a complex network of processes. Proteins serve a variety of roles in an organism's formation and functioning; they can form part of the individual's aesthetics, have the ability to develop complex structures, perform life-necessary biochemical reactions, and engage as transcription factors and receptors, and play a key role in signal transduction pathways and other molecules in regulation.

Most of the DNA of eukaryotic cells is normally incorporated into the structures called chromosomes in the nucleus. All of the genetic data in

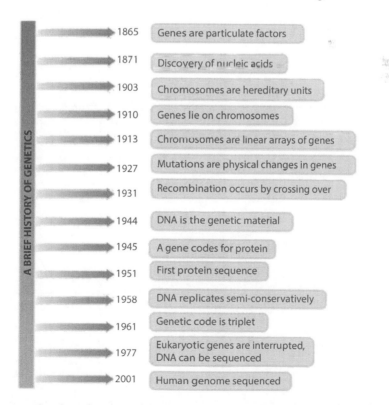

Figure 10.1 Flowchart showing a remarkable brief history of genetics from 1865 to 2001 [229].

the prokaryotic cells is found in one circular molecule of DNA, which is about one millimeter, and many times in the central region of the cell. The genome of the organism contains all of its DNA complement (Table 10.1). All normal human cells, except for eggs and sperm, have 46 chromosomes. Half of these can be linked back to mother and, therefore half of the genes can be linked to father. Physically, the genome can be divided into several separate molecules of DNA or chromosomes. In other words, it can also be said that each chromosome's DNA code is the genome. The genome is functionally divided into genes. Each gene is a sequence of DNA encoding in many cases a single type of RNA and ultimately a

Table 10.1 Types of DNA [230].

S. no.	Particulars	A	B	Z
1	Helix coiling direction	Right-handed	Right-handed	Left-handed
2	Sugar Phosphate bond	Normal	Normal	Zig-Zag
3	Helical pitch (nm)	2.8	3.4	4.5
4	Axial Rise (nm)	0.25	0.337	0.37
5	Diameter	26Å	20Å	18Å
6	Mean bp/turn	10.7	10.0	12
7	Rotation/base pairs	33.6°	35.9°	60°/2
8	Glycosyl Angle	anti	anti	C: anti, G: syn
9	Rise/bp along axis	2.3Å	3.32Å	3.8Å
10	Inclination of base pairs to axis	+19°	−1.2°	−9°
11	Pitch/turn of helix	24.6Å	33.2Å	45.6Å
12	Mean propeller twist	+18°	+16°	0°
13	Sugar puckering	C3'-endo	C2'-endo	C: C2'-endo, G: C2'-exo
14	Repeating unit	1 bp	1 bp	2 bp

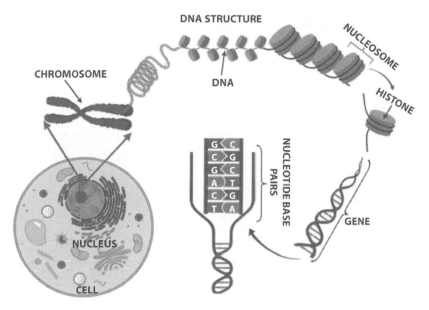

Figure 10.2 Showing the structure of chromosome at molecular level [231].

polypeptide. Each of the chromosomes of the distinct genomes may contain a large set of genes (Figure 10.2).

10.2   RNA

Ribonucleic acid (RNA) is a key polymer messenger that regulates, encodes, activates, and expresses genes in several biological activities. DNA and RNAs along with lipids, proteins, and carbohydrates constitute the four major macromolecules that are vital to all known forms of life. RNA consists of the DNA identical nucleotide series, and instead of a paired double-strand, RNA is seen as a single-strand folded on itself most often in nature. Cellular organisms use genetic information [nitrogen bases such as Guanine (G), Uracil (U), Adenine (A), and Cytosine (C)] to indicate that certain protein synthesis is driven by messenger RNA (mRNA) (Figure 10.3) (Table 10.2). Most RNAs are involved in cells through the catalyzation of biological reactions, gene expression, cellular signal responses sensing, and communication. The production of proteins is one of the most efficient fundamental systems by which RNA molecules direct protein synthesis on ribosomes (Figure 10.4) (Table 10.3). This process utilizes the tRNA molecules to transmit amino acids to the ribosome where ribosomal RNA (rRNA) attaches amino acids to form coded proteins.

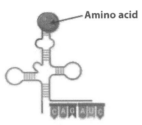

Messenger RNA: Carries instructions for polypeptide synthesis from nucleus to ribosomes in the cytoplasm

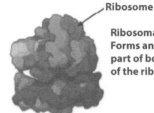

Ribosomal RNA: Forms an important part of both subunits of the ribosome

Transfer RNA: Carries amino acids to the ribosome and matches them to the coded mRNA message

Figure 10.3 Different types of RNA [232].

Table 10.2 Comparison of different types of RNA [233].

S. no.	RNA type	Size	Function
1.	tRNA Transfer RNA	Small	It assists with the conveyance of amino acids in protein synthesis to the protein synthesis site.
2.	rRNA Ribosomal RNA	Several kinds of variable in size	It assists the site of protein synthesis in conjunction with proteins to form ribosomes.
3.	mRNA Messenger RNA	Variable	It guides protein amino acid sequence.
4.	SnRNA Small nuclear RNA	Small	The initial mRNA processes in eukaryotes into its mature form.
5.	SiRNA Small interfering RNA	Small	It affects gene expression; the gene being studied is used by scientists to knockout.
6.	Micro RNA	Small	It is important in growth and development and affects gene expression.

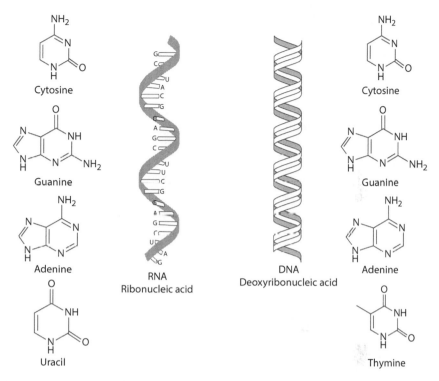

Figure 10.4 Structure of DNA and RNA [234].

Table 10.3 Difference between DNA and RNA [235].

DNA	RNA
1. DNA is the basic genetic material.	1. RNA is the genetic material of some viruses.
2. DNA is double stranded except in some viruses, e.g., (Ø × 174).	2. Most cellular RNA is single stranded with the exception of some viruses (e.g., double stranded in *Reovirus*).
3. DNA has deoxyribose sugar	3. The pentose sugar is ribose.
4. The base pairs are adenine, guanine, cytosine, and thymine.	4. The common organic bases are adenine, guanine, cytosine, and uracil.

(*Continued*)

Table 10.3 Difference between DNA and RNA [235]. (*Continued*)

DNA	RNA
5. Base pairing: AT (adenine-thymine) and GC (guanine-cytosine).	5. Adenine pairs with uracil and guanine with cytosine.
6. Pairing of bases is throughout the length of the molecule.	6. Pairing of bases is only in the helical region.
7. Purine and pyrimidine bases are equal in number.	7. There is no proportionality in between the number of Purine and Pyrimidine bases.
8. DNA is susceptible to UV damage.	8. RNA is relatively resistant to UV damage as compared to DNA.
9. In the chromosomes, most of the DNA is stored. The cytoplasm also includes some DNA, e.g., within mitochondria and chloroplasts.	9. On the chromosomes, messenger RNA is formed and is located in the nucleus and cytoplasm. Chromosomal rRNA and tRNA are also present in the cytoplasm.
10. It occurs in the form of prochromosomes, chromatin, or chromosomes.	10. It occurs in ribosomes or form association with ribosomes.
11. It is long lived.	11. Some RNAs are short-lived while others are slightly longer.
12. DNA encodes genetic messages.	12. RNA's usual function is to translate the message into proteins encoded in DNA.

10.3 DNA Barcoding

10.3.1 Introduction

A DNA barcode is a short nucleotide sequence taken from an appropriate part of an organism's genome used to define it at the level of the species. Around 1.7 million organisms using morphological (that is, Linnean) characteristics have been identified, including 200,000 angiosperms, 90,000 monocots, and 808 gymnosperms This figure may underestimate the true biodiversity of Earth [5]. Recently, vast groundbreaking DNA barcoding publications (syn.: sampling and genotyping) focused on closely preserved sequence details include modern systemic and phylogenic methods [6–9]. DNA barcodes consist of brief sequences in both 400–800 base pairs, which can be sequenced and amplified in a systemic way from the studied organisms by polymerase chain reaction (PCR). Nevertheless, the use of molecular bar coding is important to identify specific sub-species (ssp.), ecological cultivars (cv.), morphotypes, mutants, and clones. The barcode of an organism can be contrasted with sequences from the other taxa and the molecular phylogenetic analysis on the basis of MOTU, organic functional taxonomic units [10]. Barcoding of DNA is particularly useful for aquatic organisms [11], namely, fish [12, 13], meiofauna soil [2], and meiobenthos freshwater and extinct birds. In rainforests, quick enteromological inventory–based DNA have been so effective that tropical ecologists supported DNA barcoding most actively [14, 15]. In addition, DNA barcodes have been shown to be more pragmatically effective for the monitoring of bio-security, e.g., for tracking the carriers of the disease [16], as well as enforcement of law and primatology [17] and parasitic pests [18]. In the taxonomy group, barcoding has generated some confusion [19–21]. To order to delineate animals, conventional taxonomists use several morphological characteristics. Currently, DNA-based data is gradually complementing these characteristics. The classification system of DNA barcoding is based on the significantly single complex character (the element of one gene of 650-bp mitochondrial cyto-chrome-c oxidase subunit I gene often referred to as COI or COX-1) and therefore barcoding tests are deemed inaccurate and vulnerable to recognition errors [22]. Even though in a number of animal groups, the mitochondrial cytochrome oxidase subunit-I gene is a widely used barcode [23], owing to its low mutation rate, this locus is not appropriate for use in crops [24, 25]. However, complex evolution processes such as hybridization and polyploidy, which make it difficult to identify species borders, are common in plants. DNA sequences for bar coding are discussed as numbers and identities [26, 27]. The principal DNA barcode bodies and resources are (1) Consortium for the Barcode of Life (CBOL; http://www.barcodeoflife.org), which was established as early as 2004, and (2) International Bill of Life (iBOL; http://www.ibol.org), which was launched in October 2010. iBOL is a nonprofit project aimed at including developing and developed countries in the international billing campaign, establishing an active contribution to the development of DNA barcoding through more than 200 member organizations, from 50 countries and at the National Museum of Natural History of the Smithsonian Institution in Dc, Washington; (3) Barcode of Life Data Systems (BoLD; http://www.boldsystems.org). The Ontario Biodiversity Institute is the university center of the enterprise and its director. The barcode of Life Data Systems is a digital barcode DNA server, incorporating a barcode

Table 10.4 Several key articles concerning DNA barcodes have been published since 2003.

Year	Editorials and articles	References
2003	Taxonomy, DNA, and the bar code of life	[33]
	Biological identifications through DNA barcodes	[34]
	A plea for DNA taxonomy	[35]
2004	Now is the time	[36]
	DNA barcoding: promise and pitfalls	[36]
	Identification of birds through DNA barcodes	[37]
	Myth of the molecule: DNA barcodes for species cannot replace morphology for identification and classification	[38]
2005	Genome sequencing in microfabricated high density picolitre reactors	[39]
	Toward writing the encyclopedia of life: an introduction to DNA barcoding	[40]
	DNA barcodes for Biosecurity: invasive species identification	[18]
	DNA barcoding does not compete with taxonomy	[41]
	The promise of DNA barcoding for taxonomy	[42]
	DNA barcoding is no substitute for taxonomy	[43]
	The perils of DNA barcoding and the need for integrative taxonomy	[44]
	Emerging technologies in DNA sequencing	[45]
	Critical factors for assembling a high volume of DNA barcodes	[46]
	DNA barcoding: Error rates based on comprehensive sampling	[47]
	Nextgeneration DNA sequencing techniques	[48]
2006	Who will actually use DNA barcoding and what will it cost?	[49]
	A minimalist barcode can identify a specimen whose DNA is degraded	[46]
2007	Limited performance of DNA barcoding in a diverse community of tropical butterflies	[50]
	A proposal for a standardized protocol to barcode all land plants	[29]

(Continued)

Table 10.4 Several key articles concerning DNA barcodes have been published since 2003. (*Continued*)

Year	Editorials and articles	References
2008	The impact of next-generation sequencing platforms for population targeted sequencing platforms for population targeted sequencing studies	[51]
	DNA barcoding for ecologists	[52]
2010	DNA barcoding: a six-question tour to improve users' awareness about the method	[53]
	A survey of sequence alignment algorithms for next-generation sequencing	[54]
	Briefings in bioinformatics	[54]
2011	Pyrosequencing for mini-barcoding of fresh and old museum specimens	[55]
	Use of rbcL and trnL-F as a Two-Locus DNA Barcode for Identification of NW European Ferns: An Ecological Perspective	[56]
	Environmental barcoding: a next-generation sequencing approach for biomonitoring applications using river benthos	[57]
	On the future of genomic data	[58]
2012	An emergent science on the brink of irrelevance: a review of the past 9 years of DNA barcoding	[59]
	Next-generation sequencing technologies for environmental DNA research	[60]
	Environmental DNA	[61]
	Toward next-generation biodiversity assessment using DNA metabarcoding	[62]
	The golden age of metasystematics	[63]
	A bloody boon for conservation	[64]
	The future of environmental DNA in ecology	[65]
	Tracking earthworm communities from soil DNA	[66]
	Persistence of environmental DNA in freshwater ecosystems	[67]
	Bioinformatic challenges for DNA metabarcoding of plants and animals ABGD, Automatic Barcode Gap Discovery for primary species delimitation	[68]
	Soil sampling and isolation of extracellular DNA from large amount of starting material suitable for metabarcoding studies	[69]

(*Continued*)

Table 10.4 Several key articles concerning DNA barcodes have been published since 2003. (*Continued*)

Year	Editorials and articles	References
2013	DNA barcoding as a complementary tool for conservation and valorization of forest resources	[70]
	Incorporating trnH-psbA to the core DNA barcodes improves significantly species discrimination within southern African Combretaceae	[71]
	A DNA mini-barcode for land plants	[72]
	Toward a unified paradigm for sequence-based identification of fungi	[73]
	Potential of DNA barcoding for detecting quarantine fungi	[74]
	DNA barcoding in plants: evolution and applications of in silico approaches and resources	[75]
	The short ITS2 sequence serves as an efficient taxonomic sequence tag in comparison with the full length ITS	[76]
	Assessing DNA barcoding as a tool for species identification and data quality control	[77]
	The seven deadly sins of DNA barcoding	[78]
	Use of the potential DNA barcode ITS2 to identify herbal materials	[79]
2014	20 years since the introduction of DNA barcoding: from theory to application	[80]
	Ecology in the age of DNA barcoding: the resource, the promise and the challenges ahead	[81]

database, analytical tools, sample upload gateway to GenBank, a platform for species recognition and networking to international web developers and bioinformaticians (Table 10.4). It was set up by Ontario's Biodiversity Institute in 2005. The rbcL + matK Plant Working Group (2009) has been suggested as a two-piece primary combination by the Consortium for the Barcode of Life (CBOL). Nevertheless, despite the practical characteristics of these loci keys, it cannot be determined if they provide sufficiently high species resolution. The ability to differentiate closely linked or recently developed plants is one of the obstacles of crop barcoding. Many experiments have recently centered on crop DNA barcoding (e.g., [28–32]).

10.3.2   DNA Barcoding and Molecular Phylogeny

Dobzhansky said not anything makes sense in biology except in the context of evolution [82]. Phylogeny is in a resurgence that has been confirmed by the mainstream use of innovative genomic and quantitative approaches. In all evolutionary stages, phylogenetic experiments have provided insight into evolutionary tiers. The phylogenetic trees are present in all grades of the taxonomic system in animals and plants, which play an important role in relative studies in different areas of biology, molecular development, and relative genetics [83]. The basic DNA nucleotide substitution rate was estimated to be 1.3×10^8 [84] and 6.5×10^9 substitution per locus per year in grasses, and it was estimated to $1.5 \cdot 108$ in *Arabidopsis* [85, 86]. A variability analysis of an organism usually focuses on morphological characteristics. Molecular differences are primarily based on shifts in the DNA nucleotide sequences of homologous genes in plant groups and higher taxa [87]. With the advancement of molecular science, our understanding of the genetic variability in species at different tree scales has made significant progress [88, 89]. Plant genomes range from 8.8×10^6 to more than 300×10^9 bp, but DNA can be stored in a small quantity (0.1 g) of the leafy tissue. A variety of molecular and genetic methods are necessary to examine genetic diversity, including site-restriction analysis, DNA rearrangement assessment, and fragmentation of genes and intron and dominant PCR-based strategies supplemented by DNA sequencing and cladistic atomic genomes (nuDNA) [90, 91]. Several sequence alignment computer programs like MULTALIN BioEdit Sequence Alignment Editor (North Carolina State University, USA) [92, 93], CLUSTAL W [94], FastPCR [95], BLAST analysis of the National Center for Biotechnological Information (NCBI) databases [96], and MEGA5 [97] are available for inferring phylogeny. It was suggested to use DNA or protein sequences to classify species as a more effective method than conventional taxonomic approaches [5, 35]. A chloroplast gene like matK (maturase K) or an internal transcribed spacer (ITS) could be an effective barcoding target in plants [24, 98]. The efficacy of DNA barcoding in angiosperms has been shown by Kress *et al.* [24]. Ribosomal DNA (e.g., ITS) could be used to supplement the plastid gene-based results to make the identification and delimitation of species more complex by multiple elements [99]. The nuclear small subunit ribosomal RNA genes (SSU) and the highly variable inner transcribed spacing portion of the Ribosomal RNA cistron (ITS, separated into ITS1 and ITS2 regions by the 5S Ribosomal RNAs) are used to label the nuclear subunit Ribosomal RNA genes (SSU, also classified as 16S in Prokaryotes and 18S in most eukaryotes) and the nuclear large-subunit Ribosomal RNA gene (LSU). Kress *et al.* [24] stated that ITS spacer and plastid trnH-psbA had greater differentiation potential than any other locus, trnHpsbA, rp136-rpf8, and trnL-F rated highest amplification performance, with a sufficient sequence size, than any other locus [24].

10.3.3   Ribosomal DNA (rDNA) of the Nuclear Genome (nuDNA)—ITS

The nuclear ribosomal (rDNA) genes that encode ribosome structural RNAs (rRNAs) are commonly used in plant phylogenetics [100–102]. The rDNA is arranged with thousands of repeats of tandem residues of one or several chromosomal loci. Of fact, rDNA will account for up to 10% of the overall plant genome [103]. Most of the sizes of the angiosperm genome vary from 135 to 160 kb (Figure 10.5). The length of repeating unit of the ribosomal rDNA of human (18S rRNA; 28S rRNA; 5.8S rRNA; 5'ETS; 3'ETS; ITS1; ITS2; intergenic spacer; cdc27 pseudogene; p53 binding site) is 42.999 bp (NCBI # U13369). The rDNA cistron encodes into 18S, 26S, and 5.8S, and the cistron is accompanied by the 50 and 30 external spacers (50-ETS and 30-ETS) transcribed in plant genomes, which are divided into two internal transcribed spacers (ITS1 and ITS2). The regions are rather short floral sequences, ITS1 200–300 bp, ITS2 180–240 bp, and 5.8S 160 bp. The primers for amplification and decoding are extremely standardized

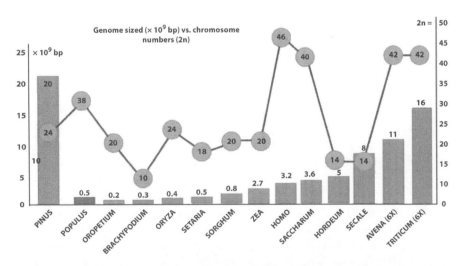

Figure 10.5 Sizes (bp) vs. chromosome numbers (2n) of various taxa plant genomes compared to the size of the human genome (3.2 ×109 bp) [236].

[104]. Two subunits with a large subunit (LSU) are made up of the eukaryotic ribosomes, about double the length of the medium subunit (SSU). The SSU is encoded by 18S and the LSU is encoded 26S and 5.8S. The ITS region contains the 5.8S gene, the most commonly distributed interspecific and intergeneric molecular marker [105]. Thanks to the efforts of concerted evolution [103], the polymorphisms are not because of the intragenomic heterogeneity of these loci, but rather to a more regular convergence of multiple ITS copies within the same genome. The 18S gene is an evolving

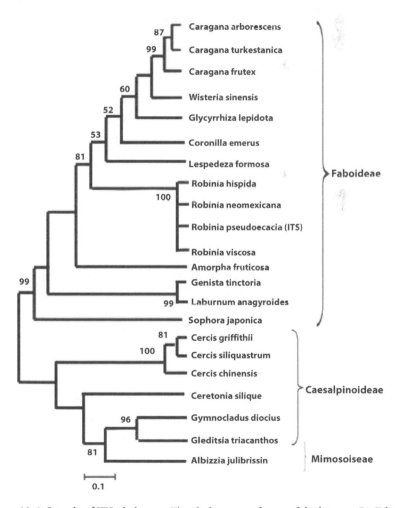

Figure 10.6 Sample of ITS phylogeny. The cladogaram of trees of the legume. BioEdit analyzed twenty-two species' ITS sequences [92] and ML (Maximum Likelihood) [89]; cladogaram was edited by MEGA4 [114] (·1,000 bootstrap). Fabaceae's three subfamilies and substitution level (0.1) are suggested [236].

marker that can be used to detect angiosperm phylogenes [87] and families like Caryophyllales.

The low variability rates in angiosperms, however, are the most significant limitation in 18S rDNA used for phylogenetic analyses. The phylogenetic utility of the 26S sequences has been little investigated. The 26S gene is approximately 3.4 kb in plants and comprises 12 segments of expansion (ES), which can be modified [106]. The 26S sequences were used to differentiate between closely related groups including Apiales [107] and to assess the phylogenetic status of plant species [108]. The external transcribed spacer (ETS) area (especially the 30-end 50-ETS neighboring 18S) was used for phylogenetic analysis. There is still a poor understanding of the frequency of ETS polymorphism. In addition, the repeated internal structure of the ETS area will confuse amplifications and sequence alignments [109, 110]. In plant phylogenetic research, ITS is the most common locus used to match all rDNA loci (Figure 10.6) [111, 112]. The advantage of the ITS Region is to amplify it in two smaller fragments (ITS1 and ITS2) using the 5.8S locus. In addition, the well-preserved 5.8S area includes sufficient phylogenetic signals for classification at order and phyla rates, but this locus is not a concern with barcoding. ITS regions also differ by addition and deletion and not by substitution, making it difficult to sequence since several ITS sequence forms are analyzed simultaneously [113].

10.3.4   Chloroplast DNA

The circular molecule is 120–217 kb in size, but an exception is found with an astounding 521.168 bp cpDNA is the green algae Floydiella terrestris (NCBI # NC_014346) [115]. There are around 100 functional genes in the chloroplast genome. It contains two inverted duplication regions (IRL – IRless), known as 10–76 kb of reverse repetitive (IR), divided into small single-copy (SSC) and large (LSC) areas by chloroplast genome.

The structural organization of the chloroplast genome is strongly conserved, i.e., completely independent of significant transpositions, deletions, inversions, insertions, and SNPs (single-nucleotide polymorphism), making it useful for evolutionary analyses. Chloroplast DNA is comparatively abundant compared with nuclear DNA (normally 50 chloroplast per cell, which is multiplied by 50 cpDNA) (usually 2n). DNA present in chloroplast is usually inherited from one parent (paternally in gymnosperms and maternally in angiosperm) with exceptions, in general, that facilitates the identification of the maternal parent in hybrids and allopolyloids [116]. Kress et al. [24] contrasted Atropa's and Nicotiana's plastid genomes and informed that nine intergenic spacers: trNH-psbA, trnK-rps16, atpB-rbcL, rp136-rps8, ycf6-psbM, trinV-atpE, trnC-ycf6, psbM-trnD, and trnL-F were compliant with the barcode requirements.

10.3.5   Mitochondrial DNA

The mitochondrial DNA (mtDNA) analysis had a significant affect on the field of animal evolutionary process and population genetics. In contrast to mammals, crop mtDNAs are rather badly studied. Plant mtDNA codes approximately 5% of the identified mitochondrial proteins. Plant mtDNA is abnormally higher than animal mtDNAs (16–25 kb), with a difference in length (300–600 kb). In Malvaceae and Cucurbitaceae, the mitochondrial genome (*Cucumis melo*) spans more than 2,900 kb [117]. In plant mtDNA, there are many foreign sequences. Chloroplast DNA sequences of 12 kB are incorporated into mtDNAs and cpDNA sequences can fill approximately 5%–10% of mtDNA. The mitochondrial genome of plants is unreliable for bar-coding because of its frequent intramolecular and intermolecular recombinations [118, 119]. The substitution frequencies for mtDNA are 3–4 times less than cpDNA, approximately 12 times less than plant nuDNA, and 40–100 times lower than mtDNA for livestock substitution rates [120]. Just a few mitochondrial markers display phylogenetic utility assurance of phylogenetic efficiency [121, 122]. Nevertheless, only a few simple pairs over 1.4 kb of sequence have been observe as a differentiated between plant and animal families on the coding region of subunit 1 (cox1), making it useful for barcoding [23, 123].

10.3.6   Molecular Phylogenetic Analysis

The barcoding region sequences were collected in DNA barcode from different individuals. A phylogenetic tree is then constructed using the resulting sequence data. Similar, putatively related individuals are grouped together in such a tree. DNA barcode appears to entail that every class is categorized by a unique sequence, but there is a significant genetic variation both contained by each species amid them. Nevertheless, hereditary differences among species are generally greater than those of the population so that each class represents a reproductive isolated species and the taxonomic tree comprises clusters of closely linked organisms and each cluster [22]. The NIH GenBank (an annotating database of all widely available DNA sequences) plays a key role in DNA barcoding. GenBank is part of Japanese DNA Databases (DDBJ), the European Molecular Biology Laboratory (EMBL and NCBI's GenBank), and is a global member of Nucleotide Sequence Databases Partnership. The GenBank sequence database is a freely accessible, illustrated compilation of all accessible combinations of nucleotides and their translations of proteins. This database was established as part of the NCBI in which International Nucleotide Sequence Database collaborated. GenBank and its associates collect sequences from more than 100,000 distinct species generated in laboratories around the world. GenBank is based on specific submissions from independent laboratories and from large submissions from sequencing centers. GenBank blends principles of natural history with concepts of science.

The Enterz Nucleotide and BLAST are the two main search and recovery methods of GenBank data (Basic Local Alignment Tool) available for sequence data analysis. You can browse a wide range of programs around the globe together with details: 1. http://bioinformatics.unc.edu/software/opensource/index.htm, 2. http://molbiol-tools.ca/molecular_biology_freeware.htm#Phylogeny, 3. http://evolution.genetics.washington.edu/phylip/software.html#recent). MP (maximum parsimony), ML (maximum probability), and BI (Bayesian inference) are the three widely employed approaches of phylogenetic analysis. Of these, it was observed that ML is the most biased [89]. In order to predict the shortest possible tree (for example, full parsimony tree), the MP algorithm searches for a smaller number of genetic occurences (e.g., nucleotide replacements) Sometimes, numerous trees are also parsimoniously generated by the study. Because developmental patterns vary significantly from each of the organisms being studied, parsimony findings can be deceptive. Parsimony research is most commonly carried out with the PAUP* 4.0 [124] and MEGA computer program [114]. The maximum likelihood approach (ML) [89, 125] analyzes an evolutionary theory as to the possibility of the observed data being properly produced by the proposed model and its presumed background. The interpretation is then chosen with the greatest chance or potential. The sampling error and adaptive marginal effects are less likely to change this method than other methods. It can evaluate various topologies of both the tree mathematically and use all sequence data. A model-based approach, the Bayesian phylogenetic inference was suggested as an option to the highest probability. MrBayes 3.0 [126] computer program, using a method of simulation called the Monte Carlo Markov chain, performs a Bayesian phylogeny estimate based on a subsequent distribution of the likelihood of trees (or MCMC). MrBayes can combine information from various data partitions or sub-sets with specific stochastic evolutionary models. This helps the user to explore heterogeneous samples of items, including anatomy and nucleotides, composed of different data. BI has made it easy to test parameter-rich evolutionary models. Table 10.5 gives a brief of the commonly used programs used for the phylogeny and DNA barcoding.

Table 10.5 A brief of the commonly used programs used for the phylogeny and DNA barcoding.

Phylogenetic analysis software	Description	Link/references
Bayesian evolutionary analysis sampling trees (BEAST)	A Bayesian MCMC program for root trees inferior to clock or clock models. It can be used for the study of sequences of amino acids, nucleotide sequence, and morphological information. Additionally, the findings can be interpreted, described, and visualized in a number of programs, including Tracer and FigTree.	http://beast.bio.ed.ac.uk
BioEdit	BioEdit is a pretty extensive analytical tool for sequence alignment. BioEdit espouses a wide range of types and provides a simple BLAST local search interface.	http://www.mbio.ncsu.edu/ bioedit/bioedit.html
ClustalX	ClustalX is a multi-sequence alignment program for ClustalW's windows interface. It offers an interconnected environment for the performance and analysis of multiple sequences and profiles.	http://www.clustal.org/

(Continued)

Table 10.5 A brief of the commonly used programs used for the phylogeny and DNA barcoding. (*Continued*)

Phylogenetic analysis software	Description	Link/references
ClustalW	This offers one with a number of possible data presentation alternatives and phylogenetic analysis matrices [PAM (Dayhoff), BLOSUM (Henikoff) or GONNET, and phylogenetic trees presentation (Neighbor-Joining, Phylip, or Distance)].	http://www.ebi.ac.uk/ Tools/msa/clustalw2/
DNA for windows	Windows DNA is a packed in user-friendly DNA study application, suitable for ventures with small scales analysis.	http://www.dna-software. co.uk/
Geneious	It offers a repository of genomic and genetic information for automated updating and for organizing and analyzing data. The software offers a fully integrated, visually sophisticated toolkit: phylogenetics and sequence alignment; BLAST sequence analysis; EMBL, NCBI, automated scanning, protein structure display, etc.	http://www.geneious. com/

(*Continued*)

Table 10.5 A brief of the commonly used programs used for the phylogeny and DNA barcoding. (*Continued*)

Phylogenetic analysis software	Description	Link/references
MAFFT	This is a unix-like system for multiple series synchronization. It offers a variety of multiple alignment processes, L-INS-I (precise for < 200 sequence alignment), FFT-NS–2 (fast; < 10,000 sequence alignment), etc.	http://mafft.cbrc.jp/alignment/software/
FigTree	It is intended to show the summarized and annotated trees created by BEAST as a visual viewer of phylogenetic trees.	http://tree.bio.ed.ac.uk/software/figtree
Format Converter v2.2.5	The program takes a sequence of sequences in an unspecified format as a source (e.g., alignment) and transforms the sequence into a user-status.	http://www.hiv.lanl.gov/content/sequence/FORMAT_CONVERSION/form.html#details_section
GARLI	A scheme that searches for maximum probability trees using genetic algorithms. It comprises the GTR+T model and can analyze nucleotides, amino acids, and codon sequences.	http://code.google.com/p/garli
Hypothesis testing using phylogenies (HYPHY)	A system with full probability of molecular evolution simulations. The vocabulary is strong, so users can use it to define templates and set up tests for the likelihood ratio.	http://www.hyphy.org

(Continued)

Table 10.5 A brief of the commonly used programs used for the phylogeny and DNA barcoding. (*Continued*)

Phylogenetic analysis software	Description	Link/references
MEGA	Windows-based software that integrates a ClustalW synchronization system, which can collect data from GenBank, and with a complete graphical user interface.	http://www. megasoftware.net
MrBayes	A phylogenetic inference software in Bayesian MCMC. This contains all models built for likelihood analysis of nucleotides, amino acids and codon substitution.	http://mrbayes.net
ModelTest	ModelTest is a system that contrasts the compatibility of the GTR (General Time Reversible) family of nucleotide substitution models with hierarchical likelihood ratio tests (hLRT). In addition, the Akaike Information Criterion calculation of probability scores is calculated.	http://darwin.uvigo.es/ software/
Oligo Calculator	Online device to find size, temperature melting, percent GC content, and DNA sequence molecular weight.	http://mbcf.dfci.harvard. edu/docs/oligocalc. html

(*Continued*)

Table 10.5 A brief of the commonly used programs used for the phylogeny and DNA barcoding. (*Continued*)

Phylogenetic analysis software	Description	Link/references
PAML	A set of applications for parameter estimation and likelihood analysis. It is used primarily in successful choice studies, ancestor rebuildings, and molecular clock estimation. For tree checks, it is not optimal.	http://abacus.gene.ucl.ac.uk/software
PHYLIP	A compilation of distance, parsimony, and probability methods for phylogenetic inference programs. PHYLIP is a kit of programs for the inference of phylogenies. PHYLIP is the most popular phylogeny package and competes for the largest number of published trees in the industry with PAUP.	http://evolution.genetics.washington.edu/phylip.html
PhyML	A simple software to scan nuclear-type or protein sequence data for total likelihood trees.	http://www.atgc-montpellier.fr/phyml/binaries.php
PAUP	PAUP (originally meant by phylogenetic analysis using parsimony), published by David Swofford of the College of Computational and Information Technology, Florida State University, Tallahassee, Florida.	http://paup.csit.fsu.edu

(*Continued*)

Table 10.5 A brief of the commonly used programs used for the phylogeny and DNA barcoding. (*Continued*)

Phylogenetic analysis software	Description	Link/references
ProfDistS	Phylogeny based on alignment of the sequence structure.	http://profdist.bioapps. biozentrum.uni-wuerzburg.de/cgi-bin/index.php
MacClade	MacClade is a software application for phylogenetic analysis. Its quantitative intensity is in character development study. It also provides other tools for information and phylogenetic entering and editing, as well as for tree diagrams and graphs.	http://macclade.org/
Neighbor-Joining	For the reconstruction of phylogenetic trees from evolutionary distance data, the neighbor-joining method is proposed.	https://www.sequentix.de/gelquest/help/neighbor_joining_method.htm
RAxML	A quick software, using nucleotide or amino acid sequences, to check for highest likelihood trees within the GTR template. The simultaneous versions are especially strong.	http://scoh-its.org/exelixis/software.html
Readseq	A tool that is especially useful for people using different phylogenesis tools to convert common sequence file formats.	http://www.ebi.ac.uk/Tools/sfc/readseq/
4SALE	A method for aligning and editing synchronous RNA sequence and secondary structure.	http://4sale.bioapps.biozentrum.uni-wuerzburg.de/index.html

(*Continued*)

Table 10.5 A brief of the commonly used programs used for the phylogeny and DNA barcoding. (*Continued*)

Phylogenetic analysis software	Description	Link/references
Sequencher	Sanger and NGS Datasets Premier DNA Sequence Analysis Software.	http://www.genecodes.com/
Tree analysis using new technology	Fast parsimony software for broad sets of data.	http://www.zmuc.dk/public/phylogeny/TNT
TreeView	TreeView offers great access to NEXUS, PHYLIP, or any other format tree file content.	http://taxonomy.zoology.gla.ac.uk/rod/treeview.html

10.3.7   Metabarcoding

During the ancient times, DNA barcoding was solely purposeful on taxonomics. DNA barcoding can now be extended to a diversity of applications and has diversified itself in the area of research. Not only is isolated and intact DNA is used, but human beings often unveil DNA (e.g., skin DNA, dentures, blood, and waste products) into the atmosphere. Such form of DNA, which is commonly known as environmental DNA (eDNA), is very damaged. It can be contained in atmospheric specimens such as air, water, or soil, and without overlapping animals, it can be obtained. The eDNA fragments are shorter than normal DNA fragments and a modified barcode method is therefore needed. Furthermore, this also includes using shorter barcodes. The use of biological samples not just to identify an individual but also to consider a wide variety of species in one sample is a second development method. This is known to be Metabarcoding. The discovery of NGS has assisted in developing metabarcoding approaches that permit a paralleling reading of the DNA sequences from one DNA extract without the need for cloning. Metabarcoding, for this reason, ranges from normal DNA barcoding and identification of retained organisms by species (e.g., of complete genomes) and is designed to be used to identify degraded DNA (eDNA) specimens up to and above the stage of families.

10.3.8 Materials for DNA Barcoding

In contrast to fresh materials, like animal specimens preserved in formalin, the DNA becomes remarkably stable matrix so that it can be obtained from museum collections. Plant DNA in herbariums up to age 100 can be obtained from collections, as well as from fossils of archeological species. Value of crop DNA depends on the technique followed after pressing for drying. Botanists also use ethanol pressurized specimens temporarily to avoid fungal attacks and deterioration when specimen-drying infrastructure, particularly in wet tropical climates, is not immediately accessible. It has been shown that alcohol is harmful to the recovery of high-quality DNA. It is promising to readily produce CO1 sequences from museum samples of insects dried from ethanol processing. Organic spices are commonly used as ingredients for meat, coloring and flavoring chemicals, preservatives, and conventional medicines. However, in the growing spice industry, substantiation and tarnishing detection of spices, especially pulverized ones, is a major face up to and concern for public health. To tackle this issue, a method of identification based on DNA barcoding has been established. Sixteen different spice forms and their specific adulterants have been successfully identified using ITS2 and psbA-trnH sequences to show that this is an effective and powerful tarnishing detection process [127].

1. DNA barcoding is very helpful for taxonomy consumers. It makes progress faster than traditional taxonomic research.
2. DNA barcoding helps taxonomists to quickly distinguish variety by recognizing divergent morphological characteristics that can reflect new organisms.
3. DNA barcode gives taxonomists the chance to expand their inventory worldwide of the diversity of life considerably and eventually complete it.
4. DNA barcoding helps many individuals to quickly and cheaply distinguish and collect information from known species and will accelerate the discovery of thousands of species that have yet to be named by making use of advancements in technologies in technology and genetics.
5. "Life Barcoders" recognizes organisms linked to other data types such as the illustrations, use, and conservation status of ecosystems via the World Wide Web by barcoding life.
6. DNA barcoding will be fully developed and able to change our perception of the complexity of living organisms and our relationship with nature.

7. Barcode has the promising to have a crucial new tool to recognize and conserve the planet's tremendous biodiversity.
8. Making comprehensive inputs accessible to the largest possible end-user community by offering uniform and high-tech detection methods such as biomedicine (parasites and vectors), agriculture (pests), environmental assessments, and customs (trade in endangered species).
9. Lift the huge load of the classification of taxonomists to concentrate on more important activities, such as the delimitation of taxa, relationship settlement, and new species identification and characterization.
10. Pair different development stages (e.g., seedlings and larvae) with the same species.
11. Provide the general public with a resource for bio-literacy.
12. Use crop DNA barcoding combined with HRM research to differentiate nutritious crops for food safety from poisonous plants.

10.4   Main Reasons of DNA Barcoding

1. DNA barcoding promotes democratic access, i.e., a structured barcode database can allow many more people to call the organisms around them by name as well as encourage species to be recognized, whether common or uncommon, endemic, or invasive, resulting in a local and global understanding for biodiversity.
2. DNA barcode mechanism works at all stages of life.
3. DNA barcoding reveals the class that look alike.
4. Barcoding of DNA eliminates uncertainty.
5. DNA barcoding provides knowledge to accelerate the recognition of known species and promote the swift acknowledgement of new species.
6. DNA barcoding is sprouting new leaves on the life tree.
7. DNA barcoding shows the value of the collections of specimens.
8. DNA barcoding speeds write life's encyclopedia, and
9. Barcoding ties biological classification to advancing boundaries of DNA sequencing digital miniaturization, automated information storage, and this convergence can contribute to mobile desktop devices and eventually handheld barcoders.

10.5   Limitations/Restrictions of DNA Barcoding

Intra-specific differentiation between interspecies genetic variations is used for the classification of DNA-based organisms. The limitations of DNA barcoding are listed as under:

1. The distributions of such variability categories are unclear and may vary from taxa to taxa. Recently, divergent organisms or new species that have evolved from hybridization may be difficult to resolve.
2. There is no universal DNA barcoding gene, no unique gene which is maintained in every area of life and demonstrates sufficient organism sequence heterogeneity.
3. Therefore, the accuracy of DNA barcoding is based on the identification of reference sequences from taxonomically confirmed samples.
4. This is supposed to be a dynamic method which requires a number of scientists and organizations to work together.
5. The sequence of barcodes is generally short (approx. 500–1,000 bp), which restricts the use of the barcode to address significant divisions of phylogenies between different classes and orders.
6. There is a certain discussion about the validity of DNA barcoding largely because of the assumption that this innovative categorization system will not strengthen but rather weaken the traditional morphological taxonomy, which may lead to inaccurate recognition of organisms by species based solely on genetic differentiation.

Nevertheless, we must retain the option of becoming a non-parallel method for taxonomical use, systematics and diagnosis with sequences of barcodes and their constantly expanded taxonomic range.

10.6   RNA Barcoding

In recent years, characterizing post-transcription gene regulation by small regulatory (20–30 nt) RNAs, especially miRNAs and piRNAs, has become a major research focus. Their identification and quantification across different developmental stages and in normal and disease tissues as well as model cell lines is a prerequisite for characterizing small RNAs. The small

(20–23 nucleotide) microRNAs (miRNAs) are direct sequentially specific epigenetic regimes and are indexed to the genomes of animal, plant, and viral animals [128–133]. Such genetic regulators are distributed in patterns that are unique to the types of tissues, cells, and developmental stage, and miRNA gene disorder or mutation induces or leads to various human diseases [132, 134–137]. Robust, reliable, and effective methods for the measurement of miRNA abundance need been developed to check miRNA expression in multiple biological or medical samples. Microarray analysis or quantitative RT-PCR (qRT-PCR) [138–142] were standard methods of miRNA profiling [143]. Such techniques, although economically effective, have been limited to analyzing existing miRNAs at miRbase (www.mirbase.org) [144, 145]. Cross-hybridization will hamper microarray assays which prohibit the identification of individual members of miRNAs sequence families or mutant variants of miRNAs, whereas qRT-PCR methods are restricted to a pre-selected subset of miRNAs. Here, we provide a step-by-step method for producing miRNA expression profiles from the deep sequencing of small libraries of RNA cDNA. As well as gathering information on the abundance of miRNA sequence-based techniques, new or mutated miRNAs and new families of small RNAs can be discovered [146–151]. Deep tissue sequenzation is sufficient to identify almost any annotated miRNA organism, although the majority of it is small [152, 153]. A small subset of miRNAs is typically the majority (>90%) of all sequences known as miRNAs (30–50 in mammalian tissues) [154–157]. The sequencing length achieved in a typical Illumina HiSeq sequence is more than sufficient to record the relative abundance of miRNAs involved in gene regulation (currently, more than 150 million sequence read). At the same time, it is time consuming and costly to prepare and sequence prototypically small library of RNA cDNA, rather than microarray and/or PCR assays. The use of a barcoding system for multiplexing multiple tests has alleviated these drawbacks. In the first stage of creating a small library of the RNA cDNA with the combination of several samples, processing time and sequencing costs decreased the use of barcode is also reduced [155, 158–163].

10.6.1   Overview of the Method

The experimental method as depicted in Figure 10.7 of small RNA cDNA library processing (Figure 10.7) involves RNA isolations, 30 adapters up to 20 separate samples, specimen pooling, 50 adapter bonds, reverse transcript, and PCR for manufacturing the cDNA library and sequencing. In comparison to a variety of RNA, cDNA library approaches for RNAseq

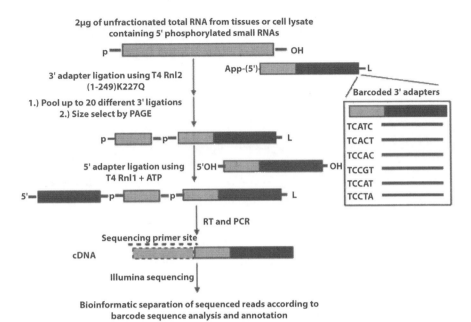

Figure 10.7 Schematic description of the preparation of the small RNA cDNA library. At the 5' end of the 3' connector oligodeoxynucleotides, the barcode reflects a 5-nt special sequence. Illumina HiSeq sequencing produces over 150 million sequence reads per sequencing lane at its smallest scale. Some sequence reads (>70%) include identifiable barcode sequences, resulting in more than 3 million sequence reads per test using the complete set of 20 barcoded adapters. L, 30 aminohexyl blocking group that inhibits the circularization of the adapter.

applications preserve orientation for the RNA insert by connecting 30 to 50 adapters with different sequences to the smaller RNA and can detect the origin of the genome or the anti-sense strand after cDNA sequence. Bioinformatics down-stream analyzes start with a barcode sequence read sequence separation, followed by an overview and definition of a derivative sequence as described by Berninger *et al.* in an accompanying protocol [164].

10.7   Methodology

Text files for each sequenced sequence and a performance score are the next generation sequence outputs. These files are processed to (1) remove from the reading the 30 barcode adapter sequence and allocate reading to a specific barcode sample, (2) generate files for each sub-sample with distinctive (non-redundant) reads that list the times each individual read is encountered, (3) exclude sequences of low-complexity and adapter-adapter binding items, and (4) map distinctive readings to the genome.

The output is a profile of the read frequencies for every miRNA that can be translated into the relative read frequencies or absolute input amounts miRNA (as contrasted to the calibrator reads for each sub-sample). These miRNA profiles can therefore be classified by clustering and analyzing the comparative expression in sequence families and genomical clusters. miRNA gene families have a sequence of MIRNAs that presumably target a single set of MRNAs, whereas miRNA genomic clusters have miRNAs adjacent to the genome. Next, we decide a cure strategy for miRNAs, an important step in identifying miRNA biological research applicants by checking their expression and possibility for prototypical miRNA hairpin structures. Finally, we uncover our strategy for identifying RNA nucleotide differences and use techniques to categorize new miRNAs. Sequence-based miRNA profiles can be deposited in the SRA (Sequence Read Archive) (www.ncbi.nlm.nih.gov/sra) both as barcode files that have not been expressly allocated to a barcode, for each sub-sample (including reads, read rate, and assigned annotation).

10.7.1   Materials Required

A software workstation or device is needed for analyzing simple, small RNA deep sequence data. Workstations have traditionally offered higher performance compared with desktop computers. Nevertheless, modern personal computers can only be used as workstations, leveraging commonly accessible software and hardware components. A computer of workstation type may have the following features: memory bug fixing support (ECC) (a style of data storage that fixed common types of internal data corruption); a higher number of memory sockets using licensed modules; numerous processor sockets; and reliable CPUs and a stable operating system (e.g., Unix-based). To obtain miRNA read frequencies, the raw deep sequence files created on Illumina Genome Analyzer II and HiSeq are processed. After image processing, one deep sequencing produces a text file in fastq format with a quality score for each nucleotide call. The size of fastq files is now multi-GB when compressed. Depending on the RNA isolation method and platform used for sequencing, a library may contain between 10 million and more than two million reads. An initial sorting phase (included in platform-specific software packages) can take place based on the performance scores.

10.7.2　Barcoded RNA Sequencing High-Level Mapping of Single-Neuron Projections

Neurons transmit information by long-range axonal projections to remote brain regions. In some instances, within a small region, functionally distinct neuron communities are intermingled. For example, neighboring hypothalamic kernels regulate fundamental drives from these nuclei projects toward separating objectives from these kernels, such as hunger, attack and sexual attraction, and neurons from these nuclei project to distinct targets [165, 166]. In the peripheral cortical area V1, the visual stimulation responses are related to the characteristics of the neurons translate to higher visual areas [167, 168]. Conclusions like these suggest that the data that each neuron transmits can be customized to its goals. This particular data routing involves an anatomical substratum, but no high-performance approach for the analysis of neuronal projection patterns is currently available. There is a good correlation between bandwidth and resolution in anatomical methods to chart long-range relations. A fluorescent or enzymatic tag is used in traditional anterograde brain mapping studies to allow light microscopy to visualize cell bodies and distal projections. Bulk approaches challenge the expected numbers of neurons on a single site and thus check the collective function of the whole neuronal community. There have been numerous massive efforts to map mesoscopic connectivity systematically, including Allen George Atlas [169] and the iConnectome [170]. While quick, these bulk methods obscure the heterogeneity in any study of the many projection neurons labeled. For example, imagine a single source region spreading into three downstream regions. The projection mechanism allows neurons to transmit information in the initial region to the three downstream regions. However, identical bulk projection patterns could be developed in several ways: (1) one-to-one architecture in which each neuron only aims at one downstream (left) area; (2) from a full structure in which each neuron targets the region (middle) downstream; or (3) a set of diverse (right) architectures. These three projection patterns cannot be distinguished with conventional bulk labeling without further experimentation with different functional implications. In addition to traditional bulk branding anterogrades, various alternatives have been developed. For example, a marker such as Cre recombinase can approach genetically determined neuronal subpopulations within an area [171, 172].

10.7.3　Using RNA to Trace Neurons

Traditional types of neuroanatomic tracking rely on color or protein loading of neurons for microscopy neural processes. An implied restriction of these methods—although seldom rigorously tested—is that, irrespective of the length from the soma, the tracer fills the neuron generously and evenly so that its force correlates to the quantity of the specified neural cycle. In distal processes, we have tried to improve barcode mRNA's abundance and uniformity, in order to serve as a comparable tag in MAPseq (Figure 10.8).

This protein was actually engineered by researchers as part of a broader project aimed at reading synaptic communication through mRNA, referred to as MAPP-nπ. A modified presynaptic protein was directly used to bind and transfer mRNA barcode in the terminal axons. Due to the fusion of the endogenous presynaptic protein NRXN1β with traffic signals, we started with pre-mGRASP, a protein designed for the presynaptic terminal [173]. Four versions of the nλ domain RNA in the cytoplasmic portion of the

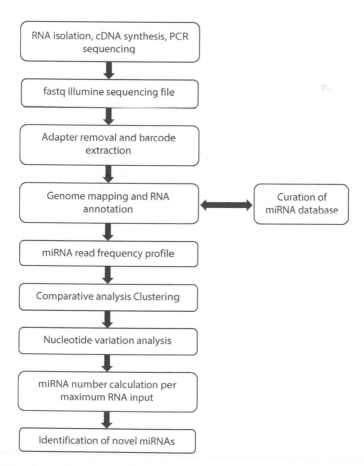

Figure 10.8 General overview of bioinformatic analysis pipeline [237].

protein were then inserted by the scientists. The nλ domain is a 22-AA peptide that strongly and particularly binds to a 15-nt RNA hairpin known as BoxB, which is derived from the λ phage λN protein. The mRNA barcode has four variants of the hairpin boxB which guarantees the attachment of the MAPP-nT to barcode mRNA to the axon terminals and therefore the transfer of the barcode mRNA [174]. Second, the researchers used Sindbis virus to deliver the barcode sequence, a virus that can achieve somewhat high expression quickly [175].

Reviewing miRNA biogenesis and structure is helpful in facilitating the understanding of miRNA profiling analysis. Mature miRNAs are omitted from primary transcripts (pri-miRNAs) by a multi-stage mechanism that contains one or more 70-nt hairpin miRNAs (pre-miRNAs) and are supported by their own promoters or share a host protein coding gene with the promoter. RNA (dsRBP), a dsRNA binding protein and RNASEN, also known as RNase III Drosha, classifies certain complexes within the nucleus, which are excised in order to produce pre-miRNAs.

Many miRNAs circumvent the basic processing order of miRNA and maybe autonomous of their maturation of DGCR8 and RNASEN or independent of DICER1.DGCR8- and RNASEN-independent miRNAs include mirtrons and tailed mirtrons that splicing and exonuclease trimming release their pre-miRNA [176, 177]. Next-generation MiRNA profiling does not only require differential expression experiments but also helps to identify the differential nucleotide (including RNA editing, 30 and 50 modifications) and new miRNAs. Read sequence reads, also known as read frequencies, are helpful in quantifying global miRNA availability in any test sample when they are included in the small RNA cDNA library preparations once standardized for comparison requirements (calibrating oligoribonucleotides) to each sample in a known amount. Ultimately, to further explain miRNA abundance, we discuss method-specific prejudices. Researchers have recently established miRNA and calibrator sequence-specific biases for the correction factors of affected miRNAs by quantifying 770 synthetic miRNAs and 50 RNAs with a barcode-like adapter and method [158].

10.7.4   A Life Conservation Barcoder

With molecular engineering refinement and the significance of the resulting database of broad molecular barcode development [46], the life of barcoding has now become more complex to use taxonomy, phylogenetics, and population genetics. This is not unique, but possibly the large scale of its technological and societal ambitions is what makes life's barcoding unique. The aim of barcoding for marker standardization, DNA banking, and proper taxonomic vouchering is another important factor. The importance for developing DNA and tissue banks has been well recognized [17, 178] and for all categories of organisms, for example, the "barcoded nematodes" [179] that first did not appear to exhibit morphological variation at the species level [180] were proven methods to associate DNA samples with taxonomic vouchers. Life coding has to be incorporated into other international taxonomic projects such as the Convention on Biological Diversity's Global Taxonomic Initiative (www.biodiv.org) or the Global Biodiversity Information Facility (www.gbif.org). Of course, the importance of preserving biodiversity can only be significantly increased if every child, leader, and science expert has such easy access to information regarding life. This is not to blindly ignore the significance of the bio-sustainability issue, but we will embrace and contribute to the development of new initiatives in such a way as in the case of bar-coding life.

10.7.5   Gene Sequencing

The identification of DNA structure by Watson and Crick contributed to discovering the physical basis of genes and inheritance. Many significant developments have been enabled with rapid advancements in genetic engineering technologies and the ability to manipulate the functioning properties of DNA molecules. Genetic engineering allows researchers to check the interaction between life molecules and the structure and function of the nervous system and gain information into how small differences in DNA, even shifts to single nucleotides, can manifest in deeper actions. Molecular biologists are using DNA in movie production, like conventional artists. If a film director would want to remove a sequence from a film reel and add to another film reel, then the entire scene will be identified, physically removed, and put into the new film cassette together. Predictably, a molecular biologist might like to split the sequence of DNA into a different vector from a specialized DNA storage system called a vector.

DNA monitoring is now a powerful tool for the study and interpretation of fundamental research. DNA sequencing has been studied in medicine in specific as a method of treatment or prognosis. The principal applications for DNA sequencing include (1) recognition and understanding of an internal cell structure, (2) the understanding of which sequence codes are used for which type of protein, (3) detecting disease-related gene mutations, (4) planning sequence-based proteins, and (5) curing sequence-based diseases.

DNA sequencing is a way of determining the sequence of nucleotides in a DNA strand (adenine, guanine, cytosine, and thymine). Since the 1970s, various methods have been created. The chemical method was invented by Fred Sanger and Alan Maxam and Walter Gilbert [181, 182]. The Sanger strategy was the most frequently used method in molecular biology until the introduction of mass sequencing technologies also called DNA sequencing methods of the next generation [183]. These include platforms for SOLiD, pyrosequencing, and Illumina. These technologies have enabled the generation in a single run of millions of reads of 50–1,000 nucleotides that are assembled in large DNA molecule thanks to powerful bioinformatics programs. The costs involved are continually decreasing; currently, for less than US\$ 1,000, a given eukaryotic genome can be fully sequenced. A comparison of many individuals' genomes can help identify disease-related genes and loci, biotic and abiotic stress resistance, yield, and phylogeny.

The sequence of nucleotides of significance in the DNA domain is determined by a DNA sequencing techniques. It can and is used in a series of steps in DNA classification, for instance, matching existing genetic sequences in order to detect a gene or to verify that recombinant DNA material is appropriate after modification.

10.7.5.1   DNA Sequencing Methods

The Sanger chain-terminating method will establish the nucleotide sequence in any pure DNA sample. This approach shows a high fidelity sequence of about 200–500 base pairs. Based on *in-vitro* DNA synthesis, the Sanger method synthesizes short pieces of DNA: the ending of the chain dideoxyribonucleoside triphosphates in the presence of nucleotide bases to which additional bases are not attachable. These nucleotides are labeled and mixed with regular bases to produce fragments of DNA in many different lengths, which are randomly stopped by adding a nucleotide ending the chains. Originally, when this procedure was done and many years later, each end of a chain nucleotide was marked as a radioactive probe, and scientists had to execute four different reactions (one for each nuclear substance) and run one gel with each reaction along a different path.

Modern methods label a different colored fluorescent dye for each chain-terminating nucleotide. In this way, it is necessary to perform just one specific reaction involving each of the clearly marked chain-terminating nucleotides and an automatic fluorescence detector will search the gel rapidly to "interpret" the identification of the last terminating nucleotide at that location. This allows you to determine the order of nucleotide bases. Modern molecular biology labs do not generate sequence reactions themselves, as a fragment of DNA is usually sent faster and cheaper to a special sequencing facility (Figure 10.9).

Each nucleotide is labeled with a particular sample, which synthesizes several DNA fragments. Each position can include a labeled chain nucleotide ending chain. When all of the synthesized DNA fragments are separated by gel electrophoresis, they are arranged according to the sizes, and a receptive lens can detect which label is producing fluorescence at each position.

Present next-generation sequence (NGS) (Table 10.6) techniques have been invented in the 1990s. In October 1990, a novel NGS technique that included reversible 30 blockers on DNA arrays was patented by Roger Tsien, Pepi Ross, Margaret Fahnestock, and Allan J. Johnston. A further NGS modification, named pyrosequencing, was published in 1996 by Pal Nyren and Mostafa Ronaghi. In 1997, Pascal Mayer and Laurent Farinelli presented a method described as DNA colony sequencing. A combination of these methods is applied by Illumina's Hi-seq genome sequencers. Lynx Therapeutics released and sold a modern NGS method in 2000 named "massively parallel decoding of signatures". A parallel model of pyrosequencing was introduced in 2004 by 454 Life Sciences.

DNA sequencing technology is undoubtedly crucial for the development of expertise in the biological sciences. Brisk advances in DNA sequence technology are therefore progressed for quicker, easier, reliable, and the most appropriate approaches.

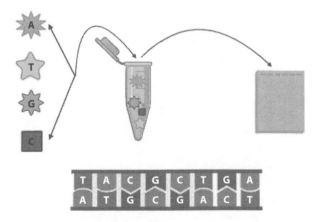

Figure 10.9 Overview of gene sequencing.

Table 10.6 Comparison of the commonly used NGS methods.

Method	Read length	Accuracy (single read not consensus)	Reads per run	Advantages	Disadvantages
Single-molecule real-time sequencing (Pacific Biosciences)	10,000–15,000 bp average (14,000 bp N50); maximum read length >40,000 bases	87% single-read accuracy	50,000 per SMRT cell or 500–1,000 megabases	Fast; Detects 4mC, 5mC, 6mA, Longest read length	Moderate efficiency; Apparatus can be expensive
Ion semiconductor (Ion Torrent sequencing)	Up to 400 bp	98%	Upto 80 million	Less expensive equipment; Fast	Homopolymer errors
Pyrosequencing (454)	700 bp	99.9%	1 million	Long read size; Fast	Runs are very costly; Homopolymer errors

(Continued)

Table 10.6 Comparison of the commonly used NGS methods. (*Continued*)

Method	Read length	Accuracy (single read not consensus)	Reads per run	Advantages	Disadvantages
Sequencing by synthesis (Illumina)	50–300 bp	99.9 % (Phred 30)	Up to 6 billion (TruSeq paired-end)	Potential for highsequence yield, depending upon sequencer model and desired application	Equipment can be very pricey; Needs high DNA concentrations
Sequencing by ligation (SOLiD sequencing)	50+35 or 50+50 bp	99.9%	1.2–1.4 billion	Low cost per base	Tools simpler than other; Includes issues with palindrome encoding
Chain termination (Sanger sequencing)	400–900 bp	99.9%	N/A	Long people read; Suitable for various implementations	With larger sequencing programs; More costly and inefficient; This method also requires plasmid cloning or PCR to take a long time

10.7.5.2   First-Generation Sequencing Techniques

DNA sequencing came for the first time in 1970s. Thanks to more technological approaches; the first type of nucleotide sequencing was RNA sequencing. With the research on bacteriophage MS2, Walter *et al.* took the first step in the sequence of RNA. Bacteriophage MS2 was the first gene identified in 1972 and the first genome identified in 1972 [184–186]. The DNA sequencing study of Frederick Sanger and Allan Maxam and Walter Gilbert (Maxam-Gilbert) contributed significantly to the development of modern DNA sequencing technology, which had an enormous impact in 1977.

10.7.5.3   Maxam's and Gilbert's Chemical Method

Maxam and Gilbert developed DNA bases sequence by chemical reaction degradation of DNA in 1973. First of all, the operator by their method based on the restriction of the terminally labeled DNA sequenced the 24 bases of the RNA transcript of *E. coli* lac at each repetition base [187]. They isolated fragments of *E. coli* approximately 1,000 bp dsDNA including the lactose promoter. Once paired with the sonicated DNA fragments that bear lac genes, the lac repressor binds to the cellulose nitrate, and only fragments belonging to the lac operator are processed. Isopropylβ-D-1-thiogalactopyranoside (IPTG), a lac operon artificial inducer, elutes pieces of DNA attached by the repressor. They obtained about 27-bp-long fragments, dsDNA. These DNA fragments then synthesize RNA molecules. RNA was resolved into single molecular organisms for the synthesis of specific regions. Exploiting the findings that an induction of triphosphate of RNA polymerase and dematured DNA is suppressed by the NTP concentration of less than 5 µM, polymerase shall activate and insert at the beginning of the RNA chain if it is supplied with di- or poly-nucleotids complementary to the template, synthesizing at a specific point a strand of operator DNA with ragged 3' ends and converting them into bands during polyacrylamide gel electrophoresis. RNA synthesis is based on a single strand of GpGpApApU Oligonucleotide, while UpA dinucleotide and ApUpCpG Pentanuclearotide on the other strand. GpU was primed for both ends and this synthesis led to the 24 bp nucleic acid e-sequencing with the *E. coli* lac operator.

In articles of Maxam-Gilbert in 1977, the chemical reaction route was outlined. DNA is marked with 32P or a 5' fluorescent stain in this procedure of which nucleotide sequence is primarily identified. DNA molecules are subsequently divided into four tubes. In each of these four separate pipes, chemical reactions for a chemical change and oxidation of a particular base (A, C, G, or T) are conducted. There are basically two steps in these chemical reactions. The first step is to break the glycosidic bond between ribose glucose in nucleotide triphosphates and the base from dimethylsulfate with purines and with hydrazine in pyrimidines. The second step is to cleavage piperidine phosphodiester bonds.

Maxam-Gilbert sequencing is the medium produced by dimethylsulfate and piperidine on the cleavage of G nucleotides. Therefore, the formic acid produces the second medium of hydrazine and piperidine, which is cleaving G and A nucleotides and also the hydrazine and the T and C nucleotides (the third medium), and in 2M Nacl, the other mixture of hydrazine and piperidine forming C nucleotides (the fourth medium).

The ssDNA, of which 5' is radioactively labeled, is extracted after unique DNA sequencing reactions after systematic DNA sequencing reactions. Packed in high percent polyacrylamide during reactions, the molecules are separated electrophoretically. Because of radioactively marked gel fragments, the autography technique allows them to be visible and the base sequence is identified. Base-specific chemical destruction reaction is sequenced by labeled fragments of DNA. Although the method can be used for both ssDNA and dsDNA, there is no need for DNA polymerase enzyme. Four bases are specifically reduced to pieces of radioactively marked bases and four bases are electrophoretically separated into poly-acrylamide planar (slab) gel separation lines [188].

10.7.5.4   Sanger Sequencing

Since Frederick Sanger and Alan R. Coulson published experiments in 1975, the modern DNA sequencing technique began [189, 190] to determine the DNA base sequence. Sanger has developed a less complicated approach, also known as "plus and minus sequencing", which is called "the chain termination method". The discovery of DNA sequence in biology at the time became a method for decoding genes, including all genomes [191]. While this method has provided unbelievable facts in the scientific world and in the year 1980, it helped Frederick Sanger to win the Nobel Prize.

Genotyping studies compete with Sanger Sequencing (accepted as a chain termination method, an enzymatic method or a dideoxy process in literature). The Sanger's DNA sequence method relies on synthesis of new fragments of DNA, which allow the new DNA synthesizing chain to be formed by combining reactions of normal deoxynucleotides (dNTPs) and dideoxynucleotides (dddNTPs). Four forms of dideoxynucleotides (ddATP, ddGTP, ddCTP, and ddTTP) are combined with the synthesis reaction in very controlled amounts and durations. In every reaction mixture, four ddNTP types, DNA Polymerase I (Klenow Fragment), four dNTP types (dATP, dGTP, dCTP, and dTTP—these are necessary for DNA polymerization), and DNA template will find out the base sequence and the DNA base complementary primers at 3' end and 32P at 5' [192].

In case of chain incorporation of such ddNTPs, the lack of oxygen in Position 3' and the presence of only H in deoxyriboses found in the structure of ddNTPs will stop polymerization during the synthesis process. Therefore, ddNTPs are unable to shape phosphodiester bond with other molecules that lack OH groups. The different DNA fragments that resulted in four forms of reaction medium were independently electrophoresized and isolated according to their lengths at the end of all procedures. They with autoradiography then become distinctive black bands and try to determine their basis sequences in relation to them. The results of Sanger sequencing reads around 800–1,000 bases in length [190, 193–196].

10.7.5.5   Automation in DNA Sequencing

Radioactive isotopes, in first-generation sequencing techniques, were used to tag DNA. For automated DNA sequencing, fluorescent tracers have been used to minimize the use of radioactive material for DNA sequencing, contributing to risks to safety for laboratory staff. The bulk of automatic DNA sequencing approaches merged PCR and fluorescence identification around the 1980s [197–199].

10.7.5.6   Use of Fluorescent-Marked Primers and ddNTPs

In the original DNA sequencing system, for separating sequencing reaction products, standard slab PAGE and authoradiography technique instruments were used. PAGE is a molecule-dimensional separation tool. PAGE is achieved by polymerizing long chains with monomers of acrylamide. Gels with pores of various sizes are created through variations in the volume of polyacrylamide contained in the solution. DNA molecules also decompose these pores with their capture. Because the pores would absorb the smaller DNA molecules, they would move more slowly throughout the solution. This will also cause large pieces of DNA to linger in proportion to small fragments in the upper part of the solution. On the other hand, smaller fragments move quicker into the gel and bands on the lower gel plates are observed.

The autoradiography procedure used for identification was carried out after identification of the DNA fragments with radioactive substances such as 32P and 35S. Gels used have been exposed to radiation and the image obtained updated the detection. Many detection-based improvements in the sequence analysis are produced in the chain termination process conducted by labeling DNA fragments with radioactive phosphorus. Among all these is the 5' end of the primer to use fluorescent dye to be numbered. Nevertheless, the need for four individual reaction media has not been replaced by this detection-based switch. The approach to allowing automation by optical system's simple, quick, and economical analysis has established dye terminator sequencing to tag DNA fragments with coloring. Hood and colleagues breakthrough is the establishment of highly automated DNA sequencing by using fluorescent primers and ddNTPs [200].

10.7.5.7   Dye Terminator Sequencing

Dye terminator sequencing is an alternative way of marking chain terminators to sequence marked primers. In contrast with the sequencing process done by means of the marked primer, the significant advantage of this procedure is a single reaction medium (four reaction mediums are used in the marked main medium). Each of the four terminators in the chain is marked with an individual fluorescent dye and has differing wavelengths for each fluorescent during the color sequence terminator sequence. The limitation of this technique is the dye effectiveness, which has a voice in inequality formation resulting from capillary electrophoresis (CE) in the length and shape of peaks. Together with DNA high-performance sample analyzer robots, the dye terminator sequencing method is employed in a number of sequencing programs. Consequently, fast and low-cost sequencing procedures are carried out [201].

10.7.5.8   Using Capillary Electrophoresis

Shortly subsequent to the development of slab gel sequencing systems, the CE-based systems were developed. With specimen size greater than slab gel systems, CE-based sequence systems offer rapid identification, convenience of use, and increased precision [202–204].

Autoradiography technological difficulties and limitations have been avoided by updating detection using color mounted on DNA fragments in CE. Similar with slab gel-based sequencing, CE isolation has various advantages. The first is capillary systems with a portable layer to enable matrix substitution during separations. The solution is sprayed between glass sheets for slab liquid separations and is polymerized.

Without creating a balloon, it is hard to pour gels, and its preparation takes time. For capillary-based automated systems, though, this has been avoided. Additionally, owing to the incorporation of capillary structures with microtiter plates, the multiple experiments performed on a sitting were unnecessary. The isolation of up to 384 samples was enabled at the same time as the incorporation of the 384 well CE-based separation. The third advantage is that rather than radioactive substances, dyes attached to DNA fragments are used to prevent damage to people's health [192, 205, 206].

Examination of several specimens can be done with the integration of a variety of techniques in an automatic DNA sequencing system single work. Fluorescent maximum chromatograms, the raw data, are collected by detecting fluorescent dyes in DNA sequencing with CE-dimensional separations [192, 206].

10.7.6   Developments and High-Throughput Methods in DNA Sequencing

Sanger sequencing is certainly a specific tool for detecting previously described polymorphism/mutations. Nonetheless, it is a commonly used tool of checking a polymorphism detected through other genotyping systems or in situations where there is no response from similar systems again. In contrast to the gold standard, though, the development of modern genotyping techniques is in trouble owing to hard labor and long-term workflow [207, 208].

Though Sanger sequence is the most frequently used simple sequencing process, it cannot differentiate between wild-type sequences at very small levels. This condition causes a problem when dealing with specimens that contain various groups of cells of different types such as solid tumors. Solid tumors have a heterogeneous tissue composition as a product of neoplastic and non-neoplastic cell types. The gain of the function mutations in oncogenes therefore becomes difficult to identify, for the reasons that neoplastic cells and non-normal cells have two alleles and one of those alleles is usually of wild-type flexible, cost-effective, and easy to use approaches are therefore necessary [209, 210]. Improved sequence-based research culminated in the emergence of high-performance sequencing technologies that allow thousands, perhaps millions of sequence analyze at a time, with the sequencing pursuits achieving low cost and rapid outcomes. Around 2005, due to the low performance of first-generation approaches, second-generation sequencing techniques appeared commercially. The most interesting aspect of these second-generation sequencing methods was the potential to rapidly execute over one simultaneous test in shorter times. In the second-generation sequencing, the "clean and test" procedure was conducted. In these processes, the marked nucleotides are inserted into freshly synthesized DNA strands in the flooding reagent; the reaction was then stopped and rinsed for the removal and testing for integrated basis phases of unnecessary reagents. The process is replicated before scanning can assess the reaction [193].

10.7.7 Pyrosequencing Method

Pyrosequencing is a pattern-by-synthesis technique used in solution with bioluminometric determination [211]. In this process, pyrophosphate (PPI) produced by the amount of nucleotide in the newly synthesized DNA chain is thus transformed by a sequence of enzyme reactions into obvious light, with a bioluminometric calculation. The enzymes which control the chemical responses in this method include Klenow Fragment (DNA polymerase I), ATP sulfurylase, apyrase, and luciferase. In the first reaction, when a nucleotide is added to the sequencing template reaction basis pairs, DNA polymerizations occur. Klenow DNA polymerase produces inorganic pyrophosphate and is used as an ATP sulfurylase substratum which contributes as a second reaction to the production of ATPs. Instead for light detection, ATP is converted into luciferase. Alternatively, apyrase extracts excess (unincorporated) nucleotides and ATP between the dissimilar simple additionals necessary for organized DNA synthesis and effective light analysis after proper nuclear addition [211]. Four-enzyme–based pyrosequencing can sequence around 1–100 bp. With a pyrosequencing system based on three enzymes, the reading duration can be increased to 300 bases; but the optimization of the method fails if a control stage is required and the DNA model failure is a restricting variable for this kind of pyrosequencing [212]. There are two big limitations on pyrosequencing. Whereas the first needs specialized equipment and training in this subject, the second requires no genome sequence induced by period limits of the baseline reading. Nevertheless, given these constraints, the abundance of experimental choices such as performing a huge number of samples using 96- or 384-well plates, disparity in alleles, methylation, and gene duplication distinguishing numbers improves its selection [213].

10.7.8   The Genome Sequencer 454 FLX System

In 2004, a Roche team (454 Life Technologies) launched the next-generation sequencing FLX method, which is also based on the methodology of pyrosequencing [214]. This is the method in which the DNA template is synthesized by using PCR (ePCR) emulsion in water drops of a fat solution [215]. Template DNA is present in each drop bound to the bead-united primer. Within this drop, the PCR procedure generates a clonal colony. Each well contains a single bead and enzymes for sequencing even picoliter-volume. gDNA, PCR, BAC, and cDNA from tiny to large organisms can be sequenced to a wide range of specimen. For smaller pieces (300,800 bp), larger fragments are necessary for pre-sequencing nebulization, and for smaller samples, no fragmentation is mandatory. Short A- and B-adapters are attached to the required fragments for purification, amplifying, and sequencing. In the ePCR procedure, DNA-fragments of a single strand (ssDNA-library) are mixed with sepharose beads with. Each bead is captured in a clonal amplification fragment that creates fragments of clonally amplified DNA with bead-immobilized properties. Then, ssDNA library beads are attached to the DNA Bead Inculbation Mix and laid with Enzyme Beads (to maintain the position of the DNA beads during sequence) in the PicoTiterPlat 454 sequencing system. In each frame, each perle fuses well within the library. PicoTiterPlate is then laden to the FLXTM Genome Sequence Instrument. When the CCD camera detects a light produced by incorporating a complementary nucleotide into the DNA, the SDNA molecules are sequenced while the fluids pass through the plate. The FLX machine can read approximately 400 to 600 Mb of sequence per cycle [216, 217].

10.7.9   Illumina/Solexa Genome Analyzer

It is a sequencing method focused on reversible coloring terminators. The terminator is subsequently cleaved to insert the next nucleotide. All four terminator-based dNTPs are present for every sequencing process, which enables more precise sequencing. A photographic instrument takes pictures of labeled fluorescent nucleotides and extracts fluorescent dye from DNA on the blocker end with chemical oxidation at the 3'-end. Illumina can yield more than 200–300 gigabase of information per phase. The exact source is 99.5% and is the most commonly employed method in sequencing [217, 218].

10.7.10   Transition Sequencing Techniques

Techniques for sequencing in the third generation eliminate the reaction delay during sequence in each base integration techniques of the second generation [193]. This evolution in the sequence sector increases rate of sequencing and sequence lengths as well as the complexity of sample preparation. The promising third-generation sequencing methods were second-molecule sequencing (sequencing single DNA/RNA molecule). Furthermore, certain innovations are not part of the third or second generation yet. These technologies demonstrate clearly the developmental stage of the third-generation sequencing techniques and let us understand that the third-generation sequencing technologies are better.

10.7.11   Ion-Torrent's Semiconductor Sequencing

High-density microwave array was developed using semiconductor technology in Ion-Torrent's sequence-sequencing technology, and the sequencing of hydrogen ions is carried out on the basis of the process of incorporation [193]. The method simplifies the process of sampling, removing the need for light to test the sample and reducing costs. The technology, however, still incorporates the "clean and sample" sequencing approach of the second generation and uses PCR for DNA template amplification in each well. Thus, the time needed for sequencing and throughput is lowered with the second-generation sequencing system [193] which allows this practice to be somewhere in between second- and third-generation sequencing methods.

10.7.12   Helico's Genetic Analysis Platform

The genetic analysis platform of Helico is the first trade system to implement sequencing technology [219–221]. This system uses the specified primers, altered polymerase, and fluorescent nucleotide analogs and visualizes the DNA molecules attached to a flat exterior during the synthesis process. Fluorescent labeling of nuclear-type analogs, known as the Virtual Terminator nucleotides, enables step-by-step sequencing of the dye due to the chemically cleavable group attachment of the dye to the nucleotide [220]. The sequential size of the nucleotide is roughly 32, and the sequence time is long similar to second-generation sequencing technology. In comparison to second-generation sequencing techniques, PCR is not necessary in this process. As with all sequencing techniques for second molecules, error reading rates exceed 5% given their high folding and 99% readability [193].

10.7.13   Third-Generation Sequencing Techniques

Third-generation sequencing strategies (second-molecular sequencing), which are predominantly being created, can be defined in three basic categories as (1) sequence by syntheses technologies in which DNA polymerase molecules are visualized during their synthesis with the single DNA molecule and (2) nanopore technologies for the sequencing of individual bases when they move across the nanopore. In specific applications, every category is used. In this chapter, we will seek to quickly clarify these different techniques of the third generation.

In the first group, the second molecule is transcription sequence, the first 3rd-generation sequence technology for detecting DNA polymerase in real time, and the sequencing approaches are real-time fluorescent resonance-energy sequence DNA sequencing (FRET) (by Visigen Biotechologien/Life Technologies). The process depends on the production of the FRET signal via a fluorophore-tagged DNA polymerase in real-time DNA sequencing with FRET when close to an accepter nucleotide with fluorophore tagging. The published fluorophore tag can be identified after the introduction of the nucleotide [193].

In the second group, the two approaches are direct microscopically advanced DNA imaging, electron microscopy (TEM) DNA imaging, and scanning tunneling microscopy (STM). Visual TEM (by Halcyon Molecular) scans of DNA sequences identifies non-periodic atoms on a planar layer and tests TEM with the use of darkfield photography [222]. Using STM, nucleotides are digitally defined from a conducting surface wherein DNA is connected by a microscope tunnel in the specific DNA sequence [223].

DNA sequence with nanopores is the third category where techniques are used by a limited amount of individual unchanged DNA molecules, and when they relocate through the nanopore due to electrical current or optical signal, they focus on the identification of basics [193].

10.8   Conclusion

DNA sequencing technology has a broad relevance. The establishment of DNA as an inherited material in several members of the same family and the observance of certain conditions of illness elevated demand for the identification of nucleotides and their relationship to certain diseases. DNA sequence has become one of the biological science milestones by exploring sequencing technology. The identification of multiple molecular disorders is due to human genome sequencing, while many still remain undiscovered. DNA sequencing is used for a number of different applications varying from complete genome sequence numerous species: DNA/RNA sequence analyses, SNP analysis, protein nucleic acid association, methylation analysis, and gene regulation research. Today, with the help of sequencing technologies, the adapted therapies for many diseases are carried out. The Sanger sequence process has been simplified by introducing fluorescent, primary-ddNTPs, and capillary gel electrophoresis to the system, which is an awkward approach in the years that it was first used and has made it possible for scientific research to be easier and more extensive. The increase in information on the method has enabled its applicability to be increased. As a consequence, the rise in DNA sequence interest led to an increase in the number of publications for this process. Due to the advantages of the DNA sequence method, studying to enhance its applicability and reduce its costs will become crucial. With these studies, new generation high-throughput sequencing devices have made it possible for scientific research to become easy and cheap. With the research results collected, what will be identified by the practical impact of the alteration at the genetic level (SNP, systemic or fragmentary copies) and this data will also be used in "social treatment" or "private counselling". The understanding of genetic differences among people can pave the way for customized treatments and enhance the value of physical treatment through such approaches. Pre-scanning of specific DNAs is necessary for possible genetic predispositions in order to have sequencing technology cheap enough [223–228]. The progress made toward customized therapy, a novel concept within the medical sector, means that the novel generation of DNA sequencing methods will be one of the fundamental laboratory methods, in particular in protection and therapeutic medical applications.

Abbreviations

%	Percentage
i.e.	That is
μM	Micromolar
μl	Microliter
bp	Base pair
DNA	Deoxyribonucleic acid

RNA   Ribonucleic acid
PCR   Polymerase chain reaction
FRET   Fluorescence Resonance Energy Transfer
UK   United Kingdom

Acknowledgement

The authors would like to express their utmost gratitude and appreciation to Director, CSIR-Indian Institute of Integrative Medicine and AcSIR - Academy of Scientific & Innovative Research. We also thank the Department of Science and Technology - India for providing research fellowship to Gifty Sawhney via fellowship code no. DST/INSPIRE Fellowship/2017/IF170212.

References

1. Marshall, E., Will DNA bar codes breathe life into classification? Biologists hope that a simple tag on all forms of life, and even a hand-held reader, will make classification a 21st century science. *Science*, 307, 5712, 1037–1038, 2005.
2. Blaxter, M., Molecular systematics: counting angels with DNA. *Nature*, 421, 6919, 122, 2003.
3. Wilson, E.O., The encyclopedia of life. *Trends Ecol. Evol.*, 18, 2, 77–80, 2003.
4. Tautz, D. *et al.*, DNA points the way ahead in taxonomy. *Nature*, 418, 6897, 479, 2002.
5. Blaxter, M., Elsworth, B., Daub, J., DNA taxonomy of a neglected animal phylum: an unexpected diversity of tardigrades. *Proc. R. Soc. Lond. Ser. B: Biol. Sci.*, 271, suppl_4, S189–S192, 2004.
6. Wyman, S.K., Jansen, R.K., Boore, J.L., Automatic annotation of organellar genomes with DOGMA. *Bioinformatics*, 20, 17, 3252–3255, 2004.
7. Leebens-Mack, J. *et al.*, Identifying the basal angiosperm node in chloroplast genome phylogenies: sampling one's way out of the Felsenstein zone. *Mol. Biol. Evol.*, 22, 10, 1948–1963, 2005.
8. Jansen, R.K. *et al.*, Phylogenetic analyses of Vitis (Vitaceae) based on complete chloroplast genome sequences: effects of taxon sampling and phylogenetic methods on resolving relationships among rosids. *BMC Evol. Biol.*, 6, 1, 32, 2006.
9. Hansen, A.K. *et al.*, Phylogenetic relationships and chromosome number evolution in Passiflora. *Syst. Bot.*, 31, 1, 138–150, 2006.

10. Floyd, R. *et al.*, Molecular barcodes for soil nematode identification. *Mol. Ecol.*, 11, 4, 839–850, 2002.

11. Schander, C. and Willassen, E., What can biological barcoding do for marine biology? *Mar. Biol. Res.*, 1, 1, 79–83, 2005.

12. Mason, B., Marine survey sees net gain in number of fish species. *Nature*, 425, 6961, 889–890, 2003, http://nopr.niscair.res.in/handle/123456789/13509.

13. Ward, R.D. *et al.*, DNA barcoding Australia's fish species. *Philos. Trans. R. Soc. B: Biol. Sci.*, 360, 1462, 1847–1857, 2005.

14. Monaghan, M.T. *et al.*, DNA-based species delineation in tropical beetles using mitochondrial and nuclear markers. *Philos. Trans. R. Soc. B: Biol. Sci.*, 360, 1462, 1925–1933, 2005.

15. Jansen, R.K. *et al.*, Analysis of 81 genes from 64 plastid genomes resolves relationships in angiosperms and identifies genome-scale evolutionary patterns. *Proc. Natl. Acad. Sci.*, 104, 49, 19369–19374, 2007.

16. Besansky, N.J., Severson, D.W., Ferdig, M.T., DNA barcoding of parasites and invertebrate disease vectors: what you don't know can hurt you. *Trends Parasitol.*, 19, 12, 545–546, 2003.

17. Lorenz, J.G. *et al.*, The problems and promise of DNA barcodes for species diagnosis of primate biomaterials. *Philos. Trans. R. Soc. B: Biol. Sci.*, 360, 1462, 1869–1877, 2005.

18. Armstrong, K. and Ball, S., DNA barcodes for biosecurity: invasive species identification. *Philos. Trans. R. Soc. B: Biol. Sci.*, 360, 1462, 1813–1823, 2005.

19. Mallet, J. and Willmott, K., Taxonomy: renaissance or Tower of Babel? *Trends Ecol. Evol.*, 18, 2, 57–59, 2003.

20. Lipscomb, D., Platnick, N., Wheeler, Q., The intellectual content of taxonomy: a comment on DNA taxonomy. *Trends Ecol. Evol.*, 18, 2, 65–66, 2003.

21. Seberg, O. *et al.*, Shortcuts in systematics? A commentary on DNA-based taxonomy. *Trends Ecol. Evol.*, 18, 2, 63–65, 2003.

22. Dasmahapatra, K.K. and Mallet, J., DNA barcodes: Recent successes and future prospects. *Heredity*, 97, 4, 254–255, 2006.

23. Hebert, P.D. *et al.*, Biological identifications through DNA barcodes. *Proc. R. Soc. Lond. Ser. B: Biol. Sci.*, 270, 1512, 313–321, 2003.

24. Kress, W.J. *et al.*, Use of DNA barcodes to identify flowering plants. *Proc. Natl. Acad. Sci.*, 102, 23, 8369–8374, 2005.

25. Fazekas, A.J. *et al.*, Are plant species inherently harder to discriminate than animal species using DNA barcoding markers? *Mol. Ecol. Resour.*, 9, 130–139, 2009.

26. Pennisi, E., Taxonomy. Wanted: A barcode for plants. *Science*, 318, 5848, 190–191, 2007.

27. Ledford, H., Botanical identities. *Nature*, 451, 7179, 616, 2008.

28. Lágler, R. *et al.*, Molecular diversity of common millet (P. miliaceum) compared to archaeological samples excavated from the 4th and 15th centuries. *Hung. Agric. Res.*, 1, 14–19, 2006.

29. Chase, M.W. *et al.*, A proposal for a standardised protocol to barcode all land plants. *Taxon*, 56, 2, 295–299, 2007.
30. Newmaster, S. *et al.*, Testing candidate plant barcode regions in the Myristicaceae. *Mol. Ecol. Resour.*, 8, 3, 480–490, 2008.
31. Steven, G.N. and Subramanyam, R., Testing plant barcoding in a sister species complex of pantropical Acacia (Mimosoideae, Fabaceae). *Mol. Ecol. Resour.*, 9, 172–180, 2009.
32. Techen, N. *et al.*, DNA barcoding of medicinal plant material for identification. *Curr. Opin. Biotechnol.*, 25, 103–110, 2014.
33. Stoeckle, M., Taxonomy, DNA, and the bar code of life. *BioScience*, 53, 9, 796–797, 2003.
34. Hebert, P.D. and Barrett, R.D., Reply to the comment by L. Prendini on "Identifying spiders through DNA barcodes". *Can. J. Zool.*, 83, 3, 505–506, 2005.
35. Tautz, D. *et al.*, A plea for DNA taxonomy. *Trends Ecol. Evol.*, 18, 2, 70–74, 2003.
36. Moritz, C. and Cicero, C., DNA barcoding: promise and pitfalls. *PLoS Biol.*, 2, 10, e354, 2004.
37. Hebert, P.D. *et al.*, Identification of birds through DNA barcodes. *PloS Biol.*, 2, 10, e312, 2004.
38. Will, K.W. and Rubinoff, D., Myth of the molecule: DNA barcodes for species cannot replace morphology for identification and classification. *Cladistics*, 20, 1, 47–55, 2004.
39. Margulies, M. *et al.*, Genome sequencing in microfabricated high-density picolitre reactors. *Nature*, 437, 7057, 376, 2005.
40. Savolainen, V. *et al.*, Toward writing the encyclopaedia of life: an introduction to DNA barcoding. *Philos. Trans. R. Soc. B: Biol. Sci.*, 360, 1462, 1805–1811, 2005.
41. Gregory, T.R., DNA barcoding does not compete with taxonomy. *Nature*, 434, 7037, 1067–1067, 2005.
42. Hebert, P.D. and Gregory, T.R., The promise of DNA barcoding for taxonomy. *Syst. Biol.*, 54, 5, 852–859, 2005.
43. Ebach, M.C. and Holdrege, C., DNA barcoding is no substitute for taxonomy. *Nature*, 434, 7034, 697, 2005.
44. Will, K.W., Mishler, B.D., Wheeler, Q.D., The perils of DNA barcoding and the need for integrative taxonomy. *Syst. Biol.*, 54, 5, 844–851, 2005.
45. Metzker, M.L., Emerging technologies in DNA sequencing. *Genome Res.*, 15, 12, 1767–1776, 2005.
46. Hajibabaei, M. *et al.*, Critical factors for assembling a high volume of DNA barcodes. *Philos. Trans. R. Soc. B: Biol. Sci.*, 360, 1462, 1959–1967, 2005.
47. Meyer, C.P. and Paulay, G., DNA barcoding: error rates based on comprehensive sampling. *PloS Biol.*, 3, 12, e422, 2005.
48. Ansorge, W.J., Next-generation DNA sequencing techniques. *New Biotechnol.*, 25, 4, 195–203, 2009.

49. Cameron, S., Rubinoff, D., Will, K., Who will actually use DNA barcoding and what will it cost? *Syst. Biol.*, 55, 5, 844–847, 2006.

50. Elias, M. *et al.*, Limited performance of DNA barcoding in a diverse community of tropical butterflies. *Proc. R. Soc. B: Biol. Sci.*, 274, 1627, 2881–2889, 2007.

51. Mardis, E.R., The impact of next-generation sequencing technology on genetics. *Trends Genet.*, 24, 3, 133–141, 2008.

52. Valentini, A., Pompanon, F., Taberlet, P., DNA barcoding for ecologists. *Trends Ecol. Evol.*, 24, 2, 110–117, 2009.

53. Casiraghi, M. *et al.*, DNA barcoding: a six-question tour to improve users' awareness about the method. *Briefings Bioinf.*, 11, 4, 440–453, 2010.

54. Li, H. and Homer, N., A survey of sequence alignment algorithms for next-generation sequencing. *Briefings Bioinf.*, 11, 5, 473–483, 2010.

55. Shokralla, S. *et al.*, Pyrosequencing for mini-barcoding of fresh and old museum specimens. *PloS One*, 6, 7, e21252, 2011.

56. De Groot, G.A. *et al.*, Use of rbcL and trnL-F as a two-locus DNA barcode for identification of NW-European ferns: an ecological perspective. *PloS One*, 6, 1, e16371, 2011.

57. Hajibabaei, M. *et al.*, Environmental barcoding: a next-generation sequencing approach for biomonitoring applications using river benthos. *PLoS One*, 6, 4, e17497, 2011.

58. Kahn, S.D., On the future of genomic data. *Science*, 331, 6018, 728–729, 2011.

59. Taylor, H. and Harris, W., An emergent science on the brink of irrelevance: a review of the past 8 years of DNA barcoding. *Mol. Ecol. Resour.*, 12, 3, 377–388, 2012.

60. Shokralla, S. *et al.*, Next-generation sequencing technologies for environmental DNA research. *Mol. Ecol.*, 21, 8, 1794–1805, 2012.

61. Taberlet, P. *et al.*, Environmental DNA. *Mol. Ecol.*, 21, 8, 1789–1793, 2012.

62. Sabatier, P. *et al.*, 6-kyr record of flood frequency and intensity in the western Mediterranean Alps–Interplay of solar and temperature forcing. *Quat. Sci. Rev.*, 170, 121–135, 2017.

63. Hajibabaei, M., The golden age of DNA metasystematics. *Trends Genet.*, 28, 11, 535–537, 2012.

64. Callaway, E., A bloody boon for conservation. *Nat. News*, 484, 7395, 424, 2012.

65. Yoccoz, N.G., The future of environmental DNA in ecology. *Mol. Ecol.*, 21, 8, 2031–2038, 2012.

66. Bienert, F. *et al.*, Tracking earthworm communities from soil DNA. *Mol. Ecol.*, 21, 8, 2017–2030, 2012.

67. Dejean, T. *et al.*, Persistence of environmental DNA in freshwater ecosystems. *PloS One*, 6, 8, e23398, 2011.

68. Coissac, E., Riaz, T., Puillandre, N., Bioinformatic challenges for DNA metabarcoding of plants and animals. *Mol. Ecol.*, 21, 8, 1834–1847, 2012.

69. Puillandre, N. *et al.*, ABGD, Automatic Barcode Gap Discovery for primary species delimitation. *Mol. Ecol.*, 21, 8, 1864–1877, 2012.

70. Laiou, A. *et al.*, DNA barcoding as a complementary tool for conservation and valorisation of forest resources. *ZooKeys*, 365, 197–213, 2013.

71. Gere, J. *et al.*, Incorporating trnH-psbA to the core DNA barcodes improves significantly species discrimination within southern African Combretaceae. *ZooKeys*, 365, 129–147, 2013.

72. Little, D.P., A DNA mini-barcode for land plants. *Mol. Ecol. Resour.*, 14, 3, 437–446, 2014.

73. Kõljalg, U. *et al.*, Toward a unified paradigm for sequence-based identification of fungi. *Mol. Ecol.*, 22, 21, 5271–5277, 2013.

74. Gao, R. and Zhang, G., Potential of DNA barcoding for detecting quarantine fungi. *Phytopathology*, 103, 11, 1103–1107, 2013.

75. Bhargava, M. and Sharma, A., DNA barcoding in plants: evolution and applications of in silico approaches and resources. *Mol. Phylogenet. Evol.*, 67, 3, 631–641, 2013.

76. Han, J. *et al.*, The short ITS2 sequence serves as an efficient taxonomic sequence tag in comparison with the full-length ITS. *BioMed Res. Int.*, 2013, 741476, 2013.

77. Shen, Y.-Y., Chen, X., Murphy, R.W., Assessing DNA barcoding as a tool for species identification and data quality control. *PloS One*, 8, 2, e57125, 2013.

78. Collins, R. and Cruickshank, R., The seven deadly sins of DNA barcoding. *Mol. Ecol. Resour.*, 13, 6, 969–975, 2013.

79. Pang, X. *et al.*, Use of the potential DNA barcode ITS2 to identify herbal materials. *J. Nat. Med.*, 67, 3, 571–575, 2013.

80. Pečnikar, Ž.F. and Buzan, E.V., 20 years since the introduction of DNA barcoding: from theory to application. *J. Appl. Genet.*, 55, 1, 43–52, 2014.

81. Joly, S. *et al.*, Ecology in the age of DNA barcoding: the resource, the promise and the challenges ahead. *Mol. Ecol. Resour.*, 14, 2, 221–232, 2014.

82. Swynghedauw, B., Nothing in medicine makes sense except in the light of evolution: A review. *Evolutionary biology from concept to application*, pp. 197–207, Springer-Verlag Berlin Heidelberg, 2008.

83. Soltis, E.D. and Soltis, P.S., Contributions of plant molecular systematics to studies of molecular evolution. *Plant Mol. Biol.*, 42, 1, 45–75, 2000.

84. Ma, J. and Bennetzen, J.L., Rapid recent growth and divergence of rice nuclear genomes. *Proc. Natl. Acad. Sci.*, 101, 34, 12404–12410, 2004.

85. Gaut, B.S. *et al.*, Substitution rate comparisons between grasses and palms: synonymous rate differences at the nuclear gene Adh parallel rate differences at the plastid gene rbcL. *Proc. Natl. Acad. Sci.*, 93, 19, 10274–10279, 1996.

86. Koch, M.A., Haubold, B., Mitchell-Olds, T., Comparative evolutionary analysis of chalcone synthase and alcohol dehydrogenase loci in Arabidopsis, Arabis, and related genera (Brassicaceae). *Mol. Biol. Evol.*, 17, 10, 1483–1498, 2000.

87. Hamby, R.K. and Zimmer, E.A., Ribosomal RNA as a phylogenetic tool in plant systematics. *Molecular systematics of plants*, pp. 50–91, Springer, Boston, MA, 1992.

88. Avise, J. and Markers, M., *Natural history and evolution*, Chapman & Hall, New York, 1994.

89. Hillis, D.M., Huelsenbeck, J.P., Swofford, D.L., Hobgoblin of phylogenetics? *Nature*, 369, 6479, 363–364, 1994.

90. Martins, L. and Hellwig, F.H., Systematic position of the genera Serratula and Klasea within Centaureinae (Cardueae, Asteraceae) inferred from ETS and ITS sequence data and new combinations in Klasea. *Taxon*, 54, 3, 632–638, 2005.

91. Mitchell, A. and Wen, J., Phylogeny of Brassaiopsis (Araliaceae) in Asia based on nuclear ITS and 5S-NTS DNA sequences. *Syst. Bot.*, 30, 4, 872–886, 2005.

92. Hall, T.A., BioEdit: a user-friendly biological sequence alignment editor and analysis program for Windows 95/98/NT, in: *Nucleic acids symposium series*, Information Retrieval Ltd., London, pp. c1979 c2000, 1999.

93. Combet, C. *et al.*, NPS@: network protein sequence analysis. *Trends Biochem. Sci.*, 25, 3, 147–150, 2000.

94. Thompson, J.D. *et al.*, The CLUSTAL_X windows interface: flexible strategies for multiple sequence alignment aided by quality analysis tools. *Nucleic Acids Res.*, 25, 24, 4876–4882, 1997.

95. Kalendar, R. *et al.*, Genome evolution of wild barley (Hordeum spontaneum) by BARE-1 retrotransposon dynamics in response to sharp microclimatic divergence. *Proc. Natl. Acad. Sci.*, 97, 12, 6603–6607, 2000.

96. Altschul, S.F. *et al.*, Gapped BLAST and PSI-BLAST: a new generation of protein database search programs. *Nucleic Acids Res.*, 25, 17, 3389–3402, 1997.

97. Tamura, K. *et al.*, MEGA5: molecular evolutionary genetics analysis using maximum likelihood, evolutionary distance, and maximum parsimony methods. *Mol. Biol. Evol.*, 28, 10, 2731–2739, 2011.

98. Kress, W.J. and Erickson, D.L., DNA barcodes: genes, genomics, and bioinformatics. *Proc. Natl. Acad. Sci.*, 105, 8, 2761–2762, 2008.

99. Chase, M.W. *et al.*, Land plants and DNA barcodes: short-term and long-term goals. *Philos. Trans. R. Soc. B: Biol. Sci.*, 360, 1462, 1889–1895, 2005.

100. Baldwin, B.G., Phylogenetic utility of the internal transcribed spacers of nuclear ribosomal DNA in plants: an example from the Compositae. *Mol. Phylogenet. Evol.*, 1, 1, 3–16, 1992.

101. Baldwin, B.G. *et al.*, Erratum: The ITS region of nuclear ribosomal DNA: A valuable source of evidence on angiosperm phylogeny (Annals of the Missouri Botanical Garden (1995) 82 (247–277)). *Ann. Missouri Bot. Gard.*, 83, 1, 151, 1996.

102. Hershkovitz, M., Ribosomal DNA sequences and angiosperm systematics, in: *Molecular systematics and plant evolution*, 1999.

103. Zimmer, E. *et al.*, Rapid duplication and loss of genes coding for the alpha chains of hemoglobin. *Proc. Natl. Acad. Sci.*, 77, 4, 2158–2162, 1980.

104. White, T.J. *et al.*, Amplification and direct sequencing of fungal ribosomal RNA genes for phylogenetics, in: *PCR protocols: a guide to methods and applications*, vol. 18(1), pp. 315–322, 1990.

105. Nieto Feliner, G., Gutiérrez Larena, B., Fuertes Aguilar, J., Fine-scale geographical structure, intra-individual polymorphism and recombination in nuclear ribosomal internal transcribed spacers in Armeria (Plumbaginaceae). *Ann. Bot.*, 93, 2, 189–200, 2004.

106. Bult, C.J., Sweere, J.A., Zimmer, E.A., Cryptic sequence simplicity, nucleotide composition bias, and molecular coevolution in the large subunit of ribosomal DNA in plants: implications for phylogenetic analyses. *Ann. Missouri Bot. Gard.*, 82, 235–246, 1995.

107. Chandler, G. and Plunkett, G., Evolution in Apiales: nuclear and chloroplast markers together in (almost) perfect harmony. *Bot. J. Linn. Soc.*, 144, 2, 123–147, 2004.

108. Simmons, M.P. *et al.*, Phylogeny of the Celastraceae inferred from 26S nuclear ribosomal DNA, phytochrome B, rbcL, atpB, and morphology. *Mol. Phylogenet. Evol.*, 19, 3, 353–366, 2001.

109. Baldwin, B.G. and Markos, S., Phylogenetic Utility of the External Transcribed Spacer (ETS) of 18S–26S rDNA: Congruence of ETS and ITS Trees of Calycadenia (Compositae). *Mol. Phylogenet. Evol.*, 10, 3, 449–463, 1998.

110. Linder, C.R. *et al.*, The complete external transcribed spacer of 18S-26S rDNA: amplification and phylogenetic utility at low taxonomic levels in Asteraceae and closely allied families. *Mol. Phylogenet. Evol.*, 14, 2, 285–303, 2000.

111. Pandey, A.K. and Ali, M.A., Molecular markers in plant systematics I: nuclear sequences, in: *Plant Sciences Research in India: Challenges and Prospects*, pp. 21–34, Botanical Survey of India, Dehradun, India, 2006.

112. Pandey, A.K. and Ali, M.A., Intraspecific variation in Panax assamicus Ban. populations based on internal transcribed spacer (ITS) sequences of nrDNA, http://nopr.niscair.res.in/handle/123456789/13509, 2012.

113. Elbadri, G.A. *et al.*, Intraspecific variation in Radopholus similis isolates assessed with restriction fragment length polymorphism and DNA sequencing of the internal transcribed spacer region of the ribosomal RNA cistron. *Int. J. Parasitol.*, 32, 2, 199–205, 2002.

114. Tamura, K. *et al.*, MEGA4: molecular evolutionary genetics analysis (MEGA) software version 4.0. *Mol. Biol. Evol.*, 24, 8, 1596–1599, 2007.

115. Gyulai, G. *et al.*, Conservation Genetics: Heat Map Analysis of nuSSRs of aDNA of Archaeological Watermelons (Cucurbitaceae, Citrullus l. lanatus) Compared to Current Varieties. *Genes Genomes Genomics*, 6, 86–96, 2012.

116. Ackerfield, J. and Wen, J., Evolution of Hedera (the ivy genus, Araliaceae): insights from chloroplast DNA data. *Int. J. Plant Sci.*, 164, 4, 593–602, 2003.

117. Alverson, A.J. *et al.*, Insights into the evolution of mitochondrial genome size from complete sequences of Citrullus lanatus and Cucurbita pepo (Cucurbitaceae). *Mol. Biol. Evol.*, 27, 6, 1436–1448, 2010.

118. Soltis, D.E. and Soltis, P.S., Choosing an approach and an appropriate gene for phylogenetic analysis. *Molecular systematics of plants II*, pp. 1–42, Springer, Boston, MA, 1998.

119. Palmer, J.D. *et al.*, Dynamic evolution of plant mitochondrial genomes: mobile genes and introns and highly variable mutation rates. *Proc. Natl. Acad. Sci.*, 97, 13, 6960–6966, 2000.

120. Cho, Y. *et al.*, Mitochondrial substitution rates are extraordinarily elevated and variable in a genus of flowering plants. *Proc. Natl. Acad. Sci.*, 101, 51, 17741–17746, 2004.

121. Demesure, B., Sodzi, N., Petit, R., A set of universal primers for amplification of polymorphic non-coding regions of mitochondrial and chloroplast DNA in plants. *Mol. Ecol.*, 4, 1, 129–134, 1995.

122. Freudenstein, J.V. and Chase, M.W., Analysis of mitochondrial nad1b-c intron sequences in Orchidaceae: utility and coding of length-change characters. *Syst. Bot.*, 643–657, 2001.

123. Vrijenhoek, R., DNA primers for amplification of mitochondrial cytochrome c oxidase subunit I from diverse metazoan invertebrates. *Mol. Marine Biol. Biotechnol.*, 3, 5, 294–9, 1994.

124. Swofford, D., *PAUP*-Phylogenetic Analysis Using Parsimony (* and Other Methods), Version 4.0 b10*, Sinauer Associate, Sunderland, MA, 2002.

125. Felsenstein, J., Confidence limits on phylogenies: an approach using the bootstrap. *Evolution*, 39, 4, 783–791, 1985.

126. Huelsenbeck, J.P. and Ronquist, F., MRBAYES: Bayesian inference of phylogenetic trees. *Bioinformatics*, 17, 8, 754–755, 2001.

127. Zhang, M. *et al.*, An efficient DNA barcoding based method for the authentication and adulteration detection of the powdered natural spices. *Food Control*, 106, 106745, 2019.

128. Bhattacharyya, S.N. and Filipowicz, W., Argonautes and company: sailing against the wind. *Cell*, 128, 6, 1027–1028, 2007.

129. Bartel, D.P., MicroRNAs: target recognition and regulatory functions. *Cell*, 136, 2, 215–233, 2009.

130. Stefani, G. and Slack, F.J., Small non-coding RNAs in animal development. *Nat. Rev. Mol. Cell Biol.*, 9, 3, 219, 2008.

131. Voinnet, O., Origin, biogenesis, and activity of plant microRNAs. *Cell*, 136, 4, 669–687, 2009.

132. Skalsky, R.L. and Cullen, B.R., Viruses, microRNAs, and host interactions. *Annu. Rev. Microbiol.*, 64, 123–141, 2010.

133. Cullen, B.R., Viruses and microRNAs: RISCy interactions with serious consequences. *Genes Dev.*, 25, 18, 1881–1894, 2011.

134. Hébert, S.S. and De Strooper, B., miRNAs in neurodegeneration. *Science*, 317, 5842, 1179–1180, 2007.

135. Ryan, B.M., Robles, A.I., Harris, C.C., Genetic variation in microRNA networks: the implications for cancer research. *Nat. Rev. Cancer*, 10, 6, 389, 2010.
136. Croce, C.M., Causes and consequences of microRNA dysregulation in cancer. *Nat. Rev. Genet.*, 10, 10, 704, 2009.
137. Calin, G.A. and Croce, C.M., MicroRNA signatures in human cancers. *Nat. Rev. Cancer*, 6, 11, 857, 2006.
138. Bissels, U. *et al.*, Absolute quantification of microRNAs by using a universal reference. *RNA*, 15, 12, 2375–2384, 2009.
139. Bissels, U. *et al.*, Combined characterization of microRNA and mRNA profiles delineates early differentiation pathways of CD133+ and CD34+ hematopoietic stem and progenitor cells. *Stem Cells*, 29, 5, 847–857, 2011.
140. Barad, O. *et al.*, MicroRNA expression detected by oligonucleotide microarrays: system establishment and expression profiling in human tissues. *Genome Res.*, 14, 12, 2486–2494, 2004.
141. Nelson, P.T. *et al.*, Microarray-based, high-throughput gene expression profiling of microRNAs. *Nat. Methods*, 1, 2, 155, 2004.
142. Baskerville, S. and Bartel, D.P., Microarray profiling of microRNAs reveals frequent coexpression with neighboring miRNAs and host genes. *RNA*, 11, 3, 241–247, 2005.
143. Fiedler, S.D., Carletti, M.Z., Christenson, L.K., Quantitative RT-PCR methods for mature microRNA expression analysis. *RT-PCR Protocols*, pp. 49–64, Humana Press, Totowa, NJ, 2010.
144. Griffiths-Jones, S. *et al.*, miRBase: tools for microRNA genomics. *Nucleic Acids Res.*, 36, suppl_1, D154–D158, 2007.
145. Kozomara, A. and Griffiths-Jones, S., miRBase: annotating high confidence microRNAs using deep sequencing data. *Nucleic Acids Res.*, 42, D1, D68–D73, 2013.
146. Aravin, A.A. *et al.*, The small RNA profile during Drosophila melanogaster development. *Dev. Cell*, 5, 2, 337–350, 2003.
147. Chen, P.Y. *et al.*, The developmental miRNA profiles of zebrafish as determined by small RNA cloning. *Genes Dev.*, 19, 11, 1288–1293, 2005.
148. Aravin, A. *et al.*, A novel class of small RNAs bind to MILI protein in mouse testes. *Nature*, 442, 7099, 203, 2006.
149. Lau, N.C. *et al.*, Characterization of the piRNA complex from rat testes. *Science*, 313, 5785, 363–367, 2006.
150. Saito, K. *et al.*, Pimet, the Drosophila homolog of HEN1, mediates 2′-O-methylation of Piwi-interacting RNAs at their 3′ ends. *Genes Dev.*, 21, 13, 1603–1608, 2007.
151. Carmell, M.A. *et al.*, MIWI2 is essential for spermatogenesis and repression of transposons in the mouse male germline. *Dev. Cell*, 12, 4, 503–514, 2007.
152. Chiang, H.R. *et al.*, Mammalian microRNAs: experimental evaluation of novel and previously annotated genes. *Genes Dev.*, 24, 10, 992–1009, 2010.

153. Friedländer, M.R. *et al.*, Discovering microRNAs from deep sequencing data using miRDeep. *Nat. Biotechnol.*, 26, 4, 407, 2008.
154. Landgraf, P. *et al.*, A mammalian microRNA expression atlas based on small RNA library sequencing. *Cell*, 129, 7, 1401–1414, 2007.
155. Farazi, T.A. *et al.*, MicroRNA sequence and expression analysis in breast tumors by deep sequencing. *Cancer Res.*, 71, 13, 4443–4453, 2011.
156. Hafner, M. *et al.*, Transcriptome-wide identification of RNA-binding protein and microRNA target sites by PAR-CLIP. *Cell*, 141, 1, 129–141, 2010.
157. Ugras, S. *et al.*, Small RNA sequencing and functional characterization reveals MicroRNA-143 tumor suppressor activity in liposarcoma. *Cancer Res.*, 71, 17, 5659–5669, 2011.
158. Hafner, M. *et al.*, RNA-ligase-dependent biases in miRNA representation in deep-sequenced small RNA cDNA libraries. *RNA*, 17, 9, 1697–1712, 2011.
159. Xu, Q. *et al.*, Design of 240,000 orthogonal 25mer DNA barcode probes. *Proc. Natl. Acad. Sci.*, 106, 7, 2289–2294, 2009.
160. Parameswaran, P. *et al.*, A pyrosequencing-tailored nucleotide barcode design unveils opportunities for large-scale sample multiplexing. *Nucleic Acids Res.*, 35, 19, e130, 2007.
161. Schulte, J.H. *et al.*, Deep sequencing reveals differential expression of micro-RNAs in favorable versus unfavorable neuroblastoma. *Nucleic Acids Res.*, 38, 17, 5919–5928, 2010.
162. Hamady, M. *et al.*, Error-correcting barcoded primers for pyrosequencing hundreds of samples in multiplex. *Nat. Methods*, 5, 3, 235, 2008.
163. Vigneault, F., Sismour, A.M., Church, G.M., Efficient microRNA capture and bar-coding via enzymatic oligonucleotide adenylation. *Nat. Methods*, 5, 9, 777, 2008.
164. Berninger, P. *et al.*, Computational analysis of small RNA cloning data. *Methods*, 44, 1, 13–21, 2008.
165. Kennedy, A. *et al.*, Internal states and behavioral decision-making: toward an integration of emotion and cognition, in: *Cold Spring Harbor symposia on quantitative biology*, Cold Spring Harbor Laboratory Press, 2014.
166. Sternson, S.M., Hypothalamic survival circuits: blueprints for purposive behaviors. *Neuron*, 77, 5, 810–824, 2013.
167. Glickfeld, L.L. *et al.*, Cortico-cortical projections in mouse visual cortex are functionally target specific. *Nat. Neurosci.*, 16, 2, 219, 2013.
168. Movshon, J.A. and Newsome, W.T., Visual response properties of striate cortical neurons projecting to area MT in macaque monkeys. *J. Neurosci.*, 16, 23, 7733–7741, 1996.
169. Oh, S.W. *et al.*, A mesoscale connectome of the mouse brain. *Nature*, 508, 7495, 207, 2014.
170. Zingg, B. *et al.*, Neural networks of the mouse neocortex. *Cell*, 156, 5, 1096–1111, 2014.

171. Gong, S. *et al.*, Targeting Cre recombinase to specific neuron populations with bacterial artificial chromosome constructs. *J. Neurosci.*, 27, 37, 9817–9823, 2007.

172. Harris, J.A. *et al.*, Anatomical characterization of Cre driver mice for neural circuit mapping and manipulation. *Front. Neural Circuits*, 8, 76, 2014.

173. Kim, J. *et al.*, mGRASP enables mapping mammalian synaptic connectivity with light microscopy. *Nat. Methods*, 9, 1, 96, 2012.

174. Daigle, N. and Ellenberg, J., λ N-GFP: an RNA reporter system for live-cell imaging. *Nat. Methods*, 4, 8, 633, 2007.

175. Ehrengruber, M.U., Alphaviral gene transfer in neurobiology. *Brain Res. Bull.*, 59, 1, 13–22, 2002.

176. Berezikov, E. *et al.*, Mammalian mirtron genes. *Mol. Cell*, 28, 2, 328–336, 2007.

177. Okamura, K. *et al.*, The mirtron pathway generates microRNA-class regulatory RNAs in Drosophila. *Cell*, 130, 1, 89–100, 2007.

178. Savolainen, V. and Reeves, G., A plea for DNA banking. *Science*, 304, 5676, 1445–1445, 2004.

179. Blaxter, M. *et al.*, Defining operational taxonomic units using DNA barcode data. *Philos. Trans. R. Soc. B: Biol. Sci.*, 360, 1462, 1935–1943, 2005.

180. De Ley, P. *et al.*, An integrated approach to fast and informative morphological vouchering of nematodes for applications in molecular barcoding. *Philos. Trans. R. Soc. B: Biol. Sci.*, 360, 1462, 1945–1958, 2005.

181. Maxam, A.M. and Gilbert, W., A new method for sequencing DNA. *Proc. Natl. Acad. Sci.*, 74, 2, 560–564, 1977.

182. Sanger, F., DNA sequencing with chain-terminating inhibitors. *Proc. Natl. Acad. Sci. U.S.A.*, 80, 2432–2436, 1983.

183. Mardis, E.R., Next-generation DNA sequencing methods. *Annu. Rev. Genomics Hum. Genet.*, 9, 387–402, 2008.

184. Bergallo, M. *et al.*, Evaluation of six methods for extraction and purification of viral DNA from urine and serum samples. *New Microbiol.*, 29, 2, 111–119, 2006.

185. Bickle, T.A. and Krüger, D., Biology of DNA restriction. *Microbiol. Mol. Biol. Rev.*, 57, 2, 434–450, 1993.

186. Biss, M., Hanna, M.D., Xiao, W., Isolation of yeast nucleic acids. *Yeast Protocols*, pp. 15–21, Humana Press, New York, NY, 2014.

187. Alberts, B. *et al.*, *Molecular Biology of the Cell*, Sixth edit., Garland Science, Taylor & Francis Group, LLC, New York, 2015.

188. Bishop, R., Applications of fluorescence *in situ* hybridization (FISH) in detecting genetic aberrations of medical significance. *Biosci. Horiz.*, 3, 1, 85–95, 2010.

189. Anguiano, A. *et al.*, Spectral Karyotyping for identification of constitutional chromosomal abnormalities at a national reference laboratory. *Mol. Cytogenet.*, 5, 1, 3, 2012.

190. Boyd, S.D., Diagnostic applications of high-throughput DNA sequencing. *Annu. Rev. Pathol.: Mech. Dis.*, 8, 381–410, 2013.

191. Boyer, H.W., DNA restriction and modification mechanisms in bacteria. *Annu. Rev. Microbiol.*, 25, 1, 153–176, 1971.

192. Kunkel, T.A., The mutational specificity of DNA polymerase-beta during *in vitro* DNA synthesis. Production of frameshift, base substitution, and deletion mutations. *J. Biol. Chem.*, 260, 9, 5787–5796, 1985.

193. Bridge, J.A., Advantages and limitations of cytogenetic, molecular cytogenetic, and molecular diagnostic testing in mesenchymal neoplasms. *J. Orthop. Sci.*, 13, 3, 273, 2008.

194. Brown, T.A., *Gene cloning and DNA analysis: An introduction*, 432pp., John Wiley & Sons, 2020.

195. Bustin, S., INVITED REVIEW Quantification of mRNA using real-time reverse transcription PCR (RT-PCR): trends and problems. *J. Mol. Endocrinol.*, 29, 23–39, 2002.

196. Bustin, S.A., Absolute quantification of mRNA using real-time reverse transcription polymerase chain reaction assays. *J. Mol. Endocrinol.*, 25, 2, 169–193, 2000.

197. Aho, K.A., *Foundational and applied statistics for biologists using R*, 618pp., CRC Press, 2013.

198. Catalina, P. *et al.*, Conventional and molecular cytogenetic diagnostic methods in stem cell research: a concise review. *Cell Biol. Int.*, 31, 9, 861–869, 2007.

199. Capuano, F. *et al.*, Cytosine DNA methylation is found in Drosophila melanogaster but absent in Saccharomyces cerevisiae, Schizosaccharomyces pombe, and other yeast species. *Anal. Chem.*, 86, 8, 3697–3702, 2014.

200. Tüzmen, Ş. *et al.*, Techniques for nucleic acid engineering: The foundation of gene manipulation. *Omics Technologies and Bio-Engineering*, pp. 247–315, Academic Press, England, 2018.

201. Clarke, G.M. and Higgins, T.N., Laboratory investigation of hemoglobinopathies and thalassemias: review and update. *Clin. Chem.*, 46, 8, 1284–1290, 2000.

202. Chuang, L.-Y. *et al.*, Restriction enzyme mining for SNPs in genomes. *Anticancer Res.*, 28, 4A, 2001–2007, 2008.

203. Dahm, R., Friedrich Miescher and the discovery of DNA. *Dev. Biol.*, 278, 2, 274–288, 2005.

204. Dahm, R. and Discovering, D.N.A., Friedrich Miescher and the early years of nucleic acid research. *Hum. Genet.*, 122, 6, 565–581, 2008.

205. Braman, J. (ed.), *In vitro mutagenesis protocols*. Vol. 634, pp. 421–430, Humana Press, Totowa, NJ, 2010.

206. Burden, D.W., Guide to the disruption of biological samples-2012. *Random Primers*, 12, 1, 1–25, 2012.

207. Harvey, D., *Modern analytical chemistry*, McGraw-Hill Companies, Inc, Boston, 2000.

208. Downie, S.E., Flaherty, S.P., Matthews, C.D., Detection of chromosomes and estimation of aneuploidy in human spermatozoa using fluorescence *in-situ* hybridization. *Mol. Hum. Reprod.*, 3, 7, 585–598, 1997.

209. Dryden, D., Murray, N.E., Rao, D., Nucleoside triphosphate-dependent restriction enzymes. *Nucleic Acids Res.*, 29, 18, 3728–3741, 2001.

210. Dussoix, D. and Arber, W., Host specificity of DNA produced by Escherichia coli: II. Control over acceptance of DNA from infecting phage λ. *J. Mol. Biol.*, 5, 1, 37–49, 1962.

211. Edwards, J. *et al.*, A new trisomic syndrome. *Lancet*, 275, 7128, 787–790, 1960.

212. Eyler, E., Explanatory chapter: nuclease protection assays. *Methods Enzymol.*, 530, 89–97, 2013.

213. Henning, F., Trifonov, V., Almeida-Toledo, L.F.d., Use of chromosome micro-dissection in fish molecular cytogenetics. *Genet. Mol. Biol.*, 31, 1, 279–283, 2008.

214. Ford, C.E. *et al.*, A sex-chromosome anomaly in a case of gonadal dysgenesis (Turner's syndrome). *Lancet*, 273, 711–713, 1959.

215. Freeman, W.M., Walker, S.J., Vrana, K.E., Quantitative RT-PCR: pitfalls and potential. *Biotechniques*, 26, 1, 112–125, 1999.

216. Frenzilli, G., Nigro, M., Lyons, B., The Comet assay for the evaluation of genotoxic impact in aquatic environments. *Mutat. Res./Rev. Mutat. Res.*, 681, 1, 80–92, 2009.

217. Galas, D.J. and Schmitz, A., DNAase footprinting a simple method for the detection of protein-DNA binding specificity. *Nucleic Acids Res.*, 5, 9, 3157–3170, 1978.

218. Goodsell, D.S., The molecular perspective: restriction endonucleases. *Oncologist*, 7, 1, 82–83, 2002.

219. Geerlof, A., *Cloning using restriction enzymes*, pp. 06–07, European Molecular Biology Laboratory, Hamburg, Retrieved, 2008.

220. Gualandi-Signorini, A. and Giorgi, G., Insulin formulations-a review. *Eur. Rev. Med. Pharmacol. Sci.*, 5, 73–84, 2001.

221. Hampshire, A.J. *et al.*, Footprinting: a method for determining the sequence selectivity, affinity and kinetics of DNA-binding ligands. *Methods*, 42, 2, 128–140, 2007.

222. Heckman, K.L. and Pease, L.R., Gene splicing and mutagenesis by PCR-driven overlap extension. *Nat. Protoc.*, 2, 4, 924, 2007.

223. Henderson, A., Warburton, D., Atwood, K., Location of ribosomal DNA in the human chromosome complement. *Proc. Natl. Acad. Sci.*, 69, 11, 3394–3398, 1972.

224. Adams, M., Activists, T., Council, A., Clinton, B., Initiative, B.H., Gene transfer in nature and traditional agriculture, http://www.truthwiki.org/genetically_modified_crops/.

225. Houldsworth, J. and Chaganti, R., Comparative genomic hybridization: an overview. *Am. J. Pathol.*, 145, 6, 1253, 1994.
226. HSU, T.-C., Mammalian chromosomes *in vitro*: I. The karyotype of man. *J. Hered.*, 43, 4, 167–172, 1952.
227. Huggett, J.F. *et al.*, The digital MIQE guidelines: minimum information for publication of quantitative digital PCR experiments. *Clin. Chem.*, 59, 6, 892–902, 2013.
228. Hughes, A., Some effects of abnormal tonicity on dividing cells in chick tissue cultures. *J. Cell Sci.*, 3, 22, 207–219, 1952.
229. Motulsky, A.G., History of Human Genetics. In: Speicher, M.R., Motulsky, A.G., Antonarakis, S.E. (eds), *Vogel and Motulsky's Human Genetics*. Springer, Berlin, Heidelberg, 2010. https://doi.org/10.1007/978-3-540-37654-5_2.
230. Dickerson, R.E., DNA Structure From A to Z. *Methods in Enzymology*, vol. 211, pp. 67–111. Elsevier Science Direct, 1992.
231. Ris, H., Chromosomes and genes - Fine structure of chromosomes. *Proc. R. Soc. Lond. B.*, 164, 246–257, 1966B.
232. Mattick, J., RNA regulation: a new genetics? *Nat Rev Genet.*, 5, 316–323, 2004.
233. Baumgarte, S. *et al.*, Prevalence, types, and RNA concentrations of human parechoviruses, including a sixth parechovirus type, in stool samples from patients with acute enteritis. *J. Clin. Microbiol.*, 46, 1, 242–248, 2008.
234. Grosjean, H., *DNA and RNA modification enzymes: structure, mechanism, function and evolution*. CRC Press, 2009.
235. Chen, T. *et al.*, The expanding world of DNA and RNA. *Curr. Opin. Chem. Biol.*, 34, 80–87, 2016.
236. Ali, M.A. *et al.*, The changing epitome of species identification–DNA barcoding. *Saudi J. Biol. Sci.*, 21, 3, 204–231, 2014.
237. Kang, W., Eldfjell, Y., Fromm, B. *et al.*, miRTrace reveals the organismal origins of microRNA sequencing data. *Genome Biol.*, 19, 213, 2018. https://doi.org/10.1186/s13059-018-1588-9.

11

Bioinformatics in Cancer Detection

**Mohit Sharma[1,2], Umme Abiha[3], Parul Chugh[3],
Balakumar Chandrasekaran[4] and Nikhil Agrawal[5]***

*[1]Post Graduate School of Molecular Medicine, Medical University of Warsaw,
Warsaw, Poland*
[2]Malopolska Centre of Biotechnology, Jagiellonian University, Krakow, Poland
[3]Amity Institute of Biotechnology, Noida, India
[4]Faculty of Pharmacy, Philadelphia University-Jordan, Amman, Jordan
*[5]College of Health Sciences, University of KwaZulu-Natal, Westville,
Durban, South Africa*

Abstract

The uncontrolled growth of abnormal cells is generally determined by the alterations in genes and epigenetic factors. Oncological research is undergoing a drastic revolution due to advanced technology improvement in the verge of exploring the relationship of molecules which make a unit cell of an organism. Molecular biologists are more aware about the genomic, transcriptomic, and proteomic data because of the obvious technology advancement in the area of molecular medicine. This has further lead to the development of novel potential targets for drug development and also establishment of molecular markers for unified treatment and therapy against cancer. Numerous cancer studies have been carried out using altered protocols, samples, and data from multiple sources in order to compare and validate new strategies with the conventional ones. Moreover, it also opens a wide arena to develop personalized or stratified medicine to counter medicinal upheaval. Bioinformatics helps to develop new methods and advancing trends in order to attain the ultimate goal of developing therapeutics and diagnostic protocols in the area of cancer research.

In this chapter, we will discuss about the contributions, applications, and importance of bioinformatics in cancer research.

*Corresponding author: nikhil.08oct@gmail.com

S. Balamurugan, Anand Krishnan, Dinesh Goyal, Balakumar Chandrasekaran and Boomi Pandi (eds.)
Computation in Bioinformatics: Multidisciplinary Applications, (229–244) © 2021 Scrivener Publishing LLC

Keywords: Cancer, bioinformatics, epigenetic factors

11.1   Introduction

Cancer is the most deadly and devastating disease, prevalence of which has claimed millions of lives worldwide. Despite advanced research and technologies that have evolved in the area of clinical diagnosis and precision medicine, cancer still remains a dreaded disease with serious health implications. This disease can either be a cause of genetic or epigenetic factors or even both. WHO reports the burden of cancer to be claiming 9.6 million lives in an estimated annual statistics record of 2018. It has been reported to be a cause of death among 1 in 6 deceased worldwide and remains an immense medical challenge [1]. Various genetic alterations and molecular aberrations aggravate cancer into a progressive disease; therefore, the best possible therapeutic intervention must target the alterations and abnormalities to evade the proliferative growth. Genetic abnormalities such as mutation, translocation, deletion, replication, and even post-translational modifications often lead to different types of cancer. Therefore, before inducing or initiating a therapy to any cancer patient, the etiological origin should be known and the exact aberrations and alteration patterns of a particular type of cancer should be confirmed. Testing through drug sensitivity, cancer bioinformatics and pharmacogenetics are major parts of PCT that are designed to unravel the genetic alterations and molecular abnormality information and select optimal anticancer drugs [2].

Use of advanced computing technology and mathematical approach to store, manage, and analyze data is one the foremost ground on which bioinformatics take a stakehold in the field of P-4 medicine. The biggest hindrance that cancer researchers faces is the lack of infrastructure to store and analyze biological data, but with the use of virtual repositories, this has improved the problem as it is readily available in the public domain from all institutions [3].

11.2   The Era of Bioinformatics in Cancer

The field of bioinformatics in the area of cancer prevention and treatment has swiftly progressed over the past many years. Since the onset of its initial implementation, epigenetic studies are now possible due to the advancement of high throughput techniques like next-generation sequencing, ChiP-ChiP, ChiP-Seq, and high-density microarrays for miRNA profiling to detect the dysregulation of tumor suppressor genes. This has further altered our understanding of cancer biology, leading to progressively competitive approaches to investigate additional and advanced datasets [4]. Bioinformatic pipelines work in conjunction of predicting a massive influence of genetic aberrations and quantifying changes of the tumor microenvironment. Extensive research has led to the development of new tools that analyze tumor-immune microenvironment and its interactions to assess tumor infiltrating leukocyte content, microsatellite instability, total alteration burden, and neoantigen presentation [5]. The enormous growth of information and technology in the area of genomics and omics is flabbergasting, as massive amounts of data is being generated with sequencing and microarray chips to integrate omics-based analysis. Furthermore, this has accelerated machine learning and integrated network–based approaches on multiple platforms to investigate assorted data within the reach of public accessible resources, like the cancer order atlas [6].

Annotating molecular and genetic aberrations as infiltrating cell states in various ideal sequencing conditions and application specific approaches are on improving verges to establish strong analysis techniques and measuring gene expression. This ability provides a scientific research to elucidate the mechanism that holds the process of genetic expression and its upheaval. These techniques that vary from improved quantification of copy variety and organic phenomenon from formal mounted tissues as applications that need high sensitivity like the quantification of tumor mutations from liquid biopsies (circulating cell free DNA) [7]. As a rigorous need to develop an efficient knowledge of understanding the constraints of processing approaches along with novel techniques to improve the flexibility of distribution and molecular impact of genes like repetitive or permutable endogenous parts, an increasing scope is felt to build well-annotated databases of simply accessible information in multi-variable

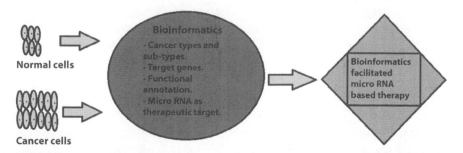

Figure 11.1 Role of bioinformatics in cancer detection.

analysis pipelines. With the advancement and isolation of SIGdb and cBio-Portal, it can establish new diagnostic and prognostic biomarkers for traditional interventional modalities still as rising areas like immuno-oncology and areas of unmet clinical want [8]. This highlights the present state of bioinformatics applications in cancer biology and infers future prospects for rising information processing applications through computer science and machine learning approaches. Figure 11.1 explains the role of bioinformatics in cancer research through facilitated micro-RNA–based therapy.

11.3   Aid in Cancer Research via NCI

National Cancer Institute or NCI has been instrumental in the advancement of cancer research by evolving the field of genomics, proteomics, and metabolomics to integrate the datasets and develop the know-how of etiological origin and molecular basis of cancers [9]. The Center for Biomedical Informatics and Information Technology (CBIIT) supervises computational data and exchange of bioinformatics-computed results among various institutions, where National Cancer Informatics Program (NCIP) uses NCIP HubExit Disclaimer and integrates the genomic, clinical, and translational studies to enhance sharing of records, regular assessments, and data visualization. It is a central operating platform, designed for researchers to exchange, share, and record important bioinformatics data to speed up cancer research. The operating platform of NCIP is a test, whether the cancer research community reveals the social and network factors of this machine beneficial for crew technological expertise and multi-investigator study teams or not [10]. NCI is a public repository that guarantees saving clinical data for a long time with collaborations among private companies to foster technology advancement and come up with fueled diagnosis and treatment approaches. This is achieved in consolidation to the Cancer Data Science Laboratory (CDSL), in NCI's Center for Cancer Research which primarily functions to collaborate laboratory statistics from cancer genomics and omics signatures and further develop computational technology to investigate it. Together, computational simulations and mathematical algorithms are instrumental in answering the critical research questions, like the etiological origin of cancer, its progression, and how can it be prevented or cured.

The Cancer Genome Atlas (TCGA) was a collaborative three year pilot project, initiated by NCI and National Human Genome Research Institute in 2005 to report various mutations in human genome that are associated with cancer progression. Researchers used high throughput genome analysis technique on more than 11,000 cancer patients with tumor and normal-healthy samples, on which various researches have been conducted and published [11]. NCI's Therapeutically Applicable Research to Generate Effective Treatments (TARGET) program has enabled scientists to isolate genetic aberrations in pediatric cancers which is predominantly observed in children during medical trials carried out by Children's Oncology Group. NCI's Clinical Proteomic Tumor Analysis Consortium (CPTAC) is a constitutive national collaboration of institutions and researchers that are involved in genomic and proteomic analysis of cancer to develop a ground of understanding on the prevalence of cancer. NCI coordinates clinical trials and provides an extensive support to intramural researchers and further foster biomedical research which is also available in public domain [12]. This extensive network has fueled the understanding of biology of cancer and isolated potential targets for novel drug-targeted therapy. Invariably, this has surfaced the establishment and development of mounted statistics and been able to discover new equipments and approaches to analyze and access the big data.

11.4   Application of Big Data in Developing Precision Medicine

The availability of volumes of biological data in the public domain was only possible because of the powerful new research technologies that evolved with time. The data has not only made the scientific community excited about the precision medicine but has also enabled the scientists and researchers to know the biological reason behind the disease.

This has made possible interventions with tailored medicines, evolution of preventive techniques, and diagnostic treatments.

The volumes of big data that are available in the databases can be retrieved by the researchers and exchanged on a platform to be useful in order to search for biological conclusions for the rare and unsolved mysteries of these deadly diseases [13].

The biggest limitation of cancer data is the fragmentation and compartmentalization; therefore, the researchers are trying to overcome the challenges that pose for fostering research. In order to speed the research, it is pertinent for the researchers to have an exchange and access of the curated data at the same time so that they are able to analyze the problem [14]. Therefore, there is a need of an infrastructure where researchers can store, analyze, visualize, integrate, and access the biological data on a common public platform which remains accessible to all the researchers and scientist all over the globe. Bioinformatics is an evolving field of study that has been observing a boom past a decade. It uses advanced computing and coding algorithms, mathematic simulations, and different technological platforms for managing, storing, and analyzing the data. Nowadays, researchers are using different tools and platforms to manage the biological data from a comprehensive analysis of the proteins, whole genome sequencing, and advanced imaging studies but integrating the data from various platforms poses a difficulty as the researchers are unable to have the access of the primary data which was created by other studies and also due to the lack of computational tools and infrastructure necessary to integrate and analyze it [15]. Recently, a big splurged boom in the use of virtual repositories, also known as Data clouds, has not only helped to integrate but also improve

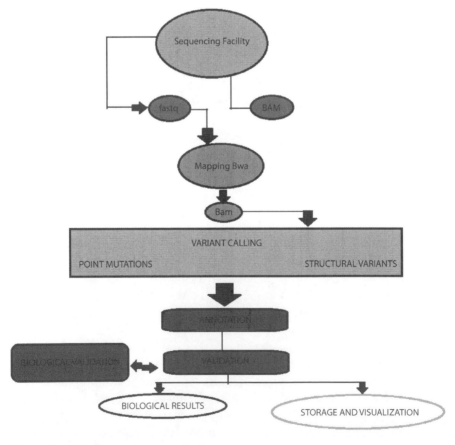

Figure 11.2 Pipeline analysis.

the access to research data. Although these steps still remain in the fetal stages and questions surround the integrated organization and coordination of these clouds and their uses. It has been possible to understand the molecular basis of cancer because of NCI that played a leading role in scientific advancement of proteomics, genomics, and metabolomics [16]. The National Cancer Informatics Program is playing a pivotal role in including clinical, genomic, and translational studies to improve the data sharing analysis and visualization in numerous research areas [17, 18]. For example, Figure 11.2 gives a detailed pipeline analysis of the structural variants and point mutations of a cancer and normal cell that can be reported via variable sequencing facilities where the data is annotated and integrated. The data is further compiled for undergoing either validation through wet laboratory procedures or a course of discussion in scientific community. The validation of the data develops a biological ground of systemic understanding which not only leads to reliable biological results but can also be stored and visualized [19].

11.5   Historical Perspective and Development

Bioinformatics and computational revolution has strengthened the approach of understanding the genetic and molecular basis of cancer. This has led the scientific community to study significant gene expressions of the expressed genome, instead of looking at the individual genes. The abundance of molecular knowledge produced, both from the laboratory as well as the amount of data stored in the patient record keeps on growing at an incredible pace. Creating fresh perspectives into the cancer genetics has been critical in discovering new ways to incorporate these results. Bioinformatics, which is the integration of genetics, information technology, and engineering, continues to evolve as a key component of research into cancer biology [20].

Cancer bioinformatics is one of several ways of focusing bioinformatics approaches in cancer, depending on the nature of disease metabolic rates, signaling, interaction, and multiplication. Clinical bioinformatics, an evolving science incorporating clinical computer science, bioinformatics, information technology, medical informatics, mathematics, and omics research, can be regarded as one of the key aspects resolving clinically important problems in early detection, successful treatments, and reliable diagnosis of cancer patients. The development of cancer-specific bioinformatics methodologies or the implementation of new and specialized bioinformatics tools to respond to the specific cancer question is desired [21].

For instance, the Semantic Web platform has been used to interpret high-throughput clinical data and to create quantitative semantic models obtained from Corvus, a data warehouse that offers a standardized interface to different types of Omics data, focused on structured biological information while using SPARQL endpoint. Semantic models including transcriptomic, epigenomic, and genomic data from melanoma samples with data from Gene Ontology and regulatory networks built from transcription factor binding information were used for the interplay between a cell molecular state and its reaction to anticancer therapy. Multivariate assays, a method for characterizing the error produced in the assay outcomes by the intrinsic error in the preparation of samples and the calculation of contributing variables, are used to support and direct clinicians to consider the use of PAM50 centroid-based genomic predictors for breast cancer care strategies and to include useful knowledge regarding the ambiguity. It can be taken seriously into account the applicability, accuracy, and convergence of methodologies, applications, computing methods, and databases that can be used to investigate cancer molecular pathways and recognize and verify novel biomarkers, network biomarkers, and individualized cancer medicines.

miRTrail is an integrative method for evaluating detailed gene and miRNA associations dependent on expression profiles to produce more rigorous and accurate data on pathogenic deregulation processes. It was proposed that miRTrail could open up opportunities to explore regulatory correlations between genes and miRNAs for human diseases, including cancer, by combining knowledge on 20,000 genes, approximately 1,000 miRNAs, and around 280,000 putative interactions. Exploring the theoretical computational mode that compares certain regulatory interactions between genes and miRNAs with clinical phenotypes would be useful, e.g., variance in gene interactions across tumor sites, phages, patient effects, or therapy responses [22].

Medical imaging must be one of the key considerations to be addressed in the development of cancer bioinformatics, as imaging in clinical pathology, tomography, NMR imaging, and positron emission tomography are one of the most appropriate and effective methods in the identification and diagnosis of cancer "early and precise". Bioinformatics-based evaluations of surface morphology of masses and other anomalies in medical images are undertaken by systematic extraction of target characteristics by mathematical morphology and by two contrast adjustment techniques improving the extracted characteristics. Based on clinical breast cancer data [23], the algorithm mentioned by Haustein and Schumacher in the Thematic Series on Cancer Bioinformatics in Clinical Bioinformatics Journal can predict tumor growth and determine the development of some metastases prior to clinical detection in cells. It could be a non-relative issue or a possible hope if cancer bioinformatics specialists will assist clinicians in defining the possible image of gene or protein associations and pathways aligned with tumor-associated shapes, densities, or positions.

11.6   Bioinformatics-Based Approaches in the Study of Cancer

There are many bioinformatics approaches to study cancers that categorize different types of cancers either on the basis of gene expression or genetic profiles. Figure 11.3 depicts three instrumental approaches: stepwise linkage analysis of microarray signatures (SLAMS), module maps, and cancer outlier profile analysis (COPA).

11.6.1   SLAMS

In order to signify the standard of care for cancer, tumors are categorized on the basis of grade, stage, and histology. Detailed analysis of histological specimens gives just a view at the molecular level, and therefore, various types of tissue appear identical but do not behave the same and several associations are not characteristic. These molecular variations are probably responsible for the result variation and treatment response for closely categorized tissues. This adds to substantial confusion as doctors have to precisely adapt a particular treatment for the patient [24]. While profiles

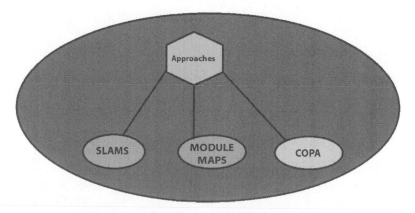

Figure 11.3 Different bioinformatics-based approaches.

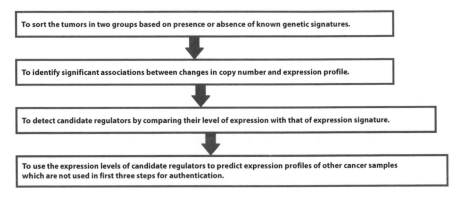

Figure 11.4 Steps involved in SLAMS.

of gene expression are not widely utilized in clinical treatment, it provides confirmation of a more systematic approach to tumor detection. Even so, this method still has its drawbacks, because the end result is not only to discover genetic markers but rather to recognize how the genes work in the disease and to establish potential targets for impacting output.

A group of scientists at Stanford University has developed a method for identifying data on gene expression by shifting the number of copies of DNA to chromosome regions consisting of candidate oncogene regulators. The gene expression profile associated with a known tumor type [25–27] is the phenotype in the linkage study.

Their method, i.e., SLAMS consists of four steps (Figure 11.4).

SLAMS was confirmed by utilizing it on the breast cancer samples and was subsequently concluded that a gene in proximity might interact with the MYC gene (oncogenic transcription factor) to express wound signature [28].

11.6.2   Module Maps

Module maps may be a possible tool [29, 30] for illustrating the normal trends of gene expression through heterogeneous tissues and cancer disease processes. Modules can be calculated by comparing specific gene sets with expression data and by retrieving a subset of co-expressed genes. The modules so acquired can be applied to all types of tissues to look for common signatures, exposing underlying processes.

Article published in Nature Genetics [31], by using module maps, indicates the expectations for cancer studies. The scientists obtained findings for various types of cancers from 2,000 microarray research and compiled them with clinical evidence. About 456 modules were identified from 3,000 gene sets and then matched across multiple cancers. The study found variations in gene expression common to different cancers, thereby offering valuable knowledge about pathways for cancer. This technique is helpful in highlighting dynamics of global disease that are not apparent from studies with a single microarray. But there are also limits. The inconsistency in outcomes from numerous techniques presents challenges as well as the lack of accurate clinical knowledge for analysis trials will influence the utility [24, 32].

11.6.3   COPA

Contemporary oncogene expression profile identification techniques are limited in their ability to distinguish patterns through multiple samples, particularly when those patterns do not predominate enough to stand out. This is attributed to the heterogeneity of patterns of expression in samples which makes it difficult to differentiate from background variations between original patterns [33]. COPA is used to address this issue to classify the variants that are found in a subset of tumor samples. From this approach, we can distinguish the outer expression profiles for the specific group of genes that have lower levels of expression, and overexpression reveals a small subset of tumor samples. COPA technique comprises of three steps (Figure 11.5).

COPA facilitates in compacting normal dynamic range of the expression profiles. It also illuminates profiles that deviate from the mean expression level. For each gene, the degree of divergence from the normal pattern of expression is then rated to produce a suitable list of outer genes.

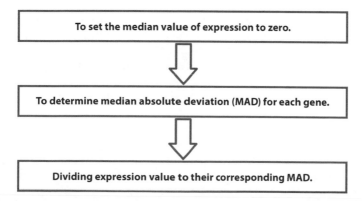

Figure 11.5 Steps involved in COPA.

COPA has been added to the oncomine database, defining a variety of outlier profiles [34]. Advances in COPA are prompting researchers to look at other tumors that may display similar rearrangements which may offer hints to potential diagnostic methods or therapeutic targets.

11.7   Conclusion and Future Challenges

There are multiple applications of bioinformatics in cancer research, but on the other hand, substantial challenges exist. More innovative approaches and techniques are needed to understand the poorly understood genetic changes associated with cancer. Methodology is also necessary for data integration and normalization algorithms for samples assembled under various conditions in different labs. Standard formats should be adopted for storing data and annotating samples.

Research is needed as positive or negative for cancer beyond the microarray sample mark; more thorough annotation is needed to understand the function of genetics in cancer subtypes, response to therapy, and other related parameters. Also, linking of microarray data with patient's clinical information should be done in computable mode and with storage of data and comes the challenge of effective mining of clinical data. caBIG™ is one of the biggest prospective to change the standard research procedure.

References

1. Ma, X. and Yu, H., Global burden of cancer. *Yale J. Biol. Med.*, 79, 3–4, 85–94, 2006.
2. Hasty, P. and Montagna, C., Chromosomal Rearrangements in Cancer: Detection and potential causal mechanisms. *Mol. Cell. Oncol.*, 1, 1, e29904, 2014, https://doi.org/10.4161/mco.29904.
3. Institute of Medicine (US) and National Academy of Engineering (US) Roundtable on Value & Science-Driven Health Care, *Engineering a Learning Healthcare System: A Look at the Future: Workshop Summary*, p. 3, National Academies Press (US), Washington (DC), 2011, Healthcare System Complexities, Impediments, and Failures. Available from: https://www.ncbi.nlm.nih.gov/books/NBK61963/.
4. Shyr, D. and Liu, Q., Next generation sequencing in cancer research and clinical application. *Biol. Proced. Online*, 15, 1, 4, 2013, https://doi.org/10.1186/1480-9222-15-4.

5. Hackl, H., Charoentong, P., Finotello, F. *et al.*, Computational genomics tools for dissecting tumour–immune cell interactions. *Nat. Rev. Genet.*, 17, 441–458, 2016, https://doi.org/10.1038/nrg.2016.67.

6. Misra, B., Langefeld, C., Olivier, M., Cox, L., Integrated omics: tools, advances and future approaches. *J. Mol. Endocrinol.*, 62, 1, R21–R45, 2019.

7. Elazezy, M. and Joosse, S.A., Techniques of using circulating tumor DNA as a liquid biopsy component in cancer management. *Comput. Struct. Biotechnol. J.*, 16, 370–378, 2018, https://doi.org/10.1016/j.csbj.2018.10.002.

8. Cesano, A. and Warren, S., Bringing the next Generation of Immuno-Oncology Biomarkers to the Clinic. *Biomedicines*, 6, 1, 14, 2018, https://doi.org/10.3390/biomedicines6010014.

9. Manzoni, C., Kia, D.A., Vandrovcova, J., Hardy, J., Wood, N.W., Lewis, P.A., Ferrari, R., Genome, transcriptome and proteome: the rise of omics data and their integration in biomedical sciences. *Briefings Bioinf.*, 19, 2, 286–302, 2018, https://doi.org/10.1093/bib/bbw114.

10. Mongkolwat, P., Kleper, V., Talbot, S., Rubin, D., The National Cancer Informatics Program (NCIP) Annotation and Image Markup (AIM) Foundation model. *J. Digit. Imaging*, 27, 6, 692–701, 2014, https://doi.org/10.1007/s10278-014-9710-3.

11. Tomczak, K., Czerwińska, P., Wiznerowicz, M., The Cancer Genome Atlas (TCGA): an immeasurable source of knowledge. *Contemp. Oncol. (Poznan, Poland)*, 19, 1A, A68–A77, 2015, https://doi.org/10.5114/wo.2014.47136.

12. Rudnick, P.A., Markey, S.P., Roth, J., Mirokhin, Y., Yan, X., Tchekhovskoi, D.V., Edwards, N.J., Thangudu, R.R., Ketchum, K.A., Kinsinger, C.R., Mesri, M., Rodriguez, H., Stein, S.E., A Description of the Clinical Proteomic Tumor Analysis Consortium (CPTAC) Common Data Analysis Pipeline. *J. Proteome Res.*, 15, 3, 1023–1032, 2016, https://doi.org/10.1021/acs.jproteome.5b01091.

13. Wooden, B., Goossens, N., Hoshida, Y., Friedman, S.L., Using Big Data to Discover Diagnostics and Therapeutics for Gastrointestinal and Liver Diseases. *Gastroenterology*, 152, 1, 53–67.e3, 2017, https://doi.org/10.1053/j.gastro.2016.09.065.

14. Tremblay, D., Touati, N., Roberge, D. *et al.*, Understanding cancer networks better to implement them more effectively: a mixed methods multi-case study. *Implementation Sci.*, 11, 39, 2015, https://doi.org/10.1186/s13012-016-0404-8.

15. He, K.Y., Ge, D., He, M.M., Big Data Analytics for Genomic Medicine. *Int. J. Mol. Sci.*, 18, 2, 412, 2017, https://doi.org/10.3390/ijms18020412.

16. Chakraborty, S., Hosen, M., II, Ahmed, M., Shekhar, H.U., Onco-Multi-OMICS Approach: A New Frontier in Cancer Research. *BioMed. Res. Int.*, 2018, Article ID 9836256, https://doi.org/10.1155/2018/9836256.

17. National Academies of Sciences, Engineering, and Medicine; Health and Medicine Division; Board on Health Care Services, National Cancer Policy Forum. *Improving Cancer Diagnosis and Care: Clinical Application of*

Computational Methods in Precision Oncology: Proceedings of a Workshop, 2019 Jun 20 National Academies Press (US), Washington (DC), Available from: https://www.ncbi.nlm.nih.gov/books/NBK544637/.

18. Liu, J., Lichtenberg, T., Hoadley, K.A., Poisson, L.M., Lazar, A.J., Cherniack, A.D., Kovatich, A.J., Benz, C.C., Levine, D.A., Lee, A.V., Omberg, L., Wolf, D.M., Shriver, C.D., Thorsson, V., Cancer Genome Atlas Research Network, Hu, H., An Integrated TCGA Pan-Cancer Clinical Data Resource to Drive High-Quality Survival Outcome Analytics. *Cell*, 173, 2, 400–416.e11, 2018, https://doi.org/10.1016/j.cell.2018.02.052.

19. Rodriguez, H. and Pennington, S.R., Revolutionizing Precision Oncology through Collaborative Proteogenomics and Data Sharing. *Cell*, 173, 3, 535–539, 2018, https://doi.org/10.1016/j.cell.2018.04.008.

20. Hulsen, T., Jamuar, S.S., Moody, A.R., Karnes, J.H., Varga, O., Hedensted, S., Spreafico, R., Hafler, D.A., McKinney, E.F., From Big Data to Precision Medicine. *Front. Med.*, 6, 34, 2019, https://doi.org/10.3389/fmed.2019.00034.

21. Wu, D., Rice, C.M., Wang, X., Cancer bioinformatics: A new approach to systems clinical medicine. *BMC Bioinf.*, 13, 71, 2012, https://doi.org/10.1186/1471-2105-13-71.

22. Laczny, C., Leidinger, P., Haas, J. *et al.*, miRTrail - a comprehensive webserver for analyzing gene and miRNA patterns to enhance the understanding of regulatory mechanisms in diseases. *BMC Bioinf.*, 13, 36, 2012, https://doi.org/10.1186/1471-2105-13-36.

23. Wu, D., Rice, C., Wang, X., Cancer bioinformatics: A new approach to systems clinical medicine. *BMC Bioinf.*, 13, 71, 2012, 10.1186/1471-2105-13-71.

24. Park, T., Yi, S.G., Kang, S.H., Lee, S., Lee, Y.S., Simon, R., Evaluation of normalization methods for microarray data. *BMC Bioinf.*, 4, 33, 2003.

25. Chen, C.N., Lin, J.J., Chen, J.J., Lee, P.H., Yang, C.Y., Kuo, M.L., Chang, K.J., Hsieh, F.J., Gene expression profile predicts patient survival of gastric cancer after surgical resection. *J. Clin. Oncol.*, 23, 7286–95, 2005.

26. Dyrskjot, L., Zieger, K., Kruhoffer, M., Thykjaer, T., Jensen, J.L., Primdahl, H., Aziz, N., Marcussen, N., Moller, K., Orntoft, T.F., A molecular signature in superficial bladder carcinoma predicts clinical outcome, *Clin. Cancer Res.*, 11, 4029–36, 2005.

27. Gyorffy, B., Surowiak, P., Kiesslich, O., Denkert, C., Schafer, R., Dietel, M., Lage, H., Gene expression profiling of 30 cancer cell lines predicts resistance towards 11 anticancer drugs at clinically achieved concentrations, *Int. J. Cancer*, 118, 1699–712, 2006.

28. Gyorffy, B., Serra, V., Jurchott, K., Abdul-Ghani, R., Garber, M., Stein, U., Petersen, I., Lage, H., Dietel, M., Schafer, R., Prediction of doxorubicin sensitivity in breast tumors based on gene expression profiles of drug-resistant cell lines correlates with patient survival, *Oncogene*, 24, 51, 7542–51, 2005 Nov 17.

29. Ihmels, J., Friedlander, G., Bergmann, S., Sarig, O., Ziv, Y., Barkai, N., Revealing modular organization in the yeast transcriptional network, *Nat. Genet.*, 31, 370–7, 2002.

30. Tanay, A., Sharan, R., Kupiec, M., Shamir, R., Revealing modularity and organization in the yeast molecular network by integrated analysis of highly heterogeneous genomewide data, *Proc. Natl. Acad. Sci. U.S.A.*, 101, 2981–6, 2004.

31. Segal, E., Friedman, N., Koller, D., Regev, A., A module map showing conditional activity of expression modules in cancer, *Nat. Genet.*, 36, 1090–8, 2004.

32. Chua, S.W., Vijayakumar, P., Nissom, P.M., Yam, C.Y., Wong, V.V., Yang, H., A novel normalization method for effective removal of systematic variation in microarray data, *Nucleic Acids Res.*, 34, e38, 2006.

33. Tomlins, S.A., Rhodes, D.R., Perner, S., Dhanasekaran, S.M., Mehra, R., Sun, X.W., Varambally, S., Cao, X., Tchinda, J., Kuefer, R., Lee, C., Montie, J.E., Shah, R.B., Pienta, K.J., Rubin, M.A., Chinnaiyan, A.M., Recurrent fusion of TMPRSS2 and ETS transcription factor genes in prostate cancer, *Science*, 310, 644–8, 2005.

34. Rhodes, D.R., Yu, J., Shanker, K., Deshpande, N., Varambally, R., Ghosh, D., Barrette, T., Pandey, A., Chinnaiyan, A.M., ONCOMINE: a cancer microarray database and integrated data-mining platform, *Neoplasia*, 6, 1–6, 2004.

12

Genomic Association of Polycystic Ovarian Syndrome: Single-Nucleotide Polymorphisms and Their Role in Disease Progression

Gowtham Kumar Subbaraj*† and Sindhu Varghese†

Faculty of Allied Health Sciences, Chettinad Hospital and Research Institute, Chettinad Academy of Research and Education (Deemed to be University), Old Mahabalipuram Road, Kelambakkam, Tamil Nadu, India

Abstract

Polycystic ovary syndrome is the frequent and a multifaceted female endocrine disorder and is one of the prominent causes of female infertility. It is also known to be a typical syndrome among South Indian women initiating high risk of infertility. Here, the aim was to explore the relationship of single-nucleotide polymorphism of FSHR, IL-10, and IRS1 gene in the pathogenesis of PCOS. A hospital-based pilot case control study was carried on PCOS and control women in the tertiary care hospital. Genotype was carried out by polymerase chain reaction. The odds ratio was calculated and it was found to be 0.71, 1.06, and 0.32 for the genes and 95% CI was estimated to assess the relative risk. The relative possibility was found to be 0.72, 1.05, and 0.35, respectively. Thus, our findings suggested no association of FSHR (rs6166), whereas IL10 (rs1800896) showed a positive association with the PCOS condition. While IRS-1 (rs1801278) polymorphisms showed a negative association and these findings should be interpreted with caution. Though, the number of investigations in different population should absolutely be increased and more intensive analysis should be done.

Keywords: Polycystic ovary syndrome, FSHR, IL-10, IRS1, single-nucleotide polymorphism

*Corresponding author: gowtham_phd@yahoo.com
†These authors have contributed equally to this work.

S. Balamurugan, Anand Krishnan, Dinesh Goyal, Balakumar Chandrasekaran and Boomi Pandi (eds.) *Computation in Bioinformatics: Multidisciplinary Applications*, (245–264) © 2021 Scrivener Publishing LLC

12.1   Introduction

Infertility is distinct as the failure to achieve clinical pregnancy after equitable time of sexual intercourse with no contraceptive methods in use [1]. Fertility involvements may be instigated in less than 1 year established on health, sexual and reproductive past, age, physical outcomes, and investigative testing. Infertility is an ailment, which creates incapacity as impairment of function [2]. The usual, young aged couples have a 25% possibility to conceive afterward 1 month of insecure interaction; 70% of the duos conceive by 6 months, and 90% of the couples have a chance to conceive by one year. Only 5% of the twosomes will conceive afterward one and a half or 2 years [3].

The cause of infertility can be categorized as i) male factor, ii) female factor, iii) collective male and female factor, and iv) inexplicable. Male infertility situations comprise of semen parameter aberration, varicocele, congenital and developed urogenital aberrations, endocrine disturbance, inherited abnormality, infection of genital track, obstruction in the reproductive track, immunological factors, and disclosure to drugs/toxins. Male infertility details for 30%–50% of the total infertility circumstances. The true occurrence of male infertility is unidentified because of the inconsistency in the incidence of infertility stated from diverse countries [4]. A normal reproductive tract contributes to the passage of spermatozoa and discharge of good quality oocyte when the endometrium is open for implantation is the two pre-basics essential in female partner for successive pregnancy.

Around 5%–10% of infertile women may have genetic abnormalities, for instance, chromosomal anomalies, single or multiple gene alterations, and polymorphisms. Infertility may have at least contact to environmental influences, endocrine interruptions, and hormonal discrepancies [5]. Endometriosis has been connected to developed rates of melanoma, asthma, auto immune syndrome, atopic ailment, cardiovascular disease, and ovarian cancer [6]. PCOS has been related with augmented waist circumference, insulin resistance (IR), raised serum insulin levels, greater lipoprotein proportions, type II diabetes, hyperlipidemia, and upsurges in central/visceral adiposity even in the setting of usual BMI [7]. Female infertility can have many reasons. The furthermost collective reasons of female infertility comprise of difficulties with ovulation, injury to the fallopian tubes or uterus, and complications with the cervix.

PCOS can be categorized by raised androgen levels, menstrual abnormalities, and minor cysts on one or both ovaries. The syndrome can be morphological (polycystic ovaries) or mainly biochemical (hyperandro-genemia). About 1:5 of women shows the presence of polycystic ovaries diagnosed by diagnostic modalities such as ultrasound scans [8] and 10% experiences extra biochemical and clinical characteristics of PCOS [9]. The ratio of women with polycystic ovaries hikes due to obesity and the recent epidemic of obesity is expected to increase polycystic ovary syndrome level more usual [10]. PCOS can be defined as an oligogenic syndrome in which the interface of number of inherited and environmental factors control the clinical, heterogeneous, as well as biochemical phenotype.

Signs and symptoms of PCOS vary. The prevalence along with the signs and symptoms of PCOS is shown in Figure 12.1.

> Random periods: A short of ovulation prevents the uterine inside layer from detaching each month.
> Substantial bleeding: The uterine inside layer builds up for a longer period of time.
> Hair growth: 70% of women by means of this situation produce hair on face and body—counting on their belly, back, and chest. Extra hair growth is named as hirsutism.
> Weight gain: 80% of women with polycystic ovary syndrome are bulky or overweight.

Although consciousness of polycystic ovary syndrome, its identification, and related disease is great, the aforementioned elementary pathophysiol-ogy is repeatedly unstated. This artefact grants an outline for coaching and widening the knowledge about the origins and controlling of polycystic

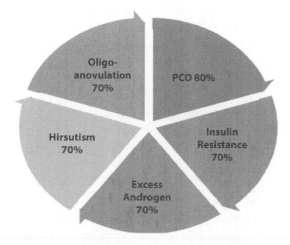

Figure 12.1 Prevalence of PCOS and its sign and symptoms.

ovary syndrome. Even skilled gynaecologists frequently find PCOS hard to recognize, mostly as the clinical sorts differ from each patient.

Even though altered specialists might have their opinions of its pathological and physiological base and approximately prospects can be examined, the subsequent prototypical contributes a beneficial background to construct and present main notions and managing pathways. In the outline, there are six phases of growth of the ovary as well as the influences which interrelate with it which aid to elucidate the contextual in the progression of polycystic ovary syndrome. Information of these phases is used as crucial for understanding the approaches existing for its management.

The initial phase in the method is toward observing the construction of the hormone, estradiol inside the follicle of ovary. The ovarian follicle has dual steroid genic cell tiers: the external theca cell coating and also the internal granulosa cell coating, detached through a vault membrane [11]. The granulosa cell layers are accountable for the production and discharge of the hormone, estradiol. It is primarily lower than the prompt of follicle-stimulating hormone by the frontal pituitary that fixes and stimulates the follicle-stimulating hormone receptor [12]. Estradiol is classified as a sexual hormone and all steroidal hormones are chemically cholesterol in nature [13].

Androgen is changed to estrogen through aromatase enzyme action. Granulosa cells comprise of huge quantities of the enzyme, aromatase; however, they do not exhibit the enzymes and proteins which are essential aimed at the cholesterol translation to androgen; thus, they cannot yield androgen. Because they are not able to produce the androgen substrate which is appropriate to create estradiol require to get androgen from alternative basis. Androgen is secreted by the theca cells and further transformed into estrogen. Theca cells secrete androgen following the stimulus of luteinising hormone (LH) from the pituitary gland that triggers the LH receptor [14]. Therefore, to enable estradiol production, LH origins the creation of androgen, and FSH encourages the alteration of those cells that are identified as the duel cell, two gonadotropin model of estrogen production, and these hormones are biologically stable [15].

Another phase in defining the progression of polycystic ovary syndrome is to focus that the expansion of a polycystic ovary is linked by means of bigger disclosure toward androgens have their specific special consequences on follicular progress and advancement. The polycystic ovary is known to contain a healthier numeral of minor antral follicles slightly fluid-filled that are apparent on ultrasound scanning. It cannot be defined as "cysts" as they comprise of a possibly fit oocyte [16] and it has also been inspired to develop usually by exogenously directed follicle-stimulating hormone [17]. This is why women with polycystic ovary syndrome are known to be at an abundant bigger threat of emerging ovarian hyper stimulation syndrome after direction of follicle-stimulating hormone in the course of aided conception. The ovarian "cysts" in polycystic ovary syndrome are hence really paused follicles, with slow cell progress along with compact cell demise. Androgen hinders the progression of superior antral follicles nevertheless fuels the development of lesser antral follicles. The differences between normal ovulation and formation of cyst is illustrated in Figure 12.2.

Clinically, the polycystic ovarian structure is related with augmented endogenic androgens. Circumstances wherein endogenic androgen quantities are systemically elevated comprise androgen-secreting cancers and delayed-onset congenital adrenal hyperplasia. In those conditions, the levels of adrenal androgen secretion may be amplified [11]. The food and factors causing PCOS is shown in Figure 12.3. Women with equally these situations progress polycystic ovaries. The reaction of the ovary to augmented androgens is thus the advancement of a polycystic morphology and hindrance of later follicular progression.

The third phase is to argue the system by which the ovary may be bare to develop the concentrations of androgen. By means of the two cells verified assuming that a hormone inequality happened, like the concentrations of circulating LH were more than follicle-stimulating hormone concentrations,

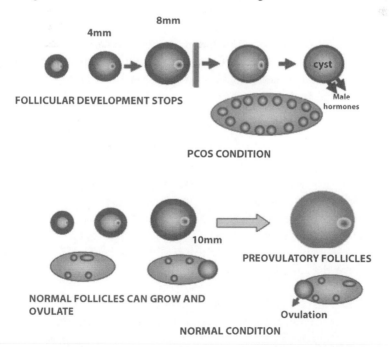

Figure 12.2 Differences between normal ovulation and cyst formation (PCOS).

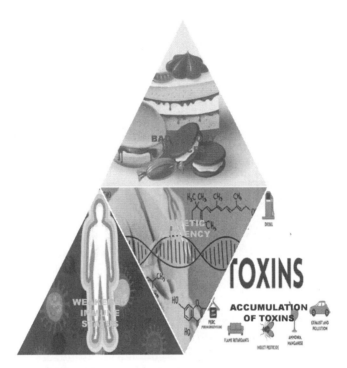

Figure 12.3 Factors and food that cause PCOS.

the production of ovarian androgen would intensify. Earlier, a bigger proportion between LH and FSH ratio was assumed as essential for the identification of polycystic ovary syndrome. This is not a part of the investigative standards, that emphasis on the subsequent elevated androgens [12]. Though, it is perfect that women with polycystic ovary syndrome are further expected to devour raised concentrations of basal LH [13] and elevated LH pulse amplitude and incidence. Whereas prolonged anovulation is capable to result in a higher LH levels, it is possible that the proportion of LH and FSH disparity is roughly that women having a predisposition to polycystic ovary syndrome and further lead to anovulation. There are growing indications from animal models and humans that polycystic ovary syndrome can be automated by enlarged fetal experience to androgen beforehand the birth [14, 15]. This might lastingly improve the secretion of basal LH [16] and enhance the quantity of the released LH which further reacts to the gonadotrophin-releasing hormone (GnRH) [16].

PCOS is a usual ailment among several countries that happen after puberty instigating infertility, particularly amid South Indian women. It is a collective endocrine condition which mainly leads to reproductive dysfunction among women [17]. The reasons causing infertility in women are shown in Figure 12.4. Polycystic ovary syndrome disorders are categorized by anovulation, hyperandrogenism, and/or polycystic ovaries (i.e., cysts in the uterus) morphology [18]. The symptoms linked with polycystic ovary syndrome are irregular periods, obesity, acne, hair growth, etc. [19]. The pathogenesis of polycystic ovary syndrome is not well distinct. This polycystic ovary syndrome condition also elevates the possibility of emerging cardiovascular disease and type II diabetes [20]. Several genetic factors comprise of polymorphisms or mutation of various genes which are linked with polycystic ovary syndrome state.

Polycystic ovary syndrome is the furthermost mutual identification made in women with heavy irregular and prolonged periods otherwise called as amenorrhoea, oligomenorrhoea. It is a common reason of infertility and hirsutism which occurs due to anovulation. Women who have polycystic ovary syndrome will experience elevated concentrations of circulating androgens as well as a noticeable link with dyslipidaemia, IR, gestational diabetes, obesity, heart disease, and type 2 diabetes. Furthermore, it is a recognized reason of endometrial hyperplasia, and it is thus associated with endometrial cancer. The short-term as well as long-term concerns of polycystic ovary syndrome denote a growing burden on health resources.

The IR at a rate of 50% of polycystic ovary syndrome women seems to associate with extreme serine phosphorylation of the insulin receptor. It seems to control the action of major monitoring enzyme of androgen biosynthesis. It is thus potential that distinct fault yields both IR and hyperandrogenism in certain PCOS women [21]. Polymorphism in the gene coding the IRS proteins, predominantly IRS-1 Gly972Arg, is linked with the phenotypic structures of PCOS [22]. The insulin receptor contains two alpha and two beta units which is considered to be a heterotetramer. The alpha subunit encloses a ligand-binding site, whereas the β-subunit

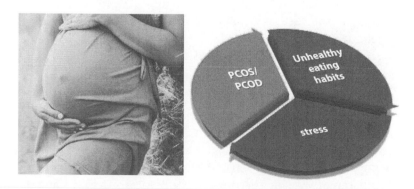

Figure 12.4 Factors and reasons behind the infertility condition.

comprises of the ligand-activated tyrosine kinase. After the tyrosine gets phosphorylated, the insulin receptor phosphorylates two intracellular substrates, insulin receptor substrate-1 as well as insulin receptor substrate-2. The IRS-1 aids as a docking molecule for signaling and hence trigger the enzyme called phosphatidylinositol 3-kinase.

The unconstrained estrogen motivation of the endometrium augments the possibility of endometrial cancer [23]. The improved free estrogens simulate the luteinizing hormone, provocating the hyperandrogenemia, which consequences in follicular atresia and scientific symbols in addition to symptoms of hirsutism. Insulin likewise upsurges the production of androgens, which again worsens hirsutism and predisposes to diabetes [23]. The pathophysiology and the molecular base of polycystic ovary syndrome are presently unfamiliar. Proof suggests that polycystic ovary syndrome is a multifaceted disease, which has mainly been examined over and done with the use of association studies of genes comprising of the insulin receptor (INSR), insulin (INS), follistatin (FST), and steroid enzymes and also has been involved, but presently, the causal molecular fault is still unidentified. Also, additional latest proof proposes the most important link of polycystic ovary syndrome is with fibrillin 3 (FBN3) on chromosome 19p 13.2 and on chromosome on 2p23.3 with numerous other genes but causative contrivances have not been determined [24].

12.2   FSHR Gene

Follicle stimulating hormone receptor (FSHR) is known to be a glycoprotein which is secreted by the frontal pituitary gland which is essential for women in follicle advancement, maturation of oocyte, and regulation of steroidogenesis [25]. FSHR fits in the G-protein coupled receptor family (Guanine nucleotide-binding protein) contains 10 exons, 9 introns, and promoter region located at chromosomal region 2p21 [26]. Due to single-nucleotide polymorphisms (SNP) changes such as Ala 307Thr and Ser 680Asn and corresponding amino acids causes PCOS [27].

12.3   IL-10 Gene

Anti-inflammatory cytokine called Interleukin-10 (IL-10) has the significant role of regulation in the immune system [28]. In human, the IL-10 gene is positioned in the chromosome1q31-1q32 [29]. This IL-10 acts as an anti-inflammatory which is connected with type 2 diabetes and obesity [30]. There are two polymorphisms such as 819C/T and −1082G/A which are reported to influence the PCOS [28]. These case studies were reported in the Caucasian population.

12.4   IRS-1 Gene

Investigation assumed to govern the IRS-1 Gly972Arg that impacts metabolic and hormonal characteristics in patients with PCOS. The IR is known to be a substantial issue involved in the pathogenesis of PCOS [31]. Figure 12.5 illustrates the symptoms and causes of insulin resistance. The binding of insulin ligand to its receptor encourages the phosphorylation of the cytosolic substrate IRS-1 [32]. The bio-kinetic reaction of IRS-1 to tyrosine protein kinases hinges on the binding likeness as well as the specificity of tyrosine phosphorylation sites in the insulin receptor substrate, which can be transformed by altered amino acid polymorphism in the phosphotyrosine-binding (PTB) domain [33].

Considering the vital role of IRS1 rs1801278G≥A polymorphism in PCOS, previous reports revealed that the vulnerability of evolving PCOS linked with SNP [34]. IR mentions to a state in which insulin does not muddle with the insulin receptor on the cell [35]. The link between IR and PCOS has substantial insight into the pathogenesis of PCOS [36]. Several studies showed that transformed insulin levels can straight arouse ovarian androgen construction in PCOS [37]. Insulin can also stimulate adrenal steroidogenesis by attracting the sympathy to ACTH (adrenocorticotropic

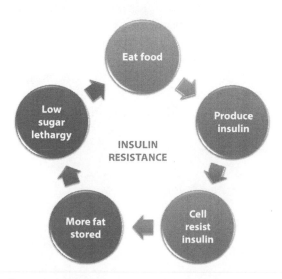

Figure 12.5 Insulin resistance (IR) causes and symptoms.

hormone) [38]. Significant physical processes including cellular glucose uptake and gene expression are controlled by insulin [39]. IR in PCOS inclines the individual to type 2 diabetes [40].

It is being recommended that extra body weight absolutely interrelates with the Arg-variant in this manner elevating the risk of type 2 diabetes. Up to date, studies have recognized numerous polymorphisms in the IRS-1 gene. Majority prevailing IRS-1 alternative, a Gly→Arg alteration at the 972 codon, which has stated to be amplified in dominance among type 2 diabetes patients. Carriers of the Arg972 are regarded as C-peptide and lesser fasting insulin levels related with the non-carriers, signifying that the Arg972 IRS-1 disparity may add to destruction toward the secretion of insulin.

Type 2 diabetes mellitus is a complicated syndrome branded by a grouping of resistance to insulin as well as insufficient compensatory insulin secretary reaction [41]. Considerable facts has been collected to put forward that heritable factors add upto the pathogenesis of diabetes, given in the high elevation of the concordance rate among the monozygotic twins [42], the increased incidence in definite racial populations [43], and the amplified prevalence in the offsprings of affected subjects [44]. The vulnerability toward both IR and insulin insufficiently seems to be genetically firm [45]. Longitudinal studies proposed that IR is the initially noticeable deficiency in the pathogenesis of diabetes.

Primarily, greater than before, the secretion of insulin by the pancreatic beta cells can recompense for IR, whereas hyperglycaemic conditions ultimately progress as beta cell reparation flops. Alterations in the insulin receptor gene have remained recognized in uncommon conditions like rigorous IR, for example, Rabson-Mendenhall and leprechaunism [46]. Defect in beta cell utility was triggered by mutations in indoctrination glucokinase gene [47, 48], hepatic nuclear factor 1α (HNF 1α), 1β (HNF 1 β), as well as (HNF 4 α) which are considered to be transcription factors [49]. The insulin-promoting factor-1 has been acknowledged in patients with development of diabetes of the immature, an unusual monogenic type of diabetes. In spite of extreme studies, genes dependable for the growth of the regular forms of type II diabetes hang about unidentified.

12.5   PCR Primers Used

FSHR - rs6166

Forward outer primer (5' - 3')	CTGCTATGAAATGCAAGCCCAAATTTAT
Reverse outer primer (5' - 3')	TGTGTAGAAGCACTGTCAGCTCTTTGTG

IL10 - rs1800896

Forward outer primer (5' - 3')	CTCCCAGTTACAGTCTAAACTGGAATG
Reverse outer primer (5' - 3')	CTCCCAGTTACAGTCTAAACTGGAATG

IRS-1 - rs1801278

Forward primer	5'-CATCCCAGCTCCAGCCAGCTCCCAGAG-3'
Reverse primer	5'-TGGGCAGGCTCACCTCCTCTGCAGCAAT-3'

12.6 Statistical Analysis

Statistical analysis of the results was carried out to compute the odds ratio and the risk ratio of the gene polymorphism. Test of significance: the P-value was considered as described by Sheskin [50]. A standard normal deviate (z-value) is calculated as $\ln(OR)/SE\{\ln(OR)\}$. PCR was performed with the isolated DNA for the detection of SNPs such as rs1801278, rs6166, and rs1800896 by using primers. After the run, PCR products were analyzed by running into 2% agarose gel electrophoresis along with control ladder (100 bp) in one lane. The PCR samples contains primers, master mix, samples (patients and control), and sterile water, and the PCR was set up. The 2% agarose gel electrophoresis was performed for the PCR samples, and the odds ratio was calculated for the gene IL-10: the odds ratio OR = 1.0625, 95% CI = 0.1559 to 7.0615, and $p = 0.95$. The risk ratio for the IL-10 was found to be RR = 1.0556. The odds ratio was calculated for the gene IRS-1: OR = 0.3269, 95% CI = 0.0275 to 3.8927, and $p = 0.37$. The risk ratio for the IRS-1 was found to be RR = 0.35. Again, for the gene FSHR, the odds ratio OR = 0.7143, 95% CI = 0.0135-37.75, and $p = 0.86$. The risk ratio for the FSHR was found to be RR = 0.72. Those odds ratio and risk ratio was calculated using the formula

$$OR = \frac{a\backslash b}{c\backslash d}$$

$$\text{and risk ratio } RR = \frac{a\backslash(a+b)}{c\backslash(c+d)}$$

The demographic data was analyzed from the patients and controls, and thus, out of the total samples, obesity is the major causative in the PCOS patients than the control. There are also data with other possible genetic inheritance like family history of diabetes, cardiovascular disease, gestational diabetes, and high blood pressure, which are comparatively higher than the control. Other conditions like difficult in losing weight, allergies, excess facial and other excess hair growth condition, and premenstrual syndrome (PMS) were also the information gathered from the patients and control.

PCOS is a common ailment causing infertility, which involves 8% in 10% of all reproductive-aged women. The etiology of PCOS was not completely understood. It is also reported that the PCOS women are increased in the androgenic levels and almost increased within the BMI range. Likewise, gene variants encode several pro-inflammatory cytokines which are linked with IR, obesity, and diabetes and also increase the risk of developing cardiovascular disease and type 2 diabetes. There are 85% of women are with bilateral PCOS and 15% are with unilateral PCOS. PCOS is linked with increased occurrence of the hypothalamic Gonadotropin Releasing Hormone (GnRH) pulse generator.

FSHR gene as a SNP changes from Ala 307Thr and Ser 680Asn corresponding amino acids variations causes PCOS. FSH is a hormone essential for the growth of follicles, maturation of oocyte, and steroidogenesis regulation and initiating phosphorylation of target proteins and adenylate cyclase. In the previous study by [51], the ovarian reply was secreted as the poor response which is a lesser amount of nearly five oocytes, and the regular responses were high in which extra oocytes [51]. There are changes in the food habits, and lifestyle modification is also one major cause of obesity, and thus, obesity is directly related to PCOS and infertility in Indian women. In the one of the studies [52], they found an important change in delivery of allele or genotypes between PCOS and controls, and they also coated that there is association of FSHR polymorphism (rs6166) with PCOS in recessive and co-dominant model [52]. A study by Huang *et al.*, [53] explains that the polymorphism in FSHR is a contributing factor among PCOS patients which leads to infertility in a Korean population [53]. The IL-10 gene polymorphism was reported that it was associated with prostate cancer development [54].

There is a variety of studies associated with cytokine like IL-6, IL-10, IL β1, and IL-18. IL-10 is an essential anti-inflammatory cytokine in pregnancy, which control the idiopathic frequent unprompted miscarriage. The down-rule of IL-10 is related by means of weekend endometrial perfusions which make the endometrium defensive that may to conclude finally source for early pregnancy loss. IL-10 is a result of monocytes and lymphocytes so as to been observed as the most important anti-inflamatory and antiatherogenic immune-regulating cytokine [55]. There are possible studies on the various genes related to cytokine, tumor necrosis factor alpha, and IL-6, and there is no information with IL-10 genetic polymorphism and PCOS. The human IL-10 gene is located on chromosome 1q31 and 1q32 [56]. They also play a role in the prostate cancer. In the previous investigation by Kelly *et al.*, they specified that the low-rating continual inflammation is in PCOS women that are further based on developed CRP levels in patients than controls [56].

There are various genes that were associated with PCOS like IL-6, IRS-1, and IRS-2, TNF alpha and PPAR are been reported most in Caucasian and some in Asian population. This PCOS condition is due to the changes in the lifestyle modification and changes in the food habitats. Due to the increase of BMI range, it leads to obesity. Because of the of environmental changes and sometimes changes in the gene can also cause PCOS. Mostly, the patients affected with PCOS have the first menstruation at the age of 11–13. This study is a pilot study in which the sample size was too small and the results were compared in the small population. The analysis for the lager sample size can able to locate the severity of PCOS condition in South Indian population. On comparing both the genes in the same population, we conclude that the gene FSHR is not associated with PCOS condition in South Indian population and the IL10 gene is associated with PCOS condition.

Biomarker of PCOS includes ovarian and adrenal steroid hormone, steroidogenesis actions, insulin secretion and action, energy homeostasis, gonadotropin action and regulation, and chronic inflammation [57]. The potential mechanisms of PCOS are very indefinable and have not been recognized systematically; familial aggregation shows that the genomic factor plays a key role in the aetiology of this disease [58]. Proof shows that IR has a significant role in the pathogenesis of PCOS [59, 60]. The insulin receptor contains two α- and two β-dimers. The ligand-binding site is present in the α-subunit, whereas the ligand-activated tyrosine kinase is present in the β-subunit. As soon as the insulin binds to its receptor, the tyrosine gets phosphorylated and the insulin receptor substrate-1 (IRS-1) and IRS-2, and two intracellular substrates also get phosphorylated. Later, the IRS-1 and IRS-2 associate and will trigger the downstream effectors, including phosphoinositide 3-kinase, to regulate the digestion and involve in mitogenic activities of insulin. The IRS-1 is situated on chromosome 2q36. The utmost mutual variant, IRS-1 rs1801278G>A polymorphism (Gly972Arg), was suggested. Newly, a meta-analysis produced an important association between IRS-1 rs1801278G>A polymorphism and the vulnerability of mounting PCOS [61].

Till now, many genes were recognized as type 2 diabetes risk genes because of its known or probable biological functions in insulin secretion, insulin signaling, adipocyte signaling, etc. by candidate gene tactic [62]. Unique of them was IRS1 which is a central molecule in the process of insulin signaling [63, 64]. As soon as the insulin binds to its receptor, the tyrosine phosphorylation of IRS1 aids as docking molecules for downstream effectors such as PI3K and phosphotyrosine phosphatase 2 (SHP-2). Prolonged insulin stimulation and other stimuli were activated by inducers of IR that triggers IRS kinases, which is phosphorylate IRS1, on Ser/Thr residues [65, 66]. On the other hand, the binding specificity and affinity of the tyrosine phosphorylation sites are significant for the response of IRS1 to tyrosine protein kinases, so polymorphisms within the tyrosine phosphorylation sites of the protein can modify those interactions [67]. Therefore, the decrease of tyrosine phosphorylation of IRS1 hinders downstream signaling of IRS1 [68]. In count, numerous new case-control studies with moderately large sample sizes stated associations of IRS-1 rs1801278 G>A alternates with PCOS, but the outcomes were differing. Outcomes of earlier meta-analyses emphasized that the IRS-1 rs1801278 A allele altered the danger of PCOS [69]. Newly, extra studies on the suggestion of IRS-1 rs1801278 G>A polymorphism with PCOS risk were shown. The IRS-1 is positioned on chromosome 2q36 and codes a 131.6 kDa IRS-1 protein. The utmost common SNP, IRS-1 rs1801278 G>A (Gly972Arg), was reflected to be associated with IR, PCOS, and T2DM [70, 71].

This study a pilot study in which the sample size was too small and the results were compared in the small population. The analysis for the lager sample size can able to locate the severity of PCOS condition in South Indian population. On comparing the both the genes in the same population, we conclude that the gene FSHR is not associated with PCOS condition in South Indian population, the IL10 gene is associated with PCOS condition, and IL-10 gene also shows no association with the disease.

12.7   Conclusion

Among the IRS1 and IRS2, polymorphism in IRS 1 gene could play a contributory role in the pathophysiology and risk of PCOS. We have analyzed PCOS participants with control DNA sample to check the FSHR rs6166, IL-10 rs1800896, and IRS-1 rs1801278 polymorphisms by polymerase chain amplification methodology. Results revealed that in SNP, rs6166 had no association with PCOS condition and rs1800896 showed positive association, whereas rs1801278 showed negative association with PCOS in the population studied (odds ratio is 0.35 and the relative risk was found to be 0.32). However, the study population should definitely be increased and more extensive study should be done to emphasize the association between PCOS and FSHR, IL-10, and IRS 1 gene polymorphisms.

References

1. Brugo-Olmedo, S., Chillik, C., Kopelman, S., Definition and causes of infertility. *Reprod. Biomed. Online*, 2, 1, 173–85, 2001;1.
2. Zegers-Hochschild, F., Adamson, G.D., Dyer, S., Racowsky, C., de Mouzon, J., Sokol, R., Rienzi, L., Sunde, A., Schmidt, L., Cooke, I.D., Simpson, J.L., The international glossary on infertility and fertility care, 2017. *Hum. Reprod.*, 32, 9, 1786–801, 2017 Jul 28.
3. Kamel, R.M., Management of the infertile couple: an evidence-based protocol. *Reprod. Biol. Endocrinol.*, 8, 1, 21, 2010.
4. Ghuman, N. *et al.*, Male infertility-evaluation and management at a glance. *Obstet. Gynaecol. Reprod. Med.*, 28, 7–14, 2018.
5. Tarín, J.J., García-Pérez, M.A., Hamatani, T., Cano, A., Infertility etiologies are genetically and clinically linked with other diseases in single metadiseases. *Reprod. Biol. Endocrinol.*, 13, 31, 2015;15.
6. Kvaskoff, M., Mu, F., Terry, K.L., Harris, H.R., Poole, E.M., Farland, L., Missmer, S.A., Endometriosis: a high-risk population for major chronic diseases? *Hum. Reprod. Update*, 21, 4, 500–16, 2015 Mar 11.
7. Ghaffarzad, A., Amani, R., Sadaghiani, M.M., Darabi, M., Cheraghian, B., Correlation of serum lipoprotein ratios with insulin resistance in infertile women with polycystic ovarian syndrome: a case control study. *Int. J. Fertil. Steril.*, 10, 1, 29, 2016.
8. Polson, D.W., Wadsworth, J., Adams, J., Franks, S., Polycystic ovaries—a common finding in normal women. *Lancet*, 331, 8590, 870–2, 1988; 6.
9. Franks, S., Polycystic ovary syndrome. *N. Engl. J. Med.*, 333, 835–861, 1995.
10. Motta, A.B., Role of obesity in the development of polycystic ovary syndrome. *Curr. Pharm. Des.*, 18, 2482–2492, 1990.
11. Adams, 2012, Peng, L. *et al.*, Effect of metformin on serum interleukin-6 levels in polycystic ovary syndrome: a systematic review. *BMC Women's Health*, 14, 93, 2014.
12. Rotterdam ESHRE/ASRM-Sponsored PCOS Consensus Workshop Group, Revised 2003 consensus on diagnostic criteria and long-term health risks related to polycystic ovary syndrome. *Fertil. Steril.*, 81, 19–25, 2004.

13. Franks, S., Polycystic ovary syndrome. *N. Engl. J. Med.*, 333, 13, 853–61, 1995; 28.
14. Abbott, D.H., Nicol, L.E., Levine, J.E., Xu, N., Goodarzi, M.O., Dumesic, D.A., Nonhuman primate models of polycystic ovary syndrome. *Mol. Cell. Endocrinol.*, 373, 1-2, 21–8, 2013; 5.
15. Padmanabhan, V. and Veiga-Lopez, A., Sheep models of polycystic ovary syndrome phenotype. *Mol. Cell. Endocrinol.*, 373, 1-2, 8–20, 2013; 5.
16. Abbott, D.H., Barnett, D.K., Bruns, C.M., Dumesic, D.A., Androgen excess fetal programming of female reproduction: a developmental aetiology for polycystic ovary syndrome? *Hum. Reprod. Update*, 11, 357–74, 2005; 1.
17. Helvaci, N. *et al.*, Polycystic ovary syndrome and the risk of obstructive sleep apnea: a meta-analysis and review of the literature. *Endocr. Connect.*, 6, 437–445, 2017.
18. Tumu, V.R. *et al.*, An IL-6 gene promoter polymorphism is associated with PCOS in South Indian women. *J. Assist. Reprod. Genet.*, 30, 1541–1546, 2013.
19. Panda, P.K. *et al.*, Genetics of PCOS: A systematic bioinformatics approach to unveil the proteins responsible for PCOS. *Genom. Data*, 8, 52–60, 2016.
20. Almawi, W.Y. *et al.*, Analysis of *VEGFA* Variants and Changes in VEGF Levels Underscores the Contribution of VEGF to Polycystic Ovary Syndrome. *PLoS One*, 11, e0165636, 2011.
21. Dunaif, A. and Graf, M., Insulin administration alters gonadal steroid metabolism independent of changes in gonadotropin secretion in insulin-resistant women with the polycystic ovary syndrome. *J. Clin. Investig.*, 83, 1, 23–9, 1989; 1.
22. Sir-Petermann, T., Perez-Bravo, F., Angel, B., Maliqueo, M., Calvillan, M., Palomino, A., G972R polymorphism of IRS-1 in women with polycystic ovary syndrome. *Diabetologia*, 44, 9, 1200–1, 2001;1.
23. Almind, K., Doria, A., Kahn, C.R., Putting the genes for type II diabetes on the map. *Nat. Med.*, 7, 3, 277, 2001 Mar.
24. Barthelmess, E.K. and Naz, R.K., Polycystic ovary syndrome: current status and future perspective. *Front. Biosci. (Elite edition)*, 6, 104, 2014.
25. Peluso, C. *et al.*, Ala307Thr and Asn680Ser Polymorphisms of FSHR Gene in Human Reproduction Outcomes. *Cell Physiol. Biochem.*, 34, 1527–1535, 2014.
26. Thathapudi, S. *et al.*, Association of follicle-stimulating hormone receptor gene ser680 asn (rs6166) polymorphism with polycystic ovarian syndrome. *Int. J. Reprod. Contracept. Obstet. Gynecol.*, 5, 9, 3126–3132, 2016.
27. Wu, X.-Q. *et al.*, Association between FSHR polymorphisms and polycystic ovary syndrome among Chinese women in north China. *J. Assist. Reprod. Genet.*, 31, 371–377, 2014.
28. Zangeneh, F.Z., Naghizadeh, M.M., Masoumi, M., Polycystic ovary syndrome and circulating inflammatory markers. *Int. J. Reprod. Biomed.*, 15, 6, 375, 2017.

29. Cordeiro, C.A., Moreira, P.R., Andrade, M.S., Dutra, W.O., Campos, W.R., Oréfice, F., Teixeira, A.L., Interleukin-10 gene polymorphism (−1082G/A) is associated with toxoplasmic retinochoroiditis. *Invest. Ophthalmol. Vis. Sci.*, 49, 5, 1979–82, 2008.

30. Barry, J.C., Shakibakho, S., Durrer, C., Simtchouk, S., Jawanda, K.K., Cheung, S.T., Mui, A.L., Little, J.P., Hyporesponsiveness to the anti-inflammatory action of interleukin-10 in type 2 diabetes. *Sci. Rep.*, 6, 21244, 2016; 17.

31. Polonsky, K.S., Sturis, J., Bell, G.I., Seminars in medicine of the Beth Israel Hospital, Boston. Non–insulin-dependent diabetes mellitus a genetically programmed failure of the beta cell to compensate for insulin resistance. *N. Engl. J. Med.*, 334, 777–783, 1996; 21.

32. Ogihara, S.D., Insulin-like growth factor II (IGF-II). *Int. J. Biochem. Cell Biol.*, 30, 7, 767–71, 1997.

33. Garzia, V., Erices, L., Valdes, P., Salzar, L., A common 34C > G variant at the peroxisome proliferator-activated receptor γ2-gene in Chilean women with polycystic ovary syndrome and controls. *Intl.*, 25, 4, 867–73, 1993.

34. Wang, Y., Wu, X., Cao, Y., Yi, L., Fan, H., Chen, J., Polymorphisms of the peroxisome proliferator-activated receptor-gamma and its coactivator-1 alpha genes in Chinese women with polycystic ovary syndrome. *Fertil. Steril.*, 85, 5, 1536–40, 2012.

35. Ciaraldi, T.P., Molecular defects of insulin action in the polycystic ovary syndrome: possible tissue specificity. *J. Pediatr. Endocrinol. Metab.*, 13, Suppl 5, 1291–3, 2000.

36. Skov, V., Glintborg, D., Knudsen, S., Jensen, T., Kruse, T.A., Tan, Q., Reduced expression of nuclear-encoded genes involved in mitochondrial oxidative metabolism in skeletal muscle of insulin-resistant women with polycystic ovary syndrome. *Diabetes*, 56, 9, 2349–55, 2007.

37. Michelmore, K., Ong, K., Mason, S., Bennett, S., Perry, L., Vessey, M., Clinical features in women with polycystic ovaries: relationships to insulin sensitivity, insulin gene VNTR and birth weight. *Clin. Endocrinol. (Oxf)*, 55, 4, 439–46, 2001.

38. Dunaif, A. and Graf, M., Insulin administration alters gonadal steroid metabolism independent of changes in gonadotropin secretion in insulin-resistant women with the polycystic ovary syndrome. *J. Clin. Invest.*, 83, 1, 23–9, 1997.

39. Plum, L., Belgardt, B.F., Bruning, J.C., Central insulin action in energy and glucose homeostasis. *J. Clin. Invest.*, 116, 7, 1761–6, 2006.

40. Chakraborty, C., Biochemical and molecular basis of insulin resistance. *Curr. Protein Pept. Sci.*, 7, 2, 113–21, 2006.

41. De Fronzo, R., Pathogenesis of type 2 diabetes: metabolic and molecular implications for identifying diabetes genes. *Diabetes Rev.*, 5, 177–269, 1997.

42. Newmann, B. *et al.*, Concordance for type 2 (non-insulin-dependent) diabetes mellitus in male twins. *Diabetologia*, 30, 763–768, 1987.

43. Lillioja, S. *et al.*, Insulin resistance and insulin secretory dysfunction as precursors of non-insulin-dependent diabetes mellitus. Prospective studies of Pima Indians. *N. Engl. J. Med.*, 329, 1988–1992, 1993.

44. Rich, S.S., Mapping genes in diabetes: genetic epidemiological perspective. *Diabetes*, 39, 1315–1319, 1990.

45. Martin, B.C. *et al.*, Role of glucose and insulin resistance in development of type 2 diabetes mellitus: results of a 25-year follow-up study. *Lancet*, 340, 925–929, 1992.

46. Taylor, S.I., Kadowaki, T., Kadowaki, H., Accili, D., Cama, A., McKeon, C., Mutations in insulin-receptor gene in insulin-resistant patients. *Diabetes Care*, 13, 3, 257–79, 1990.

47. Froguel, P. *et al.*, Close linkage of glucokinase locus on chromosome 7p to early-onset non-insulin-dependent diabetes mellitus. *Nature*, 356, 162–164, 1992.

48. Vionnet, N. *et al.*, Nonsense mutation in the glucokinase gene causes early-onset non-insulin-dependent diabetes mellitus. *Nature*, 356, 721–722, 1992.

49. Yamagata, K. *et al.*, Mutations in the hepatocyte nuclear factor-4alpha gene in maturity-onset diabetes of the young. . *Nat.*, 384, 458–460, 1996.

50. Sheskin DJ (2004) Handbook of parametric and nonparametric statistical procedures. 3rd ed. Boca Raton: Chapman & Hall/CRC.

51. Peluso, C. *et al.*, Ala307Thr and Asn680Ser Polymorphisms of *FSHR* Gene in Human Reproduction Outcomes. *Cell. Physiol. Biochem.*, 34, 1527–1535, 2014.

52. Sujatha, T. *et al.*, Association of FSHR gene ser680 asn (rs6166) polymorphism with PCOS. *Int. J. Reprod. Contracept. Obstet. Gynecol.*, 5, 9, 3126–3132, 2016.

53. Huang, X., Li, L., Hong, L., Zhou, W., Shi, H., Zhang, H., Zhang, Z., Sun, X., Du, J., The Ser680Asn polymorphism in the follicle-stimulating hormone receptor gene is associated with the ovarian response in controlled ovarian hyperstimulation. *Clin. Endocrinol.*, 82, 4, 577–583, 2015.

54. Chen, H., Tang, J., Shen, N., Ren, K., Interleukin 10 gene rs1800896 polymorphism is associated with the risk of prostate cancer. *Oncotarget*, 8, 39, 66204, 2017; 12.

55. Mosser, D.M. and Zhang, X., Interleukin-10: new perspectives on an old cytokine. *Immunol. Rev.*, 226, 1, 205–18, 2008.

56. Karadeniz, M. *et al.*, Polymorphism of the interleukin–10 gene in polycystic ovary syndrome. *Int. J. Immunogenet.*, 35, 119–123, 2008.

57. Rosenfield, R.L. and Ehrmann, D.A., The pathogenesis of polycystic ovary syndrome (PCOS): the hypothesis of PCOS as functional ovarian hyper-androgenism revisited. *Endocr. Rev.*, 37, 5, 467–520, 2016.

58. Azziz, R., PCOS: a diagnostic challenge. *Reprod. Biomed. Online*, 8, 6, 644–8, 2004.

59. Legro, J.M., Flight, I.H., Norman, R.J., Metformin in polycystic ovary syndrome: systematic review and meta-analysis. *BMJ*, 327, 7421, 951–3, 1999.

60. Chen, Z.J., Zhao, H., He, L., Shi, Y., Qin, Y., Li, Z., Genome-wide association study identifies susceptibility loci for polycystic ovary syndrome on chromosome 2p16.3, 2p21 and 9q33.3. *Nat. Genet.*, 43, 1, 55–9, 2011.

61. Ruan, Y., Ma, J., Xie, X., Association of IRS-1 and IRS-2 genes polymorphisms with polycystic ovary syndrome: A meta-analysis. *Endocr. J.*, 59, 601–609, 2012.

62. Arikoglu, H., Hepdogru, M.A., Kaya, D.E., Asik, A., Ipekci, S.H., Iscioglu, F., IRS1 gene polymorphisms Gly972Arg and Ala513Pro are not associated with insulin resistance and type 2 diabetes risk in non-obese Turkish population. *Meta Gene*, 2, 579–85, 2014; 1.

63. Yiannakouris, N., Cooper, J.A., Shah, S., Drenos, F., Ireland, H.A., Stephens, J.W., Li, K.W., Elkeles, R., Godsland, I.F., Kivimaki, M., Hingorani, A.D., IRS1 gene variants, dysglycaemic metabolic changes and type-2 diabetes risk. *Nutr. Metab. Cardiovasc. Dis.*, 22, 12, 1024–30, 2012;1.

64. Thangavelu, M., Godla, U.R., Paul, S.F., Maddaly, R., Single-nucleotide polymorphism of INS, INSR, IRS1, IRS2, PPAR-G and CAPN10 genes in the pathogenesis of polycystic ovary syndrome. *J. Genet.*, 96, 1, 87–96, 2017; 1.

65. Kilpeläinen, T.O., Zillikens, M.C., Stančakova, A., Finucane, F.M., Ried, J.S., Langenberg, C., Zhang, W., Beckmann, J.S., Luan, J.A., Vandenput, L., Styrkarsdottir, U., Genetic variation near IRS1 associates with reduced adiposity and an impaired metabolic profile. *Nat. Genet.*, 43, 8, 753, 2011.

66. Boura-Halfon, S. and Zick, Y., Phosphorylation of IRS proteins, insulin action, and insulin resistance. *Am. J. Physiol. Endocrinol. Metab.*, 296, 581–591, 2009.

67. Garzia, V., Erices, L., Valdes, P., Salzar, L., A common 34C > G variant at the peroxisome proliferator-activated receptor γ2- gene in Chilean women with polycystic ovary syndrome and controls. *Intl.*, 25, 4, 867–73, 1993.

68. Aguirre, V., Werner, E.D., Giraud, J., Lee, Y.H., Shoelson, S.E., White, M.F., Phosphorylation of Ser307 in insulin receptor substrate-1 blocks interactions with the insulin receptor and inhibits insulin action. *J. Biol. Chem.*, 277, 1531–1537, 2002.

69. Ruan, Y., Ma, J., Xie, X., Association of IRS-1 and IRS-2 genes polymorphisms with polycystic ovary syndrome: A meta-analysis. *Endocr. J.*, 59, 601–609, 2012.

70. Baba, T., Endo, T., Sata, F., Honnma, H., Kitajima, Y., Hayashi, T., Polycystic ovary syndrome is associated with genetic polymorphism in the insulin signalling gene IRS-1 but not ENPP1 in a Japanese population. *Life Sci.*, 81, 10, 850–4, 2007.

71. Haghani, K. and Bakhtiyari, S., The study on the relationship between IRS-1 Gly972Arg and IRS-2 Gly1057Asp polymorphisms and type 2 diabetes in the Kurdish ethnic group in West Iran. *Genet. Test. Mol. Biomarkers*, 16, 1270–1276, 2012.

13

An Insight of Protein Structure Predictions Using Homology Modeling

S. Muthumanickam[1], P. Boomi[1*], R. Subashkumar[2], S. Palanisamy[3], A. Sudha[4], K. Anand[5], C. Balakumar[6], M. Saravanan[7], G. Poorani[8], Yao Wang[9], K. Vijayakumar[10] and M. Syed Ali[11]

[1]*Department of Bioinformatics, Alagappa University, Karaikudi, Tamil Nadu, India*
[2]*Sri Ramakrishna College of Arts and Science (Formerly SNR Sons College) (Autonomous, Affiliated to Bharathiar University) Avinashi Road, Nava India, Coimbatore, Tamil Nadu, India*
[3]*East Coast Life Sciences Institute, Gangneung-Wonju National University, Gangneung, South Korea*
[4]*Department of Biotechnology, Dr. Umayal Ramanathan College for Women, Karaikudi, Tamil Nadu, India*
[5]*Department of Chemical Pathology, School of Pathology, Faculty of Health Sciences and National Health Laboratory Service, University of the Free State, Bloemfontein, South Africa*
[6]*Faculty of Pharmacy, Philadelphia University, Amman, Jordan*
[7]*Department of Microbiology and Immunology, Division of Biomedical Science, School of Medicine, College of Health Sciences, Mekelle University, Mekelle, Ethiopia*
[8]*Kumaraguru College of Technology, Coimbatore, Tamil Nadu, India*
[9]*School of life Science, Department of Biotechnology, Anyang Institute of Technology, Henan, China*
[10]*Department of Chemistry M. Kumarasamy College of Engineering Karur, Tamil Nadu, India*
[11]*P.G. and Research Department of Biotechnology, Mohamad Sathak College of Arts and Science, Chennai, Tamil Nadu, India*

Abstract

The homology modeling is the computational method, and it is one of the essential steps to construct the 3D protein structure using the query sequences of

Corresponding author: pboomi1983@gmaail.com

S. Balamurugan, Anand Krishnan, Dinesh Goyal, Balakumar Chandrasekaran and Boomi Pandi (eds.)
Computation in Bioinformatics: Multidisciplinary Applications, (265–278) © 2021 Scrivener Publishing LLC

amino acid and template protein. If the query sequence has similar with template structure, then the model structure can be easily predicted with high resolution. The homology modeling for structural prediction plays a crucial role to discover the novel drug target against the various diseases. Based on the two important principles such as laws of physics and evolution, the 3D protein structure can be predicted. According to the physical and evaluation principles, protein folds have stable and well-formed structure via minimizing the energy and protein molecule has outcome of gradual changes in sequence and structure. The homology modeling has different multi steps which are most accurate to predict the absolute model structure. When the sequence identity is below 15%, it cannot be used for further structure modeling which could be lead to deceptive conclusion. The maximum similarity between 30% and 40% obtained from the query and template sequences can be considered for further homology modeling. If the similarity is above 50%, then the obtained model is adequate quality which can be used for further molecular docking for protein-protein docking, protein-ligand complexes, and molecular dynamic simulation studies. This modeling technique is very comfortable, faster, and cost-effective. This chapter will discuss the different homology model for the prediction of protein structure for the drug development process.

Keywords: Homology modeling, methods, and tools used for homology modeling

13.1   Introduction

For over a decade, many organisms such as fungi, animals, and plant genomes have number of proteins. Millions of absolute 3D crystal structural for particular protein is cheerfully available in the protein dada bank (http://www.pdb.org). However, some of the protein has no identify the specific structure. The three-dimensional structure of prediction is a significant task for structural biology. Hence, the computational approach is imperative task to identify the protein structure from the data bank and to predict the new structure using various tools such as SWISS-MODEL, Robetta, I-TASSER, Phyre2, IntFOLD, Modbase, and HHpred [1, 2]. The detailed tools information is given below. When the sequence identity is below 15%, it cannot be use for further structure modeling which could be lead to deceptive conclusion. The maximum similarity between 30% and 40% obtained from the query and template sequences can be considered for further homology modeling. If the similarity is above 50%, then the obtained model is adequate quality which can be used for further molecular docking for protein-protein docking, protein-ligand complexes, and molecular dynamic simulation studies [3].

There are number of 3D protein structure available in PDB. As of January 2021, the PDB database contains 173,754 experimentally solved protein structures and UniProtKB database contains 563,927 annotated sequences. All the structures are solved from experimental method. The structural determination process in experiments involves many steps including protein expression analysis, protein purification, crystallization techniques (vapor diffusion, micro batch, and micro dialysis), and structure determined by x-ray crystallography and NMR (nuclear magnetic resonance) spectroscopy [4]. After conformation of structure obtained from above experimental and characterization techniques, the absolute 3D structure along with detailed information is available in the PDB database (http://www.pdb.org) [5]. Importantly, membrane protein is very difficult to crystallize and solve the structure due to their massive gap between the 3D protein structure and annotated sequences. Hence, computational modeling approach is innovative technique to predict the accurate structure and function of the protein [2].

Generally, three different approaches are used for the protein modeling: (i) homology or comparative modeling, (ii) *ab initio* modeling, and (iii) threading or protein folding.

The first homology or comparative modeling is the most precise computational method which can be used to build protein structure from the amino acid sequences if there is no experimental solved structure [6]. The method involves several approaches to predict their protein structure for making drug development [7]. Then, the *ab initio* modeling is an essential method to build the protein structure. If the protein structure has no available in the PDB and less quantity of similarity of protein, then this method can help to predict the new structure for the drug development process. Based on the physical principal and Monte-Carlo algorithm, the *ab initio* method has several approaches including ROSETTA, TOUCHSTONE-II, and I-Tasser to predict the protein structure. This approach is not widely used because of significant computational resources and low accuracy and to predict protein structures without any template [8]. Therefore, this is only applicable to small protein [9, 10]. Finally, threading or protein folding: this technique can be employing for sequences alignment with 3D structures to elect the suitable fold of a known sequence from a set of alternatives. There are two principles are adopted in threading or protein folding: first principle is primary sequence fold which is relatively closed into a similar structure. The second principle is limited number of protein structure folds [11]. This means that the non-homologous proteins have similar structures. The target protein sequence is folded with suitable template structure to predict the new structure and then optimized [12]. Thereby, the threading approach is usually not used, but sometimes, it is combined into other computational techniques [13].

13.2   Homology Modeling Approach

Generally, structural information for proteins is most valuable for drug discovery process than sequence alone. In biological sciences, the number of gene sequences is easily accessible, at the same time, the experimentally solved protein structure has very low. Therefore, homology modeling approach is imperative to predict the final model structure which is depending on the evolutionary relationship amidst the target and template protein sequences. Two major observations of homology modeling including three-dimensional structure determine the amino acid sequence, conserved protein structure, and small change that related to the sequence during evolution [14]. Generally, the procedure for homology modeling engages four steps such as identification potent target, sequence alignment, model constructing, and model refinement. The experimentally solved protein structure can be used as a template for protein structure modeling. From the resulting template, the structure has some criteria for selected templates such as level of similarity between the query and template sequence, the quality of the experimentally solved structure, and present ligand or cofactors. The homology modeling was predicted based on the protein structure similarity and sequence similarity. So, given experimental structure of templates to generate target sequences that share the significant sequence identity is above 30%. However, the structural prediction contains errors and experimentally accurate structures infrequently reach. Hence, the 30% identity of target template sequence is still challenging in the homology modeling. The correctness of the homology model is affected by three elements: (I) target and templates have structural similarity, (II) the accurate target template alignment, and (III) the ability to refine the model [15].

13.2.1   Strategies for Homology Modeling

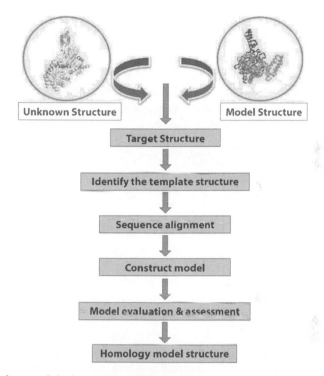

Note: If the modeled protein structure has not proper, further move for different templates for the different alignments.

13.2.2   Procedure

Several different approaches have been used for constructing protein model that has similar accuracy for model structure. The following procedures can be used to build the model structure.

1. To obtain the protein sequences from the UniProtKB database, the sequence file will be downloaded in the fasta format. The scientific community gives a unique file format for protein sequence. The fasta file is started with the symbol of ">" that gives specific information about the sequences.

>sp|-------|OPSD_
MNGTEGPNFYVPFSNATGVVRSPFEYPQYYLAEPWQFSMLAAYM
FLLIVLGFPINFLTL

2. The sequences are aligned to discover the template sequences of most similar targets to their amino acid sequences. The most extensively used algorithm for sequence alignment is BLAST (Basic Local Alignment Search Tool). The BLAST search gives a list of template PDB ID with Percentage of Identity.

3. To create a protein model, sequence alignment between the template and target sequences is needed. The ClustalW server can be used for multiple sequence alignment (MSA) which can give an evolutionary relationship. These are consensus symbols indicated by ClustalW2:

   - "*" indicates the perfect sequence alignment.
   - ":" indicates the site related to group showing strong similarity.
   - "." Indicates the site related to group showing less similarity.

After alignment, based on the higher similarity obtained from the query sequence and template sequence, the 3D protein model will be constructed for target protein. Finally, the obtained model will be used for evaluation and validation which can be performed by using PROCHECK and WHATCHECK server. Both servers provide the stereochemical assessment (bond order, bond length, bond order, polar, non-polar residues, bad contacts, etc.) for the better structural quality of the modeled protein structure.

13.3   Steps Involved in Homology Modeling

The overall homology modeling procedure consists of seven steps such as template identification, sequence alignment, backbone generation, loop modeling, side chain modeling, model optimization, and model validation.

13.3.1   Template Identification

The starting point for homology modeling process can be used for the identification of template structures from PDB, SCOP, distance-matrix alignment, and CATH [16, 17]. There are several tools with different approaches available to search the templates for target amino acid sequences. Among them, the sequence of similarity can be searched by BLAST, which can provide the pairwise sequence alignment to detect the evolutionary relationship in the range of 20%–30% sequence identify and also allows to comparing a target sequence with PDB database to identifying the best templates structure which can share a high degree of similarity. Sequence similarity of the template sequence is related to the target sequence which can generate the model 3D structures with high accuracy [18].

13.3.2   Sequence Alignment

Sequence similarity analysis is one of the most important steps to discover the homologous sequence. After selecting one or more suitable templates, how much sequence similarity is presented or not which will be analyzed by using sequence alignment tools such as ClustalW, Clustal Omega, and T-Coffee. Then, alignment correction will be done simultaneously. For the alignment correction, if any sequences are missing or more existing between the aligned sequences, then the sequences are automatically inserted or deleted, respectively. This process may enhance the quality of 3D protein structures.

13.3.3   Backbone Generation

The backbone generation is one of the crucial processes for the model structure which can be performed by using different tools such as Modeller or CASP. After sequence alignment, the real model building can be initiated to generate the backbone with the help of aligned sequence. If aligned residues are different, then the backbone coordinates (N, Cα, C, and O) and Cβ can be copied. Then, the conserved residues are completely copied and generate the 3D model [19].

13.3.4   Loop Modeling

Loop region for homology modeling is the important role for the construction of 3D model structure which can participate to active and binding sites. Several loop modeling approaches have been developed for numerous drug discovery applications. In most cases, few gaps existing in the target and template sequences through the insertion and deletion along with a little conformational change to the backbone chains. The prediction of conformational changes in loop regions is very difficult. However, the only happened in the secondary structure elements such helices and strands. But the conformational change cannot occur in secondary structure element due to several reasons. The reasons are that, first, surface loops can be involved to form crystal contacts between template and target; second is that to interexchange between the small and bulky groups; finally, if the

5 membered rings are present in amino acid side chains of Proline and hydrogen atoms present in the glycine structure, then it is very difficult to predict from the Ramachandran plot. Moreover, it is difficult to detect mutations in the loop residue from the glycine or proline [20].

13.3.5   Side Chain Modeling

The side chain modeling is an essential step to construct the protein structure by using homology modeling approaches. Generally, the side chain modeling can be done by the placing of side chain onto backbone coordinates from the parent structure and generated *ab initio* modeling simulation. The limited number of low energy conformation of protein side chain is called as the rotamers. Depending on the energy functions and search strategies, rotamers are elected with favored protein sequence and correct backbone coordinates. For side chain modeling, RAMP and SCWRL [21] servers can be utilized [22].

13.3.6   Model Optimization

When the start model optimization, the energy minimization can be done for the preparation of model protein through the molecular mechanics force fields. Every energy minimization steps, little error can be reduced and eliminated. Furthermore, few hundred steps energy minimization with suitable force filed can be used to decrease the error in the model structure. Different force fields such as CHARMM [23], GROMOS [24], and AMBER [25] have been used to correct the bond geometry and removal of bad contacts in their model protein structure. The steepest descent and conjugate gradient or other energy minimization algorithms can be used to optimize the model protein structure.

13.3.6.1   Model Validation

Finally, the constructed model structure can be further validated and verified. Depending on the sequence similarity, environmental parameters, and the quality of the templates, the accuracy of the generated model is different. Further, stereo-chemical analysis of the model is required to analysis the bond angel, bond order, torsion angle, and rotation angle parameters which can be determined through the different servers such as WHATCHECK, PROCHECK, SAVES, and molprobity. The Ramachandran plot is the most accurate method to check the quality of the protein structure through the distribution of Phi and Psi angles amino acid residues. In addition, the plot is used to understand the fall in of amino acid residues in allowed and disallowed regions. If the amino acids are fall in out of allowed region, then it will create the problem in the model structure. Furthermore, both VERIFY3D and PROSAII servers are used to determine the spatial arrangement based on their 3D conformation of the modeled protein [26–28].

13.4   Tools Used for Homology Modeling

13.4.1   Robetta

Robetta is a reliable web based interface server for the protein modeling suite. It is easily available for the fully automated structural prediction and structure information from genomic data. The Robetta server was first developed by David Baker, University of Washington. As of now, more than 44 collaborators are currently maintaining the. The protein structure can be predicted by using amino acid sequence through homology modeling or *ab initio* modeling approaches. There are number of modules such as Rosetta *ab initio*, RosettaNMR, RosettaDesign, Rosetta Dock, Rosetta Fragment Selection, Rosetta Nucleic Acids, and Rosetta Ligand, available in the Robetta server [29, 30].

13.4.2   M4T (Multiple Templates)

M4T server is a fully automated comparative protein modeling server and produce the accurate alignment by minimizing the errors associated with the comparative modeling. Two important steps are adopted: (1) to identify the one or more template candidates and (2) to decrease the error associated in the sequences alignment accuracy between target and template structure. The Multiple Mapping Method in the M4T server can gives absolute solutions for many alignment methods. In the final step, the structure building can be performed by using the modeler [31].

13.4.3   I-Tasser (Iterative Implementation of the Threading Assembly Refinement)

The I-Tasser (Iterative implementation of the Threading ASSEmbly Refinement) is the most popular web-based interface for protein structural prediction servers. The I-Tasser protocol gives new guidelines for design the web server system to protein structural and functional prediction.

It generates the super quality of 3D structure from the amino acid sequences by computer algorithms. I-Tasser server is freely available web server for academic use. The server can be used to store the data for every three months and develop the confidence scoring system [32, 33].

13.4.4   ModBase

In 1998, ModBase was developed by Sali group, and currently, ModBase contains 38,000,000 protein models from the 66 species. The ModBase software mostly relies on the modeller. ModBase is an annotated comparative modeling database.

13.4.5   Swiss Model

The Swiss model is web-based interface, fully automated protein modeling server, and its access via ExPASy proteomics web server. Globally, all biochemists and molecular biologists can be used for protein modeling in this server. Each user has a personal working interface and several modeling projects can be carried out at the same time. The template selection, modeling building, and structural quality evaluation can be implemented within the workspace [34].

13.4.6   PHYRE2 (Protein Homology/Analogy Recognition Engine 2)

PHYRE2 is a web-based interface homology modeling server that can be used to predict and analyze the structure, function, and mutations of the protein. The sophisticated BackPhyre facilities can be used for searching the protein structure toward wide range of genomes, quantity of protein sequences for homology modeling, and threading provision for user sequence onto user structure, and Phyrealarm for repeated scan for proteins that are very tricky to discover the deep analysis of model quality of protein structure, function, and mutation. Advanced Phyre2 servers, a remote homology modeling approaches to construct a 3D structure of a protein, create a binding site and find the amino acid variants of the protein sequences. The server provides the sequence information about the secondary and tertiary structure of the model protein [35].

13.4.7   Modeller

Modeller is a most frequently used programs for homology modeling which is freely available software, and it has a lot of powerful features.

Modeller is very fast and automatically calculates the non-hydrogen atoms. The modeller is not only perform the model structural and also performs some tasks the fold assessment, two or more sequence alignment, clustering of the sequence and loop modeling using *ab initio* modeling method to construct the 3D protein structures [36].

13.4.8   Conclusion

Homology modeling is the promising important computational techniques to construct the 3D model structure. For the protein structure prediction, several methods and tools have been used. Two important principles including physical and evaluation have also been applied to predict the 3D protein structure. The protein folds should be a stable and well-formed structure though minimizing the energy and protein molecule should be gradual changes in sequence and structure. From the homology modeling, we can create an absolute structural model through the sequence alignment which could be used for the development of novel target against various human diseases.

Acknowledgement

The authors thankfully acknowledge the UGC-Innovative [No.F. 14-13/2013 (Inno/ASIST)], DST-FIST [SR/FST/LSI-667/2016(C)], DST PURSE [SR/PURSE Phase 2/38 (G)], MHRD-RUSA 2.0 [F.24/51/2014-U Policy (TNMulti-Gen), Dept. of Edn. Govt. of India], and DST-SERB [EEQ/2016/000044] for the financial supports and infrastructure facilities.

References

1. Melissa, R.P. and Ian Menz, R., Methods for Protein Homology Modelling. *Appl. Mycol. Biotechnol.*, 6, 37, 2006.
2. Kuntal, B.K., Aparoy, P., Reddanna, P., EasyModeller: A graphical interface to MODELLER. *BMC Res. Notes*, 3, 226, 1–5, 2010.
3. Reddy, C.S., Vijayasarathy, K., Srinivas, E., Sastry, G.M., Sastry, G.N., Homology modeling of membrane proteins: A critical assessment. *Comput. Biol. Chem.*, 30, 2, 120–126, 2006.
4. Eswar., N., Eramian, D., Webb, B., Shen, M.-Y., Sali, A., Comparative Protein Structure Modeling Using Modeller. *Curr. Protoc. Bioinf.*, 54, 1–5, 2006.

5. Berman, H.M., Westbrook, J., Feng, Z., Gilliland, G., Bhat, T.N., Weissig, H., Shindyalov, I.N., Bourne, P.E., The Protein Data Bank. *Nucleic Acids Res.*, 28, 235–242, 2000.

6. Sanchez, R. and Sali, A., Advances in comparative protein-structure modeling. *Curr. Opin. Struct. Biol.*, 7, 206–214, 1997.

7. Kallberg, M., Wang, H., Wang, S., Peng, J., Wang, Z., Lu, H., Xu, J., Template-based protein structure modeling using the RaptorX web server. *Nat. Protoc.*, 7, 8, 1511–1522, 2012.

8. Moult, J., Fidelis, K., Kryshtafovych, A., Tramontano, A., Critical assessment of methods of protein structure prediction (CASP)-round. *Proteins*, 86, 7–15, 2011.

9. Lee, J., Wu, S., Zhang, Y., Ab Initio Protein Structure Prediction. In From Protein Structure to Function with Bioinformatics. *BMC Biol.*, 17, 3–25, 2007.

10. Rigden, D.J. (Ed.), *TASSER simulations*, pp. 3–25, Springer, Dordrecht, Netherlands, 2009.

11. Wu, S., Skolnick, J., Zhang, Y., Ab initio modeling of small proteins by iterative TASSER simulations. *BMC Biol.*, 5, 17, 2007.

12. Lesk, A.M. and Chothia, C.H., The Response of Protein Structures to Amino-Acid Sequence Changes. *Philos. Trans. R. Soc., A*, 317, 345, 1986.

13. Rayan, A., Siew, N., Cherno-Schwartz, S., Matzner, Y., Bautsch, W., Goldblum, A., A novel computational method for predicting the transmembrane structure of G-protein coupled receptors: application to human C5aR and C3aR. *Recept. Channels*, 7, 121–137, 2000.

14. Fiser, A., Template-Based Protein Structure Modeling. *Methods Mol. Biol.*, 673, 73–94, 2010.

15. Zhou, H. and Zhou, Y., Fold recognition by combining sequence profiles derived from evolution and from depth-dependent structural alignment of fragments. *Proteins*, 58, 321–328, 2005.

16. Muhammed, T.M. and Aki-Yalcin, E., Homology modeling in drug discovery: Overview, current applications, and future perspectives. *Chem. Biol. Drug Des.*, 93, 12–20, 2019.

17. Westbrook, J., Feng, Z., Jain, S., The Protein Data Bank: unifying the archive. *Nucleic Acids Res.*, 30, 245–248, 2002.

18. Saxena, A., Singh Sangwan, R., Mishra, S., Fundamentals of Homology Modeling Steps and Comparison among Important Bioinformatics Tools: An Overview. *Sci. Int.*, 1, 237–252, 2013.

19. Gromiha, M.M., Nagarajan, R., Selvaraj, S., Protein Structural Bioinformatics: An Overview, in: *Encyclopedia of Bioinformatics and Computational Biology*, vol. 2, pp. 445–459, 2019.

20. Cavasotto, C.N. and Phatak, S.S., Homology modeling in drug discovery: current trends and applications. *Drug Discovery Today*, 14, 676–683, 2009.

21. Krivov, G.G., Shapovalov, M.V., Dunbrack Jr., R.L., Improved prediction of protein side-chain conformations with SCWRL4. *Proteins*, 77, 778–795, 2009.

22. Hameduh, T., Haddad, Y., Adam, V., Heger, Z., Homology modeling in the time of collective and artificial intelligence. *Comput. Struct. Biotechnol. J.*, 18, 3494–3506, 2020.

23. Brooks, B.R., Bruccoleri, R.E., Olafson, B.D., States, D.J., Swaminathan, S., Karplus, M., CHARMM: A program for macromolecular energy, minimization, and dynamics calculations. *J. Comput. Chem.*, 4, 187–217, 1983.

24. Scott, W.R., Hünenberger, P.H., Tironi, I.G., Mark, A.E., Billeter, S.R., Fennen, J., van Gunsteren, W.F., The GROMOS Biomolecular Simulation Program Package. *J. Phys. Chem. A*, 103, 3596–3607, 1999.

25. Cornell, W.D., Cieplak, P., Bayly, C.I., Gould, I.R., Merz, K.M., Ferguson, D.M., Kollman, P.A., A Second Generation Force Field for the Simulation of Proteins, Nucleic Acids, and Organic Molecules. *J. Am. Chem. Soc.*, 117, 5179–5197, 1995.

26. Chen, V.B., Arendall, W.B., Headd, J.J., Keedy, D.A., Immormino, R.M., Kapral, G.J., Murray, L.W., Richardson, J.S., Richardson, D.C., MolProbity: all-atom structure validation for macromolecular crystallography. *Acta Crystallogr. Sect. D Biol. Crystallogr.*, 66, 12–21, 2010.

27. Carugo, O. and Djinovic, C.K., Half a century of Ramachandran plots. *Acta Crystallogr. Sect. D Biol. Crystallogr.*, 69, 1333–1341, 2013.

28. Cavasotto, C.N. and Phatak, S.S., Homology Modeling in Drug Discovery: Current Trends and Applications. *Drug Discovery Today*, 14, 676–683, 2009.

29. Chivian, D., Kim, E., Malmström, L., Bradley, P., Robertson, T., Murphy, P., Strauss, E.M., Bonneau, R., Rohl, A., Bakr, D., Automated prediction of CASP-5 structures using the Robetta server. *Proteins*, 53, 524–533, 2003.

30. Kim, D.E. and Dylan, C., David Baker. Protein structure prediction and analysis using the Robetta server. *Nucleic Acids Res.*, 32, W526–W531, 2004.

31. Fernandez-Fuentes, N., Madrid-Aliste, C.J., Rai, B.K., Jorge, E.F., Fiser, A., M4T: a comparative protein structure modeling server. *Nucleic Acids Res.*, 35, W363–W368, 2007.

32. Yang, Z., I-TASSER server for protein 3D structure prediction. *BMC Bioinf.*, 9, 40, 1–8, 2008.

33. Roy, A., Kucukura, A., Zhang, Y., I-TASSER: a unified platform for automated protein structure and function prediction. *Nat. Protoc.*, 5, 725–738, 2010.

34. Lalit, R.S., Vikrant, C.S., Abhay, C., Online Servers and Offline Tools for Protein Modelling, Optimization and Validation: A Review. *Int. J. Pharm. Sci. Rev. Res.*, 28, 123–127, 2014.

35. Kelley, L.A., Mezulis, S., Yates, C.M., Wass, M.N., Sternberg, M.J., The Phyre2 web portal for protein modeling, prediction and analysis. *Nat. Protoc.*, 10, 845–858, 2015.

36. Mellow, F. and Sali, A., Fold assessment for comparative protein structure modeling. *Protein Sci.*, 16, 2412–2426, 2007.

14

Basic Concepts in Proteomics and Applications

Jesudass Joseph Sahayarayan[1]*, A.S. Enogochitra[2] and Murugesan Chandrasekaran[3]

[1]Department of Bioinformatics, Alagappa University, Karaikudi, India
[2]Department of Physics, Dr. URCW, Karaikudi, India
[3]Department of Food Science and Biotechnology, Sejong University, Gwangjin-gu, Seoul, Korea

Abstract

Compared to genomics or transcriptomics, proteomics is often regarded as an "emerging technology," i.e., as not having reached the same level of maturity. While the successful implementation of proteomics workflows and technology still requires significant levels of expertise and specialization, great strides have been made to make the technology more powerful, streamlined, and accessible. In 2014, two landmark studies published the first draft versions of the human proteome. We aim to provide an introduction specifically into the background of mass spectrometry (MS)–based proteomics. Within the field, MS has emerged as a core technology. Coupled to increasingly powerful separations and data processing and bioinformatics solution, it allows the quantitative analysis of whole proteomes within a matter of days, a timescale that has made global comparative proteome studies feasible at last. We present and discuss the basic concepts behind proteomics MS and the accompanying topic of protein and peptide separations, with a focus on the properties of datasets emerging from such studies.

Keywords: Proteomics, mass spectrometry, data formats

*Corresponding author: jjsrbioinformatics2016@gmail.com

S. Balamurugan, Anand Krishnan, Dinesh Goyal, Balakumar Chandrasekaran and Boomi Pandi (eds.)
Computation in Bioinformatics: Multidisciplinary Applications, (279–294) © 2021 Scrivener Publishing LLC

14.1   Introduction

A bacterial cell may seem simple but it's actually a complex structure - a gel-like matrix of the cytoplasm, surrounded by both a lipid bilayer cell membrane and a cell wall. The cell should play out totally different limits together with affirming enhancements, handling those upgrades, improving, partitioning cells, and discharging waste. What is the incorporation of particles? Despite, however, water, proteins, starches, totally different particles, and sorted out varied particles are contained within the living substance, proteins do an oversized portion of the work. For development and age, a traditional bacteria desires in far more than 4,000 proteins for development and age. Not the combination of the proteins is formed, at the same time, and a few are made terribly beneath extraordinary conditions, as an example, once the cell is pushed or finds up in an exceedingly novel region. The complement of proteins found in this single cell in a particular environment is the proteome. Proteomics is the assessment of the affiliation, structure, purpose of confinement, and cooperation of the proteins composing the exercises of every living cell.

If a bacterial cell needs more than 4,000 proteins, how many can we expect to find in animals? Mammals, including humans, have probably more than 100,000 proteins. Despite the way during which the ordering contains the intrinsic course of action like an expert being, the proteins of eukaryotes provide the exceptional structure and farthest purpose that depicts a selected cell or a tissue kind and finally portrays a living being. Varied styles of cells build varied proteins; therefore, the protein of one cell is not really clone of the proteome of another. Similarly, cells that outcome from a befoulment, for example, venturesome improvement, have protein curiously with customary cells. During this manner, understanding the conventional protein of a cell is principal in understanding the developments that occur thanks to malady. This information will incite a comprehension of the atomic clarification behind the unwellness, which might then have the selection to be used to create treatment ways. Knowing how the proteome changes as the organism grows may also provide insight into the mechanisms of development in healthy organisms.

Under the standard plan of "one quality makes one force", the protein would essentially fuse the ultimate outcomes of the noteworthy variety of attribute gifts within the ordering of a living being. In any case, it is

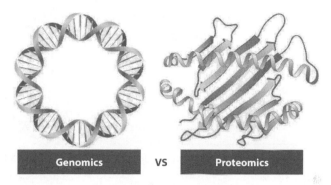

Figure 14.1 The difference between the genomics and proteomics. (Source: https://microbenotes.com/difference-between-genomics-and-proteomics/.)

not that principal. The life of attributes apparent within the human ordering is largely around 30,000–35,000. In what farthest purpose will simply 35,000 attributes code in far more than 100,000 proteins? There are many potential responses to the present solicitation, which is able to be talked regarding in additional detail beneath. One answer is that each quality could code many proteins in an exceedingly strategy known as elective connection. Elective connection proposes that one quality could build organized informational RNA things and, on these lines, various proteins. Another answer is that one lipid molecule can be adjusted incorrectly once it is consolidated with the target that it builds a substitute work. A third answer is that proteins organize with each other in complicated pathways and systems of pathways which can modification their capability. Thusly, one quality could build a few, in each sensible sense varied proteins in an exceedingly mix of how. Figure 14.1 showed the difference between the genomics and proteomics.

14.2   Challenges on Proteomics

At the end of the last century, a change of paradigm from the pure function driven biosciences to systematic and holistic approaches has taken place. Following the unbelievable genetics undertakings, customary lipid molecule science has advanced into a high output and biosciences, known as proteomics. Starting in 1995, the first attempts to deliver a "protein complement of the genome" used the established high-resolving separation techniques like two-dimensional (2D) gel electrophoresis and almost exclusively identified the proteins by the increasingly powerful mass spectrometry. Presently, head and thought difficulties were seen. Instead of the ordering, the protein is dynamic, reacting to any modification in hereditary and typical parameters. Furthermore, the proteome appears a control of being sales of degree additionally owing than an ordering, thanks to connection and modifying structures at the ribonucleic acid level and inferable from all the post-translational occasions on the lipid molecule level, as obligated addressing, post-translational changes, and befoulment. The circumstance is way logically badly designed, since different large proteins are simply gift in an exceedingly few duplicates/cells and should be seen and evaluated within observant an amazing overabundance of various compounds. The dynamic range of the abundant and the minor proteins often exceeds the capabilities of all analytical methods.

So far, only few solutions are available to handle the complexity and dynamic range. One is to reduce the complexity of the proteome and to separate the low abundant proteins from the more abundant ones. This, as a model, will be developed by multidimensional bundle steps. In any case, impulsive fiascos of proteins and countless occurring sections build this framework redundant and thus absurd. Of course, the protein to be studied will be efficient by opening with a precise traditional partition or by decreasing the whimsy utilizing an inexpensive model coming up with (for example, impulse substance chips, functionalized exterior chips, and class-unequivocal antiserum). Profitable models are assessment of vital structures, or the most interaction proteomics approaches moves to shut down. In an additional framework, a specific distinctive confirmation is performed, that envisions simply a selected variety of compound that shows categorical general functions. This could be developed by antibodies, specific recoloring seems, super molecule ligands, or categorical mass chemical analysis frameworks like MRM (particular response viewing) or SRM (single response checking) [1]. The foremost prompt utilization of this system is "based on proteomics" that screens a touch course of action of clearly got proteins/peptides.

Regardless, within the later broad stretches of the previous century, the essential issue of intermingling of proteomics undertakings was to unravel the constituents of a protein. It was realized only simply bit by bit that, for taking care of standard troubles and understanding the capability of clearing access, the developments and also the elements that vary on the super molecule range should be checked tentatively.

14.3   Proteomics Based on Gel

Since 1975, in the presentation by O'Farrel [2] and Klose [3], second gels contain charmed totally different researchers inferable from their bundle management. The combination of a concentrating structure (as an example, isoelectric centering) with a partition as appeared by mass (as an example, SDS gel electrophoresis) provides an area to subsidence in far more than 10,000 specific mixes. Hence, second gels were the strategy for call, whereas control particularly complicated lipid molecule blends similar to protein molecule. Unfortunately, gel-based proteomics had inalienable controls in duplicability and dynamic variation (Figure 14.2). Normal working frameworks should be fastidiously searched for once to induce essentially duplicatable outcomes even within one science laboratory. Results produced from identical samples in different labs in varied labs were less in each manner that actually matters and is vague on a tentative stage. An important development was the presentation of the DIGE method (GE Healthcare), a multiplexed fluorescent Cy-Dye recoloring of assorted protein states that killed, to a monster degree, the actual undependability [4]. Among the cysteine-changing "DIGE submersion checking", vital protein insight will be trained with simply a few of micrograms

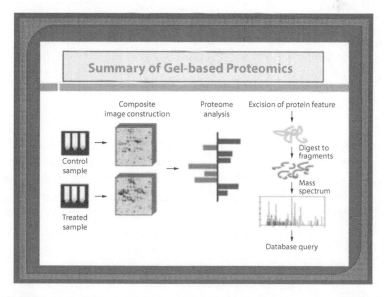

Figure 14.2 Gel-based proteomics. (Source: https://www.slideshare.net/AngelSForde/gel-based-proteomics-and-protein-sequences-analysis.)

of preliminary substance [5]. A weight is that singular two various glowing chemicals are monetarily accessible for "total DIGE" and also the expenses of the chemicals are genuinely restrictive for additional noteworthy Proteomics experiences. Additionally, limitations in load capacity, quantitative reproducibility, difficulties in handling, and interfacing troubles to mass chemical analysis make sure that the assessment noteworthiness and meticulous nature of the gel-based proteomics are considered.

14.4   Non-Gel–Based Electrophoresis Method

How to beat the preventions of gels and, at the same time, stay the compensation of an intent partition manner similar to iso-electric centering? Two or three instruments were engineered up which will prohibit proteins in strategy at any rate by the by utilize a centering structure. Probably, the most recognized realizations of these concepts are free-flow electrophoresis instruments like "Octopus" (Becton Dickinson) and the "Off-Gel" system (Agilent). Undoubtedly, when these rather new systems are compared with 2D gels, distinct advantages in recovery and improvements in the amount that can be applied have been realized, but interfacing to a further separation dimension is hampered by rather large volumes and buffer constituents. Thusly, the goals of second gels have not been return to up till this time. Sooner instead of later, specific and vital updates are to be relied on to typically beat a part of the hindrances.

14.5   Chromatography

In the restricted scene of portion systems, natural process looked as if it would have the potential as elective instrument for all around protein assessment. Regardless, from proportional font lipid molecule science, it absolutely was noteworthy that proteins did not provide quantitative recovery in several activity modes. So far, only one non-gel multidimensional approach based on chromatographic methods was commercially realized. Within the "Proteome Lab thulium PF-2D" framework (Beckman), a chromatofocusing phase got beside a turned stage natural process fractionates the model into in far more than 1,000 segments. In any case, here, what is more, the little bit of slack to stay the proteins in blueprint is undermined with the manner wherever that the destinations of the completely activity course of action is on an awfully basic level under with the intention of second gels.

14.6   Proteomics Based on Peptides

Thusly, seeing as unquestionably quantitative complex distributions of proteins looked as if it would be extensively irritating, totally different selections were scanned for. One affordable new plan was to maneuver the package and appraisal issue from the lipid molecule to the amide level. On the off probability that this might be rehearsed, another piece of speed, mechanization, and duplicability will be gotten. During this manner, new peptide-based structures, as an example, MudPIT [6], were created wherever within the wake of cutting the protein into peptides, and astoundingly computerized multidimensional fluid natural process divisions were trailed by perceiving confirmation of the peptides utilizing couple mass chemical analysis. Mainly owing to this switch to peptide based proteomics, chromatography experienced a new boom, and miniaturization of peptide separation columns to diameters below 100 μm and introduction of instruments that were capable to deliver nanoliter flow rates became available. Nano-LC with on the net or separated mass qualitative analysis territory got normal. Regardless, in complex mode, nano-LC continues to be resting on the sting of specific usefulness despite all that it experiences nonattendance of vitality and easy managing.

With the employment of the peptide-based proteomics techniques, a number of certifiable disadvantages got plainly axiomatic. By cleaving the proteins into peptides, not only the complexity of the proteome was increased by tenfold, but important information concerning the protein identification was also destroyed. Totally different peptides are indistinguishably found in essentially all varied proteins. On these lines, from an amide, the forerunner as a rule cannot be resolved without ambiguity. Moreover, furthermore, different isoforms, post-translationally modified proteins, or processing and degradation products of a protein, all produce a large set of identical peptides. Thusly, the quantitative knowledge for a selected lipid molecule finishes up being questionable. Extents of an amide that are open in additional than one lipid molecule animal varieties do not mirror the proportion of a specific protein animal types, nevertheless somewhat the proportion of the combination of all lipid molecule kinds that enclose this amide.

Due to the complexity and the necessity to analyze and identify each peptide by tandem mass spectrometry, proteome analysis time and costs increased markedly. Carefully, nowadays, even the foremost brisk mass spectrometers do not seem to be established to interrupt down intimately the whole thing of the larger half gift in one LC run. During this manner, typically significantly minor peptides do not seem to be compound. This declared that "undersampling" is insistently one reason behind the usually surprising duplicability of protein considers wherever habitually a basic abundance of the analysis provides essentially 20%–30% of covering information. Thanks to these points of read, drop-off of multifarious nature in complex proteomics got to be complete at lipid molecule stage. The lead of a lipid molecule throughout a bundle may be a trademark parameter and got to likewise be used for unequivocal ID and separation of particular protein type.

14.7   Stable Isotopic Labeling

To progress the quantitative proteomics consequences, "isotope stepping" systems be bestowed. These "isotopic weakening" techniques were by then appreciated for the appraisal of very little particles, drugs, and proteins. The pioneering work to introduce this technique into the proteomics field was done by the Aebersold group, where the cysteine residues in all proteins of two proteomic states were modified with a biotin-containing either heavy or light version of a reagent (isotope coding affinity tag, ICAT®) (7). By that time, the checked proteins are joined and secluded addicted to peptides. Essentially, the cysteine-consisting peptides passing on the engraving are inaccessible by appreciating cleansing utilizing streptavidin. Amide division Peptide separation and mass analysis revealed the identity of the peptides and at the same time determined by the signal intensity of the isotopic peptide pair the quantitative ratio of the peptides in the original proteomes. Enhanced styles of atom chemicals are created, as an example, atom cryptography lipid molecule name, ICPL® (Serva), insignificant amino event open reagents, that gave higher response yields and expanded collecting thought [8].

Of course, an introduction of the isotopic label as early as possible is desirable, since all the steps performed without the isotopic control may contribute to quantitatively wrong results. Consequently, presenting the atom engraving at a great deal of previous time of a protein assessment was created. Culture media improved with N15 atoms or constant isotope naming of amino acids in cell culture was worn in Proteomics test, significantly in cell culture or by means of microbes [9]. Regardless, with an interesting travail, a "SILAC mouse" was in like manner created in addition to use in proteomics tests [10]. The metabolic stepping approaches are conventionally confined to cell culture separates plus do not seem to be Brobdingnagian to tests from higher living things (for example, body liquids and tissues).

Thus, for peptide-based approaches, distinctive atom reagents were planned. The foremost indisputable is iTRAQ (ABI), a get-together of eight isobaric amino party open chemicals [11]. Because of the identical mass of all variants of the reagent, a certain peptide derived from different proteome states will appear with the identical mass and thus - in contrast to non-isobaric isotopic reagents – the labeling does not increase the complexity in the mass spectrum. Regardless, with a basic, unpretentious, and snappy MS analysis, no quantitative information will be picked up. Essentially throughout MS/MS analysis, unequivocal writer particles for the varied reagents are freed and might be surveyed. To create quantitative right outcomes, the mass chosen for MS/MS assessment should exist actually uncontaminated. This frequently is not true in jam-squeezed chromatograms. Thusly, the upsides of elevated multiplexing with isobaric chemicals are extremely reduced by the block to quite low down complicated amide blends in addition to by the assignment to isolate every derivative peptide by MS/MS examination to reveal tentative outcomes.

14.8   Data Mining and Informatics

One of the major difficulties in larger proteomics projects is the enormous amount of data that will be produced. Indeterminable mass spectra from every proteomic condition will be compound astoundingly by utilizing progressive programming approaches. By ideals of referencing high exposure in stuffed spectra and testing peptide/protein analytic proof and also the insignificant extent of data to be controlled nowadays, information appraisal and knowledge assessment are, by a large edge, the foremost uninteresting piece of a protein assessment. Software for automatically detecting the interesting proteins that change from one proteome state to another and filtering such proteins out of the complex proteome data can be expected in the near future.

Thriving information processing may be a mixture of knowledge science and programming operating within the territory of social security. There are numerous current areas of research within the field of Health Informatics, including Bioinformatics, Image Informatics (e.g. Neuroinformatics), Clinical Informatics, Public Health Informatics, and also Translational BioInformatics (TBI) analysis that drained health information processing (as altogether with its subfields) will connect from information checking, recovery, storing up, appraisal utilizing information mining techniques, etc. However, the scope of this study will be research that uses data mining in order to answer questions throughout the various levels of health.

The entirety of the assessments that drained a selected subfield of health information processing uses information from a specific degree of human closeness [12]. Bioinformatics utilizes atomic level information; neuroinformatics utilizes tissue level information; clinical information processing applies tolerant level information; and public health information processing uses people information (either from the bulk or on the majority). These subfields do currently and once more unfold (for instance, a solitary report ought to actually think about information from two contiguous levels); nevertheless, considering a true stress for compelling disarray, we tend to, during this work, organize AN assessment subject to the foremost raised information level used (as this paper is controlled by information use). In addition, within a given data level we will break down studies based on the type (i.e., level) of question a study attempts to answer, where each question level is of a relatively comparable scope to one of the data levels. The tissue level is of like extension to the human-scale science queries, the extent of patient information is known with clinical solicitation, and also the level of the people information is similar to the pandemic level solicitation.

The level of data used by the subfield TBI, then again, misuses information from these levels, from the atomic level to whole individual teams [12]. Specifically, TBI is, without ambiguity, based on composing information from the bioinformatics level with the additional huge levels, considering the manner that for the foremost half of this level has been withdrawn within the assessment workplace and isolated from the additional patient-challenging levels (neuroinformatics, clinical information processing, and population informatics). TBI and connection information from all degrees of human closeness is an acclaimed new heading in health information processing. The quality level of solicitation that TBI eventually tries to answer is on the clinical level, and in like manner, answers will facilitate improved HCO for patients. Research throughout all levels of accessible data, using various data mining and analytical techniques, can be used to help the healthcare system make decisions faster, more accurately, and more efficiently, all in a more cost-effective manner than without using such methods.

14.9   Applications of Proteomics

Proteomics revealed that major applications as the capacity to dissect post-translational adjustments of proteins. These changes can be phosphorylation, glycosylation, and sulphation just as some different adjustments associated with the support of the structure of a protein.

These adjustments are significant for the movement, dissolvability, and limitation of proteins in the cell. Assurance of protein change is considerably more troublesome as opposed to the recognizable proof of proteins. With respect to distinguishing proof reason, just not many peptides are required for protease cleavages followed by database arrangement of a known grouping of a peptide. Be that as it may, for assurance of change in a protein, substantially more materials are required as all the peptides do not have the normal sub-atomic mass should be broke down further.

The significant attribution of proteomics toward the improvement of protein cooperation guide of a cell is of huge incentive to comprehend the science of a cell. The information about the hour of articulation of a specific protein, its degree of articulation, and, at long last, its cooperation with another protein to shape a transitional for the exhibition of a particular natural capacity is as of now accessible.

These intermediates can be abused for remedial purposes too. An appealing method to contemplate the protein-protein associations is to clean the whole multi-protein complex by partiality-based techniques utilizing GST-combination proteins, antibodies, peptides, and so on.

Phage show is where bacteriophage particles are made to communicate either a peptide or protein of intrigue intertwined to a capsid or coat protein. It very well may be utilized to screen for peptide epitopes, peptide ligands, catalyst substrate, or single chain counter acting agent sections.

Another significant strategy to distinguish protein-protein cooperation includes the utilization of fluorescence reverberation vitality move (FRET) between fluorescent labels on connecting proteins. FRET is a non-radioactive procedure, whereby vitality from an energized contributor fluorophore is moved to an acceptor fluorophore. After excitation of the first fluorophore, FRET is identified either by discharge from the second fluorophore utilizing suitable channels or by change of the fluorescence lifetime of the benefactor.

A proteomics technique of expanding significance includes the restriction of proteins in cells as an important initial move toward understanding protein work in complex cell systems. The revelation of GFP (green fluorescent protein) and the advancement of its unearthly variations have made the way for investigation of proteins in living cells by utilization of the light magnifying instrument.

The biggest utilization of proteomics keeps on being protein articulation profiling. The articulation levels of a protein test could be estimated by 2-DE or other novel strategy, for example, isotope coded proclivity tag (ICAT). Utilizing these methodologies, the changing degrees of articulation of two distinctive protein tests can likewise be broken down.

With the assistance of the data accessible through clinical proteomics, a few medications have been planned. This intends to find the proteins with clinical pertinence to recognize a potential objective for pharmaceutical turn of events, a marker(s) for infection analysis or arranging, and hazard evaluation both for clinical and natural examinations. Proteomic advances will assume a significant job in tranquilize revelation, diagnostics, and subatomic medication as a result of the connection between qualities, proteins, and disease.

14.10   Future Scope

However, so far many proteomics experiments published did not really deliver solid and valuable scientific content. This partly is connected with the idea of holistic approaches per se, that the observation of the reactions of a perturbed system does not necessarily provide a simple and clear answer, but rather is a hypothesis generating concept. Unfortunately, the technical ability to cope with proteome complexity is still very limited despite the amazing technical progresses in mass spectrometry and nanoseparations. On these lines, it is from time to time tried to seem into a protein with monstrous travail, time, and cash; in any case with this analysis, the bulk of the force proteins is tough to achieve. Simply AN retiring quantity of the protein will be investigated, and to denounce the criticality and legality of the outcomes, trademark and real accentuations of the evaluations are deductively needed. Regardless, by prudence of the goliath travail and tremendous prices, this can be ordinarily unnoticed. The danger is that over the long term, by dominating uncommon affordable practice, the ardent plan of proteomics as a system of rules can be attended.

From now forward, we are obligated to elucidate sharp and present-day frameworks to guard in-depth and essential characteristic knowledge with these movements in check standing, section sciences, mass chemical analysis, and information processing. Closest to this goal is probably "targeted proteomics." Already, nowadays, this fashion of thinking will screen several famed proteins quantitatively and cautiously and it will increase insistence and as time goes on go into custom scientific diagnostics.

Through general relative proteomics in making an attempt the full plan, the condition is dynamically gone head to go with general close to protein science. Neither examination noteworthiness nor quantitative correctness is appealing nowadays. Post-translational modifications and analysis of many different protein species originating from the same gene present major difficulties in high throughput approaches and require innovative strategies. Atom naming techniques are in group action with mark free methodologies. After one decade of rapid improvements in analysis techniques and only slight improvement in the separation field, the acute pressure is now on the further development in separation sciences. The overwhelming majority of the problems and deficiencies are seen, and totally different professionals are handling their answers. Following multi-decade of spirited redesigns in assessment systems and primarily slight improvement within the detachment field, the unexampled weight is at the present on any movement in fragment sciences. Tangled, well-masterminded, and particularly computerized work structures utilizing each natural process and electrophoresis are basic to manage the determined proteomics section issue. Novel division systems and interfacing approaches of primarily mechanized multidimensional fractionation plans are a problematic analysis zone and can, to huge degree, choose the accomplishment of proteomics as a broad strategy afterward.

14.11   Conclusion

In the past, quite a long while, colossally helpful advances are made in the field of proteomics. The advancements are fast and touchy and give more noteworthy proteome inclusion. Moreover, blend of these innovations has made progress in refinement, investigation, portrayal, evaluation, succession, basic examination, and bioinformatics examination of enormous number of proteins in a wide range of eukaryotic and prokaryotic life forms. All fields identified with natural sciences have been profited with expanding utilization of proteomics strategies. Notwithstanding, further work is as yet required to improve the reproducibility and execution of surely understood proteomics apparatuses.

References

1. Anderson, L. and Hunter, C.L., Quantitative mass spectrometric multiple reaction monitoring assays for major plasma proteins. *Mol. Cell. Proteomics*, 5, 573–588, 2006.
2. O'Farrell, P.H., High resolution two-dimensional electrophoresis of proteins. *J. Biol. Chem.*, 250, 4007–4021, 1975.
3. Klose, J., Protein mapping by combined isoelectric focusing and electrophoresis of mouse tissues A novel approach to testing for induced point mutations in mammals. *Humangenetik*, 26, 231–243, 1975.
4. Unlue, M., Morgan, M.E., Minden, J.S., Difference gel electrophoresis: A single gel method for detecting changes in protein extracts. *Electrophoresis*, 18, 2071–2077, 1997.
5. Sitek, B., Luettges, J., Marcus, K., Kloeppel, G., Schmiegel, W., Meyer, H.E., Hahn, S.A., Stuehler, K., Application of fluorescence difference gel electrophoresis saturation labelling for the analysis of micro dissected precursor lesions of pancreatic ductal adenocarcinoma. *Proteomics*, 5, 10, 2665–2679, 2005.
6. Washburn, M.P., Wolters, D., Yates, J.R., Large-scale analysis of the yeast proteome by multidimensional protein identification technology. *Nat. Biotechnol. Mar.*, 19, 3, 242–277, 2001.
7. Gygi, S.P., Rist, B., Gerber, S.A., Turecek, F., Gelb, H.M., Aebersold, R., Quantitative analysis of complex protein mixtures using isotope-coded affinity tags. *Nat. Biotechnol.*, 17, 994–999, 1999.
8. Schmidt, A., Kellermann, J., Lottspeich, F., A novel strategy for quantitative proteomics using isotope-coded protein labels. *Proteomics*, 5, 4–15, 2005.
9. Ong, S.E., Blagoev, B., Kratchmarova, I., Kristensen, D.B., Steen, H., Pandey, A., Mann, M., Stable isotope labeling by amino acids in cell culture, SILAC, as a simple and accurate approach to expression proteomics. *Mol. Cell. Proteomics*, 1, 376–386, 2002.
10. Krueger, M., Moser, M., Ussar, S., Thievessen, I., Luber, C., Forner, F., Schmidt, S., Zaniva, S., Fässler, R., Mann, M., SILAC-mouse for quantitative proteome analysis uncovers Kindlin-3 as an essential factor for red blood cell function. *Cell*, 134, 2, 353–364, Jul 25 2008.
11. Ross, P.L., Huang, Y.N., Marchese, J.N., Williamson, B., Parker, K., Hattan, S., Khainovski, N., Pillai, S., Dey, S., Daniels, S., Purkayastha, S., Juhasz, P., Martin, S., Bartlet-Jones, M., He, F., Jacobson, A., Pappin, D.J., Multiplexed

protein quantitation in *Saccharomyces cerevisiae* using amine-reactive isobaric tagging reagents. *Mol. Cell. Proteomics*, 3, 1154–1169, 2004.

12. Chen, J., Qian, F., Yan, W., Shen, B., Translational biomedical informatics in the cloud: present and future. *Biomed. Res. Int.*, 2013, 658925, 2013.

15

Prospects of Covalent Approaches in Drug Discovery: An Overview

Balajee Ramachandran[1], Saravanan Muthupandian[2] and
Jeyakanthan Jeyaraman[1*]

[1]*Structural Biology and Bio-Computing Lab, Department of Bioinformatics,
Alagappa University, Karaikudi, Tamil Nadu, India*
[2]*Department of Microbiology and Immunology, Division of Biomedical Science,
School of Medicine, College of Health Sciences, Mekelle University,
Mekelle, Ethiopia*

Abstract

The computational methods are extensively used in the drug discovery research. The molecular modeling approach is widely employed to understand the mechanism of protein-inhibitor complex to provide more insights in the drug discovery process. The covalent inhibitor provides the plausible mechanism with the protein target which leads to identify promising drug candidates with increased potency and safety when compared to the non-covalent inhibitors. The substantial amount of computational approaches has been developed to understand the covalent interactions between protein-inhibitor complex. Still, it requires effective algorithm to overcome the challenges in the drug discovery research. In this review, we emphasize on the following themes, namely, (i) covalent inhibitors against the biological targets, (ii) applications of physical chemistry concepts in the covalent drug design, (iii) importance of the covalent target, (iv) recent framework on covalent docking, (v) S_N2 reactions in the computational approaches, and (vi) other crucial aspects in the covalent docking. The objective of this review is to highlight the components that are essential for the proper assessment and development of the novel covalent inhibitors. Further, the covalent approaches and their applications highlighted in this review will enhance the future efforts in drug designing.

Keywords: Molecular docking, drug designing, covalent targets, protease, SN2 mechanism, QM/MM approaches

Corresponding author: jjkanthan@gmail.com; jjeyakanthan@alagappauniversity.ac.in

S. Balamurugan, Anand Krishnan, Dinesh Goyal, Balakumar Chandrasekaran and Boomi Pandi (eds.)
Computation in Bioinformatics: Multidisciplinary Applications, (295–320) © 2021 Scrivener Publishing LLC

15.1   Introduction

Drug designing is a well-known concept in which the drugs are designed to interact with the macromolecular targets under the certain physiological conditions [1, 2]. The binding affinity between the macromolecular target and inhibitor maximizes their strength, leads to enhanced therapeutic response and drug efficiency, and establishes channels to the modern drug discovery on the basis of conventional and non-conventional ways. The "conventional ways" are termed as "non-covalent inhibitor", and the "non-conventional ways" termed are as "covalent-inhibitors". Covalent inhibitors usually bind with the catalytic nucleophile, for example, Serine/Cysteine proteases or can bind non-catalytic nucleophile such as GPCR and nuclear receptors [3]. The resulting covalent inhibitors will construct a bond with the macromolecular target based on the electrophile and related to the protein nucleophile which increases the rate of acylation, i.e., it retains stability and remains active for a long time. These covalent inhibitors will be calibrated according to the K_i instead of IC_{50} values, which is more appropriate prediction over the IC_{50} values to evaluate their potency against a target [4, 5]. Along with other experimental conditions, the covalent approaches help in accurate determination of the IC_{50} values based on the biological target, inhibitor and the substrate. Whereas, the K_i values consider only the target and inhibitor and it is independent of the substrate. It is exclusively determined by the intrinsic and thermodynamic quantities. The equations are shown below.

For Competitive Inhibitions

$$
\begin{array}{ccc}
& K_1 & K_{cat} \\
E + S & \Leftrightarrow ES \rightarrow & E + P \\
+ & K_{-1} & \\
I & & \\
k_i \updownarrow k_{-i} & & \\
EI & &
\end{array}
$$

Reaction (15.1)

where the $K_d = k_{-1}/k_1$ and $K_i = k_{-i}/k_i$, the overall equation is

$$
K_i = \frac{IC_{50}}{(S/K_m + 1)}
$$

(15.1)

For Uncompetitive Inhibition

$$
\begin{array}{ccc}
K_1 & & K_{cat} \\
E + S \Leftrightarrow ES & \to & E + P \\
K_{-1} & + & \\
& I & \\
K_1 & \updownarrow & K_{-1} \\
& ESI &
\end{array}
$$

Reaction (15.2)

The equation can be written as

$$
K_i = \frac{IC_{50}}{\left(\dfrac{K_m}{S+1} \right)}
$$

(15.2)

For Noncompetitive Inhibition

$$
\begin{array}{ccc}
K_1 & & K_{cat} \\
E + S \Leftrightarrow ES & \to & E + P \\
+ & K_1 & + \\
I & & I \\
K_1 \quad \updownarrow K_i \quad K_i & \updownarrow & K_{-i} \\
EI + S \quad K_4 & \Leftrightarrow & ESI \\
K_{-4} & &
\end{array}
$$

Reaction (15.3)

where $K_i = k_{-1}/k_i$ and $K_{i^\circ} = k_{-1}/k_{i^\circ}$, the equation can be written as

$$
K_i = IC_{50} \ when, \ S = K_m \ or \ S \gg K_m \ or \ S \ll K_m
$$

(15.3)

In the modern day research, the non-conventional way of drug discovery research explores more challenges in the scientific community to identify various possibilities for the worldwide threats. Moreover, the existing *in silico* tools are primarily designed to carry out study through the non-covalent inhibitors and few tools will screen for the covalent targets. However, an investigation to identify the better covalent inhibitors from the library can be achieved through the *in silico* approaches [6].

15.2 Covalent Inhibitors Against the Biological Target

Earlier reports evidenced that the covalent drugs commercially available in the later 1970s [7–9]. An emergence of aspirin in the 19th century against

COX-1 and COX-2 enzymes was the breakthrough of covalent drugs [10]. Later, the antibiotics like Penicillin and Cephalosporins are evolved for bacterial diseases, and the study has been extended to investigate for various diseases/disorders, namely, HCV proteases, proton pump (omeprazole), and type-II diabetes [10, 11]. In oncology, some covalent drugs include inhibitors of aromatase, thymidylate synthetase, and ribonucleotide reductase [12, 13]. On the other hand, the drugs like clopidrogrel, prasugrel, and ticlopidene inhibit the purnergic receptor 12 ($P2Y_{12}$) and modify the GPCR [14–16]. These inhibitors provide major breakthrough for the vascular disorder treatment, which was observed in USA, 2008 [17]. Today, more than 25 approved covalent drugs are floated in the commercial markets with the cost of US$40 billion annual worldwide sales [18]. In the present framework, the pharmaceutical and biotechnology companies are focusing more on the covalent drugs (or by mimicking the existing molecule) to float in the market [21, 22]. Therefore, the current trend will be the uplift for the medicinal chemists to discover novel potent and safe drugs [23].

Potential research on the natural products unleashes the barrier to offer effective drugs. Hence, natural products in drug discovery research with the new advancement in the pharma sector provide benefits to the scientific community [19, 20]. The bioactive natural compounds comprised of enormous amount of data in order to enhance the drug discovery research for many biological targets which will help the scientific community [24, 25]. The hydrolytic mechanism from the natural products has produced overwhelming response in the drug discovery research and turned on huge business in pharma industry. The natural products obtained from micro-organisms also play a crucial role in the pharma research to develop drugs for the antivirals, antibacterial, antifungals, etc. [18, 26–28].

In the drug discovery process, focusing on toxicity of the small molecule will be the crucial than identifying the target and lead compounds in the initial step. In the earlier days, the covalent drugs like bromobenzene and acetaminophen caused severe adverse effects. On the other hand, the drugs like beta-lactams and omeprazole have filled the vacuum to merge into the market. In the case of toxicity, the covalent drugs could be evaluated by the off-target mechanisms where the non-covalent drugs will show time-dependent values. An advancement of bioinformatics and cheminformatics approaches will provide the better understanding of the covalent drug molecules to explore their properties which will support in the drug discovery research [29–31]. Moreover, the adequate data for the covalent inhibitors related to the toxicity is being studied. Whereas, comparing the toxicity data of non-covalent inhibitors like pharmacokinetics, binding kinetics, and pharmacodynamics with the covalent inhibitors leads to the severe adverse effects. As a result, in the current stage, the pharma industry focusing mainly to deliver the product with the minimal side effects using the covalent drugs [32].

15.3 Application of Physical Chemistry Concepts in Drug Designing

The association of the target enzyme (E) and inhibitor (I) forms the protein-ligand complex. The binding affinity of the complex can be expressed by the equilibrium constant, K_i. The complex can be detailed in terms of Gibbs free energy through Equation (15.4):

$$\Delta G = -RT \ln K_{eq} \qquad (15.4)$$

Apparently, additional steps are required for the covalent binding. The enzyme-inhibitor complex forms the covalent adduct [33–35]. The covalent inhibitors were considered as safe and effective compounds when the reaction was fine-tuned toward the biological target of either activation or inactivation of metabolism to attain the remarkable mechanism of action [5]. The covalent inhibitors play a key role in the efficacy which is directly proportional to the residence time ($1/k_{off}$) of the protein-ligand complex. Hence, covalent inhibitor of the enzyme inactivation process is not an equal process with the reversible inhibition [4]. The IC_{50} is an important parameter which indicates the potency of the reversible inhibitor. The IC_{50} value can be converted to K_1/K_{-1}, called as K_i, according to the equation proposed by Cheng-Prusoff [36]. The covalent inhibitors correspond to the time and concentration dependent target inhibition, where the covalent bond formation is time-dependent mechanism. On the other hand, the reversible inhibitor shows the significance only with the concentration dependent. In few cases, the optimized ligand will neutralize the target effectively, where the Pharmacokinetic-Pharmacodynamic (PK/PD) profile of the covalent inhibitor will minimize the drug burden of the patients with no such hindrance in drug dosage/efficacy [37]. As a result of neutralization, the covalent inhibitors are difficult to interpret the IC_{50} values since it is time dependent; instead, the favorable kinetic parameters that include (i) rate of inactivation of a target (k_{inact}) and (ii) inhibition constant (k_i) are applied. Therefore, the k_{inact}/k_i ratio is usually referred to predict the potency of covalent bound complexes [38]. The strength or potency of the covalent inhibitors are determined by the biological rate constant (k_{inact}/k_i). On contrast to the IC_{50}, the determination of K_{inact}/K_i is comprised with multi-step reactions as shown in Figure 15.1. In the binding assay, the inhibition was examined over a period of time at various concentrations. The k_{obs} for each concentration will be obtained from Equation (15.5) proposed by Kitz *et al.* [39]:

$$k_{obs} = \frac{k_{inact} \times [I]}{K_I + [I]} \tag{15.5}$$

The rate at which an inhibitor reacts with the target (k_{inact}) can be determined using transition state theory (TST), which relates to the rate of reaction to the Gibbs energy profile along the reaction coordinates [3]. Using TST, the rate of reaction can be calculated by the Gibbs energy of activation ($\Delta G^{\neq}$) given by

$$k_{TST} = \frac{kB}{h} exp\, exp\left(\frac{-\Delta G \neq}{kBT}\right) \tag{15.6}$$

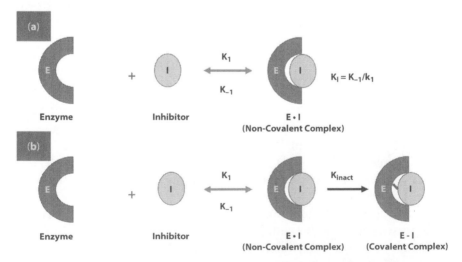

Figure 15.1 The difference between non-covalent and covalent complexes. (a) Interaction of non-covalent inhibitor with the receptor. (b) Interaction of covalent inhibitor with the receptor.

The mechanism of the covalently bound protein-ligand complex comprised of various reaction steps. For instance, in the protein mechanism of papain, the covalent adduct is formed between Cys25 and carbonyl carbon. In the initial step, the covalently modified complex will be comprised of "Michael acceptor" reaction that begins with the proton transfer step in cysteine to form thiolate. The calculation of covalent modification yields the outcomes like $\Delta G_{non\text{-}covalent}$, $\Delta G_{covalent}$, activation free energy ($\Delta G^{\neq}$), the K_{on} and K_{off} values that manage the drug residence time, which is a determinant factor to predict the pharmacological activity of the drug in contrast to the binding affinity [40, 41].

15.4 Docking Methodologies—An Overview

Computer-aided drug design, a theoretical approach, has become a common approach which is widely used in both pharmaceutical and academic sectors. The main aim of the computational approach is to predict the binding affinity between the protein and ligand to provide the valuable estimation to the experimental studies [42]. Each docking program implements their own algorithm and scoring functions in order to estimate the properties of ligand. The commonly used algorithms are AutoDock [43], AutoDock VINA [44], GOLD [45], GLIDE [46, 47], Hex Docking [48], and FlexX [49]. The main focus of these algorithms is to predict hydrogen bonding interactions and other non-bonding interactions like van der Waals interactions and electrostatics for the non-covalent bound inhibitors. An electrostatic interaction plays crucial role on determining the binding affinity between the protein-ligand interactions [50]. Some of the drugs (peptide substrates) bind tightly to the biological target in order to mimic as a natural substrate by involving in the metabolic pathways [47, 48].

Recent discovery of covalent drug has grown rapidly. Some reasons are pointed out here for the growth of the covalent drug: (i) The covalent drug has many advantages like drug dosage, adverse effects, etc., when compared with the non-covalent inhibitors; (ii) prolonged activity; and (iii) lower concentration is sufficient to achieve the pharmacological response [41]. In contrast to the non-covalent inhibitor, the covalent inhibitors require very small concentration to show either similar or increased pharmacological response. In addition to the above, the non-bonded interactions also play a key role toward the binding affinity, specificity with respect to the toxicity, and improving potency.

15.5   Importance of Covalent Targets

Many researchers reported that non-covalent affinities are directly estimated from the surface area of the interaction. Whereas, the covalent
interaction which has tight binding affinity and the complex shows significance in the pharmacological response by enabling both on-target as well
as off-target activity [52, 53]. This is more interesting when the substrate
enters in the metabolic pathway and establish as a natural substrate upon
inhibiting the targets [54]. Hence, it leads to the displacement of the inhibitor. In the case of an irreversible covalent bond between the target and the
drug, no displacement is possible, providing a more efficiency biological
target. The best example is cruzain in which a small peptide Ac-Ala-Ala-
Ala-Gly-Ala-OCH$_3$ binds with *T. cruzi* and shows the enhanced activity
toward the chagas disease as shown in Figure 15.2.

With the emergence of covalent drugs over-hooked from the non-
covalent drugs, the numerous software which are used for non-covalent
docking becomes available for the covalent docking [55]. From the available tools/softwares, the structure was modified by establishing the bond
between the target and ligand manually; this approach is also termed as
"link-atom" approach. The study can explore the significance through the
scoring evaluations [56]. This method facilitates user to determine the
nucleophilic residue in the protein and electrophilic moiety of the ligand.
However, screening the diverse set of compounds against biological target
is time consuming and encounters problem [57]. Many authors reported

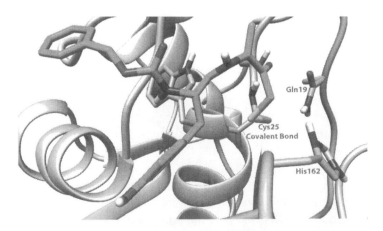

Figure 15.2 Covalent bond between protein and peptide substrate (PDB: 1AIM, www.
rcsb.org).

Table 15.1 The drug discovery process and descriptions.

Sl. no.	Process	Attributes
1	Target identification	Nucleophilic region, substrate, resistance
2	Hit identification	Covalent docking, warhead geometries, substrate based
3	Binding characterization	Mode of binding, binding kinetics, methods of experimenting
4	Optimization	Structure-kinetic relationships

that the covalent binding can be performed in two ways: (i) grid-based method and (ii) flexible side chain modification. The grid-based method was implemented with the Gaussian biasing functions. In the modification of flexible side chain, the nucleophile and electrophile are considered as reactive center [58, 59].

The drug discovery process usually proceeded with the second step (flexible side chain modification) which comprised of two steps: (i) the molecule should bind to the biological target in non-covalent form and (ii) the reactive electrophile should be located in the reasonable distance to a specific nucleophile of the target for the bond formation [60, 61] which enhances the property of the complexes. The drug discovery approach is a continuing process where it identifies the lead through the various search methods to detect the final optimized product [62, 63]. Unique features and properties of the covalent drugs are shown in Table 15.1.

15.6 Recent Framework on the Existing Docking Protocols

The present topic specifies the existing tools available for covalent docking approaches. Further, this study advocates the future perspectives in the area of covalent drug discovery research. Several authors have reported the link atom approaches using the existing molecular docking protocols for the covalent docking. These protocols are facilitated to validate the binding affinity in the respective reactive groups. Earlier, De Cesco *et al.*

2012 [64] have summed up with the recent covalent docking programs like DOCKTITE, DOCKovalent, FITTED, CovalentDock, and CovDock by exploring their challenges. The aforementioned tools have notable features as follows:

- Recognizing an electrophilic region or atom automatically uses the SMARTS pattern.
- In the case of diverse compounds, the FITTED program can be employed.
- The CovalentDock (AutoDock) supports the docking protocol by screening large set of compounds.
- The CovDock (Schrodinger Suite) is another tool which processes the reactive residue through mutating into alanine and retains the same residue after completing the covalent docking protocol. This process may not be favors the electrostatic environment and leads to docking inaccuracy.

The tools that are described here have potential to recognize the electrophile groups automatically. In the present scenario, the efficient algorithms are needed to overcome major pitfalls from the above mentioned tools.

15.7 S_N2 Reactions in the Computational Approaches

Zhang *et al.* (2012) [65] reported that existing computational approaches for the covalent drugs are inadequate in the recent scenario when compared to the non-covalent drug design. The present situations on the docking algorithms has shown more pros and cons toward covalent targets. An existing algorithm is unclear for the covalent mechanisms either to bind as well as to recognize the groups. The available tools shown favor on applying constraints to construct the bond between the reacting atoms. Secondly, apart from the bond formation, the residues are mutated to alanine or any specific residue to understand the impact on the protein complex. Moreover, applying constraints and mutating to alanine residue while docking run may impact their electrostatic and non-bonded effects. These notable issues raise more questions toward the binding energy factors. Eventually, solving the diverse set of compounds are still unclear [66].

15.8   Other Crucial Factors to Consider in the Covalent Docking

15.8.1   Role of Ionizable Residues

Predominantly, the covalent modification carries out with the deprotonation of the respective residues like Cys and Ser to yield more reactive form. Particularly, interaction between the nucleophile-electrophile can be studied to form the stable complex. In the usual instance, the thiol group of cysteine target should be deprotonated prior targeting the electrophile, which refers the whole protein complex depends on their ionizable residues and net charge. Whereas, the ionizable residues are totally depend on the net charge which governs the acid/base properties of the protein [67].

The presence of ionizable residues in the whole protein contributes about 30% [68, 69]. The ionizable residues present in the buried regions play a key role in determining the pKa values. The buried regions are mostly in the side chain of Cysteine, Histidine, and Tyrosine, and they are neutral at pH 7 and other residues like Asp and Glu (acidic residues) are charged at pH 7. The amino acid residue contains high pKa value and donates upto five hydrogen bond that is said to be Arg residue with about 12.3 pKa. The guanidinium group is considered as weakly hydrated cation in the presence of water molecule due to charge localization. The Arg residue plays a vital role on stabilization and function of proteins. Hence, the buried region of Arg residue is charged, containing high number of hydrogen bonding interactions and interaction by stacking with other planar side chain groups in proteins [70, 71]. The interaction can be evidenced by showing the class D type of beta-lactams OXA-10 of the amino acid residue Arg259 that has hydrogen bond interactions with imipenem [72, 73] and depicted in Figure 15.3.

In the biological complex, the pKa values of the ionizable residues may vary according to the environment such as solvent accessibility, charged, and polar residues of the protein [72]. The principal factors to be considered toward the ionizable groups are as follows: (i) pKa values of ionizable groups in protein can vary from the reference model with pH units; (ii) particular residue can have a different pKa value (e.g., carboxylic group and amine group); and (iii) the pKa values will differ when it exists in apo-state or when it binds with other models. The aforementioned parameters will aid to understand the free energy which have direct impacts on the protein folding and binding between the protein and ligand complexes

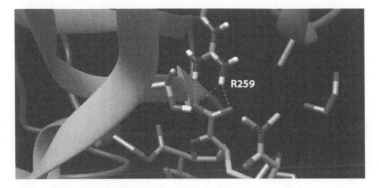

Figure 15.3 OXA23-imipenem interactions (the picture represents the significance of Arg259 with the imipenem).

upon equilibrium which corresponds to the pH of the solution. Therefore, the pH is also a crucial factor to determine the stability of the biological complex [74, 75].

15.8.2   Charge Regulation

The physical theory plays a vital role in explaining the importance of charge regulation in the protein environment. The charge regulation mechanism was elaborated by Linderstorm-Lang in 1924 [68]. In the recent years, it was considered as one of the "hot topic" in the biophysical methods to discuss more on electrostatic interaction, charge regulation, etc. [78–81]. Charge regulation includes the local charge of the protein on the solvent environment, salt concentrations, and various pH. In the recent studies, the charge regulation mechanism was extended in the transmembrane proteins [82]. The charge regulation parameters were evaluated for the biological systems to perform detailed study on the protein charge characteristics. The atom enters into the electrostatically favorable biological system; the system will be modified accordingly with positive as well as negative charged ions [83–85].

15.8.3   Charge-Charge Interactions

The pKa of the given ionizable residues carries net negative charge for the acidic residues like Asp, Glu, Tyr, and Cys and net positive charges for the other residues like His, Lys, and Arg. The energy of the interaction can be calculated with Coulomb's law [86]:

$$\Delta G_{ij} = \sum \frac{q_i q_j}{\epsilon r_{ij}} \qquad (15.7)$$

where q_i is ionizable group of interest, q_j is charge on the other groups, ϵ is dielectric constant, and r_{ij} is the distance between the two charges. Here, the electrostatic interaction has been shown as.

Zydney et al. [87] have demonstrated the electrostatic interactions using theoretical models to uncover the significance of charge regulation characteristics in the combination of ionization of ion binding reactions for the Bovine Serum Albumin (BSA) using linearized form. They reported that the change will be observed in the charge density and surface potential when the pore enters into the membrane surface due to disturbance in the electrical potentials. Further, Majee et al. [88] have reported that the repulsive forces against vdW forces are not sufficient to understand the membrane stacks. The alteration in the charge network on the membrane protein stacks impacts on the overall charge distribution which was long-standing problem in plant mechanism [89, 90]. They suggested that asymmetric form of the membrane is a crucial to the formation of the stacks. Warshel and co-workers in 2006 [91] suggested that Poisson-Boltzmann (PB) calculations are trustable than Generalized-Born (GB) calculations while exploring the challenges of microscopic, macroscopic, and semi-macroscopic calculations of electrostatic effects in proteins. They further explained that correct electrostatic energies are represented by PB results on assumed dielectric constant when compared to GB methods. Therefore, the long-range effects and boundary conditions problems will influence for the accuracy of microscopic models to attain the convergence. The PB and GB will have a directly relevant to produce similar results [92]. The GB models also produce the expected results similar to PB models in the free energy calculations on binding between small peptide ligands and protein which is referred to as dG_{bind} [93, 94].

The implicit solvent is widely used when compared to the explicit solvent, because the computational cost is more in the explicit solvent models [95, 96]. In the implicit solvent models, the environment is computed with certain dielectric and interfacial properties. As it considers few degrees of

$$R\text{-COOH} \leftrightarrow R\text{-COO}^- + H^+ \qquad pK_a \downarrow$$
$$R\text{-NH}_3^+ \leftrightarrow R\text{-NH}_2 + H^+ \qquad pK_a \downarrow$$

Figure 15.4 The pKa values of existing ionizable residues in the protein will have decreased effect in a positively charged environment [74].

freedom, it may ignore the hydrogen bond interactions, reorientation of the biological complex, and focusing partial water molecules in the protein environment. Furthermore, the protein folding for the helical structure is one of the challenging tasks where the beta-sheets are more feasible in the implicit solvent [97]. It is clearly described the purpose of accepting implicit solvent models due to their flexibility and tunable performance in the recent molecular dynamics approaches [98].

On the other hand, the explicit solvent exhibited a maximum contribution in a simulated system [99, 105] and the particle mesh Ewald (PME) approximation is commonly used in the bio-molecular simulation which accelerates the calculations by setting up an environment by interacting between all pairs of solute and solvent atoms [100, 101]. The explicit solvent model calculates the long-range interactions very efficiently by providing closest values when compared to the implicit solvent [102–104]. The existing algorithms unveil the significance of implicit solvent models. Hence, enhancement in the force fields and algorithms supports the explicit models that are highly required to determine the accuracy of the protonation states of the ionizable residues [76, 77]. Additionally, the residues like cysteine, serine, and lysine have different potential states where the experimental evaluation is required to understand the pKa's, particularly the target of targeted covalent inhibitors [78]. The wide acceptance of GB model is due to computational efficiency and accuracy. In some calculations, e.g., protein-ligand interactions, the GB and PB models encounters the problems on accepting the ions interior to the protein surface and leads to difficulties in estimating the free energies [106], where the combination of ΔG_{el} electrostatic and $\Delta G_{non\text{-}polar}$ influences the solvation free energy of the system. The interaction between the solutes in the presence of solvent (water) (ΔG_{sol}) plays a vital role to predict the free energy of the biological system [107, 108].

$$\Delta G_{sol} = \Delta G_{el} + \Delta G_{non\text{-}polar} \qquad (15.8)$$

The following equation is used to calculate the electrostatic part of the solvation of the protein-ligand system in the approximation for the Generalized Born [109].

$$\Delta G_{el} = -\frac{1}{2}\left(\frac{1}{\in in} - \frac{1}{\in out}\right)\sum_{i,j} \frac{q_i q_j}{\sqrt{d_{ij}^2 + R_i R_j\, exp\left(\frac{d_{ij}^2}{4R_i R_j}\right)}} \qquad (15.9)$$

15.9   QM/MM Approaches

The study of an enzymatic reaction requires computational methods to understand the clear picture of bond formation or bond breaking in the protein-substrate complexes. The reactant part of the system will be treated as a QM region and rest of the system will be treated with MM regions. As an outcome, the QM/MM method enables to deeply investigate on the binding mechanisms, activation free energies, and non-bonding interactions in the covalent bound complexes with the existing computational resources. The QM/MM method delivers the reliable outcome from the molecular docking protocols that leads to correlate with experimental kinetic data and the provided insights will be the benchmark for the scientists to discover or fine-tune the drug-like compounds [110].

Several authors have proposed the enzymatic mechanism on Cysteine and Serine protease enzymes using QM/MM approaches. Gao et al. (2007) [111] have reported the activation free energy of 19.8 and 16.7 kcal/mol for Cathepsin K in acylation and deacylation process in the protein environment and in aqueous solution, respectively, and the analysis shows that acylation is found to the rate determining step. They demonstrated that prior to the nucleophilic attack, the Cys25 transfers the proton to His162, and it will perform the nucleophilic attack to the carbonyl carbon to the substrate; hence, they are highly coupled. They also reported that peptide hydrolysis could be achieved by the stabilization of the oxyanion hole present in the "Michaelis complex" by the Gln19 through donating the hydrogen bond to the carbonyl oxygen.

The electrostatic effect plays a key role in determining the structure and leads to examine the functional mechanisms (molecular recognition, ligand specificity, catalytic mechanisms, and enzyme regulation) of the proteins [112, 113]. Further, electrostatic effect influences the acylation and deacylation reaction to elaborate on enzyme catalyzed reactions. Dardenne et al. (2003) [114] have reported the possible role on the formation, stabilization, and regulation of Cys25$^-$ and His159$^+$ in papain investigated through the electrostatic effects of the protein complex. They identified that the neighboring residues Gln19, Gly23, Ser24, Asp158, and Ala160 are the important residues, which contribute to the total electric field. Nobel et al. [115] have pointed out that Asp158 has pKa of 2.8 and deprotonation of Asp-COOH residue influences the Cys$^-$/His159$^+$ ion pair formation. Further, they have shown that Glu35, Glu50, Glu52, Asp55, Asp57, and Glu89 are the most relevant residues that can act as electrostatic modulators. Further, they suggested that Asp57 is a promising residue to act as an electrostatic modulator.

Arafat *et al.* [116] have explained the cysteine protease mechanism with cruzain, where they initiated their studies with transferring the proton from His162 to N1 atom of peptide substrate to form the transient intermediate, followed by Cys25 attacks carbonyl carbon. They reported that local environment is stabilized by neighboring residues rather than Cys25/His159 pair and demonstrated that Gln19, Asn175, and Trp181 could modulate the reaction with the high pKa value of the catalytic His159 in both the stages. Their investigation reveals that TS3 is the rate-limiting step by obtaining 26 kcal/mol.

15.10 Conclusion and Remarks

The covalent drugs have been extended from the known non-covalent drugs by reporting the mode of action according to the respective warheads. In the initial stage of knowing some predicted mechanism of covalent drugs, it is popularized in the pharma market. The covalent drugs are grown from the known parameters of non-covalent drug molecules, e.g., H-bond donors, acceptors, rotamers, and other physicochemical properties, where some parameters are more crucial to design the drugs. Therefore, the covalent drugs should be well accompanied in the protein (electrostatically favored environment) by targeting the respective catalytic site. Hence, the charged interactions should be carefully interpreted to make better understanding of enzyme mechanism to deliver the successful drugs.

It is quite necessary to undergo the kinetic study of the covalent inhibitors as well as other descriptors to understand how to improve the inhibitors with respect to the binding kinetics and drug solubility. The rapid growth of the covalent inhibitors which designed from the existing tools/software might delivers the inaccuracy of the data. Hence, the dedicated tool and improvised algorithms are required to explore the challenges on covalent inhibitors to attain the accuracy, safety, speed, and betterment for the usage of medicinal chemists for their day-to-day use. The purpose of this review is to provide some valuable inputs for the further investigation on the covalent inhibitors which has a good rapport on the target-directed and structure-guided drug discovery approaches. Hence, we believe that this review can be taken as benchmark for further developments to deliver the potent covalent inhibitor.

Acknowledgements

The authors BR and JJ acknowledge the financial grant supported by DST – Fund for Improvement of S&T Infrastructure in Higher Educational Institutions (FIST) (SR/FST/LSI-667/2016) (C), DST – Promotion of University Research and Scientific Excellence (PURSE) (No. SR/PURSE Phase2/38) (G), 2017, UGC-RA-2016-18-OB-AM-7124 dated: 18.04.2016, DST-SERB (File No. EMR/2016/000498 dated: 26.09.2016), MHRD-RUSA 2.0, New Delhi [F.24-51/2014-U, Policy (TNMulti-Gen), Dept. of Edn. Govt. of India, Dt. 09.10.2018] for providing computational facilities to carry out this work.

References

1. Robertson, J.G., Enzymes as a special class of therapeutic target: Clinical drugs and modes of action. *Curr. Opin. Struct. Biol.*, 17, 674, 2007.
2. Amala, M., Rajamanikandan, S., Prabhu, D., Surekha, K., Jeyakanthan, J., Identification of Anti-filarial leads against Aspartate semialdehyde Dehydrogenase of *Wolbachia* endosymbiont of *Brugia malayi*: Combined Molecular Docking and Molecular Dynamics Approaches. *J. Biomol. Struct. Dyn.*, 37, 394, 2019.
3. Drahl, C. *et al.*, Protein-reactive natural products. *Angew. Chem. Int. Ed.*, 44, 5788, 2005.
4. Krippendorff, B.F. *et al.*, Deriving K_i and K_{inact} directly from time-dependent IC_{50} values. *J. Biomol. Screen.*, 14, 913, 2009.
5. Cer, R.Z., Mudunuri, U., Stephens, R., Lebeda, F.J., IC_{50}-to-K_i: a web-based tool for converting IC50 to Ki values for inhibitors of enzyme activity and ligand binding. *Nucleic Acids Res.*, 37, Web Server issue, W441, 2009.
6. Lu, X.G., Wang, Z., Cui, Y., Jin, Z., Computational thermodynamics, computational kinetics, and materials design. *Chin. Sci. Bull.*, 59, 1662, 2014.
7. Penning, T.M., Design of suicide substrates: an approach to the development of highly selective enzyme inhibitors as drugs. *Trends Pharmacol. Sci.*, 4, 212, 1983.
8. Rando, R.R., New modes of enzyme inactivator design. *Trends Pharmacol. Sci.*, 1, 168, 1980.
9. Walsh, C., Suicide substrates: mechanism-based enzyme inactivators. *Tetrahedron*, 38, 871, 1982.
10. Chen, Y.N.P. and Marnett, L.J., Heme prosthetic group required for acetylation of prostaglandin-H synthase by aspirin. *FASEB J.*, 3, 2294, 1989.
11. Choubey, S.K., Prabhu, D., Nachiappan, M., Biswal, J., Jeyakanthan, J., Molecular modeling, dynamics studies and density functional theory approaches to identify potential inhibitors of SIRT4 protein from Homo

sapiens: a novel target for the treatment of type 2 diabetes. *J. Biomol. Struct. Dyn.*, 35, 3316, 2017.

12. Esplugues, J.V. and Marti-Cabrera, M., Safety and interactions of proton pump inhibitors: lessons learned in millions of patients. *Gastroenterol. Hepatol.*, 33, 15, 2010.

13. Ravi, M., Tentu, S., Baskar, G., Rohan Prasad, S., Raghavan, S., Jayaprakash, P., Jeyakanthan, J., Rayala, S.K., Venkatraman, G., Molecular mechanism of anti-cancer activity of phycocyanin in triple-negative breast cancer cells. *BMC Cancer*, 15, 768, 2015.

14. Xu, H., Faber, C., Uchiki, T., Racca, J., Dealwis, C., Structures of eukaryotic ribonucleotide reductase I define gemcitabine diphosphate binding and subunit assembly. *Proc. Natl. Acad. Sci.*, 103, 4028, 2006.

15. Savi, P. *et al.*, Identification and biological activity of the active metabolite of clopidogrel. *Thromb. Haemost.*, 84, 891, 2000.

16. Yusuf, S. *et al.*, Effects of clopidogrel in addition to aspirin in patients with acute coronary syndromes without ST-segment elevation. *N. Engl. J. Med.*, 345, 494, 2001.

17. Bartholow, M. Top 200 Prescription Drugs of 2009. *Pharmacy Times*, 78, 7, http://www.pharmacytimes.com/issue/pharmacy/2010/May2010/RxFocus TopDrugs-0510 2010.

18. Singh, J., Petter, R.C., Baillie, T.A., Whitty, A., The resurgence of covalent drugs. *Nat. Rev. Drug Discovery*, 10, 307, 2011.

19. Kola, I. and Landis, J., Can the pharmaceutical industry reduce attrition rates? *Nat. Rev. Drug Discovery*, 3, 711, 2004.

20. Knowles, J. and Gromo, G., A guide to drug discovery: target selection in drug discovery. *Nat. Rev. Drug Discovery*, 2, 63, 2003.

21. Zhou, S.F., Chan, E., Duan, W., Huang, M., Chen, Y.Z., Drug bioactivation, covalent binding to target proteins and toxicity relevance. *Drug Metab. Rev.*, 37, 41, 2005.

22. Kalgutkar, A.S. and Dalvie, D.K., Drug discovery for a new generation of covalent drugs. *Expert Opin. Drug Discovery*, 7, 561, 2012.

23. Ma, Y., Xu, B., Fang, Y., Yang, Z., Cui, J., Zhang, L., Zhang, L., Synthesis and SAR Study of Novel Peptide Aldehydes as Inhibitors of 20S Proteasome. *Molecules*, 16, 7551, 2011.

24. Baillie., T.A., Targeted covalent inhibitors for drug design. *Angew. Chem. Int. Ed.*, 55, 13408, 2016.

25. Sudharsana, S., Madhana Priya, N., Prabhu, D., Jeyakanthan, J., Mohanapriya, A., Conformational insights into the inhibitory mechanism of phytocompounds against SRC kinase family members implicated in psoriasis. *J. Biomol. Struct. Dyn.*, 9, 1, 2019.

26. Huggett, B., Biotech's wellspring: the health of private biotech in 2012. *Nat. Biotechnol.*, 31, 396, 2013.

27. Garber, K., Principia biopharma. *Nat. Biotechnol.*, 31, 377, 2013.

28. Prabhu, D., Rajamanikandan, S., Saritha, P., Jeyakanthan J., Evolutionary Significance and Functional Characterization of Streptomycin adenylyl transferase from Serratia marcescens, *J. Biomol. Struct. Dyn.*, 38, 15, 4418–4431, 2020.

29. Kuntz, I.D. *et al.*, The maximal affinity of ligands. *Proc. Natl. Acad. Sci.*, 96, 9997, 1999.

30. Santhosh, R., Bankoti Padmashri, N., Michael, A.M.D., Jeyakanthan, J., Sekar, K., MRPC: Missing Regions in Polypeptide Chains - A Knowledgebase. *J. Appl. Cryst.*, 52, 1422, 2019.

31. Rajendran, Santhosh., Namrata, Bankoti., Gurudarshan, Manickam., Jeyakanthan, J., Sekar, K., IMRPS: Inserted and Modified Residues in Protein Structures: A Database, *J. Appl. Cryst.*, 53, 569, 573, 2020.

32. Smith, A.J.T. *et al.*, Beyond picomolar affinities: quantitative aspects of non-covalent and covalent binding of drugs to proteins. *J. Med. Chem.*, 52, 225, 2009.

33. Ogata, M., Umemoto, N., Ohnuma, T., Numata, T., Suzuki, A., Usui, T., Fukamizo, T., A novel transition-state analogue for lysozyme, 4-O-b-Tri-Nacetylchitotriosyl moranoline, provided evidence supporting the covalent glycosyl enzyme intermediate. *J. Biol. Chem.*, 288, 6072, 2013.

34. Rojas, R.J., Edmondson, D.E., Almos, T., Scott, R., Massari, M.E., Reversible and irreversible small molecule inhibitors of monoamine oxidase B (MAO-B) investigated by biophysical techniques. *Bioorg. Med. Chem.*, 23, 770, 2015.

35. Santhosh, R., Chandrasekaran, P., Michael, D., Rangachari, K., Bankoti, N., Jeyakanthan, J., Sekar, K., ACMS: A database of alternate conformations found in the atoms of main and side chains of protein structures. *J. Appl. Cryst.*, 52, 910, 2019.

36. Cheng, Y. and Prusoff, W.H., Relationship Between the Inhibition Constant (K1) and the Concentration of Inhibitor Which Causes 50 Per Cent Inhibition (I_{50}) of an Enzymatic Reaction. *Biochem. Pharmacol.*, 22, 3099, 1973.

37. Claxton, A.J. *et al.*, A systematic review of the associations between dose regimens and medication compliance. *Clin. Ther.*, 23, 1296, 2001.

38. Strelow, J.M., A Perspective on the Kinetics of Covalent and Irreversible Inhibition. *SLAS Discovery*, 22, 3, 2016.

39. Kitz, R., Wilson, I. B., Esters of methanesulfonic acid as irreversible inhibitors of acetylcholinesterase, *J. Biol. Chem.*, 237, 3245–3249, 1962.

40. Alberty, R.A. and Hammes, G.G., Application of the theory of diffusion-controlled reactions to enzyme kinetics. *J. Phys. Chem.*, 62, 154, 1958.

41. Copeland, R.A., The drug-target residence time model: a 10-year retrospective. *Nat. Rev. Drug Discovery*, 15, 87, 2016.

42. Morris, G.M., Huey, R., Lindstrom, W., Sanner, M.F., Belew, R.K., Goodsell, D.S., Olson, A.J., AutoDock4 and AutoDockTools4: Automated Docking with Selective Receptor Flexibility. *J. Comput. Chem.*, 30, 2785, 2009.

43. Balajee, R., Srinivasa Desikan, V., Sakthivadivel, M., Gunasekaran, P., Molecular docking and DFT approaches on identification of potential

therapeutic Novel inhibitors against NS2/NS3 protease enzyme of Dengue Virus, doi.org/10.1155/2016/7264080.

44. Trott, O. and Olson, A.J., AutoDock Vina: Improving the speed and accuracy of docking with a new scoring function, efficient optimization, and multi-threading. *J. Comput. Chem.*, 31, 455, 2010.

45. Jones, G., Willett, P., Glen, R.C., Leach, A.R., Taylor, R., Development and validation of a genetic algorithm for flexible docking. *J. Mol. Biol.*, 267, 727, 1997.

46. Friesner, R.A., Banks, J.L., Murphy, R.B., Halgren, T.A., Klicic, J.J., Mainz, D.T., Repasky, M.P., Knoll, E.H., Shaw, D.E., Shelley, M., Perry, J.K., Francis, P., Shenkin, P.S., Glide: A New Approach for Rapid, Accurate Docking and Scoring. 1. Method and Assessment of Docking Accuracy. *J. Med. Chem.*, 47, 1739, 2004.

47. Guru Raj, R.R., Jayashree, B., Sureka, K., Jeyakanthan, J., Exploration of N5-CAIR mutase Novel inhibitors from *Pyrococcus horikoshii* OT3 - A Computational Study. *J. Comput. Biol.*, 26, 457, 2019.

48. Shanmughavel, P., Jeyakanthan, J., Molecular Interactions, Today & Tomorrows Printers & Pub, 2015, India, ISBN: 9788170195115

49. Ritchie, D.W., Kozakov, D., Vajda, S., Accelerating and focusing protein-protein docking correlations using multi-dimensional rotational FFT generating functions. *Bioinformatics*, 24, 1865, 2008.

50. Cross, S.S.J., Improved FlexX docking using FlexS-determined base fragment placement. *J. Chem. Inf. Model.*, 45, 993, 2005.

51. Rarey, M., Kramer, B., Lengauer, T., Klebe, G., A fast flexible docking method using an incremental construction algorithm. *J. Mol. Biol.*, 261, 470, 1996.

52. Bauer, R.A., Covalent inhibitors in drug discovery: from accidental discoveries to avoided liabilities and designed therapies. *Drug Discovery Today*, 20, 1061, 2015.

53. Swinney, D.C., Biochemical mechanisms of drug action: what does it take for uccess? *Nat. Rev. Drug Discovery*, 3, 801, 2004.

54. Lanning, B.R., Whitby, L.R., Dix, M.M., Douhan, J., Gilbert, A.M., Hett, E.C., Johnson, T.O., Joslyn, C., Kath, J.C., Niessen, S., Roberts, L.R., Schnute, M.E., Wang, C., Hulce, J.J., Wei, B., Whiteley, L.O., Hayward, M.M., Cravatt, B.F., A road map to evaluate the proteome-wide selectivity of covalent kinase inhibitors. *Nat. Chem. Biol.*, 10, 760, 2014.

55. Srinivasan, P., Prasanth, K.S., Karthikeyan, M., Jeyakanthan, J., Jasrai, Y.T., Pandya, H.A., Rawal, R.M., Patel, S.K., Epitope-based immunoinformatics and molecular docking studies of Nucleocapsid protein (NP) and Ovarian Tumor (OTU) domain of Crimean-Congo haemorrhagic fever virus (CCHFV). *Front. Genet.*, 2, 2, 2011.

56. Jones, G., Willett, P., Glen, R.C., Leach, A.R., Taylor, R., Development and validation of a genetic algorithm for flexible docking. *J. Mol. Biol.*, 267, 727, 1997.

57. Koch, A., Rode, H.B., Richters, A., Rauh, D., Hauf, S., A chemical genetic approach for covalent inhibition of analogue-sensitive aurora kinase. *ACS Chem. Biol.*, 7, 723, 2012.
58. Warshaviak, D.T., Golan, G., Borrelli, K.W., Zhu, K., Kalid, O., Structure-based virtual screening approach for discovery of covalently bound ligands. *J. Chem. Inf. Model.*, 54, 1941, 2014.
59. Ouyang, X., Zhou, S., Su, C.T.T., Ge, Z., Li, R., Kwoh, C.K., CovalentDock: Automated covalent docking with parameterized covalent linkage energy estimation and molecular geometry constraints. *J. Comput. Chem.*, 34, 326, 2013.
60. Moitessier, N., Englebienne, P., Lee, D., Lawandi, J., Corbeil, C.R., Towards the development of universal, fast and highly accurate docking/scoring methods: A long way to go. *Br. J. Pharmacol.*, 153, S7, 2008.
61. Kumalo, H. M., Bhakat, S., Soliman, M.E.S., Theory and applications of covalent docking in drug discovery: merits and pitfalls, *Molecules*, 20(2), 1984-2000, 2015, doi: 10.3390/molecules20021984.
62. Vanajothi, R., Vedagiri, H., Jeyakanthan J., Premkumar, K., Ligand-based Pharmacophore Mapping and Virtual Screening for Identification of Potential Discoidin Domain Receptor 1 Inhibitors, *J Biomol Struct Dyn.*, 38(9):2800-2808, 202.
63. Vanajothi, R., Hemamalini, V., Jeyakanthan, J., Premkumar, K., Ligand-based Pharmacophore Mapping and Virtual Screening for Identification of Potential Discoidin Domain Receptor 1 Inhibitors. *J. Biomol. Struct. Dyn.*, 4, 1, 2019.
64. De Cesco, S., Deslandes, S., Therrien, E., Levan, D., Cueto, M., Schmidt, R., Cantin, L.D., Mittermaier, A., Juillerat-Jeanneret, L., Moitessier, N., Virtual screening and computational optimization for the discovery of covalent pro-lyl oligopeptidase inhibitors with activity in human cells. *J. Med. Chem.*, 55, 6306, 2012.
65. Zhang, T., Inesta-Vaquera, F., Niepel, M., Zhang, J., Ficarro, S.B., Machleidt, T., Xie, T., Marto, J.A., Kim, N., Sim, T., Laughlin, J.D. *et al.*, Discovery of potent and selective covalent inhibitors of JNK. *Chem. Biol.*, 19, 140, 2012.
66. Liew, C. Y., Pan, C., Tan, A., Ang, K.X.M., Yap, C.W., QSAR classification of metabolic activation of chemicals into covalently reactive species, *Mol. Divers.*, 16(2), 389-400, 2012. doi: 10.1007/s11030-012-9364-3.
67. Linderstrom-Lang, K., On the ionization of proteins. Cr. Trav. Lab. *Carlsberg*, 15, 1, 1924.
68. Jordan, I. K., Kondrashov, F. A., Adzhubei, I. A., Wolf, Y. I., Koonin, E. V., Kondrashov, A. S., Sunyaev, S., A universal trend of amino acid gain and loss in protein evolution, *Nature*, 433, 633 - 638, 2005.
69. Gowri Shankar, B.A., Sarani, R., Michael, D., Mridula, P., Ranjani, C.V., Sowmiya, G., Vasundhar, B., Sudha, P., Jeyakanthan, J., Velmurugan, D., Sekar, K., Ion pairs in non-redundant protein structures. *J. Biosci.*, 32, 693, 2007.

70. Lesser, G.J. and Rose, G.D., Hydrophobicity of Amino Acid Subgroups in Proteins. *Proteins*, 8, 6, 1990.

71. Mason, P.E., Neilson, G.W., Dempsey, C.E., Barnes, A.C., Cruickshank, J.M., The Hydration Structure of Guanidinium and Thiocyanate Ions: Implications for Protein Stability in Aqueous Solution. *Proc. Natl. Acad. Sci.*, 100, 4557, 2003.

72. Malathi, K. and Ramaiah, S., Molecular Docking and Molecular Dynamics Studies to Identify Potential OXA-10 Extended Spectrum β-Lactamase Non-hydrolysing Inhibitors for Pseudomonas aeruginosa. *Cell Biochem. Biophys.*, 74, 141, 2016.

73. Saravanan, M., Ramachandran, B., Gebretsadkan G., The prevalence and drug resistance pattern of Extended Spectrum β lactamases (ESBLs) producing Enterobacteriaceae in Africa, *Microbial Pathogenesis*, 114, 180, 192, 2017. doi.org/10.1016/j. micpath.2017.11.061.

74. Pace, C.N., Grimsley, G.R., Scholtz, J.M., Protein ionizable groups: pK values and their contribution to protein stability and solubility. *J. Biol. Chem.*, 284, 13285, 2009.

75. Sinha, N., Tsai, C.-J., Nussinov, R., A Proposed Structural Model for Amyloid Fibril Elongation: Domain Swapping Forms an Interdigitating Beta-Structure Polymer. *Protein Eng.*, 14, 93, 2001.

76. Cambillau, C. and Claverie, J.M., Structural and Genomic Correlates of Hyperthermostability. *J. Biol. Chem.*, 275, 32383, 2000.

77. Ibarra-Molero, B. and Sanchez-Ruiz, J.M., Genetic algorithm to design stabilizing surface-charge distributions in proteins. *J. Phys. Chem.*, B, 106, 6609, 2002.

78. Maple, J.R., Dinur, U., Hagler, A.T., Derivation of force fields for molecular mechanics and dynamics from ab initio energy surfaces. *Proc. Natl. Acad. Sci.*, 85, 5350, 1988.

79. Spassov, V.Z. and Yan, L., A fast and accurate computational approach to protein ionization. *Protein Sci.*, 17, 1955, 2008.

80. Kirkwood, J. and Shumaker, J.B., Forces between Protein Molecules in Solution Arising from Fluctuations in Proton Charge and Configuration. *Proc. Natl. Acad. Sci.*, 38, 855, 1952.

81. Marcus, Calculation of Thermodynamic Properties of Polyelectrolytes. *J. Chem. Phys.*, 23, 1057, 1955.

82. Lifson, S., On Ion-Pair Formation in Polyelectrolytes. *J. Chem. Phys.*, 26, 727, 1957.

83. Puthiyaveetil, S., Van Oort, B., Kirchhoff, H., Surface Charge Dynamics in Photosynthetic Membranes and the Structural Consequences. *Nat. Plants*, 3, 17020, 2017.

84. Mustárdy, L., Buttle, K., Steinbach, G., Garab, G., The Three-Dimensional Network of the Thylakoid Membranes in Plants: Quasihelical Model of the Granum-Stroma Assembly. *Plant Cell*, 20, 2552, 2008.

85. Kirchoff, H., Hall, C., Wood, M., Herbstova, M., Tsabari, O., Nevo, R., Charuvi, D., Shimoni, E., Reich Z, Dynamic control of protein diffusion within the granal thylakoid lumen. *Proc. Natl. Acad. Sci.*, USA, 108(50), 20248-20253, 2011.

86. Kirchhoff, H., Structure-function Relationships in Photosynthetic Membranes: Challenges and Emerging Fields. *Plant Sci.*, 266, 76, 2018.

87. Berisio, R., Lamzin, V.S., Sica, F., Wilson, K.S., Zagari, A., Mazzarella, L., Protein Titration in the Crystal State. *J. Mol. Biol.*, 292, 845, 1999.

88. Narahari, S. and Zydney, A.L., Charge Regulation and Electrostatic Interactions for a Spherical Particle in a Cylindrical Pore. *J. Colloid Interface Sci.*, 192, 338, 1997.

89. Arghya, M., Markus, B., Ralf, B., Rudolf, P., Charge regulation radically modifies electrostatics in membrane stacks. *Phys. Rev. E*, 100, 050601, 2019.

90. Srinivasa Desikan V, C.-H. Lu, Ramachandran, B., S.-L. Lee. Effects of Microsolvation on the Electronic Properties of Sarcosine: A Theoretical Study, *Chemistry Select*, 2, 8950, 8958, 2017, DOI: 10.1002/slct.201701430.

91. Warshel, A., Sharma, P.K., Kato, M., Parson, W.P., Modeling electrostatic effects in Proteins. *Biochim. Biophys. Acta (BBA)*, 1764, 1647, 2006.

92. Jindal, G., Ramachandran, B., Bora, R.P., Warshel, A., Exploring the Development of Ground State Destabilization and Transition State Stabilization in Two Directed Evolution Paths in Kemp Eliminases, *ACS Catalysis*, 7(5), 3301- 3305, 2017, DOI:10.1021/acscatal.7b00171

93. Mustárdy, L., Buttle, K., Steinbach, G., Garab, G., The Three-Dimensional Network of the Thylakoid Membranes in Plants: Quasihelical Model of the Granum-Stroma Assembly. *Plant Cell*, 20, 2552, 2008.

94. Sanjay, K.C. and Jeyakanthan, J., Molecular dynamics and Quantum chemistry based approaches to identify isoform selective HDAC2 inhibitor – A novel target to prevent Alzheimer's disease. *J. Recept. Signal Transduction Res.*, 38, 266, 2018.

95. Zhang, H., Tan, T., van der Spoel, D., Generalized Born and Explicit Solvent Models for Free Energy Calculations in Organic Solvents: Cyclodextrin Dimerization. *J. Chem. Theory Comput.*, 11, 5103, 2015.

96. Ramachandran, B. and DhanaRajan, M.S., Molecular Docking and Simulation studies of Farnesyl Trasnferase with the potential inhibitor Theflavin. *J. Appl. Pharm. Sci.*, 1, 141, 2011.

97. Nymeyer, H. and Garcìa, A.E., Simulation of the folding equilibrium of α-helical peptides: a comparison of the generalized Born approximation with explicit solvent. *Proc. Natl. Acad. Sci.*, 100, 13934, 2003.

98. Jens, K. and Franca, F., Design and application of implicit solvent models in biomolecular simulations. *Curr. Opin. Struct. Biol.*, 25, 126, 2014.

99. Forouzesh, N., Izadi, S., Onufriev, A.V., Grid-based surface generalized Born model for calculation of electrostatic binding free energies. *J. Chem. Inf. Model.*, 57, 2505, 2017.

100. Darden, T., York, D., Pedersen, L., Particle mesh Ewald: an N·log(N) method for Ewald sums in large systems. *J. Chem. Phys.*, 98, 10089, 1993.

101. Jayashree, B., Jayaprakash, P., Suresh, K.R., Ganesh, V., Poopandi, S., Raghu, R., Jeyakanthan, J., Identification of Pak1 inhibitors using water thermodynamic analysis. *J. Biomol. Struct. Dyn.*, 38, 13, 2020.

102. Essmann, U., Perera, L., Pedersen, L.G., A smooth particle mesh Ewald method. *J. Chem. Phys.*, 103, 8577, 1995.

103. Toukmaji, A.Y. and Board, J.A., Jr., Ewald summation techniques in perspective: A Survey. *Comput. Phys. Commun.*, 95, 73, 1996.

104. York, D. and Yang, W., The fast Fourier Poisson method for calculating Ewald sums. *J. Chem. Phys.*, 101, 3298, 1994.

105. Izadi, S., Harris, R.C., Fenley, M.O., Onufriev, A.V., Accuracy comparison of generalized Born models in the calculation of electrostatic binding free energies. *J. Chem. Theory Comput.*, 14, 1656, 2018.

106. Sharp, K.A., Madan, B., Manas, E., Vanderkooi, J.M., Water structure changes induced by hydrophobic and polar solutes revealed by simulations and infrared spectroscopy. *J. Chem. Phys.*, 11, 1791, 2001.

107. Roux, B. and Simonson, T., Implicit solvent models. *Biophys. Chem.*, 78, 1, 1999.

108. Sanjay, K.C., Richard, M., Santhosh, R., Jeyakanthan, J., Identification of novel histone deacetylase 1 inhibitors by combined pharmacophore modeling, 3D-QSAR analysis, in silico screening and Density Functional Theory (DFT) approaches. *J. Mol. Struct.*, 1125, 391, 2016.

109. Still, W.C., Tempczyk, A., Hawley, R.C., Hendrickson, T., Semianalytical treatment of solvation for molecular mechanics and dynamics. *J. Am. Chem. Soc.*, 112, 6127, 1990.

110. Chaskar, P., Zoete, V., Rohrig, U., On-the-Fly QM/MM docking with attracting cavities. *J. Chem. Inf. Model.*, 57, 73, 2017.

111. Ma, S., Devi-Kesavan, L.S., Gao, J., Molecular Dynamics Simulations of the Catalytic Pathway of a Cysteine Protease: A Combined QM/MM Study of Human Cathepsin K. *J. Am. Chem. Soc.*, 129, 13633, 2007.

112. Guan, H.H., Goh, K.-S., Davamani, F., Wu, P.L., Huang, Y.W., Jeyakanthan, J., Wu, W g, Chen, C.J., Structures of two elapid snake venom metalloproteases with distinct activities highlight the disulfide patterns in the D domain of ADAMalysin family proteins. *J. Struct. Biol.*, 169, 294, 2010.

113. Dhanachandra Singh, Kh., Palani, K., Shanthi, N., Sugunadevi, S., Karthikeyan, M., Velmurgan, D., Jeyakanthan, J., Homology Modeling, Molecular Dynamics, e-Pharmacophore mapping and Docking Study of Chikungunya Virus nsP2 Protease. *J. Mol. Model.*, 18, 39, 2012.

114. Laurent, E.D., Werneck, A.S., Al de Oliveira Neto, M., Bisch, P.M., Electrostatic Properties in the Catalytic Site of Papain: A Possible Regulatory Mechanism for the Reactivity of the Ion Pair. *PROTEINS: Structure, Function, and Genetics*, 52, 236, 2003.

115. Noble, M.A., Gul, S., Verma, C.S., Brocklehurst, K., Ionization characteristics and chemical influences of aspartic acid residue 158 of papain and caricain determined by structure-related kinetic and computational techniques: multiple electrostatic modulators of active-centre chemistry. *Biochem. J.*, 351, 723, 2000.

116. Kemel, Arafet., Silvia, Ferrer., Vicent, Moliner., A Computational Study of the Catalytic Mechanism of the Cruzain Cysteine Protease, *ACS Catalysis*, 7(2), 1207 1215, 2017, doi: 10.1021/acscatal.6b03096.

Index

Also of Interest

Check out these published and forthcoming related titles from Scrivener Publishing

Smart Systems for Industrial Applications
Edited by C. Venkatesh, N. Rengarajan, P. Ponmurugan and S. Balamurugan
Forthcoming 2021. ISBN 978-1-119-76200-3

Impact of Artificial Intelligence on Organizational Transformation
Edited by S. Balamurugan, Sonal Pathak, Anupriya Jain, Sachin Gupta, and Sachin Sharma and Sonia Duggal
Forthcoming 2021. ISBN 978-1-119-71017-2

Nature-Inspired Algorithms Applications
Edited by S. Balamurugan, Anupriya Jain, Sachin Sharma, Dinesh Goyal, Sonia Duggal and Seema Sharma
Forthcoming 2021. ISBN 978-1-119-68174-8

Artificial Intelligence for Renewable Energy Systems
Edited by Ajay Kumar Vyas, S. Balamurugan, Kamal Kant Hiran Harsh S. Dhiman
Forthcoming 2021. ISBN 978-1-119-76169-3

Artificial Intelligence Techniques for Wireless Communication and Networking
Edited by Kanthavel R., K. AnathaJothi, S. Balamurugan and R. Karthik Ganesh
Forthcoming 2021. ISBN 978-1-119-82127-4

Advanced Healthcare Systems
Empowering Physicians with IoT-Enabled Technologies
Edited by Rohit Tanwar, S. Balamurugan, R. K. Saini, Vishal Bharti and Premkumar Chithaluru
Forthcoming 2021. ISBN 978-1-119-76886-9

Computation in Bioinformatics
Multidisciplinary Applications
Edited by S. Balamurugan, Anand Krishnan, Dinesh Goyal, Balakumar Chandrasekaran and Boomi Pandi
Forthcoming 2021. ISBN 978-1-119-65471-1

Fuzzy Intelligent Systems
Methodologies, Techniques, and Applications
Edited by E. Chandrasekaran, R. Anandan, G. Suseendran, S. Balamurugan and Hanaa Hachimi
Published 2021. ISBN 978-1-119-76045-0

Biomedical Data Mining for Information Retrieval
Methodologies, Techniques and Applications
Edited by Sujata Dash, Subhendu Kumar Pani, S. Balamurugan and Ajith Abraham
Published 2021. ISBN 978-1-119-71124-7

Design and Analysis of Security Protocols for Communication
Edited by Dinesh Goyal, S. Balamurugan, Sheng-Lung Peng and O.P. Verma
Published 2020. ISBN 978-1-119-55564-3

www.scrivenerpublishing.com

Printed and bound by CPI Group (UK) Ltd, Croydon, CR0 4YY